Matthew Feldman, Paul Jackson (eds.)

DOUBLESPEAK

The Rhetoric of the Far Right
since 1945

ibidem-Verlag
Stuttgart

Bibliografische Information der Deutschen Nationalbibliothek
Die Deutsche Nationalbibliothek verzeichnet diese Publikation in der
Deutschen Nationalbibliografie; detaillierte bibliografische Daten sind im
Internet über http://dnb.d-nb.de abrufbar.

Bibliographic information published by the Deutsche Nationalbibliothek
Die Deutsche Nationalbibliothek lists this publication in the Deutsche Nationalbibliografie;
detailed bibliographic data are available in the Internet at http://dnb.d-nb.de.

∞

Gedruckt auf alterungsbeständigem, säurefreien Papier
Printed on acid-free paper

ISSN: 2192-7448

ISBN-13: 978-3-8382-0554-0

© *ibidem*-Verlag
Stuttgart 2014

Alle Rechte vorbehalten

Printed in Germany

Explorations of the Far Right (EFR)   vol. 3

ISSN 2192-7448

GENERAL EDITOR: Dr. **Anton Shekhovtsov** ---------- (anton.shekhovtsov@gmail.com)

Explorations of the Far Right

edited by Anton Shekhovtsov

ISSN 2192-7448

1   Антон Шеховцов
     Новые праворадикальные партии в европейских демократиях
     причины электоральной поддержки
     ISBN 978-3-8382-0180-1

2   Florian Ferger
     Tschechische Neonazis
     Ursachen rechter Einstellungen und faschistische Semantiken
     in Zeiten schnellen sozialen Wandels
     ISBN 978-3-8382-0275-4

3   Matthew Feldman, Paul Jackson (eds.)
     Doublespeak
     The Rhetoric of the Far Right since 1945
     ISBN 978-3-8382-0554-0

CONTENTS

INTRODUCTION

Paul Jackson and Matthew Feldman

> What is really important in the construction of a world
> of doublespeak is the ability to lie, whether knowingly
> or unconsciously, and to get away with it; and the abil-
> ity to use lies and choose and shape facts selectively,
> blocking out those that don't fit an agenda or program
> [...] doublespeak is tied closely to way of looking at the
> world – political agendas and frames – that give them
> authenticity and seeming naturalness and inevitability.[1]

Having received a knockout blow at the end of World War Two, the radical right has long sought methods able to overcome the toxic legacies of
1945. The revelations of Nazi genocide in the 1940s only further added to the
discrediting of ultra-nationalist extremism. While long associated with violence, fascist ideology quickly became indelibly linked to savagery and extermination in the European and American public imagination. Even if far from
fully understood in the years immediately after the war, the Holocaust against
European Jews, the so-called 'euthanasia' program against the disabled, as
well as the murderous actions committed against a wide range of demonized
scapegoats – from homosexuals to Roma and Sinti peoples – helped to establish a powerful postwar allergy to radical right politics in Europe and the
US. This led, in turn, to anti-fascism becoming a normative, even commonsense response.[2] In the decades since, radical right protagonists have nowhere approached the heights reached by German Nazism, Italian Fascism
and the other radical right satrapies established during the 'fascist epoch' in
Europe between 1919 and 1945. For several decades thereafter, attempts to
reawaken the 'beast' of fascist ideology were marked by popular failure no
less than by attempts at ideological continuity by radical right ideologues.[3]

Over the last 30 years or so, in Europe and the US, the radical right's
self-conceptions and public influence have changed markedly. In the first

place, very few activists – let alone organizations – from these spheres would ever self-identify as fascist. The stigma of war and Holocaust, quite simply, put this term beyond the pale. As one avowedly fascist ideologue, Maurice Bardèche, already emphasized some 50 years ago:

> The single party, the secret police, the public displays of Caesarism, even the presence of a Führer are not necessarily attributes of fascism, let alone the reactionary thrust of political alliances [...] The famous fascist methods are constantly revised and will continue to be revised. More important than the mechanism is the idea which fascism has created for itself of man and freedom. [...] With another name, another face, and with nothing which betrays the projection from the past, with the form of a child we do not recognize and the head of a young Medusa, the Order of Sparta will be reborn.[4]

This thinking was subsequently repackaged by one of the more successful radical right activists since World War Two. Lyndon LaRouche, in a 1978 essay revealingly titled 'Solving the Machiavellian Problem Today', stated, 'It is not necessary to wear brown shirts to be a fascist [...] it is not necessary to wear a swastika to be a fascist [...] It is not necessary to call oneself a fascist to be a fascist. It is simply necessary to be one!'[5] For these radical right ideologues and movements, leopards have not changed their spots as much as finding better cover. Yet such an attempted obfuscation has also long being intuited by anti-racist campaigners and analysts of fascism. It has been given eloquent voice by, amongst others, the French scholar Pierre-Andre Taguieff: 'If vigilance was only a game of recognizing something already well-known, then it would only be a question of remembering'.[6]

As the essays in *Doublespeak* collectively attest, attentive observation and accurate recognition of the radical right pedigree also points beyond the ever-vexed issue of terminology. Proper recognition of the radical right, perhaps more than ever, means taking their (self-) presentation seriously; that is, taking seriously their deliberately crafted slogans, symbols and themes. As many of the specific chapters recount in detail, a deliberate process has been attempted to 'repackage' the radical right 'brand' in order to make it palatable – which in some European countries including Germany, France and Austria carries legal ramifications – to more mainstream European and American tastes. If rarely considered systematically, as this volume sets out to do, this re-presentation of fascism and radical right rhetoric has long been subject to warnings like Umberto Eco's celebrated 'Ur-Fascism' article of 1986;[7] or still earlier, Holocaust survivor and celebrated memoirist Primo Levi's warning from his *If this is a Man*: 'A new fascism, with its trail of intolerance, of abuse, and of servitude, can be born outside our country and imported into it, walking on tiptoe and calling itself by other names...'

If rarely examined at length, this 'memory of what happened in the heart of Europe', concludes Levi, 'can serve as a warning and a support'.[8] Nor has this lesson been lost decades after defeat of fascism. 'It is important that democracy in the early 21st century does not let itself be undermined by those who do not share its values but would cynically use its rhetoric', the reputed historian Richard Evans pointed out in the *New Statesman*. By this, he was referring to the notable rise of the 'extreme right' in Europe – in particular, Jobbik in Hungary and Golden Dawn in Greece, both at the extreme end of the radical right spectrum – while drawing some very loose parallels with interwar Europe:

> The far right is as aware of history as anyone else, maybe even more so. It realizes how easy it is for others to rob it of political legitimacy by labeling it as Nazi. As such, all the present-day movements of the extreme right, or at least those who are interested in gaining supporters, repudiate labels such as 'neo-Nazi' or 'neo-fascist' and adapt to the conditions of present-day democracy, at least on the surface.[9]

Using language as a kind of Trojan Horse to gain access to the liberal democratic political spectrum forms a central theme of *Doublespeak: The Rhetoric of the Far Right since 1945*. To begin to highlight what may be considered 'fifth column discourse' by radical right movements active in Europe and the United States, this Introduction can begin by briefly considering Britain's leading radical right political party, the British National Party (hereafter BNP), in order to shed some light upon this recurrent feature in the present collection of chapters.

Similar to Orwell's satirical 'doublespeak' from his dystopian masterpiece – actually a conflation of newspeak and doublethink in 1984[10] – a 'fifth column discourse' is specifically explored here in terms of the radical right's tactical, even underhand engagement with democracy; in short, making invisible a movement's radical, counter-democratic aims via the euphemized language of reform. This view is in keeping with scholars analyzing the shifting discursive registers and thematic patterns employed by the postwar radical right. One example is Cas Mudde, who argues that contemporary far right movements in Europe typically have a more 'moderate "front-stage"' intended for public consumption and 'a radical "backstage"' targeted at activists. Similarly, Michael Billig and more recently Roger Eatwell have commented on an 'exoteric' and 'esoteric' division in Britain's 1970s National Front discourse in the late 1970s, in many ways an electoral forerunner to the present-day BNP.[11]

In fact, the now-flailing British National Party offers a perfect case study of this attempted 'fifth column discourse', following the election of Nick Griffin as Party Chairman in September 1999. Founded by the uncompromising neo-Nazi John Tyndall in 1982, the BNP remained on the fringes of political life in Britain due to its association with Oswald Mosley's interwar group, the British Union of Fascists, as well as its recourse to overt symbolism from, and praise for, the Third Reich. To give just two examples underpinning this reputation for unvarnished radical right extremism, images of John Tyndall dressed as a Nazi had long done the UK media rounds; but compounding matters:

> On 25 May 1999, four days after the party's TV broadcast aired [for the London mayoral elections], the association with violent neo-Nazism reemerged when the *Mirror* newspaper exposed a link between the London nail bomber David Copeland and BNP leader, John Tyndall. In April 1999, Copeland had planted bombs in Brixton, Brick Lane and Soho [... causing] three deaths.[12]

Within six months of the *Mirror* exposé, the longtime National Front activist and Cambridge graduate Nick Griffin had taken over and set about 'modernizing' the party which, as Graham Macklin analyzes in greater detail in his contribution to this volume, first and foremost meant attempting to veil the racist, revolutionary and thuggish image of the past. As Griffin candidly laid out in his 1999 article:

Of course, we must teach the truth to the hardcore [... but] when it comes to influencing the public, forget about racial differences, genetics, Zionism, historical revisionism and so on [...] It's time to use the weight of democracy's own myths and expectations against it by side-stepping and using verbal judo techniques.[13]

It is just this type of 'verbal judo', this organizational self-censorship by an extremist party, captured by the phrase 'fifth-column discourse' and expansively analyzed across *Doublespeak*. In this vein, 'fifth column discourse' is thus a rhetorical form of deception and political cunning intended to attack an enemy from within; in this case, by aping the language of liberal democracy. Thus could Nick Griffin, facing an angry crowd at the Oxford Union in November 2007, when he was due to address the congregation, claim without irony of his opponents: 'Had they grown up in Nazi Germany they would have been splendid Nazis'.[14]

Whereas the old BNP spoke of race and forced repatriation, the 'modernized' BNP speaks of identity, for this was to be a party of cosmetically respectable politicians, in Nick Griffin's words: 'in the least controversial way possible [...] we must at all times present them [the electorate] with an image of moderate reasonableness'. Launching the tellingly entitled *Rebuilding British Democracy* in 2005, Nick Griffin correspondingly claimed that his own party manifesto was 'a tightly argued, moderately presented, blueprint for the radical transformation of Britain and British society'.[15] Griffin was thus partially able to attempt a remodel of BNP extremism, not by changing its radical right outlook so much as successfully concealing these by way of political camouflage and 'verbal judo'.

No doubt in partial consequence, the most comprehensive book on the subject, Nigel Copsey's *Contemporary British Fascism*, concludes that 'at no period throughout the entire history of right-wing extremism in Britain, has a far right party registered as much success at the ballot box as today's British National Party'.[16] While the conscious adopting of this fifth column discourse led to some limited electoral success in UK local elections in 2003 and 2004, a breakthrough arrived in June 2009 at the European elections. Mirroring the resurgence of other far right parties across Europe, BNP functionaries Nick Griffin and Andrew Brons were elected MEPs with more than 6 per cent of the proportional-representational vote. This was far and away the greatest political success the BNP had yet scored, bringing with it European funding, mainstream media appearances, and a national profile.

Had this one-time, avowedly fascist party, in short, become a conservative one? Hardly, for this conclusion would be nothing more than falling for the party's self-censorship that has been so consciously applied over the last decade. Indeed, as one internal memorandum attests, just months before their electoral breakthrough of June 2009, the BNP's employment of fifth column discourse continued to remain a central, self-conscious part of its political strategy; for example, Rule #9 from the revised, April 2009 'Language & Concepts Discipline Manual': 'Racial and ethnic epithets and insults should never be used'. And finally, in terms of the revolutionary core of the inner party, consider Rule #12 from this instructive document: 'Successful revolutions from the right have always presented themselves as restoring older traditions. Therefore, we should couch our agenda in restorationist terms whenever possible'.

In nakedly endorsing fifth column discourse, the exemplary BNP doublespeak manual also raises the issue of political framing undertaken by the contemporary radical right generally. Unlike the radical right's embrace of fifth column discourse, however, the issue of extreme right-wing 'framing' has been relatively well established by scholars. Martin Lee's survey a generation ago, for example, discerned a wider 'ideological face-lift' pushed by ideologues across Europe:

> The jackals of the extreme Right believed they found the crucial pressure point when they seized upon immigration as the main issue to rally around. While a network of ultra-right-wing cadres continued to function as the violent vanguard of xenophobia, some shock troops from Europe's neo-fascist underground split off to form mass-based political parties.

A consequence of this 'cosmetic surgery', concludes Lee, is that radical right movements often 'watered down their pronouncements' in order to gain, at given times and on certain issues, 'a significant influence on public policy'.[17] Many radical right parties, from Austria's FPÖ to Italy's *Movimento Sociale Italiano* (renamed the *Allianza Nazionale* in 1995 after claiming to jettison all links with Mussolini's historic brand of Fascism), successfully convinced national and European electorates that they shared little or no common ground with the pre-Cold War radical right.

Furthermore, as Nigel Copsey argues in the launch issue of *Fascism* (the first journal dedicated to studying the evolution of the radical right since World War One) if right-wing extremists like to forget their heritage, political scientists need to redouble their efforts to incorporate historical continuities when approaching the contemporary radical right. In particular, the surfeit of terms applied to these groups by political scientists, ranging from 'ethnonationalist' to 'far right populist', collectively runs the risk of 'consign[ing] fascism to a museum'. As Copsey continues:

> For sure, we need greater interrogation of the continuities between historical fascism and contemporary manifestations. Admittedly, the historical contexts are different, but if we are to succeed in applying historical understanding to the present, it is time for the political science community (and social scientists more generally) to engage seriously with (neo) fascism studies.[18]

Bearing out this point, Cas Mudde's *The Ideology of the Extreme Right* identified no less than twenty six competing definitions and fifty eight different characteristic features used by political scientists (most commonly xenophobia, nationalism and varying degrees of hostility to liberal democracy) to describe the phenomena analyzed in the chapters to follow here.[19] Needless to say, this number has only grown in the years since the publication of Mudde's book in 2000. This collection is concerned with the framing and rhetorical tactics deployed by the extreme right since 1945, the term increasingly favored by historians and political scientists alike to describe the 'radical right'. This term effectively captures both the continuities and ideological profile (post-, neo-) fascism of a cluster of ideologies which, in Roger Griffin's view, 'constantly evolves to accommodate changes in its habitat, producing a wide variety of new strains'.[20] A number of major publications of late have registered this mutation of radical right politics in Europe and the US, ranging from comparative studies on radical right-wing populism;[21] social movements;[22] and political violence;[23] not to mention and expanding library of national case studies collectively far too lengthy to enumerate here, let alone comprehensively address in a single volume. It also bears noting that, while often narrowly focused on contemporary developments, think-tanks and third-sector charities have also fruitfully contributed research aimed at a better understanding of contemporary radical right politics and culture generally.[24]

Yet that said, one important 'new strain' of radical right rhetoric – albeit sharing many similarities with demonized communities in the past – frequently appearing in the chapters to ensue is the turn toward anti-Muslim politics. In the aftermath of mass-casualty terrorist attacks by Islamist militants in the US on 11 September 2001; Madrid on 11 March 2004; and the UK on 7 July 2005, the emergence of a potent anti-Muslim rhetoric in the political mainstream has also offered a crucial hook for a new generation of radical right politicians to hang an extremist agenda has been palpable in some sections the mainstream media and wider public. To take a final example from the BNP's Nick Griffin, in a lecture directed to the 'back stage' of the movement in 2005, he urged activists to turn away from an unhelpful anti-Semitism and embrace anti-Muslim politics in an attempt at populist, 'front stage' campaigning:

> [...] in real politics in the real world, one's proper choice of enemy is a group who you gain a worthwhile level of extra support by identifying, who you have a realistic chance of beating, and whose defeat will take you the furthest towards your goal. With millions of our people desperately and very reasonably worried by the spread of Islam and its adherents, and with the mass media ... playing 'Islamophobic' messages like a scratched CD, the proper choice of enemy needn't be left to rocket scientists.[25]

As noted above, the biological anti-Semitism of German fascism under Hitler put paid to the biological racism so closely identified with interwar and wartime fascist movements. In its place in the twenty first century, radical right, has increasingly turned toward a 'cultural racism' of implacable difference and intractable conflict with European Muslims – in some ways playing on the same kinds of populist phobias, casual discrimination and demonization as anti-Semitism did a century ago. This cultural prejudice assumes that all Muslims are somehow responsible for the actions of an extremist minority centering on the notion that Islam – not just jihadi Islamist violence, which all citizens of goodwill naturally oppose – is an 'other' that cannot be accommodated in liberal democratic Europe. As Liz Fekete suggests, wider media narratives in particular are at the heart of this growth:

> Around much of Europe, the media is launching its own 'witch-hunts' of Muslims who display symptoms of 'unacceptable behavior' as enunciated by terrorism laws. No other communities are placed under the microscope, constantly questioned about their personal beliefs, their 'foreign allegiances', as the Muslim communities of Europe. It's former Tory minister, Norman Tebbit's cricket test gone mad.[26]

Without doubt, the more successful radical right ideologues and movements of the past generation have been acutely sensitive to shifts in the political and cultural landscape. Nowhere has this been more visible than in the embrace of populist anti-Muslim politics over the last decade.[27] Aided by recent jihadi Islamist attacks on one hand, and by longer-term demographic change on the other, Europe and the US have played witness to degrees of collective prejudice and scapegoating wholly at variance with democratic progress toward equality and individual agency. This new intolerance – as the far right has quickly grasped, and some of Anglophone literature has registered of late – would be considered unacceptable if leveled against other historical 'out-groups': Jews, Irish or black people and so on (not including Roma and Sinti peoples, who still collective stereotyping and discrimination to a shameful degree).[28] Clearly fanning these flames are windier sections of the mainstream media, thus providing an issue able to be shared by ideologues and talking heads of all right-wing stamps – 'paleo-', 'neo- 'far-' and 'extreme' alike. From this perspective, Roger Eatwell has usefully detected a link between the rhetoric of radical right activists and jihadi Islamists contributing to a 'cumulative extremism', whereby 'one form of extremism can feed off and magnify other forms'.[29] In this way, the intertwined extremes from opposing illiberal camps seek to radicalize otherwise liberal-democratic populaces rejecting both political violence and collective scapegoating – in all its forms – in favor of the clashing of supposedly hostile and monolithic civilizations.

The most violent voice in this yet in this process of 'cumulative extremism' has certainly been Anders Behring Breivik, whose attempt to start a 'European Civil War' culminating with the end of Islam in Europe led to the deaths of 77 Norwegian innocents, mostly children, on 22 July 2011.[30] Writing for the *New York Review of Books,* in the wake of Breivik's terrorist bombing and mass shootings, Malise Ruthven stressed that his anti-Muslim views are 'shared by many on the right and some in Europe's liberal mainstream'. Ruthven's article, furthermore, highlights several of the wider similarities shared between both opposing, in some ways co-dependent, extremisms:

> Just as al-Qaeda represents an extreme, activist variant of political views held by a much wider constituency of Muslim radicals, most of whom would never consider crossing the boundary between thinking and action, so Breivik (judging from his manifesto) holds a broad range of positions common to what might be called the 'counter-jihadist' or 'paranoid right'. This is represented – among others – by Robert Spencer, Daniel Pipes, and Pamela Geller in the US, the controversial Dutch legislator Geert Wilders, and Bat Ye'or and Melanie Phillips in Britain. All these writers – most of whom have denounced the Utöya massacre in the most unequivocal terms – subscribe to variants of the thesis that Europe is sleepwalking into cultural disaster or (in the case of Phillips) enabling Islamist terrorists to gain a foothold.[31]

For the radical right, correspondingly, this has become a signature issue. With the exception of a remaining hardcore of 'traditional' biological racists tending toward varying shades of white supremacism, the different manifestations of the radical right – social movements, electoral parties, and, importantly, interconnected websites – have turned toward anti-Muslim prejudice core strategy for populist mobilization.

A further example here, again drawn from the British case, offers a microcosm of the way in which anti-Muslim rhetoric quickly circulates amongst the various shades of the illiberal right – not least, online. Consider the case of a February 2012 speech delivered by Paul Weston, chairman of the British Freedom Party. Launched only eighteen months earlier, the BFP was looking seeking funding and visibility ahead of the UK's May 2012 local elections. This placed Paul Weston on a tour of the eastern US, delivering speeches and attempting to find sympathetic allies during Winter 2011, including one largely representative talk entitled 'Turning Britain into Lebanon'. Fully signed up to the 'clash of civilizations' thesis, Weston further warned of a 'slide into civil war, tit for tat atrocities becoming progressively more vicious, before the entire country goes the way of Lebanon, or more recently Yugoslavia, which of course fractured along racial, tribal and religious lines'. Weston was referring, of course, to an assumed, monolithic Islamic faith he considered 'worse than Nazism' that was acting within, and against, Britain – as apparently revealed by the 'constant news about Mosques selling literature calling for the overthrow of Britain's democracy, the murder of British Jews and homosexuals, the subjugation of the non-Muslim infidel and the desire to install a global Islamic caliphate'. Weston then concluded:

> I am going to fight for Britain, but there is no guarantee that Britain and Europe can be saved, and if we go, and America goes shortly thereafter, then so goes Western Civilization – the most humane, moral and decent civilization in the history of mankind – to be replaced by Islam, the most barbaric, illiberal and totalitarian force of pathological cruelty that can only take the Western world back to the dark ages.

Quite aside from offering a paradigmatic instance of fifth column discourse – in this case, using the language of liberal democracy to advance his anti-Muslim prejudice – perhaps just as revealing is the context for Weston's lecture. This, in turn, may be divided into two parts.

In the first instance, Weston's lecture was originally filmed and presented at the apartment of Laurence Auster, cousin of the famous writer Paul and host of the 'paleo-conservative' website and blog, *View from the Right*. The latter, a kind twenty-first century John Birch Society for the online generation, essentially opposes multiculturalism in favor of return to 'traditionalist' conservative values in the US – extending to, as noted by Auster's epigraph for his September 2008 online collection, 'What to do about Islam', 'proposals for removing jihad and sharia supporters from America, restricting or prohibiting the practice of Islam in America, and containing and isolating Islam from the rest of the world, the policy I call Separationism'. More recent blog entries have extended this religious hatred to discussions on the usefulness of nuclear attacks against Mecca and Medina and the potential necessity of killing

Muslims in the west following the outbreak of 'civil war'.[32] Still more generally, in the years both before and since Auster's particular attempts at a 'nostalgic' segregationism has extended beyond cultural prejudice toward Muslims to unreconstructed religious racism toward black Americans, as revealed by blog titles such as: 'What sets blacks off: anything or nothing'; 'What have blacks contributed to our civilization?'; 'What do whites owe blacks? And, why did God create a race whose intellectual capabilities are so far behind those of the rest of mankind?' The following comment on 'blackness' from 30 March 2012, for instance, appears a fair summary of Auster's view on 'white civilization' and its culturally and/or religiously 'inferior' rivals:

> Blacks, as I have said going back to the time of blacks' mass outburst of joy over the O.J. Simpson acquittal, are largely a criminal or criminal-sympathizing population. When a black Congressman and other black political leaders wear hoodies to express their solidarity with black thugs, they are expressing the essence of their blackness.[33]

For Auster, in short, much of the contemporary 'Muslim problem' is but an outgrowth from the perceived disaster of Civil Rights and progressive moves toward racial equality in the post-1960s, US. In this view, white Americans should retain an enshrined socio-political hegemony that Roger Griffin has elsewhere called 'ethnocratic liberalism'; as in Apartheid South Africa, democratic rights for the present majority and second class status (or worse) for ethnic minorities within the nation.[34] In this initial context, Auster's reactionary group wishing to turn back the clock on non-white tolerance and equality hosted Weston's, February 23rd speech on the 'Islamic road that Europe finds itself on, particularly so Britain, which is almost on the point of no return — or perhaps no peaceful return'.

Beyond Weston's original speech at Laurence Auster's flat, a second and wider context for Weston' speech is that of online dissemination amongst radical right groups sharing anti-Muslim rhetoric as an ideological lowest common denominator. Less than ten days' after originally being delivered in New York City, both the video and transcribed text of 'Transforming Britain into Lebanon' was posted at the now-infamous, Gates of Vienna website. Largely a single-issue website, as declared by their motto – '*At the siege of Vienna in*

1683 Islam seemed poised to overrun Christian Europe. We are in a new phase of a very old war – the *Gates of Vienna* is explicitly dedicated to resisting the so-called 'Islamification' of Europe.[35] Despite being 'relatively moderate', the *Gates of Vienna* website is consistently praised across Breivik's terrorist 'compendium', *2083: A European Declaration of Independence*. This extends to literally dozens of references and textual citations to the website; the likely reason Breivik calls this version of culturalist Islamophobia 'The Vienna School'; and most tellingly, the basis for entitling his manifesto *2083* in the first place: dating the prospective elimination of Islam in Europe precisely 400 years after the siege of Vienna (often recognized as the furthest expansion westward by the Ottoman Empire).[36]

As with Laurence Auster's position above, for the influential *Gates of Vienna* there is no attempt to separate jihadi Islamists from the overwhelming majority of peaceful, law-abiding Muslim citizens in Europe; quite simply, Islam is the enemy of western civilization *tout court.* And finally, Returning to Ruthven's NYRB text, if it is the case that 'political rhetoric can play a part in motivating extreme forms of violence', then *Gates of Vienna* surely played no small part in Breivik's radicalization – and doubtless that of other radical right activists concerned about a perceivedly imminent 'clash of civilizations'.[37] A fortnight after Weston's speech was uploaded on the Gates of Vienna website, finally, it appeared on Andrew Brons' Nationalist Unity Forum. Brons, one of two Members of European Parliament for the aforementioned BNP (the other MEP being Nick Griffin), had previously been a member of the National Socialist Movement in the 1960s, and later, from 1980, headed the neo-Nazi National Front, before joining the BNP in 2005 and successfully standing in the Yorkshire and Humber region in June 2009.[38] Unlike the 'traditionalist' conservative Auster and the single-issue, Islamophobic *Gates of Vienna*, however, Brons's website packages anti-Muslim prejudice as one among many themes in his radical right electoral stable. In this way, ideological positions held by the illiberal right on starkly contrasting issues ranging from white nationalism, revolution, and political violence, to even the importance of engaging with the electoral system in the first place, have been recently trumped by the convergence around anti-Muslim prejudice that seeks to assault liberal democracy from within.

Rounding out this instance of old wine in new bottles, shortly after returning from his trip to the US, BFP leader Paul Weston quickly formed an electoral alliance in April 2012 with the most notorious anti-Muslim street organi-zation in postwar Europe, the English Defence League. Likewise claiming to stand for liberal values against Islamist 'totalitarianism' (but again, often simp-ly collapsed into an identification of all Muslims), remarkably, the group calls itself a 'human rights organization'. The, now former, EDL joint-leaders 'Tom-my Robinson' (the pseudonym of Stephen Yaxley-Lennon) and Kevin Carroll have been in the forefront of anti-Muslim politics since the launch of this 'new far right' social movement in Spring 2009.[39] While the EDL leadership seems to share the neither the overt white supremacist views of the BNP and other neo-fascist parties in Europe and the US, nor the unabashed backward-looking racism of Auster's *View from the Right*, all three illiberal right factions can agree upon, share, and collectively advocate an anti-Muslim rhetoric only adding to a 'cumulative extremism' in Britain, the US and Europe. Following the alliance's failure in the May 2012 local elections, the BFP-EDL's other ac-tions over 2012 bear this out the predominance of anti-Muslim politics for this populist radical right milieu; from a European 'Counter-Jihad' demonstration in Aarhus (home of the newspaper publishing the inflammatory 'Danish Car-toons' in 2006) on 31 March 2012, and still more ambitiously, the First World-wide Counter-Jihad Action in Stockholm on 4 August 2012 (hosting Robert Spencer, Pamela Geller and others; both events were poorly attended by rad-ical right activists).[40] That scapegoating provocations like the so-called 'coun-ter-jihad movement' have an effect in terms of 'cumulative extremism' is simi-larly easy to locate; thus in response, Islamist extremists targeted an English Defence League demonstration in Dewsbury during Summer 2012, hoping to attack EDL-BFP supporters with guns and improvized explosive devices.[41] In this way, a similar descent into collective demonization, long familiar to radical right ideologues and movements, has been reformulated in a 'clash of civiliza-tions' discourse targeting the Islamic faith as a whole – potentially contributing to radical right violence like Brieivk's atrocities in Norway, as well as a 'cumu-lative extremism' serving only to increase already-strained community ten-sions in Europe and the US.

Yet this is not to say that the variegated forces of nationalist extremism have not found novel and innovative ways to adapt in the 21st century. They clearly have. Indeed, the modes of expression employed in the process of re-framing radical right politics – often leading to the development of public messages that differ radically to privately-held beliefs – is an increasingly important area for enquiry. In contributing to this area of scholarship, another core aim of this book is thus to offer a series of reflections on new ways of politically framing of radical right discourses. Though *Doublespeak* is not, and in a single volume cannot be, a comprehensive survey of Euro-American countries, the chapters that follow attempt provide a wide range of examinations from leading scholars in Europe and the US that are collectively concerned with historically tracing the evolution of right ideas in our new century. Regions for analysis span the post-communist in eastern Europe to postcolonial western Europe and to the contemporary American superpower, while thematic topics extend to solo actor terrorism; anti-Muslim politics and Islamophobia; populist nationalism as well as unapologetic fascism and neo-Nazism.

Despite the legacy of an instinctively anti-fascist mainstream stemming from the Second World War, a series of new political challenges facing European and American societies – from changing national immigration patterns to global banking scandals and the so-called 'Global War on Terror' – have opened political space allowing much more hospitable to reframed radical right messages than in previous decades. Over the past generation in particular, the creeping influence of radical right discourse on the mainstream agenda of politicians across Europe and America has been particularly notable. The anti-Muslim rhetoric noted above, for example, seems to be precisely the well from which the convicted Norwegian mass murderer, Anders Breivik, drank in the months and years before his terrorist attacks in Oslo and Utøya Island on 22 July 2011. In this and other recent respects touched upon below, then, far from simply waning into insignificance, the contemporary radical right has transformed in a number of pivotal ways demands further exploration.

Better historical knowledge of how radical right movements have reconfigured their politics – and often self-consciously reframed core agendas it is argued here – remains paramount for a deeper understanding of how rightwing extremism can and does adapt to new national circumstances and can manifest substantial changes over time. In turning to the often-discussed case of France, for example, Jens Rydgrens' work has exemplified this cutting-edge approach. His exploration of a new radical right 'frame' in France has identified the Front National (FN) as both a pioneering and significant case study. As he stresses, the FN's discovery of a compelling a new 'master frame' for postwar far right politics has spawned a new era of creativity among many populist nationalists. As he puts it, as a response to the discrediting of older forms of fascist politics:

> an innovative master frame was constructed in France during the late 1970s and early 1980s, and was made known as a successful frame in connection with the electoral breakthrough of the Front National in 1984. As the old master frame of the extreme right [...] was rendered impotent by the outcome of the Second World War, it took the extreme right a long time to establish a new, potent master frame that simultaneously met the conditions of: being flexible enough to fit (in modified form) different political and cultural contexts; sufficiently resonated with the lived experiences, attitudes and preconceptions of many people [...] and was sufficiently free from stigma. The master frame combining ethnonationalist, cultural racism and anti-political establishment populism met these requirements.[42]

In Rydgrens' well-received research, and indeed elsewhere, there has already been much analysis of how this new approach to re-framing radical right politics led the French Front National to inspire other nationalist movements to build upon this 'modernized' front stage approach.[43] Therefore, given the FN's wide discussion in Anglophone literature, this volume has skipped a specific chapter on the French case, even if the pan-national significance of high profile figures like Jean Marie Le Pen, as well as influential think tanks such as Alain de Benoist's GRECE, often appear in national and intellectual contexts far beyond that of France.

Rather, in order to explore in detail the approaches to reframing far right agendas, focusing on the 'doublespeak' of disparities between the inner, ideological values of radical right protagonists and their public presentation of such positions, the essays in this volume have been divided into three subsections. The first of these has an overwhelmingly thematic focus, and reflects upon the manipulation of discourse in a number of radical right settings. The section begins with an exploration by Roger Griffin into the links between the interwar period and the very different postwar dynamics operating in Europe. His analysis stretches from commentary on the use of a euphemistic language in the Third Reich pioneered by Victor von Klemperer, and especially its importance during the Holocaust, to more contemporary contexts. Griffin's chapter emphasizes the novel methods for framing a repackaged radical right among a variety of postwar movements. This includes the emergence of the New Right in France (*Nouvelle Droite*), especially the promotion of so-called differentialist and 'cultural' expressions of racism as a way to distance new strands of far right ideology from interwar biological racism. Griffin also helpfully notes the recourse to an illusory form 'doublespeak' is prevalent in other contexts of modern politics as well, meaning that a properly reflexive liberalism needs to be aware of its own limits in this regard too.

Juxtaposing Griffin's broad sweep is Janet Wilson examination of a selection of textual strategies employed by a modern 'classic' for the radical right: William Pierce's *The Turner Diaries*. Wilson examines the structure, framing and rhetorical devices employed in the novel – such as the use of an 'editor' compiling the fictional diaries long after their original composition – as ways of re-encoding key radical right, specifically neo-Nazi, themes. Her analysis extends to several overarching tropes in the book, such as the use of an apocalyptic framework, and the just battle against an oppressive multicultural regime, in order to celebrate racially-inspired violence. Wilson concludes by reflecting upon the text's often overt recourse to traditional Nazi registers raised in Griffin's contribution, rather than substantial attempts by Pierce at updating or reconfiguring radical right ideology. While the use of pulp fiction to popularize visions of a global 'race war' ideas was a landmark in radical right propaganda and culture, the context and points of reference in *The Turner Diaries* are very much unreconstructed neo-Nazism (Pierce was the one-time leader of the US-based neo-Nazi organization the National Alliance). So just as 'modernized' politicians like Nick Griffin, or more professional operators such as Geert Wilders – explored elsewhere in the volume – present cases whereby radical right ideology has been substantially reworked, Wilson's analysis of *The Turner Diaries* points to a crucial example of how traditional variants of fascist discourse (in this case, biological racism) have persisted in the postwar years.

Paul Jackson's subsequent chapter then turns to another textual case study: Anders Breivik's notorious 'compendium', or manifesto, *2083: A European Declaration of Independence*, which offers a sustained attempt to frame

23

solo-actor terrorism as legitimate political praxis. Drawing upon the notion of licence drawn from Aristotle Kallis' incisive scholarship – firstly to hate; then to develop eliminationist fantasies, and finally to advance an intellectual 'licence to kill' – this case study locates Breivik within a potent 'new' far right culture that traffics in fantasies of a Europe where Muslims are eliminated. Breivik, who sees himself as one of this movement's most radical members, dubs Europe's anti-Muslim radical right discourse 'cultural conservatism' and even – in stark contrast to the hated 'Frankfurt School', the 'Vienna School'. *2083* offers a host of framing strategies to justify revolutionary violence: Christian themes for the cultivation of a political faith; the proposition of an alternate moral code justifying violence in times of perceived 'civil war'; and a teleological meta-narrative that dates this revolutionary conflict as breaking out in 1999 (eventually culminating in 2083; the 200th anniversary of the death of Marx, and the 400th since the Battle of Vienna). Jackson characterizes wider set of discourses – found first and foremost this century on internet websites like *Jihadwatch* in the US or *The Gates of Vienna* in Europe – as offering a licence to hate. In this way, solo actor terrorists such as Breivik can nonetheless be seen to draw upon a 'community of support' that does not publically endorse violence, but, Jackson suggests, does share many of the same critiques of multiculturalism and so-called 'cultural Marxism'.[44]

Section One then concludes with the volume's first national-based case study; namely Ruth Wodak's consideration of the Austrian Freedom Party (FPÖ). After establishing the party's historical trajectory in postwar Austrian politics, her attention focuses upon how a combination of text and image has been used as a deliberately provocative communication strategy deployed in order to gain wider media attention. Her focus on this 'strategy of provocation' also adds a further nuance bearing upon radical right groups more widely: intentional ambivalence created by conflating a range of contentious issues. While openly xenophobic remarks are to an extent defended in responses to media outcries, radical right parties try to use such exposure to as ways to discuss wider issues – such as freedom of speech, or a general critique of liberal political correctness – in order to defend extremist utterances. Her analysis also stresses that the roles able to be adopted by the mainstream media are correspondingly limited: they either do not report on scandalous messages, and thus seem to tacitly endorse them, or they do report on them, giving air time and column inches to that a 'strategy of discursive provocation' was intended to generate in the first place.

Section Two then focuses turns to a handful of national case studies drawn from Western Europe and America. This section opens with an analysis of the attempted 'modernization' of the British National Party under the leadership of Nick Griffin. As noted above, when Griffin took over the party in 1999, he attempted to detoxify the BNP's brand. Yet as Graham Macklin's analysis points out, this more media savvy approach could hide neither a legacy in neo-Nazism, nor the continued promotion of neo-Nazi themes to the committed hardcore 'backstage'. Indeed, Macklin stresses how a fluidity developed between the populist messages put out to a wider public, and the continued commitment to neo-Nazism and especially anti-Semitism amongst more 'traditional' activists. Coded terms to express anti-Semitism to potentially sympathetic audiences, of the type developed by Oswald Mosley such as 'international finance', have been augmented in the BNP's coded anti-Semitic discourse with other terms, such as 'Zionist businessmen', used for example in the party's critique of the invasion of Iraq in 2003. As Macklin concludes, the very fact that he is able to analyze the extremist 'back stage' of the party in such depth suggests the limits to Griffin's modernization strategy – arguably a key reason for the party's swift decline since the relative success of the 2009 European Parliamentary elections.

Moving on, Hilde Coffé and Jeroen Dewulf offer an exploration of alternatively moderate and more extreme discourse found in the strategies of the Vlaams Blok and its more recent successor in Belgium, the Vlaams Belang. Coffé and Dewulf initially sketch out a complex regional-national context lending itself to anti-immigrant policies advanced by the Vlaams Blok – only to be followed by a gradual softening of public messages, especially with the formation of the Vlaams Belang in 2004. However, once stalling in the polls, the authors chart a return to more extreme anti-immigration rhetoric. Like many radical right politicians touting populist policies, Filip Dewinter, head of the Vlaams Belang, has no use for an older anti-Semitic register, found for example in defence of Belgian collaboration during the Second World War, but has instead turned to anti-Muslim politics. This has even led to a guarded endorsement of same-sex couples, as part of a wider strategy of demonizing 'illiberal' Muslims – a trend also seen elsewhere in Europe in recent years. Nevertheless, the conclusions reached by Coffé and Dewulf stress that, to date, despite this reframing (and renaming) of the party through a more openly aggressive, anti-Muslim agenda has not led to renewed support for its politics.

Belgium's experience is directly contrasted by its neighbour, Holland, as Koen Vossen highlights with the electoral success of populist Islamophobia in the 21st century. To contextualize this trend, his chapter provides a historical overview of the various movements to have emerged in the Netherlands since 1945. Initially, groupings like the Farmers' Party appeared to have direct linkages to the much-hated interwar fascist party, the National Socialist Movement. Following on from the limited impact of the tainted Farmers' Party in the 1960s, Vossen tracks further developments in the 1980s and 1990s via analysis of the various Centre Parties that again met with much hostility in the Netherlands. Memories of the Second World War, and a culture that thoroughly rejected interwar-style fascism lingered in the cultures of these Centre Parties. With the 2000s, Vossen turns his focus upon the emergence of two new parties, List Pim Fortuyn and Geert Wilders' Party For Freedom. Unlike the earlier radical right parties in Holland, here the framing of the political agenda was markedly different. A defence of Dutch liberal values, including rights for homosexuals and a pro-Israeli stance, was juxtaposed with a threatening Muslim 'other'. This successful approach to framing radical right illiberalism helped to distance these newer movements from the legacy of the Second World War, a profile that hampered earlier radical right groupings. Furthermore, Vossen explores the issue of backstage politics, and suggests that the rhetoric of both Fortuyn and the more extreme Wilders is something quite district from the earlier tradition of neo-Nazism.

Moving across the Atlantic, Leonard Weinberg then offers an expansive overview of the rhetoric and framing by radical right extremisms in a variety of American contexts. His analysis begins with the interwar era, a lens for assessing shifts in the postwar environment, and identifies a diverse culture whereby anti-Semitic and extreme nationalist ideas developed in the context of the Depression. Discussion spans the interwar fortunes of organizations such as the Ku Klux Klan, William Pelley's small-scale Silver Shirts movement and Father Coughlin's polemical broadcasts. Following this interwar milieu came the very different Cold War era, which provided for further critiques of the state and its power, and which also saw a growth in a host of radical right organizations often attempting to update interwar anti-Semitism to the postwar situation. Moreover, echoing Wilson's analysis of *The Turner Diaries*, Weinberg's conclusions stress that while the postwar radical right, in its various forms, has long sought to cultivate anti-Semitic messages in the US, these older movements are have been recently faced with a much more complex set of issues. Potentially, Weinberg concludes, there could be a revival of American radical right fortunes by replacing the older focus on 'ZOG' with the more widely accepted anti-Muslim politics, combined with a new embrace of nativism in response to an ever more diverse national demographic.

Following these case studies, Part Three of the volume moves analysis into Central, South and Eastern Europe. It begins with Gideon Botsch and Christoph Kopke's examination of the German case. Their exploration of key trends since the 1960s, focusing largely on the National Democratic Party, stresses the continued prevalence of anti-Semitism amongst the German radical right. Their examination reiterates the variegated ways in which anti-Semitic tropes, both coded and explicit, have marked German discourses no less than in other national contexts. This extends to Holocaust denial, expressed in recent radical right media such as White Power Music; direct action 'flash' protests, ostensibly in support of Palestinians persecuted by Israel; and coded critiques of globalization, which often advance, older anti-Semitic discourses centered upon alleged Jewish global conspiracy. While many of the other 'western' case studies encountered in Part Two, particularly Belgium and the Netherlands, stress an updating of demonized 'out-groups' from Jews to Muslims in Europe, Botsch and Kopke highlight the continued importance of anti-Semitism within the framing of the German radical right; trends also seen in Britain and the US.

Italy, another country with direct legacies to interwar fascist rule, is examined in Matthew Feldman and Anna Castriota's chapter on the avowedly fascist (not 'post' or 'neo') CasaPound movement, named after the American poet Ezra Pound. This organization, predominantly a social movement, provides a rich source for reflection upon the supra-electoral nature underpinning a great deal of radical right politics. In order to offer a 'fascism for the third millennium' it draws on left-wing themes, and a differentialist approach to racism pioneered by Alain de Benoist's French New Right, which allows members see no historical break between their politics and Mussolini's original blackshirts. Indeed, their analysis shows how the movement borrows directly from documents and ideas taken from Fascist Italy in 1930s and 1940s, but updates them via a new model for radical right activism. For example, the head of CasaPound is simultaneously the leader of their house band, *Zetazeroalfa* and retains a revolutionary core advocating a post-liberal new order and a fundamentally anti-liberal politics. Moreover, this is no mere nostalgia for the past, but an authentic re-framing of the historic Italian Fascist agenda for an era of new media technology, non-white immigration, and the Global War on Terror.

Turning to Eastern Europe, Per Anders Rudling then provides an examination in detail of the curious case surrounding Ukraine's Interregional Academy for Personnel Management, or MAUP – an institution that developed following the fall of communism and has long promoted a potent anti-Semitism via the pseudo-intellectual structure of a 'university'. Indeed, MAUP's discourse was unique in the way it presented a contemporary form of anti-Semitic conspiracism via an ostensibly academic, and therefore legitimizing, framework. In particular, Rudling reveals how the institution became a key disseminator of anti-Semitic literature addressing with the country's wartime history of Nazi and Soviet occupation. At its height, the MAUP even offered students the opportunity to be taught by notorious ex-Klansman David Duke, who defended a 'PhD thesis' at the institution. Rudling's exploration of this institution demonstrates that MAUP reflected a culture of anti-Semitism within some quarters of Ukrainian society, ultimately becoming an international liability for Ukraine as some of its more outrageous claims have an impact far beyond the confines of the academy. Moreover, fortunes have also turned against the MAUP as a result of recent developments in the Middle East; for Rudling's analysis notes that a vital financial support base for the MAUP existed in the Middle East, yet with the Arab Spring this lucrative linkup has also become destabilized.

Alexander Verkhovsky's chapter then develops an account of post-Soviet nationalism, most notably Russian radical right activity. Verkhovsky suggests both media outlets and mainstream political culture have failed to challenge an upsurge in ultra-nationalist sentiment in Russia this century. This has also created space for political opportunism, Verkhovsky notes, with particular focus placed upon both Vladimir Putin and Dmitry Medvedev. With conclusions urging a rethink by Russian society to host a more inclusive civic nationalism,

Verkhovsky chapter warns of further turbulence, and thus political opportunities, for the radical right and its hyper-nationalist discourses in the coming years. The volume then concludes with the thoughts of Chip Berlet, reflecting on the ways in which language helps to normalize violence, and offers a pathway from thinking to acting in extreme forms. He highlights how encoding reality via stark us / them dichotomies, scapegoating rhetoric, and an apocalyptic mindset urge people into more violent and confrontational ways of thinking.

Though variegated, the case studies assembled here are by no means the final word on the framing and discourse developed by the still-evolving radical right. Rather, they have been gathered to provoke fresh thinking and debate on the extent to which broad and diverse radical right movements have been able to pour old wine into new bottles, and the level to which ideologues and activists have been able to make fresh concoctions for public consumption. It is hoped by the editors and the contributors to *Doublespeak* that the explorations here will lead to a new interest among a variety of analysts – from historians to linguists, and from sociologists to political scientists – into the modes of communication employed by radical right groups. More nuanced approaches to examining the levels to which radical right politicians and ideologues have masked their ideas; successfully or otherwise, will, surely, facilitate a better grasp of how these political and social movements have responded to a wide variety of postwar changes in Europe and the US.

ENDNOTES

[1] Edward S. Hermann, *Beyond Hypocrisy: Decoding the News in an Age of Propaganda including the Doublespeak Dictionary* (Boston: South End Press, 1992), pp. 3, 6. While focused overwhelmingly on examples drawn from post-Cold War American politics and media, Herman's book also includes 'A Doublespeak Dictionary for the 1990s', containing terms of striking longevity; see p. 113ff.

[2] For two recent studies on the historiography on the Holocaust, see Tom Lawson, *Debates on the Holocaust* (Manchester: Manchester University Press, 2010). See especially chapter 7 on post-war responses to the Final Solution; and Dan Stone, *Histories of the Holocaust* (Oxford: Oxford University Press, 2010). See especially chapters 1 and 5 on European collaboration and other victims in the Nazi Holocaust, respectively.

[3] For a good overview on the post-war far right in Europe, see Martin A. Lee, *The Beast Reawakens* (London: Warner Books, 1998). Important studies on the 'failure' of the far right since 1945 include Elizabeth Carter, *The Extreme Right in Western Europe: Success or Failure?* (Manchester: Manchester University Press, 2005). Focusing upon Britain, see Mike Cronin ed., *The Failure of British Fascism: The Far Right and the*

Fight for Political Recognition (Basingstoke: Palgrave, 1996). For a more recent case study of the British far right in the generation following 1945 see Nicholas Hillman: "'Tell me chum, in case I got it wrong. What was it we were fighting during the war?' The Re-emergence of British Fascism, 1945-1958', in *Contemporary British History*, 15/4 (2001), pp. 1 – 34.

[4] Maurice Bardèche, 'What is Fascism?' [1961], translated and excerpted in Roger Griffin ed., *Fascism: A Reader's Guide* (Oxford: Oxford University Press, 1995), p. 321.

[5] LaRouche's quotation is cited is the frontispiece to Dennis King's authoritative biography, *Lyndon LaRouche and the New American Fascism* (New York: Doubleday, 1989). For an online discussion of Larouche and contextualization of his ideas, see Matthew Feldman, 'The LaRouche Organization as an Extremist Movement', on the Holocaust Education and Archive Research Team, available at: www.holocaustresearchprojec t.org/essays&editorials/larouche2.html (accessed 30/08/2012), cited note 5.

[6] While Taguieff's comment was made in the specific context of Alain de Benoist's French-based, 'right-wing Gramscian' think-tank, GRECE (*Groupement de recherche et d'études pour la civilisation européenne*), he makes the more general and relevant point that 'Neither "fascism" or "racism" will do us the favour of returning in such a way that we can recognise them easily'. For further discussion, see the 'Editorial Introduction' and 'Fascism's New Faces (and new Facelessness) in the post-fascist Epoch' in Matthew Feldman ed., *A Fascist Century* (Basingstoke: Palgrave, 2008), cited p. xxvi and 191, respectively.

[7] See Umberto Eco, 'UR Fascism', in the *New York Review of Books* (1986) reprinted in *Fascism: Critical Concepts* vol. 5 *Post-War Fascism*, eds., Roger Griffin with Matthew Feldman (London: Routledge, 2004): 'Ur-Fascism is still around us, sometimes in plainclothes. It would be so much easier, for us, if there appeared on the world scene somebody saying, "I want to reopen Auschwitz, I want the Black Shirts to parade again in the Italian squares". Life is not that simple. Ur- Fascism can come back under the most innocent of disguises. Our duty is to uncover it and to point our finger at any of its new instances – every day, in every part of the world', p. 415.

[8] Primo Levi, excerpted in Griffin ed., *Fascism*, p. 392.

[9] Richard Evans, 'Europe on the verge of a nervous breakdown', *The New Statesman*, 27 June 2012, available online at: http://www.newstatesman.com/world-affairs/world-affairs/2012/06/europe-verge-nervous-breakdown (accessed 30/08/2012). For a good overview on the issue of linguistic encoding, see Chip Berlet, 'Terms and Concepts: Use with Caution', in Feldman and Griffin eds., *Fascism* (vol. 5), pp. 397 – 404.

[10] Like Edward Herman's definition provided in the epigraph to this introduction, other theorists and writers have also employed the term 'doublespeak' – even though it does not explicitly derive from *1984* but is a conflation of two terms: 'newspeak', referred to the official language enforced by the party, hollowed out of meaning; and 'double-think', namely '[t]he power of holding two contradictory beliefs in one-s mind simultaneously, and accepting both of them', Orwell, George, *1984* (Helsinki: Kustannusoakeyhtio Otava Keuruu, 1974), p. 220.

[11] Cited in Cas Mudde *The Ideology of the Extreme Right* (Manchester: Manchester University Press, 2000), p. 20; and Roger Eatwell, 'Contemporary Fascism in the Local Arena: The British National Party and 'Rights for Whites', in Mike Cronin ed., *The Failure of British Fascism* (Basingstoke: Palgrave, 1996), pp. 99 – 117, 100.

[12] Nigel Copsey, *Contemporary British Fascism: The British National Party and the Quest for Legitimacy* (Basingstoke: Palgrave, 2008), p. 105.

[13] Nick Griffin, in the BNP's house organ, *The Patriot*, April 1999, available online at http://www.whatnextjournal.co.uk/Pages/Politics/Griffin.html (accessed 30/08/2012).

[14] Nick Griffin at the Oxford Union on 26 November 2007, cited in www.independent.co.uk/news/uk/politics/the-uprising-against-facism-students-storm-oxford-union-debate-760584.html, and www.guardian.co.uk/uk/2007/nov/27/highered ucation.studentpoliticseducation (both accessed 30/08/2012).

[15] Nick Griffin, cited in Copsey, p. 102, 161.

[16] Ibid., p. 203.

[17] For an excellent summary, see the conclusion to Lee, *The Beast Reawakens*, cited pp. 388 – 89.

[18] Nigel Copsey, 'Fascism studies (and the "Post-Fascist" era): an ideal meeting ground?' *Fascism: Journal of Comparative Fascist Studies*, 1/1 (2012), pp. 55 – 56.

[19] Mudde, *The Ideology of the Extreme Right*, p. 11. See also Cas Mudde, *Populist Radical Right Parties in Europe* (Cambridge: Cambridge University Press, 2007); as well as his edited *Racist Extremism in Central and Eastern Europe* (London: Routledge, 2005).

[20] Griffin, *Fascism*, p. 10. For a non-academic counter argument asserting that fascism is actually a doctrine of the left, see Jonah Goldberg's *Liberal Fascism* (New York: Doubleday, 2008). This text was roundly criticized by a variety of scholars in an online symposium hosted by the *History News Network* in 2010; see David Neiwert, 'Introduction' (also containing links to reviews by Roger Griffin, Robert Paxton, Matthew Feldman, Chip Berlet and more positively, Michael Leeden), as well as a response by Goldberg, available at http://www.hnn.us/articles/122469.html (accessed 30/08/2012).

[21] Recent book-length studies of far right populist parties include Daniele Albertazzi and Duncan McDonnell eds., *Twenty-First Century Populism* (Basingstoke: Palgrave, 2008); David Art, *Inside the Radical Right: The Development of Anti-Immigrant Parties in Western* Europe (Cambridge: Cambridge University Press, 2011); Mabel Berezin, *Illiberal Politics in Neoliberal Times: Culture, Security and Populism in the New Europe* (Cambridge: Cambridge University Press, 2009); Simon Bormschier, *Cleavage Politics and the Populist Right: The New Cultural Conflict in Western Europe* (Philadelphia: Temple University Press, 2010); Terri E. Givens, *Voting Radical Right in Western Europe* (Cambridge: Cambridge University Press, 2005); Michelle Hale Williams, *The Impact of Radical Right-Wing Parties in West European Democracies* (Basingstoke: Palgrave, 2006); Piero Ignazi, *Extreme Right Parties in Western Europe* (Oxford: Oxford University Press, 2003); Yves Mèny and Yves Surel, *Democracies and the Populist Challenge* (Basingstoke: Palgrave, 2002); Pippa Norris, *Radical Right: Voters and Parties in the Electoral Market* (Cambridge: Cambridge University Press, 2005); and Leonard Zeskind, *Blood and Politics: The History of the White Nationalist Movement from the Margins to the Mainstream* (New York: Farrar Straus, 2009). For more general, book-length studies of the extreme right in Europe and the US, see, Uwe Backes and Patrick Moreau eds., *The Extreme Right in Europe: Current Trends and Perspectives* (Oakville, CT: Vandenhoeck & Ruprecht, 2011); Martin Durham, *White Rage: The Extreme Right and American Politics* (London: Routledge, 2007); Roger Eatwell and Cas Mudde eds., *Western Democracies and the New Extreme Right Challenge* (London: Routledge, 2004); Paul Hainsworth, *The Extreme Right in Western Europe* (London: Routledge, 2008); Sarah Harrison and Michael Bruter, *Mapping Extreme Right Ideology: An Empirical Geography of the European*

Extreme Right (Basingstoke: Palgrave, 2011); Peter H. Merkl and Leonard Weinberg, *Right-Wing Extremism in the Twenty-First Century* (London: Frank Cass, 2003); Michael Minkenberg, *Legacies and the Radical Right in Central and Eastern Europe* (Amsterdam: Elsevier, 2009), and the Special Issue of *Contemporary European Studies*, edited by Andrea Mammone *et al.*, 'The Extreme Right in Contemporary Europe' 17/2 (2009).

[22] For selected book-length studies of radical right 'identity politics', see Kathlen M. Blee, *Inside Organized Racism: Women in the Hate Movement* (London: University of California Press, 2003); Antonis A. Ellinas, *The Media and the Far Right in Western Europe: Playing the Nationalist Card* (Cambridge: Cambridge University Press, 2010); Jörg Flecker, ed., *Changing Working Lives and the Appeal of the Extreme Right* (London: Ashgate, 2007); Paul Jackson and Gerry Gable, *Far-Right.com* (London: Searchlight, 2011); Bert Klandermans and Nonna Mayer eds., *Extreme Right Activists in Europe: Through the Magnifying Glass* (London: Routledge, 2006); Nick Ryan, *Into a World of Hate: A Journey Among the Extreme Right* (London: Routledge, 2004); Evelyn A. Schlatter, *Aryan Cowboys: White Supremacists and the Search for a New Frontier, 1970-2000* (Austen: University of Texas Press, 2006); and Anton Shekhovtsov and Paul Jackson eds., *White Power Music: Scenes of Extreme Right Cultural Resistance* (London: Searchlight, 2012).

[23] For book-length studies of radical right terrorism and political violence, see George Michael, *Confronting Right-Wing Extremism and Terrorism in the USA* (London: Routledge, 2003); Ramón Spaaij, *Understanding Lone Wolf Terrorism* (London: Springer, 2012); and Leonard Weinberg *et al.*, eds., *Political Parties and Terrorist Groups* (London: Routledge, 2009).

[24] To again cite only a selection of larger reports from leading institutions from the last few years, see Jamie Bartlett, *et al.*, *"The rise of populism in Europe can be traced through online behaviour...": The New Face of Digital Populism*, Demos, (2011), Martin Boon, ed., *Understanding the Rise of the Far Right: Survey Results, Think Tanks and Third Sector*, 2 vols., Equality and Human Rights Commission, Spring 2010; Devin Burghart and Lenny Zeskind, *Beyond FAIR: The Decline of the Anti-Immigrant Organizations and the Rise of Tea Party Nativism*, Institute for Research and Education on Human Rights (2012); Matthew Goodwin, *Right Response: Understanding and Countering Populist Extremism in Europe*, Chatham House (2011); and Goodwin, *et al.*, *The New Radical Right: Violent and Non-Violent Movements in Europe*, Institute for Strategic Dialogue (2012); Arun Kundnani, *Blind Spot? Security Narratives and Far-Right Violence in Europe*, International Centre for Counter Terrorism (June 2012); Nora Langenbacher and Britta Schellenberg, *Is Europe on the "Right" Path? Right-Wing Extremism and Right-Wing Populism in Europe*, Friedrich Ebert Stiftung, 2011; Alexander Meleagrou-Hitchens and Edmund Standing, *Blood & Honour: Britain's Far Right Militants*, Centre for Social Cohesion (2010), all available online.

[25] Nick Griffin, 'By Their Fruits (or the lack of them) Shall You Know Them' (c.2005), reproduced at: http://library.flawlesslogic.com/griffin_01.htm (accessed 30/08/2012).

[26] Liz Fekete, 'The New McCarthyism in Europe', *Arches Quarterly* 7/4 (2010), pp. 64 – 68. See Liz Fekete's related publications for the Institute of Race Relations as well: 'Integration, Islamophobia and Civil Rights in Europe' (2008); and 'Peddlers of Hate: The Violent Impact of the European Far-Right' (2012), both available online.

[27] For a selection of recent studies on this issue, see Wajahat Ali, *et al.*, *Fear, Inc: The Roots of the Islamophobia Network in America*, The Centre for American Progress, August 2011; Chris Allen, *Islamophobia* (Farnham: Ashgate, 2010), esp. Part 5; Hans-Georg Betz, 'Against the "Green Totalitarianism": Anti-Islamic Nativism in Contemporary Radical Right-Wing Populism in Western Europe', in Christina Schori Liang ed., *Europe for the Europeans: The Foreign and Security Policy of the Populist Radical Right* (London: Ashgate: 2007); Lucy James, *In Defence of British Muslims: A Response to BNP Racist Propaganda*, Quilliam (August 2009); Robert Lambert and Jonathan Githens-Mazer *Islamophobia and Anti-Muslim Hate Crime: UK Case Studies*, European Muslim Research Centre (2010); Martha C. Nussbaum, *The New Religious Intolerance: Overcoming the Politics of Fear in an Anxious Age* (London: Harvard University Press, 2012), esp. pp. 3 – 19; and Robin Richardson ed., *Commission on British Muslims and Islamophobia: Islamophobia: A Challenge for us All* (Stoke: Trentham Books, 1997).

[28] For more on the prejudice against 'Gypsies' in Europe see, for instance, a recent Special Issue by the *Journal of Ethnic and Migration Studies,* Nando Sigona and Peter Vermeersch, eds., 'The Roma in the New EU: Policies, Frames and Everyday Experiences', 38/8 (2012).

[29] Roger Eatwell, 'Community Cohesion and Cumulative Extremism in Contemporary Britain', *The Political Quarterly* 77/2 (2006), p. 205, available online at: http://people.bath.ac.uk/mlsre/PQ2006.pdf (accessed 30/08/2012).

[30] Academic studies of Breivik's terrorist atrocities include Tad Tietze *et al.*, eds., *On Utøya: Anders Breivik, Right Terror, Racism in Europe* (Kindle e-book: Elguta Press: 2011); and Veit Bachmann *et al.*, eds., 'Bloodlands: Critical Geographical Responses to the 22 July 2011 events in Norway', *Environment and Planning D: Society and Space* 30/2 (2012), pp. 191 – 206; available at: www.envplan. com/openaccess/d303.pdf (accessed 30/08/2012).

[31] See Malise Ruthven, 'The New European Far Right', available online at: www.nybooks.com/blogs/nyrblog/2011/aug/09/new-european-far-right/. Ruthven continues: 'Both Breivik and the leaders of al-Qaeda see themselves as engaged in a conflict that extends back to the Crusades, with both of them using references to medieval chivalry. Both have resorted to catastrophic violence on behalf of transnational entities: the Ummah or "community" of all Muslims in the case of al-Qaeda, and "Europe" in the case of Breivik. Both frame their struggle as wars of survival, with the emphasis placed on defending a religiously-based culture rather than a distinctive nationality or ethnicity. Both hate their respective governments for "collaborating" with the outside enemy. Both use the language of martyrdom'. (accessed 30/08/2012).

[32] See Laurence Asuter, 'What to do about Islam: A Collection', *View from the Right*, 22 September 2008; and 'How Islam – and the ever-present threat it poses to humanity – could be brought to an end in one, simple step', *View from the Right*, 17 September 2012, respectively available online at www.amnation.com/vfr/archives/011473.html# separationism; and www.amnation.com/vfr /archives/023326.html (accessed 30/08/2012).

[33] See Laurence Auster, 'What sets blacks off: anything or nothing"; 'What have blacks contributed to our civilization?'; and 'What do whites owe blacks? And, why did God create a race whose intellectual capabilities are so far behind those of the rest of mankind?', *View from the Right* blog posts of 24 March; 24 April; and 10 June 2012, respectively available at: www.amnation.com/vfr/archives/021954.html; www.amnatio n.com/vfr/archives/022271.html; and www.amnation.com/vfr/archives/022589.html.

For the 30 March 2012 quotation, see Laurence Auster, 'The Meaning of Hoodies', *View from the Right*, 30 March 2012, available at: www.amnation.com/vfr/archives/022026.html (all accessed 30/08/2012).

[34] For a discussion of this concept, see Roger Griffin, 'Ethnocracy: The Fascism of the Postwar Era?', in Sabrina P. Ramet ed., *The Radical Right in Central and Eastern Europe since 1989* (University Park: Pennsylvania State University Press, 1999), p. 308ff.

[35] See Paul Weston, 'Transforming Britain into Lebanon', 2 March 2012, *Gates of Vienna*, available at: www.gatesofvienna.blogspot.co.uk/2012/03/transforming-britain-into-lebanon.html (accessed 30/08/2012).

[36] Andrew Berwick (Anglicization of Anders Behring Breivik), *2083: A European Declaration of Independence* (July 2011), p. 1238.

[37] See Ruthven, www.nybooks.com/blogs/nyrblog/2011/aug/09/new-european-far-right/ (accessed 30/08/2012).

[38] 'Guest Colum: Transforming Britain into Lebanon by Paul Weston', *Nationalist Unity Forum*, 16 March 2012, available online at: www.nationalistunityforum.co.uk/index.php/guest-column-transforming-britain-into-lebanon/ (accessed 30/08/2012).

[39] For recent reports on the EDL, see Nigel Copsey, 'The English Defence League: Challenging our Country and our Values of Social Inclusion, Fairness and Equality', *Faith Matters*, 2011, available at: http://faith-matters.org/images/stories/fm-reports/english-defense-league-report.pdf (accessed 30/08/2012); Paul Jackson et al., 'The EDL: Britain's "New Far-Right" Social Movement', Radicalism and New Media Research Group (2011), available online at www.radicalism-new-media.org/index.php/activities/publications/reports/92-the-edl-britains-new-far-right-social-movement (accessed 30/08/2012).; and the academic article by Chris Allen, 'Opposing Islamification or promoting Islamophobia? Understanding the English Defence League', *Patterns of Prejudice* 45/4 (2011), pp. 279 – 294.

[40] For details on these small demonstrations see, respectively, Mark Townsend, 'Far right militants fail to strike blow against Islam on their Danish awayday', *The Guardian*, 31 March 2012, available online at: www.guardian.co.uk/uk/2012/apr/01/english-defence-league-european-summit-aarhus; and 'Emperor', 'Stockholm: The Grand "Counter-Jihad" Meeting of the Year Draws 50, Counter Protesters Draw Over 1,000', *Loonwatch*, available at: www.loonwatch.com/2012/08/stockholm-the-grand-counter-jihad-meeting-of-the-year-draws-50-counter-protesters-draw-over-1000/ (both accessed 30/08/2012).

[41] For example, see James Murray, 'EDL Rallies "target of a Muslim terror plot"', *The Express*, 8 July 2012, available at www.express.co.uk/posts/view/331453/EDL-rallies-target-of-a-Muslim-terror-plot (accessed 30/08/2012).

[42] Jens Rydgren, 'Is extreme right-wing populism contagious? Explaining the emergence of a new party family', in *European Journal of Political Research*, 44 (2005), pp. 413 – 437.

[43] For leading Anglophone accounts on the radical right in France see, for example, Edward G. Declair, *Politics on the Fringe: The People, Policies and Organization of the French National Front* (London: Duke University Press, 1999), esp. ch. 5 – 7; Peter Davies, *The National Front in France: Ideology, Discourse and Power* (London: Routledge, 1999) and *The Extreme Right in France, 1789-present: from de Maistre to Le Pen* (London: Routledge, 2002), ch. 6; Pascal Perrineau, 'The Conditions for the Re-emergence of an Extreme-Right Wing in France: The Front National, 1984-1998',

in Edward Arnold ed., *The Development of the Radical Right in France: from Boulanger to Le Pen* (Basingstoke: MacMillan, 2000); Gilles Ivaldi, 'The FN split: party system change and electoral prospects', in Joclyn Evans, ed., *The French Party System* (Manchester: Manchester University Press, 2003), pp. 137 – 151; James Shields, *The Extreme Right in France: From Pétain to Le Pen* (London: Routledge, 2007), chs. 7 – 11; and most recently, Gabriel Goodliffe, *The Resurgence of the Radical Right in France: From Boulangisme to the Front National* (Cambridge: Cambridge University Press, 2011), esp. ch. 8.

[44] For more on 'cultural Marxism' and its radical right genealogy, see Chip Berlet's articles in *Talk To Action*: "Anders Behring Breivik: Soldier in the Christian Right Culture Wars" (23 July 2011), available at: http://www.talk2action.org/story/2011/7/23/8287/32273/; "Breivik 2011 Manifesto Echoes Weyrich 1999 Manifesto" (25 July 2011), available at: http://www.talk2action.org/story/2011/7/25/95054/6500/; and 'Breivik's Core Thesis is White Christian Nationalism v. Multiculturalism' (9 August 2011), available online at: http://www.talk2action.org/story/2011/7/25/73510/6015 (all accessed 30/08/2012).

PART 1

MANIPULATIONS OF THE MESSAGE

'LINGUA QUARTI IMPERII':
THE EUPHEMISTIC TRADITION OF THE EXTREME RIGHT

Roger Griffin

Euphemism under National Socialism

In November 1941 Arthur Rödl, the Commandant of the Gross-Rosen concentration camp, wrote to the inspectorate for concentration camps asking what he should state as the official reason for awarding war service crosses to a number of SS members. They had performed with outstanding efficiency their assigned task of executing prisoners. In the column headed 'Justification and comments of intermediate superior', should he insert the words 'execution' (*Exekution*) or 'special action' (*Sonderaktion*)? The reply was that the reason given should be 'carrying out of special tasks important for the war effort'. The inspectorate added: 'The word "execution" may in no case be used'.[1]

This chapter seeks to place the use of euphemism by the post-1945 extreme right within a broader historical and conceptual context, starting with its most notorious episode, the Third Reich. It is well known that the Nazis used a euphemistic discourse with which to conceal their crimes to others, and probably to themselves as well. What is significant about this document is that Rödl is 'caught in the act' of asking his superiors how euphemistic he should be. This implies a level of self-consciousness about the need to find innocuous or misleading phrases for acts of inhumanity, which does not sit neatly with the stereotype of robotized soldiers, their human compassion anaesthetized, 'only doing their duty'. Here is another documented moment when the mask slipped. On April 11, 1942, SS-Major General Dr. Harald Turner, privy-councilor and chief of the German Administration in Serbia wrote to Karl Wolff, chief of Himmler's personal staff, the following:

Already some months ago, I shot dead all the [male, adult] Jews I could get my hands on in this area, concentrated all the Jewish women and children in a camp, and with the help of the SD [*Sicherheitsdienst*] got my hands on a 'delousing van', that in about 14 days to 4 weeks will have brought about the definitive clearing out [*Räumen*] of the camp, which in any event since the arrival of Meyssner and the turning over of this camp to his control, was continued by him. When the time comes that Jewish officers placed in prisoner of war camps under the Geneva Convention find out against our will that their kinfolk have disappeared, that could easily lead to complications.

Turner shows no qualms about stating that he and his subordinates had shot dead all the Jews they could lay their hands on. But when referring to industrialized mass murder, he then uses the phrase 'definitive clearing out' (*endgültiges Räumen*) of the camp for 'systematic slaughter', and places apostrophes around the expression 'Delousing Van' as the instrument of the extermination. This highlights the fact that he is deliberately using it as a euphemism for the newly-completed gas vans, the preferred technology for genocide before the perfection of the use of carbon monoxide and *Zyklon-B* in stationary gas chambers. Disinfecting prisoners is not generally supposed to 'clear out' where they are being held.[2]

In the public sphere, Nazi euphemisms played a central role in the dehumanizing process, making possible the persecution and murder of entire categories of civilians with consciences salved and seared. From his earliest speeches, Hitler used biological metaphors to allude to the forthcoming mass murder necessary to 'purify' and 'cleanse' the 'body of the nation' (*Volkskörper*).[3] 'Weeds' had to be 'rooted out'. The human carriers of 'cultural Bolshevism' had to be 'removed'. 'Life not worthy of life' became a technical term for the 'incurably insane' destined to undergo 'mercy killing', sometimes known just as 'special treatment', in the 'euthanasia campaign'. Mass murders in Poland and Russia were 'special actions' carried out by 'special forces' or 'action commandos'. Deportation to labor and death camps was called 'evacuation' or 'resettlement', and incarceration without trial was 'protective custody'. '*Ein jüdischer Wohnbezirk* '(Jewish residential area) was a ghetto. The stone path taken by those about to fall to their deaths in the Mauthausen quarries was the 'Ascension Way'. The camp 'hospital' ensured you died without treatment. The function of the 'special installations' or 'washing facilities' in Auschwitz needs no explanation.

The very phrase Third Reich was a distortion of language, implying both a revival of the imperial power of the First and Second Reich, but also a mystic, millennial state of fulfillment. It was a euphemism for a 'utopian' state that was to be constructed on the basis of military conquest and colonial pillage on an unprecedented scale, of mass-exterminations, and slave labor. Perhaps the greatest euphemism was silence, such as the silence that Himmler imposed on those responsible for overseeing the extermination of the Jews. In his speech to the *Gauleiter* in Posen on 6 October 1943, he tells them that 'At a future point we will perhaps be able to consider whether to tell the German people more about this matter', but for the moment they 'must take the secret with them to their graves'.[4]

The duplicitous language of the Third Reich

The outstanding eyewitness account of the systemic distortion of language under the Nazis is *Lingua Tertii Imperii. A Philologist's Notebook* [*LTI*]. It was written by Victor Klemperer, a Jewish intellectual who survived in Dresden until February 1945 as a social pariah under constant threat of deportation to a death camp (sorry, 'resettlement') until the night of the largest Anglo-American air-raids. The wholesale destruction of the city paradoxically liberated him, allowing him to rip off his yellow Star of David and escape as a non-Jew among the throng of refugees. Before this, he had taken meticulous notes on how the Third Reich distorted language and in turn affected the capacity of ordinary people to 'think straight'. In *LTI* he asks 'what was the most powerful Hitlerian propaganda tool? Was it the individual speeches of Hitler and Goebbels, their pronouncements on this or that theme, their rabble-rousing against the Jews, against Bolshevism?'

His answer is that these played a minimal role because most of it was not understood or was just boring to the public. Instead:

the most powerful influence was exerted neither by individual speeches nor by articles or flyers, posters or flags [...] Instead Nazism permeated the flesh and blood of the people through single words, idioms and sentence structures which were imposed on them in a million repetitions and taken on board mechanically and unconsciously.[5]

41

This insidious process involved some sinister distortions in the connotations of some everyday words. Thus *sich melden* (to report, for example, to the police, or even 'get in touch') came to refer to an individual being taken away for interrogation by the *Gestapo*, while *geholt werden* (to be collected) was something that happened when entire communities were ripped out of their existences and deported to a terrifying fate.[6] The word *Stück*, meaning 'item' in commercial German, came to be a way of referring to the number of concentration camp prisoners about to be punished or executed.[7] When the *Wehrmacht* started suffering reversals the give-away adjective that allowed the fact to be assembled from the newspaper reports was that the troops had fought *heldenhaft,* 'valiantly'.[8] Consistent with the Nazi cult of irrational, elemental, Wagnerian states of mind as the way of saving Germany from 'Jewish' decadence and intellectuality, the word 'fanatical' lost its sinister connotations. Instead, it came to refer to a positive ability to believe in Hitler, or final victory, with a total suspension of critical faculty, unleashing Titanic qualities in ordinary Germans. This made it paradoxically less a euphemism than an unwittingly honest indicator of the delusional, psychotic nature of Nazism as a belief system, as when Goebbels thus declared in November 1944 that the Reich could only be saved 'by wild fanaticism'.[9]

Perhaps one of the most telling testimonies in Klemperer's book about the cumulative impact of the drip-feed-like mechanism of Nazi euphemism for over a decade was the case of a Germanist (teacher of German literature and culture) who had a private library of German classics in Dresden. The author had animated conversations with her, a German Jewess, but could never break her out of a deep-seated doublethink forced on her as a passionate lover of German culture and devout observer of the Jewish faith, and the wife of a Jew whom the Gestapo had appointed chairman of the Jewish community. She was determined to bring her children up in the Jewish faith, but also as citizens of the 'eternal Germany'. This produced a state of controlled schizophrenia, expressed in the commitment to the principle that her children 'must learn to think the way I do, they must read Goethe like the Bible, they must become fanatical Germans', since 'only fanatical Germanness can cleanse our Fatherland of this current un-Germanness'. Klemperer's response is exemplary in its humanistic lucidity: 'Don't you realize that you are speaking the language of our mortal enemies and thus admitting defeat and thus putting yourself at their mercy, and thus betraying that very Germanness of yours?'[10] Elsa Glauber (whose surname evokes the idea of 'believer') was finally 'collected' for transport to Theresienstadt – a holding center for the death camps intended to deceive the Red Cross, an architectural euphemism.

The insights of George Orwell

Klemperer offers no general account of the relationship between totalitarianism and the contortions of language. This was left not to another philologist, but a novelist. George Orwell's wartime work for the BBC had probably sharpened his sensitivity to what happens to language under external political pressure to impose conformity of feeling, and censor out unpleasant truths or elements of dissent. In London he gleaned enough at a distance to realize the devastating impact on freedom of thought that resulted when culture was placed under the constant barrage of propaganda maintained by Nazism and Bolshevism. He was also acutely aware of how human beings instinctively use language to present their ideas in the most persuasive and flattering light. In his 1946 essay 'Politics and the English Language', Orwell asks us to consider for instance some highly articulate (and financially secure) English professor defending Russian totalitarianism:

He cannot say outright, 'I believe in killing off your opponents when you can get good results by doing so'. Probably, therefore, he will say something like this: 'While freely conceding that the Soviet regime exhibits certain features which the humanitarian may be inclined to deplore, we must, I think, agree that a certain curtailment of the right to political opposition is an unavoidable concomitant of transitional periods, and that the rigors which the Russian people have been called upon to undergo have been amply justified in the sphere of concrete achievement'. The inflated style itself is a kind of euphemism. A mass of Latin words falls upon the facts like soft snow, blurring the outline and covering up all the details. The great enemy of clear language is insincerity.[11]

In *1984*, Orwell famously dissects one of the most potent techniques used by a 'Big Brother' government for controlling the minds, and hence the behavior, of the masses, namely to replace standard English with 'New-speak', which is uniquely adapted to express the political system called 'Ingsoc' (English Socialism). This language not only actively eliminates the capacity for metaphor, irony, and satire, or any form of sophisticated inde-pendent analysis. It has also liquefied the reality principle by inducing a state of mind called 'doublethink'. The main protagonist of the novel, Winston Smith, who works for the Ministry of Truth, defines doublethink as:

> The power of holding two contradictory beliefs in one's mind simultane-ously, and accepting both of them [...] To tell deliberate lies while genu-inely believing in them, to forget any fact that has become inconvenient, and then, when it becomes necessary again, to draw it back from oblivi-on for just so long as it is needed, to deny the existence of objective real-ity and all the while to take account of the reality which one denies — all this is indispensably necessary. Even in using the word doublethink, it is necessary to exercise doublethink. For by using the word one admits that one is tampering with reality; by a fresh act of doublethink one erases this knowledge; and so on indefinitely, with the lie always one leap ahead of the truth.[12]

Once government officials are inured to doublethink, they deliberately spin lies to cover the horrific human situation over which they are wielding power, but then internalize the lies as the truth, while knowing them to be false. Thus, in the case of workers at the Records Department in the Ministry of Truth, doublethink means they are able to falsify public records, and then believe in the new history that they have just written. Himmler's compassion with the genocidal *Gauleiters* who have to walk a tightrope between being soft-hearted 'to the point of nervous breakdown', and so hard they 'lose re-spect for human life',[13] is a fine specimen of doublethink in action. Himmler very likely is serious in suggesting that the *Gauleiter* are suffering more than the Jews, because the Nazi elite is, after all, fully human, and they have the advanced moral conscience of Aryan men to find carrying out mass murder on behalf of the German people an arduous assignment. But there is double-think in his exhortation that his men must not be so brutalized by their work that they lose their respect for 'human beings',[14] unless Nazi Newspeak has genuinely obliterated any ability to recognize non-Aryans as human at all. The title of Goebbels' ministry, 'The Ministry of Enlightenment and Propaganda' and its subdivision, 'The Reich Culture Chamber' are other mind-warping examples of Orwellian concoctions for government departments.

Yet we should note that Orwell suggests that there is a major difference between the society he portrays and the one Germany promotes under the Third Reich. At the core of the Nazi leadership there was the belief in an ultimate goal: the Thousand Year Reich. The suppression of thought served a 'higher purpose', the vision of a race purged of racial and ideological enemies, a state-engineered 'joy' purged of anarchic individualism. The logical pattern of suppressing individualism in the name of a higher goal than freedom of expression is explored by Aldous Huxley in *Brave New World*, and such dystopian films as *Fahrenheit 451, 1984* and *Equilibrium*. But in Oceania those running the state *do not believe* in the propaganda and distorted language they use to delude the masses. Winston is told:

> The German Nazis and the Russian Communists came very close to us in their methods, but they never had the courage to recognise their own motives. They pretended, perhaps they even believed, that they had seized power unwillingly and for a limited time, and that just around the corner there lay a paradise where human beings would be free and equal. We are not like that. We know that no one ever seizes power with the intention of relinquishing it. Power is not a means, it is an end. One does not establish a dictatorship in order to safeguard a revolution; one makes the revolution in order to establish the dictatorship. The object of persecution is persecution. The object of torture is torture. The object of power is power.[15]

In this passage, the purpose of euphemism and doubletalk within Oceania is recognized as being manipulation for the sake of manipulation, and hence the power it gives those running the system, without any self-deluding utopianism on their behalf. The principle of deceit, recognized as integral to statecraft in both Plato's *Republic* and Machiavelli's *The Prince*, has thus been taken to its ultimate stage.

The two functions of right-wing euphemism

The purpose of Plato's 'noble lie', the myth that explained the origins of rigid class divisions in Athenian society, was to prevent it from falling into the anarchy of social conflict and the resulting descent into barbarism. There is a critical consensus that Machiavelli is open to the charge of pragmatism but not cynicism when, for example, he celebrates the virtues of 'the fox' as well as 'the lion' in a ruler. He adds:

it is necessary to know well how to disguise this characteristic [cunning], and to be a great pretender and dissembler; and men are so simple, and so subject to present necessities, that he who seeks to deceive will always find someone who will allow himself to be deceived.[16]

The Prince is intended as advice to a ruler, who must shed all trace of naivety and acquire worldly wisdom, in order to rule well. As such, the advice it gives may condone the use of euphemism in putting a convenient gloss on uncomfortable realities, or being economical with the truth, both to subjects and other heads of state. But it is not a license to create a terror state. However, the world of *1984* is one where there is no higher goal, just the machinery of a totalitarian government grinding on in the engine room of the ship of state, even though the captain who knew the itinerary has long since abandoned the bridge, if he ever went there. It is the dystopian totalitarian world that is brilliantly evoked in two other works of fiction, Terry Gilliam's *Brazil*, where a bureaucratic typing error can lead to someone's arbitrary execution; and Goddard's *Alphaville*, where words are disappearing daily from the dictionary to restrict what can be thought and imagined. In history, hell has often not been the manifestation of evil, but the product of the bureaucratic problems of running paradise. Yet in these dystopian fictions there is no paradise to run. John Lennon asked us to imagine a world without heaven or hell. But Orwell, Gilliam, and Goddard ask us to imagine one where there is not only no heaven, but no earth too, just a man made hell.

Dwelling on Orwell's disturbing concept of a totalitarian state run as an end in itself, opens up the possibility of postulating, not one, but two functions of Newspeak for the post-war far-right. The first is all too familiar: the Fascist and Nazi regimes manipulated thought extensively, through language and so-cio-cultural engineering, in order to pursue their vision of the re-born Rome and the regenerated Aryan race. The second function materializes when the revolutionary phase of a totalitarian regime is spent, or never existed at all at a populist level. Instead, the charismatic forces have been thoroughly rou-tinized and bureaucratized to a point whereby all the structures and institu-tions created have acquired a ghastly momentum of their own. At this point the state acquires the ghostly quality of a sinister horror film-set, turning eve-ryone in society into actors in a black farce in which a chasm opens up be-tween the language being used and what is actually going on. No character is charged with identifying an ideal to pursue, so that everyone either adminis-ters or colludes with the apparatus of repression or becomes its victim. The destruction of civil society, instead of being the premise of a new order, be-comes the state's primary responsibility. The site is being bulldozed with no plans for a new building.

The basic processes by which the utopian pursuit of a healthy, modern political order by an authoritarian regime degenerates into a vast prison com-plex of oppression without any windows of spiritual hope for its citizens, or eventually even its opportunist leaders, are well known to sociologists. They were first studied in depth in Max Weber's pioneering work on the 'iron cage' created by modern rationality, and the 'routinization of charisma' through bu-reaucracy. They were followed up by Zygmunt Bauman's exploration in *Mo-dernity and the Holocaust* of the links between the attempts by totalitarian so-cieties to impose order on the irreducible ambivalence and chaos of moderni-ty, and the persecution of segments of society that are seen as embodying the 'decadence' at the heart of that chaos, or even its original causes.

Together, their analyses allow a distinction to be made between forms of revolutionary right-wing totalitarian states which still enlist genuine enthusi-asm at least within ruling elites, and *nihilistic* totalitarian states, where all of the passion and utopianism is dead, but the juggernaut of power monopoliza-tion continues on automatic pilot. Such states have either, after a phase of genuine populist enthusiasm for a new future, decayed into total bureaucrati-zation devoid of utopianism. Or instead they may fall into a stage of feigned belief and counterfeited enthusiasm for the new order from the outset, be-cause the totalitarian regime was imposed by a cohort of collaborators under

47

military or imperialist coercion with no popular base, and often for the most cynical of motives.

Right-wing examples of this phenomenon are all countries that became puppet states of the Nazis before 1945. In these states almost everybody knew that they were living in a world of propaganda and lies, and few believed the official Nazi version of reality, or the official reasons given for the daily hell which life had become for the vast majority. Yet systematic disinformation about society and the world outside it, combined with a powerful instinct to survive at all costs, meant that the propaganda was both believed and not believed simultaneously. Openly acknowledging, if not the 'truth' (to which all access had been barred), then the discrepancy between official accounts of reality and actual experience, even to oneself, requires considerable intelligence and intellectual effort. It also demands considerable courage, since any dissent must be severely punished. Millions are thus forced into a permanent state of false consciousness, denial, and cognitive dissonance, more for reasons of survival than of complacency or naivety.

Such an interpretation suggests a more nuanced analysis of the role of euphemism under Nazism and Fascism. In both societies there were periods (Italy 1929 – 1936, Germany 1933 – 1941) when the regimes enjoyed some measure of genuine popular support, and a large percentage of the new ruling elites was fanatically committed to the totalitarian project. Once these projects started demonstrably failing, the propaganda was intensified while genuine belief haemorrhaged from the system. By 1938 in Italy and 1944 in Germany the speeches of Mussolini, Hitler and Goebbels and the slogans on posters exhorting the public to ever greater self-sacrifices, rang hollow to practically everyone, especially to those Germans suffering the Allies' terror bombing; but the state machine churning out what had now become blatant lies had no reverse gear or stop button. The doubletalk continued flowing, the doublethink was perpetuated. Meanwhile, deep down inside, crushed egos with still a spark of authentic life waited desperately to be released from the prison of falsehood and mendacity into a new life under an alien system of 'democratic' values that had been systematically demonized by propaganda. Those fortunate enough to survive into a life within liberal democracy, rather than a new dictatorship under the communists, would find that it too runs its own economy of truth.

The post-war euphemization of the extreme right

We can now turn to the much reduced, but nevertheless still potent 'Fourth Empire', (Imperium Quartum) of the extreme right, that has resisted six decades of liberalization in the West. Having identified the existence of a nihilistic-bureaucratic variant of euphemism in the extreme right before the watershed year of 1945, it is clear that there are several right-wing regimes lacking a genuine popular base which must offer good specimens of this Newspeak: Franco's Spain and Salazar's Portugal, certainly after 1945, the right-wing military dictatorships in Latin America, Hussein's Iraq, Suharto's Indonesia, the Greece of the Colonels, and Gaddafi's Libya.

However, the very impotence of the anti-state right since the defeat of Hitler has meant it could never take power and has been spared bureaucratization, so that its euphemism is necessarily of the utopian variety. Of course, there is no shortage of un-euphemistic forms: the websites of White Aryan Resistance or Stormfront; the lyrics of 'hate music'; the two books by William Pearce, leader of the National Alliance, *The Turner Diaries* and *Hunter*, or the mood of violence whipped up at Aryan Fests, are just some examples of the flood of literature making no secret of the depth of hatred which is felt for the alleged destroyers of White civilization: Jews, liberals, One-Worldists, multiculturalists, and more recently Islamists.

However, some within the far-right recognized fifty years ago the need for a radical change of discourse if the obstacle posed to the credibility of the extreme right by Nazi war-crimes and atrocities in the name of racial rebirth was to be overcome. Three basic strategies have been adopted to make extreme-right ideas palatable in a post-Holocaust liberal West. The first is historical revisionism, a particular version of which is the Holocaust Denial. The sophisticated variants of both use the full paraphernalia of academic discourse to 'prove' that there was no deliberate genocide of the Jews, that the numbers of dead have been inflated, that the persecutions were simply a feature of war (as shown by the Dresden terror bombing), and were eclipsed in violence by atrocities committed in other countries. The fact that no written order given by Hitler to carry out mass exterminations exists, demonstrates that they were carried out by over-zealous underlings, rather than being directed by the Nazi regime, and that their scale has been exaggerated. An important technique used by revisionists is to take Nazi euphemism at face value. The showers were showers.[17] 'Selection' did not mean selection for the gas chambers. Protective custody was protective custody.[18] In this case taking euphemism literally has become part of a much more sophisticated and large scale exercise in euphemism in the etymological sense, 'speaking well' of genocide and war-crimes.

The second strategy is the European New Right's deliberate translation of the Nazis' nationalist biological racism into culturalist, metaphysical, and pan-European terms, with a stress on the need to maintain cultural difference and separation rather than assert cultural superiority, let alone exterminate inferior races. As has been shown extensively elsewhere,[19] this tactic was adopted in the mid-60s in French neo-fascist circles, which recognized the ineffectiveness of any discourse directly reminiscent of the inter-war period, except among hard-core fascists. The task of forging a new discourse was carried out with considerable intellectual verve by Alain de Benoist, who drew on a host of intellectual sources not tainted by Nazi associations, including Antonio Gramsci's concept of 'cultural hegemony', to argue for an attempt to win cultural hegemony for right-wing ideas rather than staging a revolution by force. This would be done not through party-politics, but through 'metapolitics', or by what Pierre Krebs of the German New Right called 'taking over the laboratories of thinking'.[20]

It was a vision taken up enthusiastically in various countries, notably Italy, Germany and Russia, all of whom produced a prolific stream of publicity designed to undermine the hegemony of liberalism and establish the credentials of an 'organic' cultural nationalism. Again, doublethink is a helpful term here. It is difficult not to read the highly intellectual and scholarly works of New Right intellectuals without gaining the impression that they simultaneously know deep down that they have a direct lineage to interwar fascists, and yet at the same time *believe* they are laying the foundation for a Conservative Revolution that is utterly unconnected with Nazism or Fascism. Armin Mohler, famous for his highly influential (in New Right circles) 1949 book *The Conservative Revolution in Germany,* called the Nazis the 'Stalinists of the Right',[21] showing that post-war neo-fascists position themselves as the right-wing equivalent of 'healthy' Marxists in their cultural war against the creeping 'totalitarianism' of liberalism. At the same time this acknowledges that they are a 'healthy' part of an organic revolutionary right-wing tradition.

One of the most powerful euphemisms to emerge from the New Right was 'differentialism', the claim that all cultures should strive for hegemony in their own cultural space, and that multiculturalism and egalitarianism should thus be vigorously opposed as a form of cultural genocide. In a passage in *Les Idées à l'Endroit* (1979) De Benoist talks of the:

> joy which is experienced during a journey from seeing differentiated ways of living which are still well rooted, in seeing different people living according to their own rhythm, with a different skin colour, another culture, another mentality — and that they are proud of their *difference*. I believe this is the wealth of the world, and that egalitarianism is killing it.[22]

On the basis of this, he argues that those who reject diversity and welcome multiculturalism are 'dangerous racists' who do not tolerate the 'Other'. The political correlative of restoring the organism of original cultures is what Yann Fouéré called 'a Europe of a hundred flags',[23] with each ethnicity enjoying its own culture within its own space. No matter how liberal and un-Nazi this sounds on the surface, it is evident that illiberal, biologically racist ideas concerning the organic relationship between people and soil and notions of ethnic purity have been translated into the sanitized discourse of culture and identity. The implications of not just stopping mass immigration from outside Europe, but recreating a patchwork quilt of self-contained 'ethnies' with their own culture and traditions is an anthropological myth, since nationalities have never existed as self-contained territorial and cultural units in history except in the racist imagination. Nor is multiculturalism a deliberate policy of liberalism. It is the ineluctable effect of modernity, which liberalism can attempt to regulate but not turn off like a tap without becoming illiberal.

A case study in the unsustainable results of a sustained attempt to create an island of ethnic purity within a multi-ethnic area is provided by the Transylvanian Saxons of Siebenbürgen (Sibiu, Romania) in the 1920s and 1930s.[24] An even more disturbing case study in what happens when an ethnie tries to achieve independent hegemony is provided by the two Balkan Wars of the 1990s. The logical consequence of securing ethnic homogeneity or a Europe of a thousand flags is persecution, mass migration and ethnic cleansing.

The New Right's Herculean, but generally successful exercise, in creating a total Newspeak to rationalize the extreme right-wing rejection of liberal democracy and multiculturalism in favor of a 'rooted' and 'organic' society was paralleled by an even more abstruse development within the neo-fascist terroristic right. Instead of recycling Mussolinian Fascism or Hitlerian Nazism (both not only discredited ideologies but historical failures), terroristic organizations such as Terza Posizione and Ordine Nuovo, based their rationale for violence in the 1970s and 1980s on the works of Julius Evola. Since the 1930s, Evola created an entire alternative history of the world based on cyclical development: from a society based on the Tradition, and hence on a hierarchical society led by a caste of warrior-priests, to the 'decadent' egalitarianism and materialism of the Kali Yuga, the Black Age. This deeply esoteric and convoluted Philosophy of History, contained in such key works as *The Revolt against the Modern World*, *Man among the Ruins*, and *Riding the Tiger*, inspired a number of bombings against civil society in the 'Years of Lead' (1968 – 1980). Civilians were blown up in squares and railway stations or on trains at random, either to bring about 'the disintegration of the system'[25] as the premise for a new Traditional Society, or simply to demonstrate that the 'spiritual elite' forced to live among the ruins of a degenerate society were still metaphysically awake enough to carry out acts of wanton destruction.

The Evolian 'vision of the world' is so utterly dense and outlandish, reminiscent of a cocktail of Spengler with Tolkien, that it is difficult not to believe that Evolianism served as an elaborate, pseudo-intellectual pretext for attacks on civil society, which were essentially neo-fascist in inspiration, but rationalized through an unusually elaborate form of ideological euphemism. Otherwise the link between nostalgia for a Traditional feudal society and blowing up ordinary civilians in Piazza Fontana or Bologna Station is simply unintelligible. The process of ideological euphemization can be seen clearly at work in the case of Aleksandr Dugin's Pan-Slavist version of the Right, as is promoted by his Arctogaia movement. It draws on both De Benoist and Evola as well as a vast array of the most incongruous intellectual and artistic sources, but is a thinly disguised legitimation of Russian xenophobia, anti-liberalism, and fascism. In all these cases the degree to which the protagonists, and especially the activists, of the esoteric, abstruse, or simply obscurantist 'metaphysical right' actually take their own bizarrely eclectic ideas seriously is difficult to resolve. It makes sense to postulate once again, a sort of 'doublethink' in which fascists concoct or adopt an elaborate rationale for raw hatred; in a spirit that combines cynicism and belief, in the same way that the hate music scene cultivates Holocaust denial, but also implicitly celebrates the genocide in the name of the group No Remorse.

However it was not only among extreme right intellectuals that the New Right's metapoliticization and euphemization of fascism had a major influence. Starting with Jean-Marie Le Pen's *Le Front National*, neo-populist parties all over Europe have adopted differentialist racism and defended their xenophobic rejection of immigration in terms of the threat it poses to identity and culture, rather than racial hatred and superiority. Anti-Islamist groups, such as the English Defence League and Geert Wilder's Party for Freedom, also use a differentialist discourse, rather than any sort of biological racism. Again, how far the New Right's euphemisms about the importance of cultural difference have been internalized as the 'real' reasons for a campaign against Muslims rather than 'traditional' xenophobia is difficult to assess. The latent violence in radical neo-populist anti-Islam surfaced dramatically in July 2011 in Anders Breivik's twin-attacks on Norway. It was the first major terrorist attack from the European extreme right whose rationale was heavily influenced by concerns with cultural hegemony, identity, and the threat of Islam to 'Christian' society, rather than by neo-Nazi ideas of white supremacy and anti-Semitism.

One interesting development in this respect has been the attempt by Nick Griffin to turn the British National Party (BNP) into a neo-populist party. This involved drastically overhauling the overtly neo-Nazi discourse used by his predecessor John Tyndall, both in his journal *Spearhead* and in *The Eleventh Hour* (his attempt to emulate *Mein Kampf* while in prison). Here is a sample of neo-Nazi Oldspeak:

If we are seriously to grapple with the chaos of the present day and formulate a creed and movement for national rebirth, our thinking must begin with an utter rejection of liberalism and a dedication to the resurgence of authority [...] For all these reasons, our creed and cause, though they must begin with nationalism, must ultimately rise beyond nationalism to serve the paramount interest of race.[26]

Note the phrases 'utter rejection of liberalism' and 'resurgence of authority', which allude to a Hitler-style destruction of parliamentary democracy, with all the violence, persecution, murder, and broken lives that it involved. It was 'serving the interests of race' that created Sobibor, Belsen, and Auschwitz. After Nick Griffin's make-over of the party which started in 1999, any hint of revolutionary violence has been airbrushed out. The 'modern' (i.e. pseudo-neo-populist) BNP uses its website to position itself instead as an anti-immigration party deeply concerned with the conservation of British identity. There is no revolutionary call for national rebirth and a studied avoidance of the word 'race':

> Given current demographic trends, we, the indigenous British people, will become an ethnic minority in our own country well within sixty years – and most likely sooner. Each nation has the right to maintain its own identity. The right of India to remain Indian, the right of China to remain Chinese, the right of Pakistan to remain Pakistani and the right of Saudi Arabia to remain Saudi does not mean that any of these nations 'hate' anybody else. All it means is that they wish to preserve their identity and national existence.
>
> This is all the British National Party seeks for Britain – the right to be British. This is not an extreme demand – it is actually just perfectly normal and completely in line with the rights granted to every other nation and with international law.[27]

This exemplifies BNP Newspeak. It would be impossible to glean anything about the hardcore neo-Nazi ideology of the BNP without studying the history of its leader, Nick Griffin,[28] or the Party, and scrutinizing the many times in the past in which the party's key activists have let their populist mask slip, to reveal a violent racist who looks to Hitler and not Le Pen, as his avatar. How many activists actually believe in the neo-populism of the official website rather than see it as a form of 'entryism' for an extremist agenda into the electoral system, is difficult to judge. Again doublethink may come into play. Nick Griffin knows he is a Nazi but then again knows he is not: like an ex-smoker who is still a smoker who does not smoke, rather than a non-smoker. In his racist past he certainly inhaled.

The danger of right-centrism in considering euphemism

Having established some basic concepts in approaching the double-speak of modern right-wing extremism, it is important to locate it in the wider context of the general abuse of language by politics. Euphemism is a fundamental feature of all totalitarian societies, left or right, because of the extensive recourse to social engineering and social control, which is integral to carrying out an anthropological revolution and the creation of an alternative modernity. Thus, under Bolshevism, Marxism-Leninism inevitably spawns a whole system of euphemism, including the term 'Marxism-Leninism' itself, which covered a multitude of sins. For example, in reference to the Ukrainian famine and genocide presided over by the Soviet regime, Stalin expressed in a letter to Lazar Kaganovich on 11 August 1932, his suspicions about the Ukrainian peasantry and of the loyalty of the entire Ukrainian party apparatus, which he described as dominated by followers of Symon Petliura and agents of the Polish leader, Jozef Pilsudski. Stalin expressed fears that 'Ukraine could be lost' [to Russian communism] and that it should be transformed in the shortest time possible into 'a true fortress of the USSR' and an 'exemplary republic'.[29] A Ukrainian historical website comments:

> According to the historian Yuri Shapoval, these Stalinist euphemisms implied the following actions, regardless of the number of victims: (1) squeezing out of Ukraine the maximum amount of grain possible (justified by the need to modernize and feed the city populace); (2) conducting a thorough purge of all social spheres (justified by the supposed presence of latent Ukrainian nationalists and other enemies).[30]

Similarly a study of the collectivization of the Kulaks reveals euphemisms reminiscent of Nazispeak, the forcible deportment of two million peasants being referred to as 'administrative measures' undertaken to bring about 'special resettlement'.[31]

If this is a sample of Soviet euphemism at the height of the destructive phase of the revolution, we do not have to go far to find examples of 'nihilistic bureaucratic' euphemism for Soviet communism in Russia and its satellites after 1945. The following is the text of a 1962 brochure from the GDR defending (indeed, boasting about) the Berlin Wall. It was published in English for foreign distribution.

> Thus did the anti-national, aggressive NATO policy create the wall which today separates the two German states and also goes through the middle of Berlin. The Bonn government and the West Berlin Senate have systematically converted West Berlin into a centre of provocation from where 90 espionage organizations, the RIAS American broadcasting station in West Berlin [Radio in the American Sector] and revanchist associations organize acts of sabotage against the GDR and the other socialist countries. Through our protective measures of 13 August 1961 we have only safeguarded and strengthened that frontier which was already drawn years ago and made into a dangerous front-line by the people in Bonn and West Berlin. How high and how strongly fortified a frontier must be, depends, as is common knowledge, on the kind of relations existing between the states of each side of the frontier.[32]

The same systemic abuse of language established itself in all communist societies, in Communist Hungary, Poland, and Czechoslovakia, in Communist China, in Pol Pot's Cambodia, and in North Korea. Its diffusion in post-Stalinist Russia is wonderfully satirized in Aleksandr Zinoviev's satirical novels *Yawning Heights*, *Radiant Future*, and *On the Threshold of Paradise* written in the 1970s, before he became a retrospective admirer of Stalin and supporter of the extreme forms of Serbian ultra-nationalism in the Balkans.

Yet it would be a grave error to assume that liberal democratic politics is immune to this language disease. Liberal economics has sprouted a host of euphemisms, from downsizing to structural readjustment and qualitative easing. US citizens of ethnic Japanese were held without due process in 'relocation centres'. [33] The two Gulf wars and their aftermath spawned a host of new ways of minimizing the brutality of war, such as 'collateral damage', 'friendly fire', and 'extraordinary rendition'. 'Expectant' does not mean pregnant in military jargon but expected to die because of severe injuries.[34] In 1982 Noam Chomsky commented:

> When the United States moves to overthrow the government of Iran or

Guatemala or Chile, or to invade Cuba or Indochina or the Dominican Republic, or to bolster murderous dictatorships in Latin America or Asia, it does so in a noble effort to defend free peoples from the imminent Russian (or earlier, Chinese) threat. Similarly, when the USSR sends in tanks to East Berlin, Hungary, Czechoslovakia, or Afghanistan, it is acting from the purest of motives, defending socialism and freedom against the machinations of U.S. imperialism.[35]

Chomsky also notes in his *Failed States: The Abuse of Power and the Assault on Democracy,* the official judicial euphemization of the term torture by Bush's legal advisors:

> In 2002, White House counsel Alberto Gonzales passed on to Bush a memorandum on torture by the Justice Department's Office of Legal Counsel (OLC). As noted by constitutional scholar Sanford Levinson: 'According to the OLC, "acts must be of an extreme nature to rise to the level of torture. Physical pain amounting to torture must be equivalent in intensity to the pain accompanying serious physical injury, such as organ failure, impairment of bodily functions, or even death"'. Levinson goes on to say that in the view of Jay Bybee, then head of the OLC, 'The infliction of anything less intense than such extreme pain would not, technically speaking, be torture at all. It would merely be inhuman and degrading treatment, a subject of little apparent concern to the Bush administration's lawyers'.[36]

To paraphrase Lord Acton: 'All power corrupts language, but absolute power corrupts language absolutely'.

ENDNOTES

[1] See the 'Glossary of Some Terms Used by the NS Regime in Connection with the Murder of European Jews' reproduced on the basis of expert testimony produced during David Irving's libel action against Deborah Lipstadt in 2000. Available at: http://www.fpp.co.uk/Legal/Penguin/experts/Longerich/glossary/part1.html (accessed 09/11/2011).

[2] See the article '"The Delousing Van", Euphemism for Murder' published by the Holocaust History Project. See: http://www.holocaust-history.org/19420411-turner-wolff/ (accessed 09/11/2011).

[3] 'Nazi Euphemisms', The Holocaust Chronicle, see: http://www.holocaustchronicle.org /staticpages/215.html (accessed 09/11/2011).

[4] Bradley Smith and Agnes Peterson eds., Heinrich Himmler. Geheimreden 1933 – 1945 (Berlin: Propyläen, 1974), p. 171.

[5] Victor Klemperer, The Language of The Third Reich, (London: Continuum, 2002), p. 15.

[6] Ibid., pp. 185 – 187.

[7] Ibid., p. 149.

[8] Ibid., p 8.

[9] Ibid., p. 61.

[10] Ibid., pp. 190 – 193.

[11] George Orwell, 'Politics and the English Language' (1946), at: http://www.george-orwell.org/Politics_and_the_English_Language/0.html (accessed 09/11/2011).

[12] George Orwell, Nineteen Eighty-Four (London: Penguin, 2000), pp. 40 – 41.

[13] Smith and Peterson, Heinrich Himmler, p. 171.

[14] Ibid.

[15] Orwell, Nineteen Eighty-Four, p. 302.

[16] Nicolò Machiavelli, The Prince (1513), ch. 18, 'Concerning The Way In Which Princes Should Keep Faith', at: http://www.gutenberg.org/files/1232/1232-h/1232-h.htm#2HCH0018 (accessed 09/11/2011).

[17] See Samuel Crowell's article written for the Institute for Historical Review focusing on how the evidence that there were basement showers for Crematorium III refutes allegations that the showers disguised gas-chambers (a sort of design euphemism), at: http://www.ihr.org/jhr/v20/v20n2p17_Crowell.html (accessed 09/11/2011).

[18] For a refutation of some of the tactics used by historical revisionists to 'play down' or relativize the Nazi atrocities see: http://www.jewishvirtuallibrary.org/jsource/Holoca ust/denial1.html (accessed 09/11/2011).

[19] Roger Griffin, 'Plus ça change!: The Fascist Pedigree of the Nouvelle Droite', in Edward Arnold (ed.,) The Development of the Radical Right in France 1890 – 1995 (London: Routledge, 2000), pp. 217 – 52; 'Between Metapolitics and Apoliteia: The New Right's Strategy for Conserving the Fascist Vision in the 'Interregnum', Modern and Contemporary France 8/2 (February 2000), pp. 35 – 53.

[20] Pierre Krebs, Die europäische Wiedergeburt (Tübingen: Grabert, 1982), p. 86.

[21] Armin Mohler, Die Konservative Revolution in Deutschland 1918 – 1931 (Stuttgart: Friedrich Vorwerk, 1950). Introduction.

[22] Alain de Benoist, Les Idées à l'endroit (Paris: Éditions Libres Hallier, 1979), p. 36.

[23] Yan Fouéré, L'Europe aux Cents Drapeaux (Paris: Presses d'Europe, 1968).

[24] See Tudor Georgescu, 'Dreaming of a Eugenic Fortress: The Transylvanian Saxon Eugenic Discourse in Interwar Romania'. See: http://www.pulse-project.org/node/81 (accessed 09/11/2011).

[25] Franco Freda, La Disintegrazione del Sistema (Padova: Edizioni del Ar, 1969).

[26] John Tyndall, The Eleventh Hour. A Call for British Rebirth (London: Albion Press, 1988), pp. 589 – 603.

[27] See: http://www.bnp.org.uk/policies/immigration (accessed 09/11/2011).

[28] See Roger Griffin, 'Alien Influence? The International Context of the BNP's "Modernization"', in Nigel Copsey and Graham Macklin eds., The British National Party: Contemporary Perspectives (London: Routledge, 2011), pp. 190 – 206.

[29] R.W. Davies, Oleg V. Khlevniuk, E.A. Rees eds., The Stalin-Kaganovich Correspondence, 1931 – 1936 (New Haven: Yale University Press, 1972), p. 108.

[30] See: http://www.artukraine.com/famineart/cius3.htm (accessed 09/11/2011).

[31] Lynne Viola, 'The Aesthetic of Stalinist Planning and the World of the Special Villages', *Kritika: Explorations in Russian and Eurasian History* 4/1 (Winter 2003), pp. 101 – 128.

[32] See: http://www.calvin.edu/academic/cas/gpa/wall.htm (accessed 09/11/2011).

[33] See: http://www.discovernikkei.org/forum/en/node/2401 (accessed 09/11/2011).

[34] See the list of 'politically honest words' at: http://www.vizettes.com/kt/ae/page s/euphemisms-glossary.htm (accessed 09/11/2011).

[35] Noam Chomsky, *Towards a New Cold War* (New York: Pantheon, 1982), p. 192.

[36] Tom Engelhardt, 'Noam Chomsky on War Crimes in Iraq' at: http://www.tomdispat ch.com/post/73753/noam_chomsky_on_war_crimes_in_iraq (accessed 09/11/2011).

TOXIC RHETORIC:
THE LANGUAGE OF *THE TURNER DIARIES*: *A NOVEL*[1]

Janet Wilson

In his right-wing dystopian novel, *The Turner Diaries* (1978), the neo-Nazi, William Luther Pierce III (1933 – 2002), ideologue of the white national-ist movement in America, lays out his scheme of a white, racist revolution against the US Government, followed by the extermination of all Jews and people of color, leading to the ultimate control of the planet. In recounting this war between the pro-Nazi ideologues and guerrilla fighters, and their enemies who represent democracy, Pierce introduces a range of rhetorical strategies in order to manipulate contemporary language. Key linguistic signifiers of the existing social structure are 'cleansed' and redefined in his post-apocalyptic vision for humanity, in order to celebrate a nuclear holocaust and a new fas-cist order.

Originally a Professor of Physics at the University of Oregon, Pierce had a life-long engagement with the US extreme right and 'Universal Nazism'. He was editor of the *National Social World*, the organ of the World Union of Na-tional Socialists founded in 1962; he headed the National Youth Alliance in the early 1970s and in 1974 founded the National Alliance, through launching the white revolutionary tabloid *Attack*. Pierce virtually became *the* voice of the National Alliance: he broadcast half-hour weekly programs from its headquar-ters in West Virginia, and sent them out in audio cassettes (with a subscrip-tion publication called *Free Speech*); he wrote a monthly National Alliance newsletter and from 1978, the intellectually elitist glossy magazine, *National Vanguard*. At its height the National Alliance was the largest neo-Nazi organi-zation in the US with over 1000 members and 16 cells.[2] Pierce published un-der the pseudonym of Andrew Macdonald. He wrote one other novel, *The Hunter* (1989), based on the case of Joseph Paul Franklin who was impris-oned for killing interracial couples in the 1970s. Its story of interracial assas-sinations carried out by an ex-Vietnam hero who joins a white nationalist group and believes the system has to be destroyed because it is corrupt, preaches xenophobia against blacks and Jews even more vehemently than in *The Turner Diaries*.

This chapter analyses the function of the linguistic techniques of *The Turner Diaries* in implementing and promoting its neo-Nazi, anti-Semitic, racist ideology, with reference to the theory and practice of Critical Discourse Analysis. This theory argues that 'racist opinions and beliefs are produced and reproduced by means of discourse [...] through discourse discriminatory exclusionary practices are prepared, promulgated and legitimized'.[3] *The Turner Diaries* is an extreme example of these practices: everyday language is appropriated and revised into a 'normalized' discourse of violence, racial bigotry and terrorism. The process of 'denaturalization', of exposing what is accepted as common sense, is in Critical Discourse Analysis usually the responsibility of the critical linguist;[4] in *The Diaries* this role is assumed by the narrator, who exposes and revises the commonplace in order to emphasize the polarization of two regimes of power, and to confirm the overturning of western civilization. Specifically, familiar words and terms are redefined through newly imposed meanings in order to validate racial cleansing and genocide. To the critical reader who might be ideologically opposed, what is presented as the new common sense appears uncommon, unacceptably violent and toxic.

The novel illustrates Norman Fairclough's argument that discourse, as a theory of ideological processes in society, can be seen in terms of hegemony and changes in hegemony.[5] But the extreme denaturalization processes of the novel can also be read as distorting the 'double movement' of discourse analysis that Margaret Wetherell and Jonathan Potter identify, the movement back and forth between 'established' and 'constitutive' elements of discourse. Double movement is now radicalized as the text performs linguistically the annihilation and replacement of key terms in established discourse used in the USA, terms that convey the nation's categorization and organization and the formation of its subjects and agents. Written from the fascist angle of diarist and revolutionary guerrilla fighter, Earl Turner. *The Diaries* show a new piece of discourse developing from the established one and replacing it, as *constitutive* of a different, substitute reality, that of the post apocalyptic New Era.[6]

The chapter also considers the novel's status and Pierce's neo-Nazi ideology in relation to the radical right-wing populist parties (RRP) that have emerged in Europe since the mid 1990s, gaining popularity by mastering a double-edged political rhetoric that masks their far right ideology. Their electoral successes stem from an ideological identity based on negative expressions of identity through cultural and civic references, and discursive support for forms of social and political authoritarianism.[7] The Danish Peoples' Party, which gained 12 per cent of the vote in 2001 following the politicization of immigration issues and the creation of a niche in the electoral arena, now functions as the government's main coalition partner. Like other RRPs such as Le Pen's *Front National* and the Austrian Freedom Party (FPO), its success can be explained in terms of a master frame of ethno-nationalist xenophobia, and anti-political establishment populism.[8] Another example is the Italian National Alliance (*Alleanza Nazionalle*, AN), which has positioned itself on the democratic far right, having recovered from post-war political stigmatization as the *Movimento Sociale Italiano* (due to perpetuating the Fascism of Mussolini's era, although these traditional ties are still covertly maintained). The AN has contributed to all three of Berlusconi's governments; it increased its numbers in parliament again in 2008 and then fused with the *Forza Italia* and the Social Alternative of Alessandra Mussolini from the People of Freedom (*Popolo della Liberta*) in early 2009.[9]

The rise of the far right throughout Europe since the turn of the century has been aided by the 'repressive radical media' which has encouraged a right-wing discourse to be normalized in the public sphere, and allowed for cyber cultures to be developed by sub groups on the internet.[10] This chapter therefore asks whether the dangerous and influential text *The Turner Diaries*, described by historian of fascism, Roger Griffin, as 'the *Mein Kampf* of Universal Nazism', has made stronger inroads in this changing political climate than at any other time since its publication in 1978.[11] In the 1990s Pierce's status as a white racist revolutionary was heightened by the notoriety of *The Turner Diaries* when it was linked with the Oklahoma bombings of Timothy McVeigh, and then given commercial publication. Increased distribution possibilities in the twenty-first century – the internet with list servers (Google), chat lines, on-line book ordering services, as well as DVDs and CDs – is enabling Pierce's message to spread globally.[12] This chapter will also consider how far his neo-Nazi racist discourse is reinscribed in the duplicitous rhetoric that appears in the current shift within right-wing parties. That is, a move away from issues of race and revolution to focus on cultural ideological battles through metapolitics or towards transcending nationalism through Europeanization.[13] Finally, how can the novel be interpreted in relation to other terrorist networks, given its extremist discourse of essentialized racial whiteness?

The Turner Diaries *as a far right neo-Nazi text*

European far right parties, adopting a revised political discourse based on anti-immigration and Islamophobia, have recently abandoned the explicit anti-Semitic, racist discourse that dominated post-1945 far right politics with its claims of white genetic superiority. Positioning themselves against the discourses of multiculturalism that underpin national immigration policies, they favor the euphemistic term, 'ethno-differentialism', namely the preservation of the hegemony of different cultures, referring to notions of a racially pure, historically embedded culture,[14] and whiteness 'as an essentialized social identity which is under threat'.[15] A pro-racist dystopian fiction like *The Turner Diaries*, an example of the 'uneuphemistic' discourses of the extreme neo-Nazi – in the forms of texts, websites and festivals which are overt in their hatred of those who threaten the so-called 'white Aryan'[16] – seems far removed from such political readjustments and developments, and might serve as an anachronistic reminder of this earlier framing of right-wing extremism. Stigmatized as a neo-Nazi text and linked to now discredited organizations of which Pierce was once leader, the National Youth Alliance and the National Alliance, *The Turner Diaries* has, with notable exceptions such as the popularity surge following the Oklahoma bombings, been ignored or vilified because of its discourses of hatred and violence.

Pierce's novel, written in a fictional diary form, portrays a grim, extreme dystopia. Most of the world has been destroyed in a nuclear holocaust, and the extermination of non-white groups and of racial elements among the remaining whites announces the triumph of a fascist revolution and new world order (the 'New Era').[17] Earl Turner's diaries recount how a guerrilla terrorist campaign conducted by the 'Organization' – a group of 'revolutionaries' including its elite cadre, 'the Order', to which Turner belongs – positions itself against the 'System' in a conflict that results in a seizure of power by racists in California and the spread of 'The Great Revolution' to North America, Europe and the rest of the world: the whole planet is claimed as the homeland of the white race, 'uncontaminated' by non-Aryans. An editorial voice in the Foreword states that the diaries of Earl Turner, a martyr of the revolution after his death as a suicide bomber in 1993, have been discovered in the 100th year anniversary of the New Era when the ruins of Washington are being excavated. As a text that crucially links two world orders, the *Diaries* display a rhetorical structure designed to validate and reinforce the fascist ideology behind the Organization's 'revolutionary' annihilation of western civilization:

> We are forging the nucleus of a new society, a whole new civilization that will rise from the ashes of the old. And it is because our new civilization will be based on an entirely different world view than the present one that it can only replace the other in a revolutionary manner.[18]

The samizdat-type dissemination of *The Turner Diaries* after the novel was completed in 1978 – through advertisements in right-wing magazines, gun shops, or by word of mouth – before being published by Pierce's own company, National Vanguard Books, in 1986, means that, apart from the neo-Nazi circles that Pierce was associated with, its impact in terms of the kinds of social relations that coalesce around certain texts is difficult to measure. After gaining some notoriety as the alleged blueprint for the Oklahoma City bombings in 1995, it was published briefly by a commercial publisher, Barricade Press, who invoked the American First Amendment of Freedom of Speech as justification.[19] National Vanguard Books published a second edition in 1996, claiming that the novel was a bestseller (since it had sold more than 350,000 copies without the aid of a commercial publisher). Although respected internet bookseller sites such as Amazon still advertise *The Turner Diaries* (now available on Kindle), and it is freely downloadable on right-wing internet sites, there are often dire warnings attached such as: this is 'a bigoted book, a dreadful book, full of hate, it offends almost everyone', 'many would like it banned', and 'this book contains racist propaganda'. It also offers 'prior knowledge' to the USA of how to understand the causes of racist and extremist behavior.

The novel's outsider status as being beyond the bounds of social acceptability, however, has not stopped it achieving cult status as 'the bible of

65

the racist right' (according to the FBI), and read as a prototype for terrorist activities.[20] *The Turner Diaries* inspired the Order, a terrorist group which operated inside the US in 1983 – 1984;[21] it influenced the copy-cat crime by the terrorist Timothy McVeigh, who imitated the Organization's blowing up of the FBI HQ in planning the Oklahoma bombings (the FBI incident also appears in the film *Arlington Road* by Jeff Bridges); while a race war like the one at the novel's center is strongly believed to be imminent by many grassroots BNP supporters.[22] The novel contributes to trans-Atlantic links between US white terrorism and other solo terrorists, such as the London nail-bomber, David Copeland, who attacked homosexuals and blacks in 1999 and admitted to influences from Christian Identity, the UK-based National Socialist movement and *The Turner Diaries.*[23]

As a dystopian narrative that also contains mini-lectures on post-war fascist ideology, and editorial annotations that explain previous key social values and concepts now eradicated in the New Era, *The Turner Diaries* can be differentiated from non-fictional media publications by right-wing political parties (pamphlets, election manifestos, feature articles, TV and radio broadcasts, websites, postings and blogs) in which fascist aims and political extremism are masked by a forked-tongued rhetoric.[24] Written without any political imperatives such as the aim for greater legitimation and wider acceptance, the novel confirms the greater opportunities that fiction offers for reimagining human destiny. Pierce, making no attempt to mask the depth of his hatred, presents to a pre-existing neo-Nazi readership his template for political revolution: the destruction of key symbols of American power, the Pentagon and the FBI, and the nuclear erasure of most of western civilization. Originating as twenty-six monthly episodes written over three and a half years for *Attack,* the tabloid of the National Youth Alliance and National Alliance organizations, the novel was assured of a continuing audience;[25] there was no need to vary and disguise its rhetoric in order to seek a new one. Similar to the great Victorian writers of serialized fiction like Dickens in novels such as *Great Expectations,* Pierce had to meet regular deadlines, a need which undoubtedly controlled the novel's shape and content, making the narrative predictable: each episode contains some explosive deed in order to hold the reader's attention. But the extreme racist discourse of the *Diaries,* used to justify the Organization's acts of violent destruction is undoubtedly antithetical to the avowedly non-revolutionary public goals of contemporary European right-wing parties, which are currently seeking a more acceptable public face.

There is little evidence, therefore, of the covert or 'euphemistic' rhetoric that Roger Griffin finds in post-war rhetorical strategies of the extreme right, or of the divisions between surface propaganda and the underlying ideological commitments that are a feature of the current BNP's 'make-over'.[26] Instead, several rhetorical strategies pervert language, serving the aims of revolutionary discourse, such as authorizing violent acts of destruction. Discourse becomes related more overtly to intent and practice in the service of the Organization's nihilistic agenda. The attributes of undesirable groups such as Jews and liberals are redefined as justification for racial purification and the eradication of non-Aryan elements; more radically, the manipulated terms and linguistic recordings acquire extended 'prophetic' status in light of the Organization's revolutionary takeover in 1999. An 'editorial' revising terms, concepts, imagined values, and ideologies of the Old Era for readers of the New Era, constitutes a metatext that reinforces this process. In this combination of fiction with 'factual' lexicographic, editorial discourses, newly marginalized terms like 'woman's lib.', 'libertarian', and 'liberal', exist as traces of a past reality; while new 'mainstream' words like 'revolutionary', 'patriot' and 'holy martyr', gain enhanced semantic value. Linguistic revisions and reinterpretations become metaphorically toxic, as terms are either partly eviscerated or highly recharged in their semantic 'reincarnation' in the New Era, forcing a verbal displacement of the old reality.

Overturning reality: referential and predicational strategies

The Organization's attacks on the System (i.e. the US Government and its Allies) stigmatize cherished values like fairness, equality, justice, and they include renaming and relabeling society in keeping with its revolutionary, anti-Semitic, racist ideology. Comparison with this revision of values and meanings can be made with the linguistic model of Newspeak, the new language in George Orwell's dystopia, *1984,* whose purpose:

> was [...] to make all other modes of thought impossible. [...] Its vocabulary was so constructed as to give exact and often subtle expression to

every meaning that a Party member could properly wish to express, while excluding all other meanings. This was done by the invention of new words, but chiefly by eliminating undesirable words and by stripping such words as remained of unorthodox meanings, and so far as possible of secondary meaning whatever.[27]

Like the 'Party' of *1984*, the Organization envisages a world in which plural discourses and discordant voices are reduced to a single mode of thought. Turner invents new meanings for some words, eliminates undesirable ones, and excludes so-called unorthodox meanings. But as the New Era is never fully realized as a functioning social order in the way that the society of *1984* is, there is no invention of new words or neologisms. Instead, in keeping with its narrative of a racial war, and a world destroyed by nuclear bombardment, *The Turner Diaries* presents a textual site of confused and contested linguistic interpretations and meanings.

The novel's semantic contradictions and destabilizations of language also exemplify the Orwellian concept of doublethink, outlined in *1984*, as 'the power of holding two contradictory beliefs in one's mind simultaneously, and accepting both of them'.[28] The ability to tell a lie that is unconsciously believed in, informs *The Turner Diaries'* process of relabeling and renaming. This appears in definitions of the System's activities through terms that mirror those of the Organization, recalling Nazi anti-Semitic propaganda of World War II in which the victim/perpetrator dichotomy is reversed. As a key insight into fascist mass psychology on Pierce's part, this distorted polarization is undoubtedly one reason for the novel's popularity with its neo-Nazi readership. The System is represented as tyrannical and oppressive, yet also corrupt, degenerate and in urgent need of cleansing. Its total annihilation is required as a matter of urgency, for 'if the Organization fails in its task now everything will be lost'; the System qua Enemy will 'destroy the racial basis of our existence', Turner claims, for it is a cancer and 'if we don't cut it out of our living flesh, our whole race will die'.[29] The Organization on these grounds thereby justifies its campaign of violent sabotage. Turner goes so far as to stress the greater destructive possibilities available through 'political terrorism', a superior strategy to the System's 'vandalism' with its directionless behavior leading to acts of random violence due to a 'massive venting of frustrations'.[30]

In order to validate a pure Aryan racial hierarchy Turner's prejudicial discourse foregrounds individuals associated with the Organization and pushes to the background those associated with the System, creating a polarized, racialized 'them' and 'us'. This reflects an 'ideological square' – a Positive Self-Presentation and a simultaneous Negative Other Presentation – in which the out-group is represented in negative ways and the values of the in-group represented in positive ways.[31] Although Turner's ideological framework consists of oppositions between the System and the Organization, with the latter pitting itself against the former and seeking to destroy it, its representation is hardly *less* negative than that of the out-group, the System. Neither has any positive attributes according to the novel's system of representation, which has few positive signifiers, and persistently represents key social terms like equality and fairness with negative connotations; for example, in warning of the dangers of the 'racial integration of the police', Turner argues that the '"equal opportunity" boys have lost their efficiency'.[32]

Similar to the ideological square are referential strategies or naming options, that is, choices made in describing a group, foregrounding one social category over another,[33] represented in the Organization's anti-Semitism and its elevation of the Aryan race to the pinnacle of racial perfection. Crude stereotypes appear, for example, the hypothetical figure 'Kappy the Kike' who allegedly commits 'Jewish' crimes: he buys white women and sells them into the white slave trade, or dismembers them in gruesome rituals. 'Kike', a pejorative name of abuse made familiar by Nazi Germany, is used to justify violence: 'A civilization that tolerates the existence of Kappy and his filthy business should be burned to the ground'.[34] Predicational strategies – that is, the use of attributes, predicates, collocations and allusions to distort and pervert the meaning of nouns – are also introduced to promote fascist extremism.[35] Concepts of equality, for example, are defined as a 'hoax' constructed by the Jews for their own benefit. Equality consists of the 'ferment of decomposition of races and civilizations', which the Jews in their 'unique historical role' have initiated and fostered.[36] The rejection of the Enlightenment principle of human equality has long been a defining criterion of right-wing extremism; this attack recalls the conspiratorial anti-Semitism promulgated by the National Front in the UK at about the same time as the *Diaries* were written, when it was claimed that the Jews 'were encouraging the mixing of racial groups and an apocalyptic style race war'.[37] It confirms the long-held belief among Anglophone fascists that multiculturalism and mass immigration are part of a Jewish conspiracy designed to weaken the white race, and it reinforces the fascist tradition of Jewish conspiracy theories like the infamous *Protocols of the Elders of Zion* forgery.[38]

Relabeling validates the Organization's extreme fascist ideology, and traces of a euphemistic discourse can be discerned in the way that individuals are aligned to the Organization so that coherent relations between them and other social actors are established.[39] But they are labeled in ways that reflect radical semantic contradictions: a 'revolutionary' is not a freedom fighter seeking liberation but a perpetrator of genocide and ethnic cleansing in order to purify the race; a 'martyr' is someone who has lost his life by attacking a symbol of American power and causing wholescale slaughter of innocents; while a 'patriot' is an armed guerrilla fighter, opposed to national values. Another predicational strategy is the assigning of new attributes to familiar political distinctions, so revising the political spectrum. 'Relatively naïve "Conservatives"' and 'right-wingers' – usually upholders of the status quo – are 're-sponsible' and therefore questionable, because they champion reform of the System rather than its overthrow; liberal whites and libertarians are 'inherently hostile to all government', and 'pseudo-sophisticated "liberals"' – usually associated with intellectual independence – are defined as decadent, with a 'spiritually debilitating lifestyle', brainwashed by the 'unnatural ideology peddled by the mass media and government'. Their 'submissive world view', in short, lacks the 'moral toughness and spiritual strength to stand up and do single combat with life'.[40]

Negative naming strategies denounce the System as harshly repressive and controlling; the term 'Big Brother' invokes Orwellian images of surveillance. A new passport system is installed by the System, allegedly to seek out 'illegal aliens' – namely, the unemployed and migrants – but in fact to find and root out so-called 'racists',[41] i.e. members of the Organization who have committed acts of terrorism. Another exclusionary, duplicitous technique appears in the use of scare quotes, a form of shorthand to indicate hostility to alleged attributions of racism: these critically distance Turner's point of view from the language of the System. A '"responsible conservative"', a member of the Chicago Jewish community, is reported as having described the Organization as a '"gang of racial bigots"' and '"racists"', while the US Attorney General, in his address to the nation, labels the Organization's members as '"depraved racial criminals"' who 'want to "undo the progress towards true equality" made by the system': all are scored by scare quotes.[42] Once more Pierce plays directly to the core neo-Nazi beliefs of his readership by appropriating words and phrases from post-war anti-Nazi discourse, and signaling their controversial status to indicate ideological struggle, division and antagonism:

> All the liberals and Jews had to do was to begin screeching about 'inhumanity' and 'injustice' and 'genocide', and most of our people who had been beating around the edges of a solution took to their heels. Because there was never a way to solve the race problem which would be 'fair' for everybody.[43]

Turner's most insidious and far-reaching semantic manipulations are reserved for those so-called 'treasonous' individuals and groups within the System who, he argues, are targeting and 'victimizing' the Organization. 'Conservatives' and 'right-wingers' are led by the Attorney General who demands that the '"racist conspiracy" be broken up' in the cause of law and order. Those who hold such views are 'morally bankrupt' because, as 'conspiracy mongers', they spread lies about the Organization:

> The current conspiracy theory being circulated among the Conservatives is that the Organization is actually in the pay of the System. We are the hired provocateurs whose job is to raise enough hell to justify the repressive counter-revolutionary and anti-racist measures the System is taking.[44]

Identifying a common enemy through the belief in a sinister, Jewish-based conspiracy in order to scapegoat and demonize a minority group, is commonplace in far right parties.[45] The allegation that the System is circulating a 'conspiracy theory' deflects responsibility for the very rhetorical act by which Turner perpetrates this idea. That the System labels the Organization's members as its 'hired provocateurs' – whose violence is needed in order to justify its repression – is another fantasy about the lack of agency and victimhood in order to preempt charges of mal-intent. The linking of the terms 'anti-

71

racist' (i.e. eradicating racism) and 'anti-revolutionary' (i.e. perpetrating violence leading to a nuclear holocaust) through the adjective 'repressive', as if
they are ideologically equivalent, further distorts and confuses the message
of *The Turner Diaries*.

The Turner Diaries' revision of political labels like 'Conservative' and
'right-winger' through these predicational strategies, in order to justify the Organization's program of sabotage and guerrilla warfare against the System,
recalls the non-aggression of Hitler's so-called 'peace speeches' of 1933,
such as the one made on 27 August which commemorated the Battle of the
Franco-Prussian War (1870 – 1871):

> If we have said it once, we have said it twice: we want peace with the
> rest of the world. We ourselves have experienced the dreadfulness of
> war. None of us want it. None of us want foreign property. None of us
> wants to annex foreign people. But what God has given to the Volk be-
> longs to the Volk. And if treaties are to be sacred then not only for us but
> for our opponents. The treaties clearly provide that the Volk of the Saar is
> entitled to choose its own fate.[46]

In contrast to the homogenizing of different groups (for example: blacks,
Jews, race traitors and so on) within the System to represent it as a uniform
organization and hence a common enemy, Turner repeatedly articulates the
revolutionary ideology of the Organization and symbolically represents its practices through distinguishing between different types of member: such as those
who seek to retain their present situation and those who wish to move into the
elite and secretive 'Order'. One member named Powell, who 'rebelled' for re-
fusing to carry out an assassination order, is labeled a Mutineer, a term that in
army or navy discourse refers to someone planning an armed revolt, and de-
serving instant execution. Powell simply refuses to obey inhumane orders, yet
he is executed; so the label reflects the punishment, not the deed. Powell, thus
showing himself to be a 'responsible conservative', is negatively targeted in
ways that undermine his role in the Organization by the suggestion that economic self interest lies behind his hatred of conventional government: 'His
were the motivations of a libertarian, the sort of self-centered individual who
sees the basic evil of government as a limitation on free enterprise'. These hi-

erarchies of value reinforce a new contrast between the economic man (Powell) and the spiritual man (Turner). Defining Powell as someone governed by material and selfish motivations, Turner then introduces – for the first time – the higher purpose of the Organization, its spiritual and religious ethos, which is ultimately linked to his own fate as martyr–to-be.[47]

The Turner Diaries' *'editor' and readers*

The Turner Diaries' different time frames and discursive modes that both recount the events leading to the holocaust and record the diaries' chance survival as a record of these events, construct an imagined model of text-reader-reception. Turner's narrative is framed by a Foreword which tells of the diaries' discovery 110 years after the Great Revolution, and an Epilogue which tells of the fate of the rest of the world and the Organization's worldwide victory after the diaries conclude: this is just before Turner's suicide mission in November 1993.

Through the device of a contemporary 'editor' (a fictional counterpart to the actual author, Andrew Macdonald/Pierce), who records the twentieth-century phenomena that have been erased in the destruction of western civilization, the process of relabeling, renaming and rewriting reinforces the institutionalization of the fascist New Era. The edited narrative produces particular indexical meanings involving social norms, roles and identities, so that the reader may be oriented around the new 'centring institution' of the New Era.[48] The editor who prepares Turner's narrative for public consumption is descended from the survivors who, at school, 'memorized the names of the Martyrs in the sacred record handed down to us by our ancestors'.[49] As another mouthpiece for the Organization's anti-Semitic ideology, he venerates the diaries and hero-worships Turner, who has been memorialized in the Record of Martyrs. He uses a prestigious indexical naming strategy with implied deference and politeness in identifying the scholar who discovered the diaries by giving his full name, title, institution and profession as 'Professor Charles Anderson from the Historical Institute', and praising him as the author of *The History of the Great Revolution*. This strategy contrasts with the naming practices in Turner's diary entries in relation to the earlier centering institutions. Politically influential, distinguished figures of the System, such as the US Attorney General and other community and national

73

leaders, are scantly identified and never named, while members of the Organization are known by their first name only, suggesting brotherhood, loyalty, and shared goals, thus preserving a degree of anonymity consonant with its underground position. Yet again, Pierce manipulates his readership with a narrative technique that dramatizes the fortuitous unearthing of the diaries in the New Era, the awe and jubilation on the part of the NE survivors upon reading their version of the Revolution, a vital link to the past. In this way the elitist and prophetic powers of Turner's voice are highlighted. The editorial fetishization of the *Diaries* as a rediscovered relic of the inaccessible, annihilated past, and the potent suggestion of the text's cult status, crosses the boundary between fiction and reality. Pierce thus promotes one possible paradigm for the novel's current use by right-wing extremists who might wish to identify themselves with those fictional readers (and survivors) of the Foreword and Epilogue.

This editorial presence intrudes on the text in the form of explanations and identification of events and phenomena that have been erased in the nuclear holocaust. They are interpolated in parentheses within the text and signaled as 'Note to the reader'. Some define historical phenomena neutrally. English units of measurement are converted into the metrical measures used in the New Era; a 'Bazooka' is 'a portable launcher for small rockets, used primarily as an infantry weapon against armored vehicles in World War II'. Other terms, however, mark the nuclear devastation: Tel Aviv, 'the largest city in Palestine during the period of Jewish occupation', was nuked; 'The ruins of the city are still too radioactive for human habitation'; while selected nouns are redefined to justify the eradication of unwanted practices associated with the 'System and its liberalism': 'Women's lib.', for example is

a form of mass psychosis which broke out during the last three decades of the Old Era. Women [...] denied their femininity and insisted they were 'people' not 'women'. This was encouraged by the System as a way of dividing our race against itself.[50]

The information imparted in the notes confirms the erasure of some aspects of the past in the present, the success of the Organization's genocidal policies of racial and ethnic cleansing and, crucially, the purification of language in the New Era.

The editor's Notes to the Reader create a fictional narratee, defined as 'the agent implicitly addressed by the narrator',[51] for whom the editorial explanations are intended. This figure can be identified with the unknown readers, those inhabitants of the New Era who have lost access to their heritage. The editor's narratee can also be distinguished from the implied reader, an imaginary addressee whose values, preoccupations, and commonsense understandings are usually attributed to the values of groups and communities of reader. The implied reader is more of a reading position inscribed or encoded in the text than an individual or name, representing 'the integrating of the data and the interpretative process invited by the text'.[52] Thus, it encourages the real reader's complicity in producing authorial meaning and is a potential entry point for ideology in interpretation.[53]

Yet, as a controversial text, *The Turner Diaries* generally demonstrates a reduced level of reader awareness from what would be expected with an implied reader. The ideological conflict culminating in a violent race war and nuclear holocaust, represented by destabilized meanings, scare quotes, predicational and referential strategies, indexical meanings and other narrative devices, makes the positioning of the implied reader problematic and any readily collusion with 'meaning-making' unlikely. Unless already committed to neo-Nazi views or political terrorism, readers are more likely to be drawn to the normative values and positions represented by the overturned System than by the absolutist views of the Organization. Furthermore, although recruitment is a theme of the story – 'to attract new members with a militant disposition and purge it of the fainthearts and hobbyists, the "talkers"'[54] – the novel's rhetorical strategies are not directed towards persuasion or conversion. Finally and crucially, there is never a direct address to the reader as 'you', a device that might encourage reader involvement.

Limited possibilities for reader participation in the text are characteristic of other right-wing discourses. Chris Atton and others have recently observed of the practices of the far right media, notably the BNP's sanitized websites, that audiences are not co-producers of meaning, counter-discourses are not invited, and unlike the more liberal media, they construct a 'community with closure'.[55] The *Turner Diaries* acts as a prototype of such textual practices that deter potential new readers for, despite its being a fiction, many readers would position themselves among the excluded liberal, liberationist or conservative groups to take up an oppositional reading, based around disbelief or anger at such a negative, violent and vituperative world vision: national life (i.e. American society) has been sacrificed in order to pursue a genocidal policy of racial warfare. So although linguistic techniques such as semantic redefinition and referential and predicational strategies can be identified in this text, only selected readers will be hospitable to or receptive of the revised frameworks of meaning which they represent because, cumulatively, these changes are antithetical to the aspirations of those who inhabit the contemporary public domain.

Conclusion: The Turner Diaries *in the twenty-first century*

The false historical consciousness in the novel, constructed largely as a reaction to post-war stigmatizing of the Nazi genocide and the final solution, suggests it can be read as an outright apologia for Nazi war crimes, indeed as a form of Holocaust denial. Turner attacks the discursive methods by which the media perpetuated anti-Nazi themes, reversing the time-frame of history and attributing the outbreak of World War II to alleged Jewish stories about Hitler that circulated at the time:

stories about Hitler flying into rages and chewing carpets [...] babies being skinned alive to make lampshades and then boiled down into soap, girls kidnapped and sent to Nazi stud farms – the Jews convinced the American people these stories were true and the result was World War II with millions of our best race butchered – by us – and all of eastern and central Europe turned into a huge communist prison camp.[56]

The persistence of Nazi propaganda is crucial to the voice and ideology of the novel; most notably in the informing framework of a post-apocalyptic new world, introduced in messianic terms: 'We are truly the instruments of God in the fulfilment of his Grand design'.[57] In its depiction of a new, racially purified world order the novel suggestively fulfills the vision of the Third Reich, (a name that proclaims the belief in the ultimate achievement of the Thousand Year Reich), and of Nazi and Fascist aspirations for a 'reborn Rome and regenerated Nazi race' which, as Roger Griffin points out, were to come about through linguistic, social and cultural engineering.[58] Pierce's inspiration for writing the novel as a diary apparently came from an equally clandestine text, the anonymous *John Franklin Letters*, written in letter form, set in the future of the 1970s, and concerning a revolt against those in control of the USA. Published in 1959 by the John Birch Society, the *John Franklin Letters* was given to Pierce by another neo-Nazi member of the National Alliance, Revilo P. Oliver, a Professor of Classics at the University of Illinois.[59] If this was his source, rather than fictions like Jack London's *The Iron Heel*, then *The Turner Diaries* can be further read as a characteristic manifestation of late-twentieth-century neo-Nazism rather than through broader discursive interpretations of the movement in its historical and cultural contexts. In every sense the novel is a continuation of the old ideological formulae of 1930s fascism, and the well-known Nazi arguments about race and genetic superiority based upon biological and hierarchical lines, as well as being a fictional reimagining of the Third Reich's visionary aspirations that were demolished by World War II.

The toxic rhetoric of *The Turner Diaries* contrasts superficially with the more sophisticated rhetorical strategies used by contemporary twenty-first century European right-wing parties. The BNP's revised website displays 'liquid ideologies' associated with a range of discourses; for example, using a partial liberalism advocating forcible repatriation of non-whites, adopting terms like equality, fairness and rights, and appropriating postcolonial discourse to suggest that its members are being threatened by the 'other' – aliens and immigrants – while being oppressed by those who have previously been victims of the party's racism.[60] Such manipulations are responses to the general disfavor with which earlier biologically racist, anti-Semitic and anti-democratic discourses are now regarded. But, as J. E. Richardson stresses, in the end the new practices often only camouflage the same hard-core ideologies;[61] and in many cases the rhetorical sleights of hand remain the same. Ruth Wodak, for example, points out the effectiveness of the reversed victim/perpetrator position – the core strategy of the Organization's attack on the System in *The Turner Diaries* – in the tactics used by the far right Austrian Freedom Party of late.[62] Finally, in its messianic overtones and in Turner's destiny as savior and martyr, the *Diaries* look ahead to other potential apocalyptic movements. Earl Turner's selection for death as a suicide bomber, whose mission is to fly into the Pentagon, anticipates the current Islamic suicide bombers of 9/11, with their conviction of engaging in Jihad and entering Paradise at the moment of death. As a text written in 1978, this positioning of the novel recalls the imaging of the diaries in the text itself as existing liminally between two world orders, for *The Turner Diaries* straddles two discourses and moments belonging to two entirely different cultures and historical eras. Although an analysis of the readership of this text over the last thirty-five years is outside the scope of this paper, it is impossible not to see in the figure of Turner-as-martyr a forerunner of recent devastating acts of destruction, anticipating lone wolf terrorists like David Copeland and the London nail-bombings in 1999, and the anti-Islamist, Anders Breivik and his bomb attack on Oslo and massacre on Utøya Island, Norway in July 2011.

ENDNOTES

[1] The term, 'toxic rhetoric', is adopted from Lawrence Buell, 'Toxic Discourse', *Critical Enquiry* 24 (Spring 1998), pp. 639 – 665; Buell links it to green protests against the desecration of the environment, such as the anti-toxic resistance movement that fears contamination of the world by occult toxic networks. In this chapter it refers to language that is manipulated due to racial cleansing, 'purged' of its original semantic value, and now 'toxically' charged following nuclear fallout that inaugurates a neo-Nazi fascist era.

[2] See the biography of William Pierce by Robert S. Griffin, *The Fame of a Dead Man's Deeds: An Up-Close Portrait of White Nationalist William Pierce* (2001), p. 10, 116 – 118. Available at: http://www.euvolution.com/library/fame-of-a-dead-mans-deeds.pdf (accessed 12/12/2012).

[3] Martin Reisigl and Ruth Wodak, *Discourse and Discrimination: Rhetorics of Racism and Anti-Semitism* (London: Routledge, 2001), p. 1; cited by John E. Richardson, 'Race and Racial Difference: The Surface and Depth of BNP Ideology', in Nigel Copsey and Graham Macklin eds., *British National Party: Contemporary Perspectives* (London: Routledge, 2011), pp. 38 – 61, 38.

[4] Mary Talbot, *Media Discourse: Representation and Interaction* (Edinburgh: Edinburgh University Press, 2007), p. 46.

[5] Jan Bloomaert, *Discourse: A Critical Introduction* (Cambridge: Cambridge University Press, 2005), p. 30.

[6] Margaret Wetherell and Jonathan Potter, *Mapping the Language of Racism: Discourse and the Legitimation of Exploitation* (New York: Harvester Wheatsheaf, 1992), pp. 86 – 87.

[7] Sarah Harrison and Michael Britten, *Mapping Extreme Right Ideology: An Empirical Geography of the European Extreme Right* (London: Palgrave, 2011), p. 22.

[8] Jens Rydgren, 'Explaining the Emergence of Radical Right-Wing Populism: The Case of Denmark', *West European Politics* 27/3 (2004), pp. 474 – 502, 475.

[9] See Roger Griffin, 'Introduction', in *Post-War Fascisms*, ed. Roger Griffin and Matthew Feldman, vol 5 of *Fascism: Critical Concepts in Political Science* (London and New York: Routledge, 2004), pp. 3 – 4; Antonio Carioti, 'From the Ghetto to Palazzo Chigi: The Ascent of the National Alliance', *Post-War Fascisms*, pp. 91 – 110.

[10] See Chris Atton, 'Far-Right Media on the Internet: Culture, Discourse, Power', *New Media*

and Society 8/4 (2006), pp. 573 – 587, 574; citing John Downing, *Radical Media: Rebellious Communication and Social Movements* (Thousand Oaks, CA: Sage, 2001).

[11] Roger Griffin, ed., *Fascism* (Oxford: Oxford University Press, 1995), p. 372.

[12] Michael Reynolds, 'Virtual Reich', in *Post-War Fascisms*, 347; Griffin, *Fame of a Dead Man's Deeds*, p. 223.

[13] Roger Griffin, 'Alien Influence? The International Context of the BNP's *British* Modernization', in *British National Party*, pp. 190 – 206, 195.

[14] Matthew J. Goodwin, *New British Fascism: Rise of the British Labour Party* (London: Routledge, 2011), pp. 67 – 69; and 'The Extreme Right in Britain: Still an "Ugly Duckling" but for how long?', *The Political Quarterly* 78/2 (April-June 2007), pp. 241 – 25l.

[15] Les Back, 'When Hate Speaks the "Language of Love"', unpublished paper presented at the Social Movement Studies Conference, London School of Economics, April 2002. Cited by Atton, p. 374.

[16] For further examples see Griffin, '"Lingua Quarti Imperii": The Euphemistic Tradition of the Extreme Right', chapter 1 of this volume.

[17] This in itself is based on the '110 years after the birth of the Great One'; that is, Hitler's birth in 1889, which was celebrated in 1999. *The Turner Diaries* by Andrew Macdonald (Fort Lee, NJ: Barricade Books, 1996). This chapter uses the online version available from SolarGeneral.com (White National News Portal). As page numbers are not given, references are provided only to the chapters. See Epilogue.

[18] *The Turner Diaries,* chapter 16.

[19] On the history of the novel's publication see Griffin, *Fame of a Dead Man's Deeds*, pp. 141 – 142.

[20] See the online version on the anti-Semitic White Nationalist News Portal, SolarGeneral.com.

[21] Roger Griffin, ed., 'The Cleansing Hurricane: William Pierce', in *Fascism,* p. 373. For this and other groups influenced by *The Turner Diaries*, see Robert Griffin, *Fame of a Dead Man's Deeds*, pp. 10 – 12.

[22] Goodwin, *New British Fascism*, p. 6; Roger Griffin, 'Paper Tiger or Cheshire Cat? A Spotter's Guide to Fascism in the Post-Fascist Era', in *Post-War Fascisms*, p. 392; on Pierce's denial of any links between the National Alliance and McVeigh, see Robert Griffin, *Fame of a Dead Man's Deeds*, pp. 161 – 166.

[23] Griffin, 'Paper Tiger or Cheshire Cat?', p. 392; 'Hooked Crosses and Forking Paths', in Matthew Feldman, ed., *A Fascist Century: Essays by Roger Griffin* (London: Palgrave, 2008), pp. 111 – 112; Michael Reynolds, 'Virtual Reich', in *Post-War Fascisms*, p. 343.

[24] Nigel Copsey and Graham Macklin, '"THE MEDIA = LIES, LIES, LIES!": The BNP and the Media in Contemporary Britain', *British National Party*, pp. 81 – 102.

[25] Griffin, *Fame of a Dead Man's Deeds*, p. 138.

[26] Griffin, '"Linguistic Quarti Imperii"', chapter 1 of this volume; Richardson, 'Surface and Depth of BNP Ideology', p. 39.

[27] George Orwell, *1984* (Harmondsworth: Penguin, 1986), p. 237.

[28] George Orwell, *1984*, p. 220. See further in Griffin, '"Linguistic Quarti Imperii"', chapter 1 of this volume.

[29] *Turner Diaries*, chapter 7.

[30] *Turner Diaries*, chapter 12.

[31] J.E. Richardson, *Analysing Newspapers: An Approach from Critical Discourse Analysis* (Houndmills: Palgrave Macmillan, 2007), p. 51, 239 – 40. The concept was developed by Teun van Dijk.

[32] *Turner Diaries*, chapter 1.

[33] J.E. Richardson, *Analysing Newspapers*, pp. 49 – 51; citing Reisigl and Wodak, *Discourse and Discrimination*, p. 47.

[34] *Turner Diaries*, chapter 12.

[35] Richardson, *Analysing Newspapers*, p. 52 – 53, citing Reisigl and Wodak, *Discourse and Discrimination*, p. 54.

[36] *Turner Diaries*, chapter 4.

[37] Goodwin, *New British Fascism*, pp. 6 – 26.

[38] Richardson, 'Surface and Depth of BNP Ideology', pp. 52 – 54.

[39] Richardson, *Analysing Newspapers*, p. 50.

[40] *Turner Diaries*, chapter 6.

[41] *Turner Diaries*, chapter 5.

[42] *Turner Diaries*, chapter 3.

[43] *Turner Diaries*, chapter 6.

[44] *Turner Diaries*, chapter 9.

[45] Ruth Wodak, 'The Strategy of Discursive Provocation – A Discourse-Historical Analysis of the FPÖ's Discriminatory Rhetoric', chapter 7 of this volume.

[46] M. Domarus, *The Essential Hitler: Speeches and Commentary*, ed., P. Romane (Wauconda, Ill: Bolchazy-Carducci Publishers Inc., 2007), pp. 163 – 165.

[47] *Turner Diaries*, chapter 7.

[48] On indexicality see Jan Bloomaert, *Discourse: A Critical Introduction* (Cambridge: Cambridge University Press, 2005), pp. 11 – 12, 252, 253.

[49] *Turner Diaries*, Foreword.

[50] *Turner Diaries*, chapters 9 and 6.

[51] Shlomith Rimmon-Kenan, *Narrative Fiction; Contemporary Poetics* (New York and London: Routledge, 1983).

[52] Rimmon-Kenan, *Narrative Fiction*, p. 119.

[53] Talbot, *Media Discourse*, pp. 46 – 48.

[54] *Turner Diaries*, chapter 1.

[55] Atton, 'Far-Right Media', p. 12.

[56] *Turner Diaries*, chapter 7.

[57] *Turner Diaries*, chapter 10.

[58] Griffin, '"Linguistic Quarti Imperii"', chapter 1 of this volume.

[59] Griffin, *Fame of a Dead Man's Deeds*, pp. 137 – 141.

[60] Atton, 'Far-Right Media', p. 8.

[61] Richardson, 'Surface and Depth of BNP Ideology', p. 58.

[62] Wodak, 'The Strategy of Discursive Provocation', chapter 7 of this volume.

2083 – A EUROPEAN DECLARATION OF INDEPENDENCE: A LICENSE TO KILL

Paul Jackson

In Anders Behring Breivik's now notorious manifesto, *2083 – A European Declaration of Independence*, one finds from pages 1070 to 1074 a short but revealing discussion on what he calls the role of the Grand Master Overseer. This, Breivik proposes, is a 'civilian administrator, care-taker and logistical officer' who supports clandestine, 'military' terrorist operations, such as his own, which are part of a wider, self-styled 'crusade'. One of the purposes of the 'Grand Master Overseer', after a terrorist action, would be to offer ideological framing and support, to establish a wider audience for the messages that the act of terrorism sought to advance: in this case, alerting the public to an alleged 'Islamization' of Europe. Moreover, after an act of terrorism, the Grand Master Overseer figure would be in a difficult position, as 'he' (note gender) could not simply condone the actions of the terrorist. This would impact negatively on the propaganda message being cultivated. As Breivik puts it on page 1074 of the manifesto:

> It should be noted, that due to legal limitations concerning the support for 'so called terrorism' he [the Grand Master Overseer] can not openly support the activities of any fallen Knight. He must use deceitful approaches, speak with 'two tongues' in order to ensure that he doesn't incriminate himself in any way.[1]

In other words, the Grand Master Overseer needed to support the far right ideology underpinning such terrorism, but also needed to openly reject the actual use of violence.

Elsewhere in the manifesto, the theme of 'two tongues' enters the discussion in some greater detail. Breivik regularly talks of those who share his ideological concerns of a Muslim conspiracy to over-run Europe, yet do not openly advocate violence. Again, the value of such non-violent polemicists is discussed positively, in terms of high profile figures that secretly support terrorism, but also need to preserve what he calls 'reputational shields'; that is, a non-violent profile that offers them a measure of acceptability.[2] According to this argument, while active militants, like Breivik, develop terrorist violence to publicize the cause, non-violent figures within the new, Islamophobic far right (what Breivik calls the 'Vienna School') should articulate, in parallel, messages that support these same concerns, while also publicly distancing themselves from violent extremism. So throughout the manifesto there is an awareness that to openly endorse the violence of extremists would damage the reputations of potentially influential figures, who need to perform 'doublespeak' to develop their Islamophobic, far right concerns.

To examine this tension between a wider discursive field marked by hateful rhetoric, and actual acts of extremist violence, this chapter will unpick how Breivik's manifesto has drawn upon a 'license' to hate Muslims that has been offered by a range of ideologues since 9/11. Moreover, *2083* also actively attempts to present fellow travellers with a more extreme 'license' to go on and commit extremist violence themselves, as well as offering a recipe for how to do so. It will not only examine Breivik's relationship with the wider milieu of contemporary, far right Islamophobia, but will also draw on a range of critical concepts – in particular 'community of support', 'political religion' and 'projective narratives' – to develop a culturalist assessment of how extreme discourses can be mutated into messages promoting extreme violence. It will conclude that the wider Islamophobic messages, which Breivik drew upon to radicalize his own position, represent a facilitating culture for acts of far right violence. Moreover, Breivik himself has set a disconcerting precedent, one potentially giving license to others who may want to act in a similar, murderous manner.

Breivik and the license to 'hate' and to 'kill'

First and foremost, it is important to stress that Breivik was a 'solo actor' terrorist. His interpretation of how people should react to his acts of terrorist violence was a vision that he created himself. He was thus, of course, in no position to actually promote someone to the role of Grand Master Overseer. Indeed, though he now has a diffuse coterie of clandestine support, Breivik should not be viewed as part of a formalized network of far right terrorists capable of managing a wider media message. His belief that his 'mentors', namely those he cites at length in his manifesto, would have secretly approved of his actions is not one that we can back up in fact. Rather, all evidence points to the fact that he was a self-radicalizer, though one in loose contact with others within far right and Islamophobic circles.

Yet despite this, in the time since his actions, a number of prominent far right figures, such as Stephen Yaxley-Lennon from the English Defense League,[3] inevitably played out Breivik's call for non-violent (or at least less violent) spokesman figures to react to his terrorist activities in the summer of 2011. A variety of figures on the far right spectrum at this time condemned violence yet used Breivik's terrorist atrocities as a means to develop, in the ensuing media interest, the broad diagnosis of a crisis created by a growth in Europe's Muslim populations. As Breivik repeatedly stressed in his manifesto, such 'patriotic' figures needed to capitalize on the publicity generated by terrorist massacres; using it as a platform to articulate more broadly new far right concerns, while also condemning terrorist violence in order to protect their 'reputational shields'. The reason why we can see this matchup between what Breivik wanted to achieve on the one hand, and how independent figures within Europe's new far right have behaved subsequently on the other, is simply because Breivik did not develop his outlook in a vacuum. Indeed, it is quite clear that, to a great extent, he copied the views of others – even plagiarizing large portions from well-known texts,[4] which he then further radicalized. So it is not surprising that we find many far right figures agreeing with his ideas while rejecting his actions. Breivik merely set in place a more extreme form of praxis; one based upon the fantasies and desires of a wide range of anti-Muslim commentators, movements and politicians who are currently operating within the contemporary far right. In other words, he was a solo actor terrorist who was able to rationalize his killing spree by immersing himself in a wider discursive field of contemporary far right Islamophobia.[5]

In his manifesto Breivik cites a range of ideological mentors, while much of his voluminous text is simply cut and pasted from Islamophobic blogger sites. *2083* makes no secret of this, and frequently references a wide range of influential authors who comment negatively on the impact of Muslim communities across Europe and the US. Among the most notorious and significant of these sources for establishing Breivik's general critique of Islam in European history and contemporary society has been the controversial blogger Fjordman, an alias for Peder Jensen, who is referenced 114 times in the document, with many of his articles reproduced at length. Fjordman has produced many lengthy essays strongly criticizing the role of Muslims in modern Europe, which have been hosted on a number of Islamophobic websites, including Gates of Vienna. This crucial website for Breivik has become a central source for the dissemination of far right, Islamophobic rhetoric. Moreover, it is named after one of Breivik's most important historical reference points, the Siege of Vienna of 1683. Another key website, Robert Spencer's Jihadwatch, is cited 116 times, and thus represents one of the major outlets of 'populist' Islamophobia drawn upon by Breivik. It is also notable how *2083* builds upon the narratives developed by Fjordman and similar bloggers, while synthesizing these views into what he calls the 'Vienna School' of ultra-nationalist thought; one that is marked by more conservative and more radical strands.[6] Breivik sees himself as part of the more radical strand of this Vienna School, while clearly setting his concerns over the Muslim 'other' within a wider discursive framework.[7]

Aside from promoting the expulsion of Muslims from Europe, Breivik's 'Vienna School' is also characterized in *2083* as holding an ultimately revolutionary attitude towards existing western governments, while also promoting a Christian culture and tradition, alongside a pro-Israeli stance. Unsurprisingly, as well as Fjordman, Breivik develops specific praise for figures such as Bat Ye'or (a figure who has contributed a number of books on the 'Eurabian' theme, again proposing a gradual overtaking of Europe by Muslim populations) and Pamela Geller. Lengthy country-by-country analyses of the performance of a variety of far right movements are also included in *2083* which, broadly speaking; represent ultra-patriotic and ultra-nationalist associations in most European countries. Special mention is reserved for the English Defense League, which he characterizes as a prime example of the youth movements that his preferred form of extreme nationalism should be generating. It is notable, however, that he is also critical of the EDL, which he sees as a movement lacking a fully developed ideology.[8] Moreover, Breivik is openly hostile towards neo-Nazism, and in particular claims he disagrees with its biological and anti-Semitic underpinning.[9] Indeed, he sees the baggage of Nazism and the stigma of the Holocaust as another major hindrance to far right figures preserving their reputational shields. So, clearly one can see that Breivik is a politically savvy figure, a protagonist critically engaged with the contemporary far right who is careful of how he locates himself within this wider milieu. Moreover, Breivik drew upon the online sphere to construct a wider sense of a radicalized community, highlighting the importance of virtual spaces for such radicalization. As will be discussed further below, generating an 'imagined community' of like-minded activists is vital for solo actor terrorists, and there is now no better tool for developing such an imagined realm of perceived support than the Internet.[10] As I have argued elsewhere, even if their contributors are ignorant of their full significance to such unpredictable extremists, these perceived communities of support are a vital part of the radicalizing dynamic for solo actor terrorists.[11]

Indeed, it is important to stress that, aside from being overtly violent in intent, acts of solo actor terrorism are simultaneously attacks carried out in the name of a wider group that the solo actor identifies with. Far right terrorism is an ideologically motivated action, and Breivik's case is no exception. Solo actor terrorists need to gather together a 'community of support' that they believe will approve of their actions. Arguably, terrorism is distinguishable from many other forms of violent criminality by the way its perpetrators perceive their actions as, in some manner, both altruistic and part of a wider political project.[12] Nevertheless, when approaching self-radicalizers such as Breivik, it is difficult to view the people he chose as his touchstone, such as Fjordman or even the British newspaper columnist Melanie Phillips, as writers who directly caused him to commit his actions. Such figures cited by Breivik have cultivated a heightened, often scare-mongering, discourse to target a specific community, but they do not express the need to symbolically or literally kill en masse – the type of action that Breivik came to believe had become an essential task. So the diverse set of anti-Muslim figures Breivik cites in his manifesto, sometimes at great length, did not develop for him the terrorist strategy he felt compelled to live out, nor did they directly encourage him to commit violence. Breivik did all of this himself. Nevertheless, it seems obvious to suggest that there must be some connection between a complex discursive field promoting hatred towards Muslim communities – driven by a call for Islam's impact on Europe to be overturned – and someone taking it upon themselves to violently respond to this sustained culture of hatred towards a defined scapegoat community. Consequently, it becomes valid to enquire how the many writers and commentators cited by Breivik were indeed developed by him within his more extensive community of support. The wide range of far right and anti-Muslim commentators referenced in *2083* were figures contributing to a heightened general milieu that has surely lent itself to more extreme radicalization. But how can we frame this connection? Here we can develop some observations from the existing literature on cultures of genocide.

To develop this link between violence found in genocide and that in terrorism, it is intriguing to note that one recent analysis of the case, by Raffaello Pantucci, highlights the connection between Breivik and the radicalizing impact of the anti-Muslim agenda of Serbia during the breakup of Yugoslavia in the 1990s. Not only was the NATO war against Serbia highlighted as a key 'tipping point' in his path to radicalization, but as Pantucci puts it:

he praises Radovan Karadic as a great man and lists him as one of his most revered leaders. He sees the wider victimization of Serbia within Europe as a fundamental part of Europe's surrender to Islam.

Moreover, as with other analysts, Pantucci doubts the utility of understanding Breivik through the simple lens of insanity (though some form of mental instability may well become an established part of the overall picture). Rather, Pantucci stresses that there seems to be extensive elements of rational planning behind the terrorist actions, highlighting that they were, in many ways, considered as carefully crafted killings,[13] as is the case with many perpetrators of genocide. With this identification of echoes of genocide during the breakup of the former Yugoslavia, we can even turn to some of the recent analyses of genocide, and the thinking on the mentality of perpetrators of such politicized violence, to help consider the fuzzy links between an ideology that promotes fantasies of exclusion and violent responses.

It is notable that some of the recent literature on genocide has been concerned with examining the relationships between extremist ideologies and later acts of extreme violence, unfolding via a two-stage process. The work of Aristotle Kallis has been especially relevant here: theorizing the combination of extreme, primitive desires to eliminate a designated 'other', and highly rational behavior to achieve this goal, which does appear to characterize such murderous forms of extreme political violence. Kallis argues that all genocides radicalize individuals into mass murderers through two key stages: developing a 'license to hate' a discrete other – such as Jews or Muslims – within a wider population. This is then followed by an extreme situation – such as direct orders from a respected superior; the removal of sanctions when indulging in killing; entering into an arena where the precedent for systematized killing has been established; or even simply a hyper-paranoid state of 'self defense' – sparking a more radical 'license to kill'. In order to reconsider Breivik's action and manifesto, this sort of general modeling is extremely useful in linking an exclusionary ideology and a language of hatred on the one hand, and extreme violence on the other, when approaching a pan-European, Islamophobic discursive field 'licensing' extremist violence.[14]

When considering this point, it is also worth stressing that Kallis reflects on the psychology of this process. His work asserts that the rhetorical cultivation of an ever-greater 'license to hate' through a variety of media messages, and perceived injustices, generates a powerful sense of cognitive dissonance between what is becoming ever more desirable regarding the elimination of a targeted community, and what is morally permissible. This can generate quite extreme tensions between desire and permissibility that lead to radical methods for resolution. These resolutions can come when such radicalized figures are given a 'license to kill', namely to act in violently extreme ways. Such violence can also become easily accepted, for it resolves the disconnection between conventional morality and the extremes of what has become desirable through extended exposure to a culture of extreme hatred.[15] So when we look at the wider discursive frame of Islamophobic messages that have been promoted by a number of far right figures,[16] we can view such an engagement with this discourse as an essential aspect of the process of radicalization. These messages helped to produce what can be dubbed a 'license to hate' in Breivik (and many others). The contributors to this discourse promote a worldview that normalizes an extreme desire – in this case, to eliminate all Muslim influence from European cultural life. Yet this more general license to hate needed to be further radicalized by Breivik himself, to create the license to indiscriminate murder that he believed justified his actions.

Exactly what triggered this crossover into violent extremism remains difficult to establish. After further scrutiny of the Breivik case, we may well come to know more details about the mental health explanations of his actions. His trial has shown that he was legally culpable for his actions, though exactly how his psychological makeup impacted on his actions has yet to be fully established. Moreover, there is a pattern here. Many commentators on solo actor terrorists argue that a variety of mental health vulnerabilities can help to explain the turn of individuals to terrorism. Unlike group terrorists, there is a propensity for solo actors to suffer from mental health issues, although it is also recognized that mental health concerns alone do not explain the need to murder others.[17] Just as with other acts of extreme political violence, a variety of explanatory factors feed into the reasons why an individual decides to kill for a political cause.

Turning to some of the recent literature on terrorism is helpful in further considering this issue. In particular, such a perspective raises important discussions that seek to unpick the cultural milieu of terrorist violence. Indeed, in order to think about terrorism as involving a two-stage process of extreme hatred preceding extreme violence, it is advantageous to adopt what can be broadly described as a 'culturalist approach'. One academic figure developing such an approach, Mark Juergensmeyer, stresses in his *Terror in the Mind of God* the need for a culturalist view for analyzing terrorism. Here, terrorist ideologies are regarded as socially constructed phenomena, a position that clearly chimes with what has been discussed above. Broadly akin to Michel Foucault's concept of the 'episteme' or Pierre Bordieu's notion of the 'habitus', for Juergensmeyer understanding the framing, ideological assumptions that underpin terrorist motivations and actions are crucial to interpreting the acts of such figures. Even for solo actor terrorists – figures such as Breivik who carry out terrorist acts unaided by a wider terrorist network – setting one's actions within the views and discourses of a wider cultural milieu, often interpreted by terrorists themselves as broadly supportive of their action, is a vital component to the functioning of extremist cultures. As Juergensmeyer stresses:

Even those acts that appear to be solo ventures conducted by rogue activists often have networks of support and ideologies of validation behind them, whether or not these networks and ideologies are immediately apparent [...] Behind convicted bomber Timothy McVeigh and Buford Furrow, the alleged attacker of a Jewish day-care center, was a subculture of militant Christian groups that extends throughout the United States. Behind Unabomber Theodore Kaczynski was the strident student activist culture of the late 1960s, in which one could easily become infected by the feeling that 'terrible things' were going on [...] In all of these cases the activists thought that their acts were supported not only by other people but by a widely shared perception that the world was already violent: it was enmeshed in great struggles that gave their own violent actions moral meaning.[18]

By developing this perspective, alongside Kallis' model of the discrete licenses to 'hate' and to 'kill', we can consider terrorist violence as a phenomenon embedded in wider cultural networks, even if these wider networks are not fully cognisant of their role in supporting an actual terrorist. This is the phenomenon that we see clearly articulated in the Breivik case.

Strikingly, the far right discourse discussed above seems to have been particularly significant in helping Breivik define his enemy. There are two key categories of opponents set out in Breivik's *2083*: not only Muslims but also those he dubs 'cultural Marxists'. While drawing much of his Islamophobia from figures such as Fjordman and Bat Ye'or, another key influence also feeds into this analysis: American ideologue William S. Lind, alongside others connected to the radical conservative think tank the Free Congress Foundation. This directly relates to the assertion, in Breivik's worldview, of the pernicious impact of the general phenomenon he summarizes as 'political correctness' and the critical term 'cultural Marxism'. As with his development of the threat of the Islamization of Europe, Breivik again simply cuts and pastes much of the analysis directly from others, in this case Lind and other 'paleoconservative' writers who have written on this theme.[19] This American influence is also important to note, not least because, when looking at the people he actually killed, Breivik did not target Muslims, but rather left wing students and the government establishment.

According to Lind (and Brevik), twentieth century Marxism diverged into two distinct forms: economic and cultural. While economic Marxism rose and fell during the twentieth century, epitomized by the dissolution of the USSR in the late 1980s and early 1990s, a parallel strand of 'cultural Marxism' was developed in the west by key figures such as Antonio Gramsci, Theodor Adorno and Herbert Marcuse. In what is essentially a wildly over-inflated assessment of the impact of the Frankfurt School on contemporary Western society, Breivik argues that the much-mythologized year of 1968 represented a key turning point in modern history – one where the cultural Marxists became dominant in the West. Adherents of this ostensibly pernicious ideology thereafter used positions of cultural power in order to promote a 'politically correct' agenda of ideas and policies such as multiculturalism and feminism. For Breivik, this represented the creation of a totalitarian society, one that promoted a weakening of national traditions and longstanding European cultural identity. So while it is certainly correct to look at his actions and see extremism, it is also worth bearing in mind that when Breivik himself looks at European society he, too, sees an extreme situation. Most worryingly for him, this extreme scenario allowed a crusading Islam to establish a stronghold in Europe, which needed to be forcefully rebuffed.

With this bifurcation of enemies, cultural Marxist and Muslim, we can also see clearly that Breivik had an obvious notion of who he was fighting for and against, and ultimately stresses that cultural Marxists are the greater danger. To this end, *2083* goes so far as to divide European cultural Marxists into the categories of A, B, and C level 'traitor', with a further category D for those who support higher-level 'traitors'.[20] Most of the people reading this book, in fact would be classified as B level traitors (although Breivik considers 'professors' at least to be level A traitors), as would many of those he killed and injured on 22 July 2011. Level B traitors are people well integrated into the functioning of the modern state, from the politically active, to employees of government organizations, university lecturers and teachers. Such people are seen as legitimate targets during a terrorist action, according to Breivik's framework. For Breivik, all level A traitors are legitimate targets too, although terror actions that are able to kill more level B traitors are deemed preferable to ones directed at smaller numbers in the level A traitor category. Essentially, he stresses that level B traitors have far less security surrounding them than level A traitors (such as high-end politicians), so terrorist violence against level B traitors are more likely to succeed, and create mass killings that will generate publicity.[21] It is also important to stress that such distinctions justifying violence against figures deemed to be 'traitorous' is also underpinned by a sense of moral justification, raising the question: how does Breivik develop the idea that he is morally correct to kill such traitors?

Morality and violence: the politicized language of religion

Another key analyst of terrorist cultures, Albert Bandura, stresses the importance of examining the 'moral' paradigm within which terrorist actors like to believe they operate. We saw earlier that Kallis' approach highlights the need for extremist perpetrators to develop a new morality in order to overcome a mismatch between revolutionary viewpoints on the one hand, and what most people would consider morally acceptable on the other. This construction of an alternate moral framework, one where violence becomes permissible, is another central component in the creation of a viable terrorist culture that offers not only a license to hate, but also a license to kill. To this end Bandura argues that, by developing a 'moral sanction of violent means, people see themselves as fighting ruthless oppressors who have an unquenchable appetite for conquest'. *2083's* rhetoric vis-à-vis cultural Marxists and Muslim 'invaders' within Europe clearly fit this paradigm of fending off ruthless oppressors, as does his equation of liberalism with totalitarianism. Furthermore, Bandura stresses that, for the terrorist, the 'task of making violence morally defensible is facilitated when nonviolent options are deemed to have been ineffective'.[22] So two further key tropes within terrorist cultures, then, are a language of morality (usually developed in terms of the 'purification' of decadence), and the argument that non-violence has been tested and found wanting. Unsurprisingly, we can find this type of rhetoric across Breivik's manifesto too. We will come back to the latter point further on in the chapter, but for now we can focus more on the creation of a morality that promotes violent extremism.

In such alternate 'moral' worlds, drawing upon the language of religion becomes a key element of terrorist propaganda. Indeed, while Islamist terrorists can be best viewed as essentially secular political extremists who steep their ideology in a skewed reading of Islam in order to justify indiscriminate violence,[23] religious discourse has also been appropriated in the terrorist cultures developed by other forms of violent extremism. In American neo-Nazi circles, for instance, David Lane's doctrine of Odinism grew into his own political religion, Wotanism.[24] Indeed, the apocalyptic and revolutionary themes underpinning extremist ideologies can potentially be developed from writings of all major religions, as well as from pagan faiths. Such tropes allow terrorists to gut religious texts for apparent endorsements of violence, which can greatly help in evoking the necessary moral justifications for terrorism, setting it within a wider set of cultural justifications that offer gravitas to extremist actions.

When unpicking such selective and deeply politicized recourse to religious language within a fascist mind-set, the conceptual term 'political religion', developed by Emilio Gentile among others,[25] presents an effective model for examining such political appropriation of religious tropes. As with all variants of political religion, Breivik's turn to the religious is selective and intended to create a sacred aura around his actions. Indeed, though his tenor can become clearly religious in places – even going so far as to cite scripture – his understanding of the past and vision for the future are firmly rooted in a historical sense of time: his is a secular vision of a European Christendom, but one drawing on mythic and religious themes in order to enhance the ostensible moral gravitas of terrorist violence. In particular, his understanding of the past is defined by a historical meta-narrative outlining how this 'Christian Europe' has been in a centuries-long conflict with waves of Muslim invaders. So essentially, this is a typically fascist 'good' against 'evil' historical myth – structurally akin to those of other fascists, such as the historicized anti-Semitic conspiracy theories developed by Hitler in *Mein Kampf*. Meanwhile, Breivik's vision for the future redemption of Europe is an emphatically secular, 'this worldly' one, while his deployment of a Christian language is primarily used to evoke a sense of European tradition and culture.

Political religion theory also highlights the evocative power of myth and ritual in helping to create a sense of faith – especially a 'higher' sense of purpose – within revolutionary ideologies like fascism. Typically, the Breivik manifesto repeatedly highlights to its readers a sense of duty to commit acts of violence, or to privately support them, while also drawing on a range of mythic tropes to structure the fantasy of war. Drawing on our earlier discussion, we can view such utterances in *2083* as Breivik offering his readers a license to kill by repeatedly instructing the reader to take his own actions both as inspiration, and as setting a precedent for further violence to follow. In order to place a mythic aura around this idea of a terrorist act as future inspiration, *2083* repeatedly returns to The Crusades and the Knights Templar as central to the mythopoeic register in later sections of the manifesto. These later writings, for the most part at least, comprise of a text that (more so than earlier in the manifesto), is actually authored by Breivik.

In turning to the third part of Breivik's manifesto in particular, we find he devotes scores of pages to the nature of the new Knights Templar order – which he believes will redeem European Christianity by recruiting a small but fanatically loyal elite. In eliding a romanticized impression of the historical Knights Templar with the idea of modern terrorist cells, *2083* then outlines the various rituals to be performed in order to bring potential terrorists into the new Knights Templar. This fantasy extends to many detailed pages on the uniforms and medals to be worn by members, alongside a commentary that highlights the existence of a special, higher role in protecting Europe from an enemy that only a select few can fully recognize. The level of nuance here is important to stress. In terms of uniforms and medals, for example, there are a variety of illustrations printed alongside lengthy accompanying texts setting out the meaning behind symbolic clothing and awards. Breivik also develops an oath of initiation for new Knights, which regularly taps into ontological concerns: for example, we can find a detailed discussion on the nature of gravestones that are suitable for the twenty-first century Knights Templar. By again evoking the mythic register when discussing those Knights 'martyred' during their attacks, Breivik underscores the important role of personal sacrifice to a higher cause. Furthermore, a sense of righting injustice is also a notable component in Breivik's 'moral' framework: he regularly stresses that Knights of the new order are figures carrying out a higher form of justice than that currently exercised by European states – which helps explain his personal rejection of the authority of the court that tried and convicted him in 2012. Indeed, his proposed new Knights Templar order is conceived as one functioning as a legal system superior to that of individual states and multi-national institutions such as the European Union. In this fantasy world, the Knights Templar is an institution that has the right to act as judge, jury and executioner in particular situations.

Finally, political religions have often drawn on aspects of traditional religions to further develop a sense of gravitas and legitimacy. With respect to discussions regarding Christianity in the manifesto, Breivik identifies strongly with the Christian faith – albeit in a cultural rather than a theological manner – and is particularly opinionated on the theme. Firstly, what is notable here is that he is broadly critical of Protestantism, and claims that cultural Marxism has infected many Protestant churches of late. Moreover, he argues that only one denomination truly represents the Christian tradition in Europe: Catholicism. Yet for Breivik, the most significant aspect of Christianity is its ability to convey a sense of a rooted, historicized identity to otherwise decadent Europeans. Thus his critique of Protestantism centers upon his view that the Reformation ultimately led to a fragmentation of the Christian tradition. Although key figures of reform, such as Martin Luther, may have had important points to make, for Breivik the break with Catholicism only served to weaken Christian identity in Europe in the long term. Contrastingly, a strong culture of Catholicism in the contemporary world is styled as a vital force against any weakening of the European character.[26] Indeed for Breivik, the appropriation of Christianity is not ultimately theological: *2083* does not call for a return to some golden age of Christianity, or a simple reversion to Medieval Europe. In fact, Breivik repeatedly suggests that Europe will remain largely secular in his version of the future.[27] Nor, for the most part, is there a clear sense that the ideology is derived in any meaningful sense from readings of the Bible. In the final section of the document we can find less central chapters that do develop some specific points from scripture, in order to further help legitimize acts of warfare, again with reference to a Crusader context, but these do not appear central to the vision.

Undoubtedly, the language of religion has a clear legitimizing role within Breivik's manifesto – serving to steep acts of terrorism within a quasi-moral framework – even if his cause remains primarily a political one. In order to understand this justification of violence, it is important to comprehend how such terrorists try to situate themselves within a narrative wider flow of history. In particular, it is vital to understand how Breivik styles the present as a time where peaceful options are no longer available.

From non violence to terrorism: the projective narrative

Another leading theorist who has linked political religious theory and terrorism is Roger Griffin, who has also commented in detail on the specific appropriation of idealized hero myths within the far right terrorist mind-set. Griffin argues that terrorists often like to think of themselves as comparable to mythical and heroic figures from previous eras, and even generate their own pantheon of heroes to whom the terrorist likens him or herself. Not surprisingly, Breivik's manifesto is shot through with just such references to past figures – not least in his self-presentation as a modern day Knights Templar; a 'warrior' akin to historical military 'hero' figures such as Richard the Lionheart. There is a pronounced narcissistic quality to the way Breivik presents himself as such a hero, one that many psychological interpretations will undoubtedly focus attention on in future analysis. Yet in terms of analyzing the rhetorical styles of the manifesto, Griffin adds a further term for scrutinizing this appropriation of heroic identities among far right terrorists: 'projective narratives'. This term refers to connections made by such terrorists that connect their individual actions in the present to idealized readings of the past, especially to utopian visions for the transformation of a whole society.[28]

As far right terrorists often consider themselves archetypal hero figures – a 'chosen' elite invested with the belief they have superhuman powers of perception and ability – they believe they have moved beyond simply diagnosing a crisis, and are resolved to take decisive action. To achieve this, such terrorists construct a narrative arc to justify their on-going actions, to sustain the fantasy that they may actually succeed in precipitating revolutionary change. This sense of linking personal actions with a wider flow of events is powerfully evoked in Breivik's understanding of European history, and his meticulous creation of a 'sacralized' moral framework for legitimizing violence. But as Griffin states, these projective narratives also need to offer a connection between the present and the future in order to allow terrorist praxis to be viewed not merely as an isolated incident, but rather as an act leading towards a more extensive scheme of revolutionary change. Indeed, a terrorist's projective narrative is essentially the 'story' connecting individual extremists' actions with the political aim of the overthrowing of one society and replacing it with another. In *2083*, Breivik's projective narrative is particularly detailed, and typically culminates in a vision of revolution.

In *2083*, Breivik regards Europe as a continent in constant battle with Muslim domination; and moreover, in the present, Muslims are now being aided by the ever more powerful force of cultural Marxism, one which has given them the upper hand. In terms of Griffin's projective narrative linking his terrorist violence to a wider cause, Breivik divides the more recent past and future into four phases. These periods set out Europe's perceived invasion by Muslim 'outsiders', and their eventual defeat in the year 2083 (which also happens to be 200 years since Marx's death). He is quite specific on the timing of these phases. First, he finds that a 'Phase of Dialogue' lasted from 1955 to 1999, a period where a more peaceful means could have remedied his concerns, and Muslims could have been removed from Europe without the need for 'civil war'. This was followed by what he calls the 'First Phase of the European Civil War' meaning that, between 1999 and 2030, Europe has been, and will continue to become, ever more marred by the Muslim 'threat'. During these years, this danger will increasingly be rebuffed by terrorist resistance fighters and small groups, of which his own solo act was an early instance. This will be combined with a growing consolidation of non-violent conservative and patriotic movements who will fight, in parallel, the propaganda war against Muslims and their cultural Marxist defenders. By thus presenting Europe as already gripped by civil war, Breivik situates himself in a period where all peaceful means have already been exhausted – as we have seen a key trope within terrorist radicalization. Building on this wild speculation, Breivik's projective narrative contends that, from 2030 to 2070, this civil war will enter a more advanced, second phase – one where the Knights Templar will develop complex cellular terrorist operations, leading to a groundswell of cultural conservative forces preparing the way for the final phase of conflict. This is 'Phase 3 of the European Civil War', lasting from 2070 to 2083. At this point, precisely four hundred years after the Siege of Vienna, a 'cultural Conservative' worldview will finally overthrow cultural Marxism, and the cause that lies at the core of the Breivik vision will be victorious. At this point, all remaining level A and level B traitors will be executed, and all remaining Muslims will be deported from Europe.[29]

What is striking about Breivik's discourse is the blurring of an extremist fantasy, containing a Europe free from Muslims, with a rationalized approach to how this fantasy will be achieved. In this complex blurring of the rational and the irrational, one again finds echoes of a genocidal mind-set.[30] Breivik sees himself as but one early visionary in a war of civilizations that has been underway for centuries, and is just entering into a revolutionary phase. His

96

early act in the 'civil war' was thus intended to inspire long-term revolutionary change; but he is not expecting that his being in the world alone will achieve results in the foreseeable future. In particular, we can see from this narrative that Breivik's breakdown of recent history and future occurrences offers an explicit justification for the targeting of civilians. Apparently, this would not have been acceptable before 1999, but becomes so after this point. Elsewhere in his manifesto, Breivik justifies such a position by making bold statements surrounding the need to 'awaken' wider society to this coming war through acts of mass violence that would help to bring attention to the cause.

Finally, Griffin's theoretical work setting out the ideas animating fascist revolutionaries also highlights the importance of the myth of rebirth within extremists' interpretations of their own importance to a project of redeeming a national community.[31] Here too, this trope is central to the construction of Breivik's projective narrative. Acts of terror are presented as a necessary part of a mythic process of awakening the wider population to the dangers posed by the alleged Islamization of Europe, alerting them to the supposed conspiracy of cultural Marxism. Mass murder therefore aims to stir up a wider public consciousness to the threat he believes he has identified (Breivik even argues that it is better for operations to kill too many people rather than not enough). A point he underscored, when at the conclusion of his trial on 24 August 2012, he 'apologized' for not killing more. Patently, the link between death and renewal is inescapable in Breivik's fantasy – thus legitimizing extreme violence.

Conclusions

The analysis set out in this chapter demonstrates that *2083 – A European Declaration of Independence* exemplifies the potential extremism within contemporary anti-Muslim cultures and other forms of far right activism. Contemporary Islamophobia should not be dismissed as mere colorful but harmless 'populism', and is a discourse that can give a potent license to hate. Moreover, as with group terrorists, solo actors also operate within larger counter-cultural arenas. Via a culturalist approach to understanding the impact of extreme ideological concerns upon self-radicalizers it is possible to see the role played by the wider discursive field from which Breivik drew his violent ideas. For the most part, contributors to Europe's Islamophobic far right field do not directly incite terrorist violence. Though just as a wide variety of Nazi propaganda images helped to establish a license inciting hatred towards Jewish communities in the 1930s, so the license to hate Muslims promoted by a diverse range of far right politicians, movements and blogging websites has helped to normalize an extreme hatred towards Muslims. Breivik has predicated his own actions on this strand of far right ideology. Although the new far right Islamophobes have not directly given him a license to kill, they certainly furnished him with more than enough material to develop a heightened license to hate and to cultivate the desire for a Europe free from Muslims.

In examining what Breivik has added to this formula, it is clear that there are a number of additional features too. The evocation of mythic themes to give a quasi-religious quality to his 'crusade' helped steep his actions in a profound sense of 'moral' purpose. Though this 'morality' involved the mass slaughter of children as young as 14 on 22 July 2011, it is notable that he justified these actions in terms of fighting a war against a ruthless and powerful enemy. Within his projective narrative, moreover, the theme of historical phases is projected into the future, carefully delimiting when violence becomes permissible, while rationalizing his present situation as a special time -- civil war – where violence has become licensed. Throughout this civil war period, *2083* forecasts a conflict on two fronts; namely, terrorist violence and propaganda. Often the propagandists will have to publicly distance themselves from the terrorists. Indeed, moving away from Breivik's fantasy of civil war itself, it is notable to see that the responses from figures who cultivate a license to hate – such as Stephen Yaxley-Lennon and Peder Jensen – followed Breivik's expected trajectory in 2011: condemning terrorism while using the media interest generated by his extreme actions as yet another opportunity to develop the core ideological concerns of Europe's Islamophobic far right.

Finally, it is important to stress that Breivik himself considered his manifesto, as well as his actions, to be an inspirational offering to others, promoting a license to kill for those who may be persuaded by the contemporary views of new far right Islamophobes. *2083* offers both the ideology and the practical advice on how to carry out massive terrorist violence. Yet even in light of Breivik's murderous language and incitement to likeminded 'patriots', predicting future solo actor violence is notoriously problematic. From this analysis of the Breivik case, however, it seems clear that the more powerful the license to hate – in this case, by the Islamophobic far right – the greater the likelihood of someone else, probably with a set of psychological vulnerabilities, will take up Breivik's license to kill.

ENDNOTES

[1] *2083 – A European Declaration of Independence*, p. 1070.

[2] Ibid., pp. 663 – 665.

[3] For a reproduction of Tommy Robinson talking about the Breivik case on 25 July 2011, see: http://www.youtube.com/watch?v=4RdJ4dpRQeE&feature=player_embedded (accessed 22/02/2012).

[4] For more detail here, see: cf Chip Berlet at: http://www.talk2action.org/story/2011/7/23/8287/32273 (accessed 22/02/2012).

[5] Paul Jackson, 'Solo Actor Terrorism and the Mythology of the Lone Wolf', in Gerry Gable and Paul Jackson eds., *Lone Wolves: Myth or Reality?* (Ilford: Searchlight, 2011), pp. 79 – 88.

[6] This 'Vienna School' is a neologism, and is not to be confused with either the 'Vienna Circle' of early Twentieth Century philosophers, or the subsequent 'Vienna School' of economists.

[7] For a fuller analysis of the Islamophobic discursive field that Breivik developed within his manifesto, see: 'Breivik, The Conspiracy Theory and the Oslo Massacre' *European Race Audit Briefing Paper* 5 (September 2011), at: http://www.irr.org.uk/pdf2/ERA_B riefingPaper5.pdf (accessed 22/02/2012).

[8] *2083 – A European Declaration of Independence*, p. 1241.

[9] For example, when commenting on potential Grand Master Overseer figures, Breivik was clear that such representatives could not have a Nazi heritage, Ibid., p. 1073. Also, Breivik sets out his opposition to the historical legacy of Nazism as follows: 'I remain a staunch anti-Nazi and I blame the NSDAP for the situation we are in. Had it not been for the actions of the cultural right-wing extremists known as the NSDAP, our Western European countries would not be dominated by the cultural Marxist extremist regimes we witness today. If the NSDAP had been isolationistic instead of imperialistic (expansionist) and just deported the Jews (to a liberated and Muslim free Zion) instead of massacring them, the anti-European hate ideology known as multiculturalism would have never been institutionalized in Western Europe, because the Marxists would never have been so radicalized to begin with'. Ibid., p. 1435.

[10] For wider analysis of the significance of new media for the contemporary far right, see: Paul Jackson and Gerry Gable eds., *Far-Right.com: Nationalist Extremism on the Internet* (London: Searchlight, 2011).

[11] Paul Jackson, 'Solo Actor Terrorism and the Mythology of the Lone Wolf', in Gerry Gable and Paul Jackson eds., *Lone Wolves: Myth or Reality?* (Searchlight, 2011), pp. 79 – 88.

[12] Ramón Spaaij, *Understanding Lone Wolf Terrorism: Global Patterns, Motivations and Prevention* (New York: Springer, 2012). Chapter 3.

[13] Raffaello Pantucci, 'What Have We Learned about Lone Wolves from Anders Behring Breivik?' in *Perspectives on Terrorism* 5/5–6 (2011). Available at: http://www.terrorismanalysts.com/pt/index.php/pot/article/view/what-we-have-learned (accessed 22/02/2012).

[14] For a summary of this perspective, see: Aristotle Kallis, '"Licence" and Genocide in the East: Reflections on Localized Eliminationist Violence', *Studies in Ethnicity and Nationalism, 2007 ASEN Conference Special* 7/3 (2007), pp. 6 – 23.

[15] Ibid.

[16] For a clear summary of the turn to Islamophobia in the contemporary far right, see: Jose Pedro Zuquete, 'The European Extreme-Right and Islam: New directions?', *Journal of Political Ideologies* 13/3 (2008), pp. 321 – 344.

[17] See: Ramón Spaaij, 'The Enigma of Lone Wolf Terrorism: An Assessment', *Studies in Conflict and Terrorism* 33/9 (2010), pp. 854 – 870.

[18] Mark Juergensmeyer, *Terror in the Mind of God: The Global Rise of Religious Violence* (Berkley: University of California Press, 2000), p. 11.

[19] For more detail on this aspect of the Breivik manifesto, see Chip Berlet, 'Updated: Breivik's Core Thesis is White Christian Nationalism v. Multiculturalism'. See: http://www.talk2action.org/story/2011/7/25/73510/6015 (accessed 22/02/2012).

[20] *2083 – A European Declaration of Independence*, pp. 930 – 931.

[21] Ibid., pp. 941 – 942.

[22] Albert Bandura, 'Mechanisms of Moral Disengagement', in W Reich ed., *Origins of Terrorism: Psychologies, Ideologies, Theologies, States of Mind* (Washington: Woodrow Wilson Centre Press, 1990), pp. 161 – 191.

[23] Hendrik Hansen, 'Islamism and Western Political Religions', *Religion Compass* 3/6 (2009), pp. 1026 – 1041.

[24] George Michael, 'David Lane and the Fourteen Words' *Totalitarian Movements and Political Religions* 10/1 (2009), pp. 43 – 61.

[25] Emilio Gentile, *Politics as Religion* (Princeton: Princeton University Press, 2006).

[26] *2083 – A European Declaration of Independence*, p. 1132.

[27] Ibid., p. 1135.

[28] Roger Griffin, 'Shattering Crystals: The Role of 'Dream Time' in Extreme Right-Wing Political Violence' *Terrorism and Political Violence* 15/1 (2003), pp. 57 – 95.

[29] One can find much reference to this model throughout the manifesto, but the phases are neatly summarized on pages 803 – 804 of *2083 – A European Declaration of Independence*.

[30] For a discussion on the blurring of rational and mythic elements in the 'transgressive violence' of genocide, see Dan Stone, 'Genocide as Transgression', *European Journal of Social Theory* 7/1 (2004), pp. 45 – 65.

[31] Roger Griffin, *The Nature of Fascism* (Abingdon: Routledge, 1993).

THE STRATEGY OF DISCURSIVE PROVOCATION: A DISCOURSE-HISTORICAL ANALYSIS OF THE FPÖ'S DISCRIMINATORY RHETORIC

Ruth Wodak

Socio-political and historical context

In their political discourse in general, and especially in their past election campaigns, the FPÖ (the Austrian Freedom Party; *Freiheitliche Partei Öster-reichs)*[1] has developed specific discursive patterns that have been widely discussed in the media, as well as in scholarly research.[2] When summarizing the results of these studies, particular dynamic patterns have been shown to emerge time and again, albeit with certain variations.

The campaigns have integrated a range of traditional means of election campaigning (which include events both small and large, spanning speeches and other performances by the top candidates in public spaces, beer tents and discotheques; posters, advertisements, party-run newspapers, media appearances, distribution of printed materials, and so on) with new social media (the World Wide Web, brochures designed to look like comic books, a rap-song specifically written for, and performed by, the party leader).[3] This has effectively opened up new avenues of communication with diverse target groups, as well as created a whole network of texts and images intertwined in subtle inter-textual ways with each other. The contents distributed by such means include open and coded constructions of marginalizing and discriminatory statements that draw on xenophobic, Islamophobic, anti-Semitic, homophobic and other resentments.

Examples from earlier election campaigns include, for instance, the slogans '*Daham statt Islam*' ('at home instead of Islam')[4] in 2006 or '*Abendland in Christenhand*' ('The Occident in Christian hands') in 2009. While such statements regularly test the boundaries of the socially acceptable and legally permissible, it is rare for a slogan to cross the legal boundaries of freedom of speech, although moral thresholds defined by mainstream society are often violated. The FPÖ MP Susanne Winter, for instance, was tried, and convict-ed,[5] by a criminal court of justice for hate-incitement (*Verhetzung*) and the vili-fication of religious teachings,[6] because she had used her speech at a New Year's meeting of the FPÖ, to claim that the founder of the Islamic religion had written the Koran during epileptic fits, and had been a pedophile.[7]

It is through precisely this type of provocative rhetoric labeled as 'strate-gy of provocation' that the FPÖ has placed the general public, and particularly its political competitors, in a dilemma.[8] Even if it is one of the basic rules of politics that any reaction raises the attention given to a political adversary and should therefore be avoided, the common sense slogan 'by saying nothing, we agree' also applies here. There are, however, statements that cannot be left unchallenged. The by now predictable response to such reactions on the part of the FPÖ is, in turn, an integral part of the campaigns themselves and is used to both construct and reinforce the FPÖ's status as a victim, thus in-viting voters through a strengthened sense of group identity against a com-mon, external enemy (a conspiracy). Haider, the then leader of the FPÖ, used the poster slogan: '*Sie sind gegen ihn, weil er für Euch ist*'[9] in the national election of 2006 ('They are against him, because he is for you!'). Thus, reac-tion and counter-reaction can lead to an escalation of the discourse that virtu-ally guarantees the FPÖ unanimous attention, a process through which it can dominate the political agenda.

The Austrian radical right after World War II

The history of the party, widely known as the 'Freedom Party of Austria' (FPÖ), dates back to the early years after World War II, and the political set-up, both created and supported by the Allied Powers of the USA, the UK and the Soviet Union. This enabled them to keep control over Austria until the *Staatsvertrag* (State Treaty) of 1955 marked the 'rebirth of the Austrian Re-public' and the withdrawal of Allied Forces from Austria.[10] During the period between 1945 and 1955 (prior to the *Staatsvertrag*), the Allies clearly sup-ported the development of a bi-polar political scene by encouraging (a) the cooperation of socialist-democratic movements on the left of the political spectrum and the formation of what would somewhat later evolve into the So-cial Democratic Party of Austria (SPÖ; *Sozialdemokratische Partei Öster-*

reichs), and (b) the merging of various fairly moderate right-wing, conservative and pro-clerical movements into the Austrian People's Party (ÖVP; *Österreichische Volkspartei*).

It was in response to the externally-supported bi-polar arrangement of the Austrian political scene that the Association of Independents VdU (*Verband der Unabhängigen*) (the forerunner of the FPÖ) was formed in 1949 by incorporating a vast array of political movements comprising of 'old Nazis, German nationalists and a fair number of liberals',[11] who were deliberately prevented from joining, or being subsumed into, either of the two mainstream parties of the left and right. Interestingly, the VdU came into being with the 'active assistance of the Socialist Party (SPÖ) [...] [which] hoped that the new movement – 688,000 previously disenfranchised former members of the NSDAP [Nazi Party] who were allowed to vote for the first time in the 1949 parliamentary elections – would split the bourgeois vote, cutting into the support of the ÖVP',[12] as well as with the support of the Austrian Communist Party (*Kommunistische Partei Österreichs*, KPÖ) which also believed that the creation of the VdU would enhance the chances for the left. In the 1949 parliamentary elections, the VdU won 12 per cent of the national vote, giving it a fairly strong position in the post-election political scene. It was not long before the VdU issued the call 'for its main objective – the abolition of all laws governing de-Nazification procedures'.[13] To this end, the argument employed by the VdU rested, above all, on the reversal of the perpetrator-victim dichotomy: the real victims were not those persecuted by the Nazi regime, but those who had profited by acquiring Jewish property (Aryanizers) and former members of the NSDAP'.[14]

Accordingly, the VdU used a 'grotesque conception of fascism' based on a crude view of totalitarianism 'to attack the de-Nazification policies of the government and to equate Nazism with other political systems'.[15] Hence, 'when the VdU spoke about fascism, it mentioned neither National Socialism nor the Holocaust, at best indicating the 'positive aspects' of German fascism, such as full employment and economic growth', thereby allowing for a revival of Austrian 'pro-fascist' sentiment on a national scale and making it a significant element of the country's political agenda for many years to come.

Given the early VdU ideology, as well as the fact that the party was a conglomerate of people sharing a very broad spectrum of visions of the role and form of an Austrian 'third political force', it did not take long before the party entered a significant crisis which ended with even stronger pan-Germanist and pro-fascist agendas coming to the fore. It was amidst this crisis that the FPÖ was established in 1955/56, clearly 'funded as a German nationalist party of the far right, in which former, seriously incriminated National Socialists took the leading functions.'[16] For example, the first FPÖ chairman, Anton Reintaller, had once been:

> a member of the National Steering Committee of the Austrian NSDAP and the *SS-Brigadenführer* who held the position of Minister of Agriculture in the treacherous Austrian government of Seyß-Inquart in 1938.[17]

Reintaller's Nazi past, as well as that of other key members of the FPÖ at the time of its founding (such as Lothar Rendulic or the later FPÖ chairman Friedrich Peter), made the FPÖ the 'successor to the Austrian NSDAP'.[18] This also shaped its character in a way that precluded any treatment of the party 'as a normal third party like the German Liberals (FDP) or other small liberal parties in West European Countries'.

When Friedrich Peter (also a former *Waffen*-SS member) took over the chair of the FPÖ following Reintaller's death in 1958, the profile of the party did not change dramatically. However, a series of (more or less superfluous) attempts to take the FPÖ into the mainstream of Austrian politics gradually began to have an effect. Hence, throughout the 1960s, the drive to 'open up' the FPÖ (in a moderate direction) could be observed in the party's actions under Friedrich Peter, when 'both liberal and national' views were given a voice. The culmination of this 'opening up' took place when, in 1970, the newly elected Chancellor Bruno Kreisky of the SPÖ formed a minority government with the support of the FPÖ and appointed 'four former NSDAP members to ministerial posts'.[19] It was at this juncture that the FPÖ's participation in mainstream Austrian politics was finally confirmed. The isolation of the pro-Nazi elements of the Austrian political class (embodied by the FPÖ) ended, thus sending 'a signal to the FPÖ that the SPÖ, in order to gain power, could do business with former Nazis in a pragmatic way'. These developments, however, did not occur without huge resistance from parts of the SPÖ who unsurprisingly opposed a coalition with the FPÖ and its leader, purely because of Kreisky's obvious *realpolitik*. Specifically, the disclosure of Friedrich

Peter's Nazi past by Simon Wiesenthal led to a new kind of justification rhetoric, while employing doublespeak via a range of discursive strategies, such as those of calculated ambivalence and provocation. Bruno Kreisky defended his decision to invite Friedrich Peter into the government. On the one hand, he tried to appease anti-fascist resistance in his own party, the SPÖ, while on the other hand, he denounced Simon Wiesenthal and thus played in to the hands of the FPÖ. This specific justification discourse also paved the way for explicit anti-Semitic rhetoric and related indirect devices such as insinuations and the so-called *Waldheim Affair* 1986.[20]

The government career of the FPÖ did not last long: with Kreisky's SPÖ winning three consecutive elections in 1971, 1975 and 1979, it had no further need to turn to the FPÖ for support. The pragmatic-liberal views among FPÖ members gradually decreased, both at the regional party level and in the federal parliamentary party. The feeling of dissatisfaction with the 'liberal' tendency within the party continued to grow under the leadership of the FPÖ's 'liberal' chairman Norbert Steger (between 1980 and 1986), when the FPÖ took part in yet another (highly unsuccessful) federal government with the SPÖ (between 1983 and 1986). Evidence of the clear split within the party was made explicit on 14 September 1986, when the FPÖ national convention witnessed a coup led by the leader of the Carinthian FPÖ – Jörg Haider – who became the new federal chairman of the party. Haider's arrival as FPÖ chairman marked the turn of the majority of the FPÖ to radical and nationalist views. It also denotes a shift in the balance of power within the party, towards that tendency which in 1966 had partly left the FPÖ to form the National-Democratic Party (NDP), and which had grown stronger after many members of the FPÖ had left to join the NDP in response to the FPÖ's 1970 'coalition with Kreisky, the Jew'[21].

With the aid of strongly anti-Semitic, anti-foreigner and Nazi-sympathizing slogans, it was not long before Haider – a rhetorically skillful, well educated politician who, despite his youth, pleaded allegiance to the Nazi traditions of his family[22] – took the FPÖ on the path to successful elections at both federal and regional levels. By November 1986, the party already enjoyed significant increases in its electoral support at the parliamentary elections, gaining 9.7 per cent of the national vote (a rise on the previous elections of 1983 of 4.7 per cent). In 1989, the FPÖ came second (after the ÖVP) in regional elections in Carinthia, and Haider was elected as the governor of the province. With the FPÖ leaving its 'perpetual' third spot for the first time, the party's 'walk to power' began. Even after Haider was forced to step down as Carinthian governor in 1991 (following his infamous remarks praising Nazi Germany's so-called 'employment policies'),[23] he returned to power in Carinthia after winning the regional elections later in the same year.

Throughout the late 1980s and the early 1990s, the nationwide anti-foreigner initiatives by the FPÖ under Haider, such as the 1989 'Declaration of St. Lorenzen', the backing of the 1992 Foreigners Act, the 1992 'Austria First Petition' and the 1997 'FPÖ Party Platform',[24] secured for the FPÖ a significant rise in its electoral support. It is mainly due to the party's stance on migration-related matters that the FPÖ increased its share of the vote in the 1994 parliamentary elections to 22.5 per cent and secured the same result in the elections held in December 1995.

The latter part of 1999 marked another turning point in the history of the FPÖ. In the parliamentary elections held on 3 October, the FPÖ received an unprecedented 26.91 per cent of the national vote, and, for the first time in the party's history, took second place in the federal parliamentary election. After a period of negotiations, the FPÖ signed the coalition agreement with the ÖVP and entered the federal government in early 2000.[25] It must be emphasized that with the FPÖ entering the federal government, a radical right party which had frequently expressed both coded and explicit praise for Nazism had come to power in an EU member state for the first time ever.[26] Apart from the already mentioned praise for Nazi employment policies (which, of course, implies the praise of slave labor and concentration camps), Haider, for example, also praised former members of the *Waffen SS* at a World War II veterans' meeting and claimed that they were 'honourable men'.[27]

Although sanctions against the Austrian government (*Maßnahmen gegen die österreichische Regierung*) were eventually introduced by the 14 EU member states, it is not this fact, as much as the 'fragile' performance of Wolfgang Schüssel's ÖVP-FPÖ government, which pushed the FPÖ into gradual decline. Midway through the parliamentary tenure of the first ÖVP-FPÖ government (2000 – 2002), Haider stepped down as FPÖ party chairman. Yet he continued to influence the party's federal activities by guiding his successor, a deputy chancellor in the ÖVP-FPÖ government and the new

FPÖ chairwoman, Susanne Riess-Passer. Haider's influence on the party de-creased as the chairmanship of the FPÖ was taken over, successively, by Mathias Reichhold and Herbert Haupt. Despite this, Haider organized another coup at the party convention in Knittelfeld in the autumn of 2002, where FPÖ ministers were forced to step down, thus breaking the federal government coalition. In the aftermath of the Knittelfeld coup, new parliamentary elections took place in November 2002. Although the elections proved highly detri-mental to the FPÖ's national electoral success (as the party received just 10 per cent of the vote, thus losing almost a 16 per cent share of the vote), the FPÖ, led by Herbert Haupt, entered later that year into another coalition gov-ernment with the ÖVP, led again by Wolfgang Schüssel.

When, in June 2004, the FPÖ suffered a severe defeat in elections to the European Parliament (scoring only 6.3 per cent in comparison to the 23.4 per cent obtained in 1999) and Herbert Haupt was forced to step down as the party chairman, Haider began yet another comeback. In the first instance, Ur-sula Haubner, Jörg Haider's sister, was elected as the new federal chairwom-an of the FPÖ in July 2005. Although Haubner's chairmanship of the party was clearly guided by the 'patronage' of her brother, the influence retained by Haider over the FPÖ no longer satisfied the far-reaching political ambitions of the Carinthian governor. Thus, when it became clear in early 2005 that 'abort-ing' the party would be easier for Haider and his trusted followers than at-tempting, yet again, to take over power in an already widely scorned FPÖ, Haider established a new party called the 'Union for the Future of Austria' (*Bündnis Zukunft Österreichs* – BZÖ). On 4 April 2005, leaders of the FPÖ in-cluding its chairwoman Ursula Haubner, the federal vice-chancellor Hubert Gorbach and the leader of the FPÖ's parliamentary group, Herbert Scheibner, joined the BZÖ, thereby enabling a Haider-led party of the radical right to en-ter the Austrian federal government.

The national parliamentary elections of 1 October 2006 marked a consid-erable defeat for both FPÖ-originated political groupings. The FPÖ, (now headed by H.-C. Strache, a former friend of Haider), and the BZÖ (headed by Haider) managed a combined 15.1 per cent of the national vote. However, the electoral result of 2006 obviously proved to be too modest for the FPÖ and BZÖ to become (either separately or combined) a government coalition party, particularly in the light of the almost 70 per cent share of the vote gained by the two mainstream parties (SPÖ and ÖVP). Therefore, following a (typically) long period of negotiations, the radical right movements did not become part of the Austrian government which was formed early in 2007 by the SPÖ and the ÖVP, headed by the chairman of the SPÖ, Alfred Gusenbauer. And so, after eight years spent in the Austrian government, the radical right groupings of the FPÖ and the BZÖ returned to their oppositional roles. After the death of Jörg Haider in October 2008 (Haider died in a car accident in a small Carinthian village after having spent half the night in a gay bar in Klagenfurt. He crashed into a tree while speeding and completely drunk on Vodka), the BZÖ gradually lost (and continues to lose) votes, except in Carinthia; the FPÖ, on the other hand, under H.-C. Strache is growing rapidly and stands the chance of becoming Austria's strongest party at the next national election in 2013.

It is obvious from this – briefly summarized – history of the Second Austrian Republic that radical right-wing parties have not been successful when governing; their success seems to lie in the oppositional 'campaign habitus'.[28] This is particularly apparent if one observes the rise of H.-C. Strache, the leader of the FPÖ, after the schism of the BZÖ. Once again, his appeal seems to grow, with his slogans and rhetoric becoming increasingly xenophobic, EU-sceptic and anti-Turkish. To date, he has frequently stated that he does not want to be part of any government.

In the following, I focus on some typical characteristics of the FPÖs recent rhetoric, although – as mentioned above – the 'strategy of calculated ambivalence' and the 'strategy of provocation' are certainly not new. Quite the contrary, they have both been part of the FPÖ's rhetorical repertoire for many decades. The strategy of provocation aims at raising awareness to the FPÖ's agenda by practically forcing the media to report on it. In this way, the FPÖ's agenda became hegemonic; all other parties react to the respective provocation and thus neglect their own values and frames. The strategy of calculated ambivalence is linked to the strategy of provocation in intricate ways: this discursive strategy implies addressing multiple audiences simultaneously with the same utterance that accordingly allows for several interpretations. Usually, this strategy is employed once the pressure on the FPÖ to apologize for their provocative and offensive statements becomes too big.[29]

The Viennese election campaign 2010

Ahead of local elections on 10 October, the summer of 2010 saw a poster campaign featuring subjects that did not correspond to well-known patterns in various ways: One of them read *'We finally give our Viennese security'*, *'Wir geben unseren Wienerinnen und Wienern ENDLICH SICHERHEIT')*[30] and featured the front-runner, H.-C. Strache, in conversation with a woman and a man in police uniforms. This new 'discourse of safety' relates both to the number of police officers in Vienna (which the FPÖ would like to be bigger), as well as to a second thematic strand that links criminality with certain groups of offenders from foreign countries. Put in these terms, the poster's subject did indeed conform to the usual topics raised by the FPÖ. However, it did not constitute a discursive provocation in the sense defined above. Such a provocation was, however, delivered by a poster first spread across the city in mid-August 2010 (see Figure 1).

Figure 1: Poster used by the FPÖ in the Vienna election campaign of 2010.

The poster is very bright overall, predominantly using white and blue. The latter is the traditional color of the party, derived from the cornflower, also known as blue-bottle, worn by the German Nationalists of the nineteenth century. The poster also uses red, the second color of the party logo, not discernible in a black-and-white reproduction. The letter O is printed in red, F and P are both blue. [31]

Red is also the color of the slogan used on the right-hand side of this poster. The call to vote for the party in the upcoming election, spread across the lower end of the poster, is printed in white over a blue background and provides some cohesion for the different elements of the poster.[32] In accordance with the reading habits of a culture using a writing system running from left to right, the reading path begins on the left, and thus the candidate is presented as the actual subject of the poster. The presentation of a man, born in 1969, is youthful, casual, clean and healthy: a spotless white shirt, unbuttoned at the top, no jacket or tie, brilliant blue eyes and white teeth, a tanned complexion, dense brown hair with only a touch of grey at the temples, and smiling self-confidently from the poster's surface.

It should be made clear that this focus on the persona of the leading candidate is at odds with the fact that Strache, though first on the election list of his party for the Vienna election, was, and still is, a member of the Austrian Parliament. No one seriously assumed that he would resign his position in the parliament and assume a position in Vienna's municipal government, except in the very unlikely event of being elected mayor. The voters were thus called upon to give their votes to someone who was actually only running as a figure-head without any intention of working at the city level. This strong focus by a campaigning party on a 'charismatic' leader figure, completely removed the question of who would actually sit on the seats won in the election (no other candidates on the FPÖ's list made any appearance on further posters in this campaign), is not a phenomenon exclusive to right-wing populist parties, yet is more commonly seen here than elsewhere.[33]

The poster's upper-right corner shows the party logo, a combination of the letters FPÖ, the acronym for the full name, and the self-styled reference *'Die soziale Heimatpartei'*, literally 'The social homeland-party.' Already, in their 1992 petition for a popular referendum *'Österreich zuerst'*, literally 'Austria first', the FPÖ had demanded a 'right to one's homeland for all Austrian citizens.'[34] The ambiguous term *'Heimat'*, translated here as 'homeland', is well suited to evoke stronger feelings of belonging rather than a reference to the citizenship of a nation.[35] In contrast to the changeable legal category of citizenship or residence status, '*Heimat*' refers to an enduring and essentializing entity that determines who 'really' belongs and who *is* a 'real Austrian' (*der echte Österreicher*). The central statement of the poster, positioned beneath the logo, speaks directly to this question of who 'really' belongs and reads '*Mehr MUT für unser "Wiener Blut"*', which translates to 'More COURAGE for our "Viennese Blood"', and the addition of '*Zu viel Fremdes tut niemandem gut*', i.e. 'Too much of the Foreign is not good for anybody'. So here it is again, strategic and deliberate provocation via the reference to 'blood'. The slogan makes clear the distinction between an in-group of 'us' (linguistically realized through the possessive pronoun '*unser*', i.e. 'our') and an 'other' kept vague (realized by the abstract noun '*Fremdes*' i.e. 'the foreign'). In large bold red letters, the poster calls for more courage that presupposes that there must be some (unspecified) danger emanating from this 'other'. It is obvious from the start – and the text also acknowledges this through its choice of words – that taking the side of 'our "Viennese blood"' will provoke huge opposition, because it violates the social taboo on open racism and explicit xenophobia, which corresponds to the human rights principle that all human beings are born as equals in dignity and rights. The opposite of courage, the slogan implies implicitly, is cowardice.

Thus, those who do not also take the side of 'our "Viennese blood"' must be considered cowards. Those of a different political persuasion are implicitly discredited: 'they' are not prepared to protect 'us'! In this way, a salient discursive strategy is triggered, namely 'the victim-perpetrator reversal' ('they are stronger than we are'), linked to the so-called 'saviour strategy' (like Robin Hood, Strache would come and support and fight for the poor). This combination of strategies condenses an argument in the form of a contended argument, a *topos*: if the 'real' Viennese are in danger, H.-C. Strache (i.e. the FPÖ) will save them.

The use of the word 'blood' in the context of the construction of the 'self' and the 'other', i.e. of 'us' vs. 'them', is essential to the success of the discursive provocation evident in this case. Political positions advocating ever more strict and severe regulation of immigration and residency have been part of the political mainstream for some time now; throughout Europe, legislation designs more and more difficult requirements for those who want to immigrate or acquire residency, even where right-wing populist parties are not part of the respective government. 'Blood', however, is both a conventional metaphor and metonymy for ancestry and descent, and firmly rooted in language use (for example: in the somewhat antiquated, but generally comprehensible figure of speech 'one's own flesh and blood'). So far, the discourse of the political mainstream has shied away from drawing on this immutable feature of human beings.[36]

The demand for *'limpieza de sangre'*,[37] i.e. the 'purity of blood', is, of course, a crucial aspect of the history of racism in Europe, as this argument was used after 1492 to deny Spanish Jews the possibility to convert to Christianity and thus avoid being murdered or banished from Spain – a converted Jew, the law stated, was still a Jew and hence to be excluded from Spanish society (a racist postulate that would later re-emerge in the Nazis' *Nürnberger Gesetze*[38] of 1935). The notion of 'pure blood' pervades the history of racism throughout the centuries. Of course, we cannot assume that everyone who sees the poster is aware of that history. What we can assume, however, is that the racist aims ('pure blood') underlying the atrocities of National Socialism have become part of the collective memory in Austria (as in Germany), not least because of its treatment in school curricula.[39] The content of collective memory can certainly be evoked through associations, making it easy to allude to; yet those who designed and produced the poster in question can deny, as an unfounded accusation, the notion that they did so knowingly and deliberately, precisely because of the implicit nature of allusions.[40]

Since accusations of racism are social stigmata that must be averted in Western democracies, neither the party's candidate nor the voters should suffer it – which leads right back to the pattern of provocation, reaction and counter-reaction described above. Even the quotation marks used to bracket *'Wiener Blut'*, the reference to 'blood' can be seen as part of the strategy of pre-emptively warding off accusations of racism. For one, quotation marks are generally used in written communication as a means of creating distance between the text's producer and the text itself (i.e. this word, this phrase is not my own, but another's). Secondly, the phrase *'Wiener Blut'* is known, to at least part of the population, as the title of a famous waltz by Johann Strauss (junior).[41] Significantly, however, the poster would not be meaningful if the reference were simply to the waltz or the operetta of the same name. In this context, the quotation marks mean first and foremost: 'We don't mean this literally, so please don't "misunderstand" our meaning...'

As a matter of fact, the FPÖ did indeed reject all criticism as a deliberate misreading and produced a new advertisement, rich in text and on the topic 'What do we mean by "Too much of the foreign is not good for anybody,"' in response.[42] On the surface, this creates the appearance of a rational discourse, but the content of its arguments do not withstand close examination: they are quickly recognizable as a mixture of insinuations and half-truths, couched in conditional clauses, which makes it difficult to reject them explicitly (in addition to the persistent dilemma that any detailed response would again draw attention to the political adversary). The arguments brought forth in this poster do, however, immediately clarify what is meant by 'the foreign': on the one hand, these arguments and slogans attack the FPÖ's main political opponent, the SPÖ, for its alleged political position regarding immigration and integration; and on the other hand, they focus on religion, in particular on Islam.

Conclusions and Perspectives

In his 2009 lecture entitled 'Europe of Strangers', Zygmunt Bauman stated that:

in the language of vote-seeking politicians, the widespread and complex sentiments of *Unsicherheit* are translated as much simpler concerns with law and order (that is with bodily safety and the safety of private homes and possessions), while the problem of law and order is in its turn blended with the problematic presence of ethnic, racial or religious minorities – and, more generally, of alien styles of life. [43]

Thus, Bauman argues that globalization and the vast complexity of our societies, lead politicians to search for simple answers to unsolvable problems, such as the financial crisis, and so forth. It is easy, he claims, to find culprits and scapegoats who can be blamed for the causes of our current woes: everybody who is 'different' and who does not 'belong' to 'us'.

As the causes for present troubles, Bauman implies, are not immediately visible and are instead frequently distant, and as politics always remains a more 'local affair', explanations and remedies are sought in areas closer to the home-ground of daily experience. Bauman also comments on the specific metaphorical language used by politicians to explain the roots of problems as a language 'in which we can speak of cures and medicines', i.e. as if our societies were suddenly overwhelmed by dangerous illnesses.[44] Threats to collective identity (stemming from individual insecurity), Bauman continues, are easily countered:

> local state powers may still be used to close the borders to the migrants, to tighten the asylum laws, to round up and deport the unwelcome aliens. The governments cannot honestly promise its citizens secure existence and certain future; but they may for the time being unload at least part of the accumulated anxiety (and even profit from it electorally) by demonstrating their energy and determination in the war against foreign job-seekers and other alien gate-crashers, the intruders into once clean and quiet, orderly and familiar, native backyards.

Rarely has the essence of current xenophobic and frequently racist politics been as neatly summarized as in Bauman's argument. The search for local scapegoats has lent itself – for centuries – to quick electoral success. Of course, not all 'others' are discriminated against: our societies, we are told again and again by our governments, need qualified experts, but poor and unqualified migrants are not welcome.[45] Moreover, the threat frequently does not only relate to a fear of unemployment and of losing one's position in the working sphere, if foreigners also 'look or behave differently', racist and nativist stereotypes can be evoked and instrumentalized for political ends.

The rise of right-wing populist movements in recent years – and related to this phenomenon, the frequently repeated requests for more discrimination against out-groups in more and more blatant and explicit rhetoric – would not have been possible without massive media support. This does not, of course, imply that all newspapers share the same position. Although some tabloids do, leading populist politicians have to be – and usually are – media-savvy: they undergo rhetorical training (such as Neurolinguistic Programming, NLP), employ qualified spin-doctors and are educated in performance techniques which lead to a softer 'front-stage' image, adapted to mainstream values. Anthropologist André Gingrich rightly describes such a leader as 'a man/woman for all seasons'.[46]

Thus, right-wing populists intentionally provoke the media by violating publicly accepted liberal norms. In this way, the media are forced into a 'no-win' situation: if they do not report a scandalous racist remark, they might be perceived as endorsing it. If they do write about it, they explicitly reproduce the xenophobic utterance. A predictable dynamic is triggered which allows right-wing populist parties to set the agenda and distract the media from other important news as any new scandal would be publicized immediately in great detail. The dynamic consists of several stages: the scandal is first denied; then once some evidence is produced, the scandal is re-defined and equated with entirely different phenomena. Predictably, the provocateurs then claim the right to freedom of speech for themselves, as a justificatory strategy. Such utterances immediately trigger another debate – unrelated to the original scandal – about freedom of speech and political correctness. Simultaneously, victimhood is claimed by the original provocateur and the event is dramatized and exaggerated. This leads to the construction of a conspiracy: somebody must be 'pulling the strings' against the original producer of the scandal and scapegoats (Muslims, Jews, Turks, Roma, foreigners, and so forth) are quickly discovered. Once the accused member of the respective minority finally receives a chance to present substantial counter-evidence, a new scandal is launched. Possibly, a 'quasi-apology' might follow in case 'misunderstandings' should have occurred; and the entire process starts all over again.

This dynamic of discursive provocation implies that right-wing populist parties strategically manage to frame media debates. Other parties and politicians are thus forced to continuously react and respond to ever newly staged scandals. Few opportunities remain to present other agendas, frames, values and counter-arguments. In this way, radical right-wing populist parties succeed in dominating the media and public debates. Moreover, in this way, the dissemination of discriminating rhetoric persists and is continuously (re)produced.

115

ENDNOTES

[1] For elaborate analyses of the right-wing populist Austrian Freedom Party and the so-called *Haider Phenomenon*, see: Ruth Wodak and Anton Pelinka eds., *The Haider Phenomenon in Austria* (New Brunswick: Transaction Press, 2002); Anton Pelinka and Ruth Wodak eds., *'Dreck am Stecken'. Politik der Ausgrenzung* (Vienna: Czernin, 2002); and Michał Krzyżanowski and Ruth Wodak, *Politics of Exclusion: Institutional and Everyday Discrimination in Austria* (New Brunswick: Transaction Press, 2009).

[2] While these analyses cannot be discussed here in detail, see: Martin Reisigl, 'Discrimination in Discourses', in Helga Kotthoff and Helen Spencer-Oatey eds., *Handbook of Intercultural Communication* (Berlin/New York: De Gruyter, 2007), pp. 365 – 394; Ruth Wodak and Katharina Köhler, 'Wer oder was ist ‚fremd'? Diskurshistorische Analyse fremdenfeindlicher Rhetorik in Österreich', *SWS-Rundschau* 1 (2010), pp. 33 – 50; Katharina Köhler and Ruth Wodak '"Mitbürger, Fremde und, echte Wiener"– Ein- und Ausgrenzungen über Sprache. Diskursive Konstruktion von Macht und Ungleichheit am Beispiel des Wiener Wahlkampfes 2010', *Deutschunterricht* 6 (2011), pp. 64 – 73; and Jakob Engel and Ruth Wodak, 'Kalkulierte Ambivalenz, "Störungen" und das "Gedankenjahr": Die Causen Siegfried Kampl und John Gudenus', in Rudolf de Cillia and Ruth Wodak eds., *Gedenken im "Gedankenjahr": zur diskursiven Konstruktion österreichischer Identitäten im Jubiläumsjahr* (Innsbruck: Studienverlag, 2009), pp. 79 – 100. For detailed examples of the application of the discourse-historical approach (DHA) to radical right-wing populist rhetoric in Austria, see: Jakob Engel and Ruth Wodak, '"Calculated Ambivalence" and Holocaust Denial in Austria' in Ruth Wodak and John Richardson eds., *Fascism in Text and Talk* (London: Routledge, 2013, pp. 73 – 96).

[3] See: www.hcstrache.at/ (accessed 12/12/2012).

[4] Literally a rhymed form of 'At Home Instead of Islam'; German *'Daham'* is a dialectal form of *'daheim'* ('at home'). In particular, in Viennese dialect, diphthongs are monophthongized. The use of very simple rhymes is something of a trademark of FPÖ-campaigns.

[5] Oberlandesgericht Graz, 17 July 2009.

[6] See § 283 Section 2 and § 188 *Österreichisches Strafgesetzbuch*.

[7] John Richardson and Ruth Wodak, 'Recontextualizing Fascist Ideologies of the Past: Right-Wing Discourses on Employment and Nativism in Austria and the United Kingdom', *Critical Discourse Studies*, 6/4 (2009), pp. 251 – 267; and John Richardson and Ruth Wodak, 'The Impact of Visual Racism. Visual Arguments in Political Leaflets of Austrian and British Far-Right Parties'. *Controversia*, 2 (2009), pp. 45 – 77.

[8] Such statements by the FPÖ are intentionally offensive; the speakers (or writers) are aware of the provocative content; they are also aware of the fact that the FPÖ will receive a maximum of media coverage because of such statements; see Katharina Köhler and Ruth Wodak, '"Mitbürger, Fremde und, echte Wiener" – Ein- und Ausgrenzungen über Sprache. Diskursive Konstruktion von Macht und Ungleichheit am Beispiel des Wiener Wahlkampfes 2010', *Deutschunterricht* 6 (2011), pp. 64 – 73, where we propose the notion of 'Strategy of Discursive Provocation' to cover such rhetorical dynamics.

[9] Literally 'They are against him, because he is for you'. FPÖ poster during the national election campaign, October 1994, see: http://www.demokratiezentrum.org/bildstrategi en/personen.html?index=21&dimension= (accessed 12/12/2012).

[10] See, for example, Oliver Rathkolb, *The Paradoxical Republic: Austria 1945 – 2005* (New York: Berghahn Books, 2009) (translated by Otmar Binder from the German 2005

version); Ruth Wodak, Rudolf de Cillia, Martin Reisigl and Karin Liebhart, *The Discursive Construction of National Identity* Second Revised Edition (Edinburgh: Edinburgh University Press, 2009); Ruth Wodak and Rudolf de Cillia, 'Commemorating the Past: The Discursive Construction of Official Narratives about the 'Rebirth of the Second Austrian Republic', *Discourse and Communication* 1/3 (2007), pp. 337 – 363.

[11] Herbert Schiedel and Wolfgang Neugebauer, 'Jörg Haider, die FPÖ und der Antisemitismus', in Anton Pelinka and Ruth Wodak, eds., *'Dreck am Stecken'. Politik der Ausgrenzung* (Vienna: Czernin, 2002), pp. 11 – 32, 16.

[12] Walter Manoschek, 'FPÖ, ÖVP and Austria's Nazi Past', in Ruth Wodak and Anton Pelinka eds., *The Haider Phenomenon in Austria* (New Brunswick: Transaction Press, 2002), pp. 3 – 17, 5.

[13] Ibid., p. 7.

[14] For more details, specifically related to the history of the FPÖ and the various election campaigns since 1986, see Michał Krzyżanowski and Ruth Wodak, *Politics of Exclusion: Institutional and Everyday Discrimination in Austria* (New Brunswick: Transaction Press, 2009).

[15] Herbert Schiedel and Wolfgang Neugebauer, 'Jörg Haider, die FPÖ und der Antisemitismus', in Anton Pelinka and Ruth Wodak, eds., *'Dreck am Stecken'. Politik der Ausgrenzung* (Vienna: Czernin, 2002), pp. 11 – 32, 15.

[16] Ibid., p. 16.

[17] Walter Manoschek, 'FPÖ, ÖVP and Austria's Nazi Past', in Ruth Wodak and Anton Pelinka eds., *The Haider Phenomenon in Austria* (New Brunswick: Transaction Press, 2002), pp. 3 – 17, 6.

[18] Ibid., p 7.

[19] Herbert Schiedel and Wolfgang Neugebauer, 'Jörg Haider, die FPÖ und der Antisemitismus', in Anton Pelinka and Ruth Wodak, eds., *'Dreck am Stecken'. Politik der Ausgrenzung* (Vienna: Czernin, 2002), pp. 11 – 32, 17.

[20] For an extensive analysis of the so-called Kreisky-Peter-Wiesenthal Affair, see Ruth Wodak, Peter Nowak, Johanna Pelinkan, Helmut Gruber, Rudolf de Cillia and Richard Mitten, *"Wir sind alle unschuldige Täter!" Diskurshistorische Studien zum Nachkriegsantisemitismus* (Frankfurt a M.: Suhrkamp, 1990). For a short summary in English, see Ruth Wodak, 'Suppression of the Nazi Past, Coded Languages, and Discourses of Silence: Applying the Discourse-Historical Approach to Post-War Anti-Semitism in Austria', in Willibald Steinmetz, ed., *Political Language in the Age of the Extremes* (Oxford: Oxford University Press, 2011), pp. 351 – 379.

[21] Herbert Schiedel and Wolfgang Neugebauer, 'Jörg Haider, die FPÖ und der Antisemitismus', in Anton Pelinka and Ruth Wodak eds., *'Dreck am Stecken'. Politik der Ausgrenzung* (Vienna: Czernin, 2002), pp. 11 – 32, 17; Ruth Wodak, Peter Nowak, Johanna Pelinkan, Helmut Gruber, Rudolf de Cillia and Richard Mitten, *"Wir sind alle unschuldige Täter!" Diskurshistorische Studien zum Nachkriegsantisemitismus* (Frankfurt a M.: Suhrkamp, 1990).

[22] Michał Krzyżanowski, 'Haider: The New Symbolic Element of the Ongoing Discourse of the Past', in Ruth Wodak and Anton Pelinka, eds., *The Haider Phenomenon in Austria* (New Brunswick: Transaction Press, 2002), pp. 121 – 157.

[23] See Haider's utterance which praised the 'good/adequate employment policies of the Third Reich' and contrasted these to post-war employment policies (*ordentliche Beschäftigungspolitik im Dritten Reich*) in *Protokoll der Sitzung des Kärntner Landtages*, 13 June 1991.

See: http://www.doew.at/projekte/rechts/fpoe/fpoezitate.html (accessed 12/12/2012).

[24] Reinhold Gärtner, 'The FPÖ, Foreigners and Racism in the Haider Era' in Ruth Wodak and Anton Pelinka, eds., *The Haider Phenomenon in Austria* (New Brunswick: Transaction Press, 2002), pp. 17 – 33; Martin Reisigl and Ruth Wodak, '"Austria First". A Discourse-Historical Analysis of the Austrian "Anti-Foreigner Petition" in 1992 and 1993', in Martin Reisigl and Ruth Wodak eds., *The Semiotics of Racism. Approaches in Critical Discourse Analysis* (Vienna: Passagen Verlag, 2000), pp. 269 – 303; Bernd Matouschek, Ruth Wodak and Franz Januschek, *Notwendige Maßnahmen gegen Fremde? Genese und Formen von rassistischen Diskursen der Differenz* (Vienna: Passagen Verlag, 1995).

[25] Haider himself, however, did not join the government due to imminent EU sanctions and the growing international turmoil surrounding the FPÖ as a member of the coalition forming the federal government.

[26] See Anton Pelinka, 'Die FPÖ in der vergleichenden Parteienforschung. Zur typologischen Einordnung der Freiheitlichen Partei Österreichs' in *Österreichische Zeitschrift für Politikwissenschaft* 31 (2002), pp. 281 – 290; Walter Manoschek, 'FPÖ, ÖVP and Austria's Nazi Past', in Ruth Wodak and Anton Pelinka, eds., *The Haider Phenomenon in Austria* (New Brunswick: Transaction Press, 2002), pp. 3 – 17; André Gingrich, 'A Man for all Seasons' in Ruth Wodak and Anton Pelinka, eds., *The Haider Phenomenon in Austria* (New Brunswick: Transaction Press, 2002), pp. 87 – 102.

[27] Haider claimed that former members of the *Waffen-SS* were '*anständige Menschen*', who remained loyal to their former beliefs ('*ihrer Überzeugung treu geblieben sind*') on 30 September 1995, in Krumpendorf, Carinthia, at a commemoration meeting of a veterans' society *Kameradschaftsbund IV*).

[28] Ernst Grande, 'Charisma und Komplexität: Verhandlungsdemokratie, Mediendemokratie und der Funktionswandel politischer Eliten', *Leviathan* 28/1 (2000), pp. 122 – 141; Ruth Wodak, 'Old and New Demagoguery. The Rhetoric of Exclusion', available at: http://www.opendemocracy.net/ruth-wodak/old-and-new-demagoguery-rhetoric-of-exclusion, published on-line, 5 May 2011. This is also obvious from the recent exposure of various FPÖ/BZÖ ministers during the black-blue government, many of which were involved in huge corruption cases, and will probably be brought to court in the near future.

[29] Haider usually apologized after one of his big public provocations by saying: 'Actually, I have to apologize', thus apologizing but also simultaneously indicating that he is forced to do so and does not really mean this ('*Eigentlich muß ich mich entschuldigen*') (see Jakob Engel and Ruth Wodak, 'Kalkulierte Ambivalenz, "Störungen" und das "Gedankenjahr": Die Causen Siegfried Kampl und John Gudenus', in Rudolf de Cillia and Ruth Wodak eds., *Gedenken im "Gedankenjahr": zur diskursiven Konstruktion österreichischer Identitäten im Jubiläumsjahr* (Innsbruck: Studienverlag, 2009), pp. 79 – 100; Jakob Engel and Ruth Wodak, '"Calculated Ambivalence" and Holocaust denial in Austria', in Ruth Wodak and John Richardson, eds., *Fascism in Text and Talk* (London: Routledge, 2013, pp. 73 – 96).

[30] Literally 'We FINALLY give SAFETY to our Women and Men of Vienna'; for more details of the campaign and its analysis, see Katharina Köhler and Ruth Wodak, '"Mitbürger, Fremde und, echte Wiener" – Ein- und Ausgrenzungen über Sprache. Diskursive Konstruktion von Macht und Ungleichheit am Beispiel des Wiener Wahlkampfes 2010', *Deutschunterricht* 6 (2011), pp. 64 – 73.

[31] For a general discussion of visual design, see Gunther Kress and Theo Van Leeuwen, *Reading Images. The Grammar of Visual Design* (London: Routledge, 1996).

[32] See Theo Van Leeuwen, *The Language of Colour* (London: Routledge, 2011).

[33] See Ruth Wodak, *The Discourse of Politics in Action: Politics as Usual* (Basingstoke: Palgrave, 2011); John Corner and Dick Pels eds., *Media and the Restyling of Politics* (London: Sage, 2003).

[34] See Martin Reisigl and Ruth Wodak, "'Austria first'. A Discourse-Historical Analysis of the Austrian "Anti-foreigner Petition" in 1992 and 1993', in Martin Reisigl and Ruth Wodak eds., *The Semiotics of Racism. Approaches in Critical Discourse Analysis* (Vienna: Passagen Verlag, 2000), pp. 269 – 303.

[35] Martin Reisigl and Ruth Wodak, *Discourse and Discrimination. Rhetorics of Racism and Antisemitism* (London: Routledge, 2001), p. 155.

[36] Legislation regulating citizenship in many European countries privileges the descendants of citizens over persons descended from non-citizens (*'ius sanguinis'*, i.e. 'law of blood' or 'law of descent', as opposed to *'ius soli'*, i.e. 'law of soil' which emphasizes the place of birth). However, regulations always specify ways in which persons of other descent can acquire citizenship under certain conditions. The website http://eudo-citizenship.eu/ provides more information for those interested in how citizenship can be gained or lost; see also Ruth Wodak, 'Language, Power and Identity' *Language Teaching*, FirstView Articles, pp. 1 – 19 (accessed 25/04/2011).

[37] See Werner Conze and Antje Sommer, 'Rasse', in Otto Brunner, Werner Conze and Reinhart Koselleck eds., *Geschichtliche Grundbegriffe. Historisches Lexikon zur politisch-sozialen Sprache in Deutschland*. Vol.5 Studienausgabe mit beigefügten Korrigenda (Stuttgart: Campus, 2004), pp. 135 – 178, 140.

[38] See, in particular, the so-called *'Gesetz zum Schutze des deutschen Blutes und der deutschen Ehre'*, i.e. a law to 'Protect German Blood and German Honour' (*Reichsgesetzblatt* p. 1146).

[39] See Rudolf de Cillia and Ruth Wodak eds., *Gedenken im "Gedankenjahr": zur diskursiven Konstruktion österreichischer Identitäten im Jubiläumsjahr* (Innsbruck: Studienverlag), pp. 79 – 100.

[40] See John Richardson and Ruth Wodak, 'Recontextualizing Fascist Ideologies of the Past: Right-Wing Discourses on Employment and Nativism in Austria and the United Kingdom', *Critical Discourse Studies* 6/4 (2009), pp. 251 – 267; Katharina Köhler and Ruth Wodak, '"Mitbürger, Fremde und, echte Wiener" – Ein- und Ausgrenzungen über Sprache. Diskursive Konstruktion von Macht und Ungleichheit am Beispiel des Wiener Wahlkampfes 2010', *Deutschunterricht* 6 (2011), pp. 64 – 73 for more details.

[41] Strache also used the waltz in his appearances during the election campaign and thus used the medium of music to reinforce this connection in the network of associations, i.e. insinuations, for those in the know.

[42] Accessible at: http://www.hcstrache.at/bilder/mediaordner/g10,14110782715,0830.jpg (accessed 12/12/2012).

[43] See Zygmunt Bauman, 'Europe of Strangers', (2009), available from: http://docs.google.com/viewer?url=http://www.transcomm.ox.ac.uk/working%20papers/bauman.pdf (accessed 23/07/2011).

[44] Ibid., p. 13.

[45] Sarah Harrison and Michael Bruter, *Mapping Extreme Right Ideology* (Basingstoke: Palgrave, 2011).

[46] See André Gingrich, 'A Man for all Seasons', Ruth Wodak and Anton Pelinka eds., *The Haider Phenomenon in Austria* (New Brunswick: Transaction Press, 2002), pp. 87 – 102.

119

PART 2

WESTERN EUROPE AND THE USA

'TEACHING THE TRUTH TO THE HARDCORE':
THE PUBLIC AND PRIVATE PRESENTATION OF BNP IDEOLOGY

Graham Macklin

These are people who will use pseudonyms to conceal their true identities. Their emails are encrypted, with only the chosen few possessing the codes needed to decipher their messages. They are people who employ carefully-coded language to express their views, and who will, before speaking plainly, quite literally look over their shoulders.[1]

Rule # 5: **The BNP does *not* tell lies** about what it stands for, what it has stood for in the past, and what its intentions are. We do not have a secret doctrine of what we 'really think' which we conceal from the public. We make no secret of the fact that we are an ethno-nationalist party or that our ultimate goal is the orderly, humane and voluntary repatriation of the resident foreigners of the UK. Activists should never deny or squirm when asked about these things but defend them with good conscience.[2]

The idea that a far right party operates an acceptable 'front-stage' persona in order to mask an unacceptable, exclusionary 'backstage' ideology is not a new concept.[3] That a politician or political party might do one thing and say another is often taken for granted; the rise of 'political lying' is by no means a far right phenomenon.[4] However, ideological bifurcation functions as an innate component of the operating system of post-war fascist ideology. It serves as a mode of communication and as a 'coping strategy' enabling far right groups to organize themselves around certain forms of 'rejected knowledge' which, since the Second World War, have been profoundly out of step with the values of the societies in which they organize. This duality co-exists without contradiction, resulting in an 'exoteric' articulation of its ideology for public consumption and an 'esoteric' truth understood by an initiated hardcore of political activists.[5]

To understand the genesis of this development one need look no further than the defeat of fascism during the Second World War. Despite being victorious against the Axis powers, there was no military or ideological reckoning with domestic Fascism after the war in Britain. There was no *épuration* as in France. Nor indeed any attempt to 're-educate' fascists as in post-war Germany. There was no need. British fascists, for all their professed patriotism, found themselves completely and utterly on the wrong side of the national narrative, central to which was the concept of an 'anti-fascist' war fought against Fascism and Nazism. It was a war of 'resistance' against the very creed espoused by Britain's fascists. Viewed as a threat to national security, hundreds – including Sir Oswald Mosley, leader of the British Union of Fascists (BUF) – were interned. This event marked a 'watershed' in the history of British fascism. It forever tarnished its 'patriotic' image. This was reinforced in 1946 by the hanging of William Joyce, one of Mosley's former lieutenants, who had broadcast for the Nazis as 'Lord Haw Haw'. His sobriquet became synonymous with collaboration and treachery. The emerging horrors of the Holocaust, first revealed to the British public through newsreel footage of the Belsen concentration camp, set the seal on British fascism's estrangement from mainstream politics.

This chapter examines the 'front-stage' and 'backstage' strategies employed by the British National Party (BNP) leadership in its recent attempts to recontextualize its racial nationalist ideology and in doing so to keep it center-stage.[6] The BNP chairman, Nick Griffin, a life-long far right activist has, since his election in 1999, sought to 'modernize' the party. For the first two decades of its existence, the BNP operated on the periphery of British politics, more a street gang than a political party, where it enjoyed a well-deserved reputation for violent, racist extremism. That Griffin should have assumed the mantle of 'modernizer' is in many ways deeply ironic. During the 1980s, he was centrally involved in the 'political soldier' faction of the National Front (NF), which developed and espoused a revolutionary ideology that only served to further marginalize the party in the wake of its catastrophic defeat in the 1979 general election. Following a further split in the organization and his involvement with the International Third Position ITP – a small revolutionary nationalist *groupuscule*, which Griffin now argues was a cult[7] – he entered the political wilderness. His route back into organized far right politics was to be via *The Rune*, the mouthpiece of the Croydon BNP, through which, as editor, Griffin established a reputation for himself as a political hardliner and got himself convicted for inciting racial hatred in 1998. Paradoxically, rather than disbarring him from political office as it would in a liberal-democratic party, such credentials boosted his popularity with other party hardliners, signaling that he was 'one of them'. Their backing proved crucial to him winning the 1999 leadership contest against the party founder John Tyndall. Installed as the leader of the BNP, Griffin quickly became a leading advocate of 'modernization', a key term, and indeed fault-line, for the party in the years immediately after his assumption of power. It is within the context of this drive for 'modernization' that Griffin's 'doublespeak' needs to be evaluated.

The program of ideological overhaul upon which the BNP embarked after 1999 was one designed to remove the overly National Socialist roots of its ideology and personnel, not to mention its addiction to both anti-Semitism and biological racism. Looking askance at 'the winning formula' or 'master frame' employed by the Front National (FN) in France – indicating that modernization was not a process that took place in isolation – BNP strategists sought to replicate the approach. In essence, this entailed downplaying its neo-Nazi antecedents and exchanging 'biological' identity for 'cultural' identity. This would enable them to construct what political scientist Elizabeth Ivarsflaten subsequently dubbed a 'reputational shield' that would deflect accusations of extremism and render the BNP a viable political alternative in the eyes of the British electorate.[8]

The party's failure to sufficiently insulate itself from its past was highlighted in a 2006 Sky News poll which found a large reservoir of support for its policies but rather less for the BNP itself.[9] The idea of constructing a reputational shield had been a cornerstone of the 'vocabulary battle'; spearheaded by extreme right-wing intellectuals in France in the 1960s who were cognizant of the fact that their path to power would be blocked, more or less permanently, as long as the 'left' defined the terms of political discourse.[10] The legacy of this struggle is reflected in the 'mobility' of FN ideological discourse which eschews 'fixed' rhetorical 'signifiers' in favor of a fluidity and ambiguity that has enabled it to synthesize contradictory viewpoints and in doing so appeal to the broadest possible constituency without endangering party unity or alienating public support.[11]

Griffin's recalibration of how the party expressed itself drew upon these debates and demonstrated an understanding of the power of semantics as a means of achieving ideological hegemony as a precursor to achieving political hegemony. Indeed Griffin was particularly keen that the party's local election gains be insulated from the 'careless extremism' emanating from within his own party, stressing that there was no longer any room for the 'Three H's': 'hard talk', 'hobbyism' and 'Hitler'.[12] Boiled down to its essentials, Griffin's message to party activists, noted one observer, was to 'be careful about racist language, violence, Holocaust denial or Nazi-worship'.[13] In its place four unobjectionable 'apple pie' concepts were enunciated: 'freedom', 'security', 'ideology' and 'democracy', which the party now promoted as the embodiment of its ideals, described by Nigel Copsey as the 'surface gloss' beneath which its revolutionary ideology was concealed.[14]

Taken at face value, Griffin appeared to be promising that the party was putting its extremism behind it and embracing democratic politics. There was, so the official mantra stated, no room for those unable to reconcile themselves with this cathartic process, which included, as it transpired, party founder John Tyndall. This supposed break with the past was in fact nothing of the sort. This much was evident in the reaction of external and internal party publications in Griffin's election as leader in 1999. *The Patriot*, the mouthpiece of the BNP modernizing faction, proclaimed Griffin's election with the headline 'New Millennium, New Leader' which drew a line under the past and signaled a new direction for the future. Internal party publications, however, directed at party activists alone were more candid. Signaling that Griffin's election meant merely the re-calibration of how BNP ideology was presented, rather than any root and branch transformation of its content, the internal BNP membership bulletin reassured readers: 'New Leader, Same Cause'.[15] Expanding upon this in *The Patriot*, Griffin argued that it was not an ideological overhaul that was needed but 'new tactics'. 'More guile' instead of 'careless extremism'. As he stressed:

Of course we must teach the truth to the hardcore, for like you, I do not intend to allow this movement to lose its way, but when it comes to influencing the public, forget about racial differences, genetics, Zionism, historical revisionism and so on – all ordinary people want to know is what we can do for them that other parties can't or won't.[16]

There are two tiers to the rhetorical strategy employed by Griffin in attempting to convey BNP ideology. The 'populist' strategy, aimed at the general public, is predicated upon a 'common sense' opposition to immigration. Party strategists made the 'discursive choice' to shift party rhetoric and publications away from explicitly racialized articulations of national identity as part of its search for a 'winning formula'.[17] The development of this 'banal' or 'routine' racism was based upon everyday concerns such as the competition for social housing, and not upon biological racism or Holocaust denial – concerns that are alien to voters. On doorsteps this approach helped to create 'cognitive dissonance' between the perception and reality of the BNP at a local level. Based upon 'community activism' this approach enabled the BNP to build a certain level of legitimacy and fend off accusations of extremism in some localities.[18] Party canvassers were issued with instructions on what to wear and how to talk in order to dispel images of thuggery. This part of the party's 'normalization' strategy aimed to foster the impression that the BNP is a party of 'family values' giving substance to its propaganda that 'people like you' were voting for the BNP, a slogan taken from the French FN. This strategy of de-toxification sought to make the BNP an acceptable and viable political alternative.

The second tier is then reached through membership and participation in the inner life of the party itself, attending local meetings, reading internal 'ideological' publications and participating in the full gamut of party activities. The net result of this process of radicalization was that they would be transformed into ideologically committed party cadres. Behind closed doors, Griffin and other party leaders are more forthright on issues of race relations than they are in public. Indeed it was this practice of 'teaching the truth to the hardcore'[19] that led to Griffin's (unsuccessful) prosecution for inciting racial hatred in 2006, as a result of secret filming that took place at a BNP meeting – highlighting once more the duality of BNP politics.

There is also a third tier, which is an extension of the second. This is the foreign political meeting. Indeed, on an international level, Griffin presents an even more candid account of party policy and strategy. To take but one example, at a meeting in the United States in 2002, Griffin used his 'keynote' speech to castigate his American listeners for failing to adequately exploit 9/11 for political gain. 'It's a disgrace, from what I've seen,' stated Griffin,

> that we made more out of September 11 in Britain in terms of finding ways to prise open cracks in multi-racial society and destroy it, which has to be our aim, we made more out of September 11 in Britain than American nationalists made in America and that is unbelievable. It really is. You should be ashamed of yourselves.[20]

The same holds true for the behavior of party activists. For instance in August 2011, Chris Hurst, a rising star within the party and frequently lauded on its website, was filmed in Hungary giving Nazi salutes at a white supremacist concert; an act he was unlikely to have performed on British soil.[21]

Ultimately, Griffin appears to have regarded language as a malleable political tool, a form of linguistic 'entryism', to be manipulated and utilized, in accordance with political expediency.[22] As Griffin wrote in 1999, this was to be effected by using 'the weight of democracy's own myths and expectations against it by side-stepping and using verbal judo techniques'.[23] The origins of this 'political ju-jitsu' technique of seeking to portray liberalism as the real 'totalitarianism' and its proponents as 'tyrants' in contrast to the BNP 'who stand for freedom', can be found in the 'revisionist' underground. Griffin borrowed the concept, tellingly, from the German Holocaust denier Ernst Zündel who had counseled the adoption of 'revisionist ju-jitsu' in order 'to turn the massive strength of the Exterminationists against themselves, so that they trip over their own lies and repressive laws'.[24] Griffin asserted that 'The Six Million lie is dead', and that 'revisionism' now required 'publicists' like himself to help 'dig the grave'. However, Griffin's career among the vanguard of such publicists concluded with the chastening experience of a criminal conviction which has tarnished his political career since 1998 and perhaps explains his insistence that the party abandon Holocaust denial in public. The party's 'revisionist' intent is now altogether more subtle in its tone and content due to this belated recognition that overt Holocaust denial tarred the party with the brush of extremism and damaged its chances of gaining public office and thus political power.

However, coded anti-Semitism continues to underpin Griffin's attempts to re-position his party as the champions of the white working class, abandoned by 'New Labour'. It has been the articulation of 'grievance' and 'victimhood' that has allowed the BNP to mobilize 'angry white men' to their cause,[25] rather than previous attempts to rehabilitate the Third Reich through the practise of Holocaust denial. Indeed Griffin and the BNP have sought to utilize the terminology of the Labour Party and trade union movement for their own ends. On many occasions, Party literature has claimed that it is the BNP that now encapsulate the values of 'Old Labour' and the working class. This attempted political inversion is also to be found in the aural culture of the BNP which has recorded its own version of 'This Land, is Your Land' written by folk singer Woodie Guthrie and popularized by musician (and anti-BNP campaigner) Billy Bragg, giving it a new meaning altogether.[26] BNP videos have also used the song 'If you tolerate this then your children will be next' by the Manic Street Preachers, a song about the anti-fascist International Brigades in the Spanish Civil War, which, in a similar example of 'verbal ju-jitsu' is used to buttress the claim that the 'great multicultural experiment' has brought nothing but 'violence, hatred, fragmentation and despair' to London. 'You can interpret the lyrics any way you want,' argued a BNP spokesman in defense of its usage following complaints. This statement was not simply an unconscious post-modern flourish but rather the recognition that language can be ambiguous, can have several layers of meaning, and will be heard and interpreted differently by different audiences.[27]

Griffin articulates this narrative of righteous resistance in his opposition to British liberal democracy and the European Union, both of which are portrayed as oppressive, neo-Marxist 'totalitarian' regimes. As part of this political critique, Griffin has appropriated the lexicon of anti-fascism, accusing protestors of using 'fascist methods' to deprive him of his 'free speech'.[28] This could be seen in his verbal attack upon anti-fascist protestors who had gathered outside the Oxford Union debate to demonstrate against his invitation to address this August body in October 2007. 'I have seen them beat up old men and women who are wearing war medals and try and kill them', claimed Griffin, 'had they grown up in Nazi Germany they would have been splendid Nazis'. Such verbiage, whilst ostensibly in defense of his right to freedom of speech, betrays a linguistic calculation on Griffin's part that deliberately inverts Britain's national narrative of anti-fascist struggle against Nazism in order to de-legitimate his opponents who are portrayed as the real extremists.[29]

Academics and journalists who have investigated the party's ideological antecedents are tarred with the same brush. 'Dredging up quotes from 10, 15, 20 years ago is really pathetic and, in a sense, rather fascist', argued the party in response to renewed revelations of Griffin's well-documented record of Holocaust denial.[30] This tendency to turn history on its head was also evident in 2009 following the leaking of the party's entire membership list on-line, which resulted in a handful of members having their homes or cars vandalized. The BNP claimed they were the victims of a 'sustained and political witch-hunt' which, lacking propriety or proportion, was likened to the Nazi pogrom 'Kristallnacht'.[31]

Similarly, the language of liberal human rights is invoked in support of its anti-immigration platform. Immigration, maintains the BNP, has led to the 'systematic destruction' of the white working class, which they consider to be an act of 'genocide'. To support their contention that 'indigenous' (i.e. white) Britons are being 'ethnically cleansed', the BNP cite the Convention on the Prevention and Punishment of the Crime of Genocide, adopted by Resolution 260 (III) A of the United Nations General Assembly on 9 December 1948, which states that genocide 'means any of the acts committed with intent to destroy, in whole or in part, a national, ethical, racial or religious group'. Section 2 (c) of this convention further states that 'deliberately inflicting on the group conditions of life, calculated to bring about its physical destruction in whole or in part' also constitutes genocide. By thus turning the language of liberal democracy against itself, the BNP seeks to validate its case against immigration without recourse to traditional racist argumentation.[32]

Such rhetorical idioms are used by the BNP to facilitate its racial separatist agenda, without reference to an older set of anti-Semitic arguments claiming that immigration is a tool deliberately used by the 'money power' or 'international finance' (a euphemism for Jews) to break down white racial solidarity and self-interest as a precursor to the creation of a 'one world government'. Griffin's reinvented lexicon, cloaked in the language of the left, instead seeks to retain the conspiratorial framework of its opposition to the forces of globalization without mentioning, in public at least, those forces traditionally supposed to be controlling the conspiracy. For the interests of public consumption the BNP has been willing to neuter the full implications of its argument.

Griffin has also sought to use these tactics to outmaneuver his 'neo-Nazi' political rivals on the far right, using their actions and pronouncements to detoxify his own image in a bid to shift public perceptions of the party and its policies. His use of a more extreme but ideologically identifiable opponent to make its own pronouncements appear less extreme, and therefore more publicly palatable, is classic BNP strategy. Indeed in asserting that there was no one who was more disliked by 'neo-Nazi cranks' than he, Griffin has regularly employed such a rhetorical device in order to buttress his own supposed 'moderation'.[33] This tactic was particularly evident when Griffin sought to outmaneuver his opponents during the course of a serious internal schism within the party during 2007 – 2008, during which dozens of local organizers and activists resigned in protest at Griffin's treatment of several leading activists accused of plotting a 'coup' against him. Simon Darby, the party's deputy chairman, branded the leading protagonists of the protest as 'Neo-Nazis that they have purged from the Party', on BBC Newsnight, a strategy employed to discredit them in the eyes of the 'modern' party members.[34]

The BNP 'modernization' strategy has taken place within, and been aided significantly by, the national and international context in which it has taken place. Following serious rioting in the deprived Northern towns of Burnley, Bradford and Oldham in the summer of 2001, coupled with the attacks on the World Trade Centre of 9/11, the BNP began to base its campaigns against Islam. Beneath this 'common sense' populist campaign against Muslims lies a strategy based upon short to medium term political expediency. There had been some internal conflict when Griffin announced this anti-Islamic platform, not least with party founder John Tyndall, who continued to believe that Jews were the principle threat to white civilization. Partly in response to such arguments, Griffin justified his stance on the grounds that Islam was *the sin qua non* upon which the BNP had to campaign:

This is the factor which is going to dominate politics for decades to come. *This* is the enemy that the public can see and understand. *This* is the threat that can bring us to power. *This* is the Big Issue on which we must concentrate in order to wake people up and make them look at what we have to offer all around.[35]

This populist platform, manifested in campaigns against visible targets such as mosques, halal meat, the burka or in neologisms such as 'paedostani' – an amalgam of paedophile and Pakistani – through which to attack Muslims, pushes the party's anti-Semitic ideology further backstage rather than serving to repudiate it. As Griffin explained to a 2006 BNP meeting in Burnley, Lancashire, the spectre of anti-Semitism had to be banished from party discourse and replaced with a campaign against 'Islam' because 'it's the thing they [the general public] can understand, it's the thing the newspapers, the newspaper editors, sell newspapers with'. The decision not to openly condemn the 'Zionist Jews around George Bush' was a calculation based on racial *realpolitik* and the current balance of political power. The BNP had no political power and had to choose their targets carefully. To 'bang on' about the Jews was electoral suicide Griffin noted:

the British public haven't the faintest idea of this group behind George Bush pushing him to war. The public would just think we were barking mad. They would think 'oh you're just attacking Jews just because you want to attack Jews. You're attacking this group of powerful Zionists just because you want to take poor Manny Cohen the tailor and shove him in a gas chamber'. That is what the public would think. It wouldn't get us anywhere other than stepping backwards. It would lock us in a little box, which the public would think extremist, cranks, lunatics, nothing to do with me and we wouldn't get power. Whereas by making Islam the issue, when every time someone turns on the television, every time they pick up a newspaper, in areas like Burnley and Blackburn, every time they talk to their neighbours, they get a drip, drip, drip, something else, which tells them that yeah, Islam is a real serious problem.[36]

Speaking later on that year to an audience of white extremists in the United States, Griffin underlined this point. 'The proper enemy to any political movement isn't necessarily the most evil and the worst', he stated. 'The proper enemy is the one we can most easily defeat'.[37] Despite being tactically conceived, this is not to argue that BNP hostility towards Islam and indeed Muslims is not perfectly genuine. Indeed since becoming the mainstay of BNP political campaigns, particularly in the Northern towns from which it drew some support and which have large Muslim populations, a generalized anti-Muslim sentiment has hardened into an ideological platform, one that has popular traction and which allowed the party to make a limited break from the political periphery to which it was previously confined.

Running in tandem with this strategic refocusing of the party was an attempt to 'soften' its image. This was particularly evident in its public presentation. BNP leader Nick Griffin often held press conferences surrounded by female BNP activists in an attempt to eschew its 'thuggish' image. Again, the approach was quite deliberate. As Griffin explained to party activists:

> Let me make it absolutely plain that this is not some BNP version of Politically Correct sex and disability quotas. It has nothing to do with who we would actually like to sit in Parliament for us; in many cases – almost certainly the majority, for that would simply reflect the realities of inborn human nature – that would be well educated and already successful white males. It is simply about having as many candidates as possible who, simply by being what they are, will help 'soften' our rough image and so help to open the hearts and minds of more ordinary people to us.[38]

This was not a particularly successful strategy, however. Despite several ephemeral 'puff pieces' in the media with female BNP members, the remarks of a London BNP organizer who stated that rape was 'simply sex' did little to dispel the perception of far right politics for misogyny.[39]

Race is omnipresent within the BNP. It is the party's *raison d'être* and the part of its platform best known to the public. In a bid to become mainstream, and in recognition that the multi-racial society was a permanent fixture, the BNP dropped its commitment to 'compulsory repatriation' in 1999. The party remains committed, however, to 'voluntary repatriation' which carries with it less of a stigma than the spectre of force contained in the word 'compulsory'. This was a more 'saleable' position. 'We can stand on that ground without for a moment giving up our eventual idea of a mono-racial Britain', wrote Griffin.[40] Despite its symbolic importance this was no 'Clause Four' moment. For the

BNP changing one word in its constitution made little difference to the over-arching eventual ideological imperative.

There has however been a major difference in how this is expressed. Richard Edmonds who, until recently, was a leading figure in the BNP and one of its founding members, once proudly declared that he was '100 percent racist'. Such modes of forthright expression from leading party members are now no longer the norm. Having infiltrated the BNP, rising to become its central London organizer, *Guardian* journalist Ian Cobain recalled being told about 'the problems we face' by another London BNP official in a conversation, which speaks volumes about the internalization of codes employed to voice racial views:

I heard phrases like this uttered by BNP members many times and, after several months, came to understand their precise, nuanced meanings. 'Nice areas' I quickly understood to signify predominantly white areas. 'Quiet areas' are places where black and minority ethnic people live, but keep a low profile, and don't compete too hard for jobs, school places or sexual partners. 'Troublesome areas' are places where black people do just the opposite. 'No-go areas' are places where black and minority ethnic people are in a majority. 'Ethnics' speaks for itself, as does 'our people'. And 'the problems we face'? They are, quite simply, that there are black people living among us whites.

In my seven months as a party member I heard very few racist epithets, and no anti-Semitic comments. Such language appears almost to be frowned upon in Griffin's post-makeover BNP. Perhaps it is a tribute to the Race Relations Act 1976 and the Public Order Act 1986, and to the gently shifting mores of British life, that racists rarely feel able to express themselves, even among like-minded people. But some of the fear and the hatred remains: it just emerges in code.[41]

Cobain's observations reflect the internalization of the party's modernization process at work with regard to its changing discourse on race, which, though superficial and linguistically evasive, highlights a degree of coded self-censorship through which key ideas and concepts can be enunciated without fear of falling foul of the law. Party activists have internalized the encoding of language in an attempt to reflect the broader shift in far right rhetoric, one that has seen the party move away from 'race' to 'culture' in its articulation of the 'threats' facing British society. Expanding upon the rhetorical repudiation of biological racism pioneered by the French Nouvelle Droite, Griffin explained that the party's new 'formula' was to talk in terms of the decline of human diversity,

> which is the thing which gives people their sense of identity and belonging [...] Now I can defend that on *Newsnight* or *Question Time* in a way that everyone of vaguely good will or independent thought out there will think 'yeah, that's reasonable enough, that's not racist bigotry'.[42]

During the past decade this shift in the rhetoric of the far right in Britain with regard to its championing of 'ethno-plurality' has been expressed around the idea of the 'cultural' rather than 'biological' incommensurability of 'Islam' to the British 'way of life'. However, as the reliance on such coded phraseology in itself reveals, below the 'surface' the BNP critique of multicultural society continues to be underpinned by principles of biological determinism and racial difference.[43] The evolution of this linguistic practice means, not just that activists can communicate amongst themselves, and indeed with others, without fear that their remarks will immediately alienate listeners or, worse, lead to their own prosecution for inciting hatred, but that the party can maintain its platform of 'separation' without overt recourse to the biological idioms of 'race'.

The employment of deliberately neutral synonyms is also evident in how Nick Griffin discusses race and immigration in the public sphere. This came to the fore following his defeat in the East London constituency of Barking in the 2010 general election. During the campaign itself, Griffin was reminded of a statement he had made in 1997, when he thought he was speaking privately to several officials from the Front National. He was in fact speaking to undercover reporters for the ITV *Cook Report*. Griffin had said to them, with regard to the white working class in London that:

> the people who have the brains and ability got out [of London] years ago, one way or another. The people who are left are either the 15 per cent of the population who are happy to put up with it, they're so decadent they

actually like it, or they are too stupid to do anything about it. They will vote BNP, but you can't build a movement on those people.

When challenged by a reporter pondering why Griffin was now appealing to the self-same people he had earlier dismissed, Griffin stated that

I wasn't talking about this part of London [...] We were talking about the likes of Brixton and Hackney. People here have still got fight in them [...] we can't organize in a place like that [Brixton or Hackney]. They're good, decent people. But to organize something, you have to have people who've got an unusual flair and spark.

Reminded that he had said they were 'too stupid to do anything about it' Griffin claimed he was 'drunk'.[44] It was clear, however, that Griffin believed he was in 'foreign' territory. Campaigning in Barking was 'like leafleting in central Nairobi' (the Kenyan capital), he alleged.[45] Following his defeat, Griffin lamented that Barking was 'finished' and that 'London is gone' for the English. The BNP now had to become a 'civil rights organization' for the British 'minority'.[46] Untangling the meaning of such codes is not difficult and is entirely in keeping with the observations made by Cobain: London was 'finished' for white people. Such rhetoric was reflective both of the generalized belief that immigration is 'invasion' and settlement is 'colonization' – of the internal self-image many party cadres have of belonging to a movement for racial survival – not merely an 'ordinary' political party.[47]

The development of coded communication, to internalize and enshrine core party values – which speak to the layman, but whose 'true' meaning can only be deciphered by veteran activists – can be seen during the course of a fractious BNP meeting for party activists held in the European Parliament in May 2010 (and subsequently placed on-line by a disgruntled member). As discussion degenerated into an unseemly squabble between activists and Griffin, the chairman was criticized for appointing BNP activist Steve Squire as his new London regional organizer, instead of an activist with a longer track record of involvement within the party. Griffin dismissed the length of service as immaterial, responding that Squire's family 'has been in nationalism since the 1930s and that 'his father was jailed under the race act. He's grown up with it [...] he's a very good man'.[48] What this meant, in plain terms which members would have understood, was that at least one member of the London regional organizer's family had been involved with one or more of the interwar fascist groups of the 1930s and that his father's political activities had led to a criminal conviction. This political pedigree was, for Griffin, evidence that Squire was a committed activist and 'a very good man'.

Beneath the 'official' façade of populist anti-Islam campaigning and coded anti-black prejudice, anti-Semitism continues to exert a powerful hold over the racial nationalist tradition. Since 1945, however, the historical memory of the horrors of the Holocaust has served as a brake on the political success of far right parties who have refused to shelve such rhetoric. Those who continued to support the racial nationalist cause could no longer give open voice to anti-Semitism if they sought to gain widespread public support. Even before the passing of a raft of Race Relations legislation in the late 1960s British fascists, well aware of the odium that shrouded their politics, censored themselves. No longer did they speak openly of those they perceived to be their racial enemies. The Jews were referred to as 'four-by-twos', 'kangaroos' or even as 'Eskimos'.[49] Such a rhetorical sleight of hand fooled few. Whilst such crude rhyming slang and the oblique reference to the Inuit were the preserve of hard line racial fascists like Arnold Leese, a former leader of the Imperial Fascist League (IFL) others, such as Sir Oswald Mosley, erstwhile leader of the British Union of Fascists (BUF), employed a slightly higher register in order to cloak their anti-Semitism. Indeed, as Mosley was noted to have observed in 1954:

We can still get our point across by playing up 'characteristics' without name calling. We used to talk about international Jewish bankers; now, when we talk about American capitalists our followers know exactly whom we're talking about. We have been identified long enough as fighting Jews for our followers to know what we mean.[50]

Exercizing even more caution, the BNP's *Language and Concepts Discipline Manual* of 2005 – an internal party document providing guidance for party organizers on the bare minimum expected of them when communicating with the general public – stated *pace* Mosley that 'we do not believe that Jews *per se* are bad, though we do of course, reserve the right to condemn individual Jews that are doing something bad'. Nevertheless, in recognition of the party's past record of anti-Semitism the manual concluded that, all things considered, 'it is *best to simply never speak or write of Jews at all* [emphasis in the original]'.[51] Rarely, however, has the party heeded its own advice with regard to its front-stage presentation. Since 1999 the BNP has substituted the word 'Jew' for 'Zionist' but done little else to signal a principled rejection of anti-Semitism. Indeed, during its campaign against the war in Iraq, *Voice of Freedom*, the party newspaper, claimed that Britain sent troops to serve in Iraq because 'Tony Blair swapped British blood for donations from a clique of filthy-rich Zionist businessmen'.[52] This short sentence succeeded in invoking a number of anti-Semitic stereotypes: the Jew as capitalist, the Jew as rootless and disloyal, the Jew as war profiteer, not to mention the more medieval image of the Jew feeding off British and *ergo* Christian 'blood' – the 'blood libel'. A virtually identical point, made in slightly less lurid prose, was enshrined in the 2005 BNP manifesto, which pledged to immediately withdraw British troops from Iraq and that 'we will never again involve British troops in any more American "wars for oil" or neo-con adventures *on behalf of the Zionist government of Israel* [my emphasis]'.[53]

Such arguments against the war in Iraq bear all the hallmarks of Mosley's opposition to the Second World War as a 'Jews War' whose injunction to followers, commonly quoted by apologists, that BUF members 'do nothing to injure our country, or help any other power [...] to obey [their] orders and in particular obey the rules of their service' was in fact a truncated version of his original message which was hardly representative of Mosley's actual attitude to the war – a 'quarrel of Jewish finance' – in which he expressly refused to fight. This episode is also a prime example of how the far right uses language to reframe its own history for present political exigency.[54]

Like Mosley, Griffin has sought to exploit the world financial crisis through an increase on his attacks on 'banksters' (a fusion of the word 'banker' and 'gangster').[55] Within the far right underground, the evocation of 'New York bankers' and the 'International Money Power' is likely to trigger images of specifically 'Jewish' bankers in the minds of his followers. Indeed the utilization of the myth of Jewish financial control of world affairs and its role in encouraging revolution and war was advanced with regard to recent events in

Libya. The party journal *Identity* blamed Libya's internal turmoil upon the 'Rothschilds' and the 'banksters' leaving seasoned readers in little doubt that they meant 'Jewish' interests were again manipulating world events – in keeping with the age old idea of a 'Hidden Hand' working behind the scenes, all the more convincing for its invisibility.[56]

Griffin's own personal ideological framework appears to be very much as it was twenty years ago, albeit with some refinement. Discussing events in Libya, whilst neglecting to mention his previous praise of Colonel Gaddafi, Griffin attacked the conflict as another example of a 'neo-conservative' war for oil, fought by so-called 'rebels' who served as proxies for 'New World Order puppet masters such as George Soros'.[57] That Griffin should have alighted on George Soros, a Hungarian-born Jewish billionaire financier, when he could have chosen any other arch capitalist, is reflective of the continuities in con-spiratorial thinking. The name 'Soros' alone, whose Jewish lineage is well known, serves as a signifier. There is no need to be so crass as to point out that he is Jewish. As Mosley noted back in the 1950s 'we have been identified long enough as fighting Jews for our followers to know what we mean'.[58]

Reverting again to a line of argument first employed by Mosley in the 1930s but forgotten in subsequent decades by hardliners like Tyndall, (photos of whom dressed in Nazi uniform in front of portraits of Adolf Hitler, provided a fairly clear visual indicator of his political preferences) internal BNP publica-tions have argued that they must reject 'Judeo-obsessivism' as an impedi-ment to future growth. This injunction comes with the caveat that:

> Lest anyone misunderstand, the BNP has not 'embraced Zionism', 'sold out to the Jews', or anything like it. We remain well-aware that subversive Jews exist, that some Jews tend to have a characteristic style of (material-istic and scheming, like Karl Marx and George Soros) subversion, and we remain committed to fighting them, *when this is really the case.*[59]

Whilst claiming to reject anti-Semitism – and to follow the line propound-ed by Mosley that they only attack Jews for what they do, not because they are Jews – this article also re-affirmed and reworked, through its linking of Marx and Soros, the image of the 'Jew' as involved in a specifically com-munist/capitalist conspiracy against Gentile interests.

Even in denying charges of anti-Semitism Griffin thus reinforces the politics of racial exclusion. Stating that he had 'no time for anti-Semites' Griffin stated that fraudster Bernie Madoff 'didn't steal OUR pension funds [...] He mostly stole from Jewish charities. He may be a Jewish crook, but his Jewishness is irrelevant'.[60] Madoff's Jewishness could not be more relevant for Griffin, however. Indeed it is precisely these attributes, racial, religious or both, that makes Jews not British. The pension funds were Jewish, not 'ours'. In such a manner, the idea of race is reinforced and Jews are denied 'our' national identity – despite the seeming restraint placed upon an anti-Semitism clearly placed 'backstage' since 1999.

Doublespeak can also be visual. *Identity* uses images to convey its racial ideology in code to its readers. In January 2005, for instance, *Identity* featured an article praising A. K. Chesterton, the founding chairman of the National Front (NF) in 1967 and author of *The New Unhappy Lords* (1965, a contemporary 'classic' of anti-Semitic conspiracy theory), alongside another anti-Semitic author S. E. D. Brown, editor of the *South African Observer*. Both individuals were lauded for their work in revealing that the Bilderberg Group, 'are without doubt the sinister black heart of western "democracy"'. The article, entitled 'The Hidden Hand' – a traditional euphemism for Jews – did not mention 'Jews' in print, but signaled its true meaning by juxtaposing a picture of Chesterton, the 'Jew wise' British patriot, against one of his racial nemesis, Henry Kissinger, so that readers would have been in no doubt as to who and what lay behind the Bilderberg Group: the Jews.[61] This visual message could be easily decoded by its readership. Recent polling data reveals that 33 per cent of BNP voters subscribe to the proposition that there exists a major international Jewish / Communist conspiracy to undermine the traditional Christian values of Britain and other western countries. There is no need to voice such sentiments openly for them to be clearly understood by a large proportion of the hard core membership.[62]

While such ideas may resonate internally, an attempt to mobilize such prejudice for electoral gain has been more divisive among party strategists. During the Barking general election campaign in 2010 – in which Griffin stood against the incumbent Labour MP Margaret Hodge – Griffin's campaign team sought to mobilize anti-Semitic prejudices which they believed existed amongst the Black and Muslim electorate to vote, if not for them, then at least against Hodge. To this end, thousands of copies of a publication entitled *The Barking and Dagenham Sentinel* were distributed, consisting of a forthright attack upon Hodge's political record underpinned by an assertion that she herself was a rich, foreign Jew: 'Hodge', asserted the publication, 'was born in Egypt as Margaret Oppenheimer, the daughter of a *refugee millionaire German Jewish steel trader* [my emphasis]'.[63] If seasoned party activists on the ground agreed with the sentiment they nevertheless realized that it would be very damaging for their campaign. Indeed, as one leading activist observed, it made for disastrous propaganda:

> It was incredibly long winded and was about the least effective propaganda item ever produced by the BNP. It also contained an anti-Semitic slur that had to be blacked out with marker pens. This ridiculous newspaper destroyed the last week of the BNP's Barking and Dagenham campaign as it had to be censored (which took our activists days and days) and then they were ordered to distribute it. It will not have benefitted our campaign in the slightest.[64]

Thus, whilst such private dialogue remains diametrically opposed to the public persona that the 'modern' BNP wishes to project, there is clearly a disagreement between party strategists, as to whether or not the use of anti-Semitism in public electioneering is really beyond the pale. That there is still such a conflict within the upper echelons of the party signals just how far the modernization strategy has yet to travel. This is also reflected in the party's attitude to the media. The BNP is, perhaps understandably, profoundly hostile to the media, and in particular the British Broadcasting Corporation (BBC), whose documentary teams have mounted a number of 'stings' against the party in recent years. Griffin, who has been the 'victim' of several of these programs – leading in 2006 to his prosecution as a result of the screening of *The Secret Agent* (2004) – is markedly more hostile than most. His hostility pre-dates any direct personal encounter with such programming, however. Griffin was the author of a notorious pamphlet entitled *Who Are the Mindbenders?* (1997), which claimed that Jews controlled the media. The pamphlet increased his notoriety as an anti-Semite, a reputation he has been unable to lose. Griffin certainly no longer refers to the Jewish control of the

141

media. He now refers simply to the 'controlled media', which allows him to discuss his beliefs unimpeded by any major revision to the intellectual framework in which they function.

Griffin also appears to be unable to categorically distance himself from Holocaust denial, a propensity which saw him convicted of inciting racial hatred in 1998 and given a two year suspended sentence. Despite the fact that Holocaust denial (or 'historical revisionism' as it was euphemistically styled within the far right), no longer plays any public part in BNP discourse, Griffin has not unreservedly disassociated himself from it. Asked in 2007 whether he still denied the Holocaust, Griffin stated that he did not: 'European law now says the Holocaust did happen, precisely as understood, so I accept European law, so yeah, I believe in the Holocaust'.[65] Such a statement, with its Orwellian echoes, was hardly an emphatic denial. Griffin believed in the Holocaust now because European law, which criminalized Holocaust denial, compelled him to. Rather than reject Holocaust denial unequivocally, Griffin retained the same stance during his 2009 *Question Time* appearance, when he refused to even discuss his past proclivities claiming that 'I cannot tell you why I said those things in the past, or why I have changed my mind' because European law prevented him from doing so. Despite reassurance from Justice Secretary Jack Straw that no such law existed, Griffin refused to be drawn on the subject, displaying a further extension of the notion of denial as a 'thought crime' which paints the state as seeking to oppress 'free speech'.[66]

'As a credible vehicle the BNP is finished. It is dead. It is over', wrote one former party strategist in July 2011. The BNP had become 'a tainted and toxic brand'. As former party cadres began leaving the BNP in droves, strategic discussion again centered upon the failure of the party to erect a sufficiently robust reputational shield. 'Organized nationalism has a bad public reputation in this country', conceded Eddy Butler, the party's former national elections officer. 'Whether we like it or not, it is associated with Nazism, anti-Semitism, violence and hatred. That is some reputation to live down'. Nor was the reputation invented, Butler admitted.[67] That the party's modernization strategy stalled was hardly surprising. The 'surface' articulation of ideology is ultimately reflective of the 'depth' of its ideological concerns. The insulation from public calumny that this front-stage strategy was supposed to bring the party was compromised from the start by the failure of party ideologues, and in particular by its chairman, to alter or successfully veil, in any meaningful way, the backstage 'depth' of its racial *Weltanschaung*. There was no root and branch transformation of core values that would have enabled it to become a genuine 'post-fascist' party. Indeed had there been a Herculean cleansing of the Augean stables in order to rid the party of its 'baggage', then the key architects of the 'modernization' strategy, Griffin included, would have all had to leave the party.

The culture of careless extremism against which Griffin railed in 2001 remains just as much an issue in 2013. Moreover, the failure to genuinely modernize has implications for civil society. Griffin's own predilection for careless extremism 'creates the climate where a BNP member has been arrested for burning the Koran', one disaffected party strategist has argued.[68] The failure to genuinely overhaul the center, he implies, has given license to a more concrete expression of racist extremism on the periphery, which in turn has fuelled the party's reputation for racism. The effect, it was argued, is cumulative. Griffin's extremism 'creates a breeding ground for freaks and justifies nutters doing all manner of things'.[69] Sour grapes perhaps, but given that it is possible to write a chapter on BNP doublespeak indicates the limited and cosmetic nature of the party's modernization. The increasingly sophisticated coded phraseology of the BNP's critique of multiculturalism has not masked the fact that, largely because its core ideological allegiances remain unaltered, the 'new' BNP appears little different from the 'old'. Following a major split within the party after the 2010 general election, many BNP ideologues and strategists have begun contemplating life outside the BNP. Searching for a way to outrun history, figures such as Butler have begun to look again at why the first wave of modernization did not remove the taint of extremism. This, unsurprisingly, was because the BNP was anchored in an historical and ideological tradition that was defined by its extremism. Their arguments for further reinvention were not, as Griffin dismissed them, a betrayal of core values or an appeal for 'civic' nationalism. Rather it was an acknowledgement that, though the BNP will undoubtedly remain a part of the political landscape for some time to come, the party had failed to move with the times and, in its present incarnation at least appeared unable in eyes of many of its members and activists to further advance the cause of racial nationalism.

ENDNOTES

[1] Ian Cobain, 'The Guardian Journalist who became the Central London Organizer for the BNP', *The Guardian*, 21 December 2006.

[2] *BNP Language and Concepts Discipline Manual:* BNP Policy Research, July 2005.

[3] Cas Mudde, *The Ideology of the Extreme Right* (Manchester: Manchester University Press, 2000), p. 20.

[4] Peter Oborne, *The Rise of Political Lying* (London: Simon and Schuster, 2005); and John Mearsheimer, *Why Leaders Lie: The Truth about Lying in International Politics* (London: Duckworth Overlook, 2011).

[5] Michael Billig, *Fascists: A Social Psychological View of the National Front* (London: Harcourt Brace Jovanovich, 1978).

[6] Ruth Wodak and John E. Richardson, 'European Fascism in Talk and Text – Introduction' in Ruth Wodak and John E. Richardson (eds.), *Analysing Fascist Discourse: European Fascism in Talk and Text* (Abingdon: Routledge, 2013), pp. 1 – 17. For a discussion of this practice in an earlier incarnation of the BNP see John E. Richardson, 'Racial Populism in British Fascist Discourse: The case of COMBAT and the British National Party (1960 – 1967),' pp. 181 – 202 in the same volume.

[7] See: http://www.youtube.com/watch?v=ohLMemktE18 (accessed 19/04/2010).

[8] Herbert Kitschelt, *The Radical Right in Western Europe* (Michigan: University of Michigan Press, 1995); Jens Rydren, *The Populist Challenge: Political Protest and Ethno-Nationalist Mobilization in France* (New York: Berghahn, 2004); and Elizabeth Ivarsflaten, 'Reputational Shields: Why most Anti-Immigrant Parties failed in Western Europe, 1980 – 2005'. Available at: www.nuff.ox.ac.uk/politics/papers/2006/ivarsflatena psa2006.pdf (accessed 07/11/2011).

[9] 'Sky Poll Shows Backing for BNP Policies', 25 April 2006. Available at: http://news.sky.co m/story/422131/sky-poll-shows-backing-for-bnp-policies (accessed 04/07/2012).

[10] Harvey G. Simmons, *The French Front National* (Boulder: Westview Press, 1996), pp. 217 – 221.

[11] Steve Bastow, 'The Ideological Mobility of Front National Discourse', *Essex Papers in Politics and Government*, 10 (October 1998), pp. 1 – 25.

[12] Nigel Copsey, *Contemporary British Fascism: The British National Party and the Quest for Legitimacy* (Basingstoke: Palgrave, 2008), p. 142.

[13] Ian Cobain, 'Racism, Recruitment and how the BNP Believes it is just "One Crisis Away from Power"', *The Guardian*, 22 December 2006.

[14] Copsey, *Contemporary British Fascism*, p. 103 and p. 123.

[15] *British Nationalist*, October 1999.

[16] Nick Griffin, 'BNP – Freedom Party', *Patriot* 4 (Spring 1999).

[17] Daphne Halikiopoulou and Sofia Vasilopoulou, 'Towards a "Civic" Narrative: British National Identity and the Transformation of the British National Party,' *The Political Quarterly* 81/4 (October – December 2010), pp. 583 – 592.

[18] James Rhodes, 'The Banal National Party: The Routine Nature of Legitimacy,' *Patterns of Prejudice* 43/2 (2009), pp. 142 – 160.

[19] Griffin, 'BNP – Freedom Party'.

[20] Nick Griffin, *American Renaissance Conference 2002* (VHS cassette 2002).

[21] Brian Flynn, 'BNP chief's Hitler salute to Breivik Heroine,' *The Sun*, 4 August 2011.

[22] Nick Griffin, 'Time to go to the Ball', *Spearhead* 335 (January 1997).

[23] Griffin, 'BNP – Freedom Party'.

[24] Nick Griffin, '"Populism" or Power?' *Spearhead* 324 (February 1996).

[25] On which see Robert Ford and Matthew J. Goodwin, 'Angry White Men: Individual and Contextual Predictors of Support for the British National Party', *Political Studies* 58 (2010), pp. 1 – 25.

[26] 'Town Folk Musician records CD for British National Party', 23 February 2006. Available at: http://www.doncasterfreepress.co.uk/news/doncaster-news/town-folk-musician-rec ords-cd-for-british-national-party-1-499357 (accessed 23/02/2006).

[27] Sam Jones, 'Manics' Tribute to International Brigades crops up on BNP Website', 28 March 2009. Available at: http://www.guardian.co.uk/music/2009/mar/28/manic-street-preachers-bnp-website (accessed 04/07/2012).

[28] 'BNP Leader says Opponents of Trinity Debate used "Fascist Methods" to stop it', 8 November 2011. Available at: http://www.thejournal.ie/bnp-leader-says-opponents-of-trinity-debate-used-fascist-methods-to-stop-it-274375-Nov2011/ (accessed 07/11/2011).

[29] Matthew Taylor, 'Irving and Griffin Spark Fury at Oxford Union Debate', 27 November 2007. Available at: http://www.guardian.co.uk/uk/2007/nov/27/highereducatio n.studentpoliticseducation (Accessed 04/07/2012).

[30] 'BNP FAQs – Countering the Smears', Available at: http://www.bnp.org.uk/articles/counte ring_smears.html (accessed 12/03/2007).

[31] For the 'Peoples' Defence Fund' see: https://appeals.bnp.org.uk/defence.html (accessed 13/01/2009).

[32] 'Cockneys become First Victims of the Immigration Invasion Genocide', available at: http://www.bnp.org.uk/news/cockneys-become-first-victims-immigration-invasion-genocide (accessed 07/11/2011).

[33] 'BNP Leader Nick Griffin: Everyone is Against me', 29 October 2011. Available at: http://www.bbc.co.uk/news/uk-politics-15499805 (accessed 07/11/2011).

[34] 'Sadie's story', 22 December 2007. Available at: http://enoughisenoughnick.blogspot. co.uk/2007/12/sadies-story.html (accessed 04/07/2012).

[35] Nick Griffin, 'Our Fight in the Culture Clash', *Identity* 64 (March 2006).

[36] BNP, *Tameside Election* (BNP DVD 2006).

[37] Jonathan Tilove, 'White Nationalist Conference Ponders Whether Jews and Nazis Can Get Along', 3 March 2006. Available at: http://www.forward.com/articles/white-nationalist-conference-ponders-whether-jews/ (accessed 03/03/2006).

[38] Nick Griffin, 'The Big Picture Behind our Electoral Targets', *Identity* 83 (October 2007).

[39] Andrew Gilligan, 'Women More Troubled by Bag Theft than Rape, BNP Candidate Claims', *Evening Standard*, 1 April 2008.

[40] Nick Griffin, 'No Time for Peter Pan', *Spearhead* 357 (November 1998).

[41] Ian Cobain, 'The Guardian Journalist who became Central London Organizer for the BNP', *The Guardian*, 21 December 2006.

[42] Quoted in Matthew Goodwin, *New British Fascism: Rise of the British National Party* (Abingdon: Routledge, 2011), p. 66.

[43] John E. Richardson, 'Race and Racial Difference: The Surface and Depth of BNP Ideol-ogy', in Nigel Copsey and Graham Macklin eds., *British National Party: Contempo-rary Perspectives* (Abingdon: Routledge, 2011), pp. 38 – 62.

[44] John Harris, 'Griffin vs Hodge: The Battle for Barking', *The Guardian*, 13 March 2010.

[45] Russell Myers and Lee Sorrell, 'Nick Griffin: Barking's just like Central Nairobi,' *The People*, 25 April 2010. Available at: http://www.people.co.uk/news/tm_headline=nick-griffin-barking-s-just-like-central-nairobi%26method=full%26objectid=22210082%26si teid=93463-name_page.html (accessed 07/07/2012).

[46] 'Nick Griffin Talking About Barking and The Rest London After The Elections', uploaded 8 May 2010. Available at: http://www.youtube.com/watch?v=fr0LmLz0jXk (accessed 07/11/2011).

[47] Goodwin, *New British Fascism*, pp. 157 – 161.

[48] 'Altercation in Brussels (Part 2 of 2)', uploaded 31 May 2011. See: http://www.you tube.com/watch?v=I8XJFTaNVDw (accessed 07/11/2011).

[49] See for instance 'Arnold Spencer Leese', 15 March 1944, in TNA HO 45/25571.

[50] *The ADL Bulletin*, March 1954.

[51] BNP, *Language and Concepts Discipline Manual* (2005). Available at: http://www.bnp.or g.uk/organisers/store/general_guides/language_discipline.pdf (accessed 12/01/2009).

[52] 'Blair's Evil War', *Voice of Freedom*, August 2004.

[53] *Rebuilding British Democracy: British National Party General Election 2005 Manifesto* (London: BNP, 2005), p. 52.

[54] Richard Griffiths, 'A Note on Mosley, the "Jewish War" and Conscientious Objection', *Journal of Contemporary History* 40/4 (2005), pp. 675 – 688. See also Graham Macklin, 'Modernizing the Past for the Future' in Nigel Copsey and Graham Macklin eds., *British National Party: Contemporary Perspectives* (Abingdon: Routledge, 2011), pp. 19 – 37.

[55] 'Banksters Live the Highlife on Your £1.3 Trillion Bailout' available at: http://www.bnp.org.uk/news/banksters-live-highlife-your-%C2%A313-trillion-bailout (accessed 07/11/2011).

[56] 'Those Who Cannot Remember the Past are Condemned to Repeat it (Part 2)'. Available at: http://eddybutler.blogspot.com/2011/04/those-who-cannot-remember-past-are.html (accessed 07/11/2011).

[57] 'Attack on Libya – Nick Griffin Slams "Puppet" Cameron', available at: http://www.bnp.org.uk/news/attack-libya-%E2%80%93-nick-griffin-slams-puppet-cameron (accessed 07/11/2011).

[58] *The ADL Bulletin*, March 1954.

[59] *Identity* 66 (May 2006).

[60] 'Matthew Bell: The *IoS* Diary', 4 January 2009. Available at: http://www.independent.co.uk/opi nion/commentators/matthew-bell-the-iiosi-diary-1224213.html (accessed 07/11/2011).

[61] *Identity* 51 (January 2005).

[62] YouGov poll 'European Elections' – Fieldwork Dates: 29 May – 4 June 2009. Available at: http://www.channel4.com/news/media/2009/06/day08/yougovpoll_080609.pdf (accessed 02/08/2009).

[63] 'The Millionaire "Socialist"', *The Barking and Dagenham Sentinel*, No. 1, 2010. The offending phrase was removed from PDF copies of the newspaper that subsequently circulated.

[64] 'The Highly Irregular Lifestyle of Patrick Harrington' available at: http://eddybutler.blogs pot.com/2011/03/highly-irregular-lifestyle-of-patrick.html (accessed 07/11/2011).

[65] *Lincolnshire Echo*, 15 March 2007.

[66] 'Question Time', 22 October 2010. Available to view at: http://www.bbc.co.uk/iplayer/epis ode/b00nft24/Question_Time_22_10_2009 (accessed 13/11/2010).

[67] 'It isn't all Greek to me', available at: http://eddybutler.blogspot.com/2011/07/it-isnt-all-greek-to-me.html (accessed 07/11/2011).

[68] 'Those Who Cannot Remember the Past are Condemned to Repeat it (Part 2)'. Available at: http://eddybutler.blogspot.com/2011/04/those-who-cannot-remember-past-are.html (accessed 07/11/2011).

[69] 'Every Finishing Line is the Beginning of a New Race' available at: http://eddybutler.blo gspot.com/2011/07/every-finish-line-is-beginning-of-new.html (accessed 07/11/2011).

WAVERING BETWEEN RADICAL AND MODERATE: THE DISCOURSE OF THE VLAAMS BELANG IN FLANDERS (BELGIUM)

Hilde Coffé and Jeroen Dewulf

Despite considerable losses in the 2010 federal elections, the Vlaams Belang (Flemish Interest, VB) remains one of the largest radical right-wing parties in Western Europe. Indeed, gaining 12.3 per cent of Flemish (Dutch-speaking Belgian) votes in the federal elections of 2010, the party is a major political player and has a strong foothold in both the (regional) Flemish and the (federal) Belgian party system. The party's growth began at the end of the 1980s, when it decided to put more emphasis on the migration issue rather than on Flemish independence, which had been the party's main focus when it was founded in 1978. Aiming at further electoral growth, the party softened its discourse during the second half of the 1990s. This change in strategy was also a consequence of the *cordon sanitaire*; namely, an agreement by all other parties in Belgium's Parliament to refuse any political deal with the radical right party. Since 2007, however, the Vlaams Belang is returning to fiercer stances on migration and Flemish nationalism, partially as a consequence of the development and growth of new conservative right-wing competitors.

In examining these trends, this chapter provides an overview of the changes in the party's discourse, while relating these to the party's political and social environment, including the existence of the *cordon sanitaire*; rulings on charges of racism; and the development and electoral success of new right-wing conservative parties. In order to understand changes in the discourse of the Vlaams Belang, however, it is crucial to consider the political and social context in which the party acts. In keeping with Dézé's approach, this chapter will argue that parties are partly-dependent variables of the political systems in which they operate and to which they are likely to adapt.[1] This is obviously not a phenomenon unique to radical right parties. Indeed all parties, of whatever ideology, may be seen as part of a particular party system to which they react. Yet radical right parties represent a particular case given their extremist and (often) populist, anti-establishment discourse.[2] As radical right parties in Europe often position themselves explicitly outside the political party system, they have to balance the *adaptation* of their discourse to the political system with the need to *distinguish* themselves from this system by sticking to their radical discourse. Analyzing party texts, campaign materials, speeches of – and interviews with – party leaders, the following sections chronologically discuss the discourse of the Vlaams Belang, and changes therein, particularly in relation to the party's political and electoral environment.

The Roots of Flemish Nationalism (1830 – 1945)

When the Southern Netherlands became an independent kingdom under the name of Belgium in 1830, it was ruled as an entirely Francophone nation. Despite the fact that about 57 per cent of the Belgian citizens were Dutch-speaking, there was little protest against the country's language policy.[3] The population in Belgium's poor Dutch-speaking north had other concerns than matters of linguistic pride. In the early years of Belgium, the only form of protest against the nation's language policy came from a small circle of middle-class intellectuals who formed the 'Flemish Movement'.[4] Despite the fact that Belgium's Dutch-speaking provinces had never built a political or cultural entity in the past, this movement claimed that its inhabitants formed a specific people, a 'volk'. The movement referred to these provinces with the medieval term 'Flanders' and to its inhabitants as 'the Flemish', arguing that there existed a specific 'Flemish spirit' that found its reflection in a Flemish mentality, morality and traditions, but above all in its language. Although the Flemish Movement played an essential role in maintaining concern for the Dutch language and in popularizing the terms 'Flanders' and 'Flemish', its message did not reach the masses.

By the end of the nineteenth century, however, the once lucrative metallurgic industry in the French-speaking south suffered due to competition with the German Ruhr, while the expansion of the port of Antwerp attracted increasing numbers of investors to Flanders. This economic shift made the Flemish people more confident, which was reflected in slogans such as 'I'm proud to be Flemish!' or 'In Flanders, Flemish!'[5] Inspired by Germany's victory over France in 1870, young members of the Flemish Movement increasingly adopted German nationalist rhetoric about the superiority of the 'Kulturnation', a nation defined by a single ethnicity and language, and shifted the demand for the equality of Dutch and French in Belgium to the exclusivity of Dutch in Flanders. Radical 'flamingants' now even pleaded for Flemish independence.

In contrast to these hardliners, the moderate 'flamingants', looked for compromises and achieved a major success in 1898 with the Equality Law which recognized the equality of the Dutch and French language in judicial matters. This process of moderate reform was violently interrupted in 1914 when German troops invaded (neutral) Belgium and occupied most of its territory. With its 'Flamenpolitik' (Flemish policy), the German occupier attempted to divide Belgium along linguistic lines in the hope of winning Flemish support. While most of its members refused collaboration, some hardliners in the Flemish Movement seized the opportunity to push through a radical reform of Belgium. Shortly before the end of the First World War, these 'activists' even declared the independence of Flanders. Due to individual acts of collaboration, the Flemish Movement as a whole lost much of its credibility and became marginalized in the wave of Belgian patriotism that erupted after Germany's defeat.

Just as has occurred during the First World War, anti-Belgian resentment prompted radical Flemish nationalists to collaborate with the occupiers during the Second World War. They hoped to win German support for their cause. Yet, after the liberation in 1944, their radical ambitions were again thwarted.[6]

Radical Flemish nationalism from (1945 – mid 1980s)

In 1954, a group of politicians linked to the Flemish Movement founded the Volksunie (Peoples Union, VU). The party's main goal was to contribute to the gradual transformation of Belgium into a federal state. In 1978, Karel Dillen (1925 – 2007) broke with the VU and founded the Vlaams Blok (Flemish Block, VB). Dillen, a radical anti-Belgian Flemish nationalist with fascist sympathies,[7] aimed to make the Vlaams Blok a kind of *whip party* that would spur the VU to adopt a more radical policy. Dillen believed that the VU had made too many concessions to Francophone parties in the negotiations over the federalization of Belgium. He claimed that, unlike the VU, the Vlaams Blok was a radical party:

hard, uncompromising, always zoning in on the other parties' shortcomings, but not itself tempted by the fleshpots of Egypt. In view of our programme, we are not cut out to be a leading party, in any sense whereby we would be expected to share power with another party.[8]

Dillen advocated an autonomous Flemish republic. In the party's formative years, immigration had not yet become the dominant issue. Only in its 1980 manifesto, *Fundamental Principles*, did the Vlaams Blok for the first time include a paragraph about immigration. In that paragraph, alongside advocating a ban on new immigration was a proposal for the gradual reduction of guest workers. Nonetheless, this anti-immigration measure was overshadowed by the central theme the party had made itself known in the 1980s: the demand for a fully independent Flanders.

Prioritizing migration over Flemish nationalism (mid 1980s – early 1990s)

In 1983, the Vlaams Blok changed course. The party decided to reach out to youth activists by giving a platform to a new generation of party members, including the rhetorically talented Filip Dewinter, Gerolf Annemans and Frank Vanhecke, who would soon play major roles within the party. Under pressure from these and other ambitious, younger party members, the Vlaams Blok gave increasing attention to the immigration issue. On 25 March 1984 – the International Day Against Racism – the party held, for the first time, an ideologically centered congress dedicated to the *foreigner problem*. Dillen subsequently submitted a bill proposal to the Belgian Chamber of Representatives that offered a cash incentive for immigrants to return to their countries of origin. Also in 1984, during the campaign for the European Parliament, the Vlaams Blok ran the populist slogan 'We say what you are thinking', making the point that out of political correctness, concerns in the population about the growing number of (predominantly Moroccan and Turkish) immigrants were not addressed by mainstream political parties or in the mainstream media. With the combined pressures of immigration and a high unemployment rate in Belgium during these years, the Vlaams Blok hoped to make deep inroads with sectors of the population hit hardest by the concessionary politics of the center-right government then in power.

Also during these years, the success of France's National Front (FN) in mobilizing voters around the core theme of resistance to immigration was another prompt for the Vlaams Blok to focus on the issue.[9] Furthermore, there is nothing strange or surprising in an ideological wedding between Flemish-nationalist separatism and a strong position on immigrants. The premise of radical nationalism is that a certain cultural group should be able to exercise, as much as possible, sovereignty within the territory to which it has historically been tied. The unabated presence or unchecked influx of new population groups can therefore trigger negative feelings, as the concern may arise that these groups represent a threat to the cultural homogeneity of the region or nation.[10]

In the 1987 elections, the party continued to prioritize the immigration issue and organized an aggressive campaign under the provocative slogan 'One's own people first'; itself based on the FN's motto 'The French First'. This campaign proved to be successful: the Vlaams Blok went from having zero seats in the Senate and one in the Chamber of Deputies, to holding one seat in the Senate and two in the Chamber. Despite this success, tensions emerged over the emphasis on the immigration issue to the detriment of Flemish nationalism. This tension was essentially between what paid electoral dividends and what represented the party's original core ideology. Those who wanted to place the emphasis on Flemish nationalism dubbed Filip Dewinter and others *Lepenists* (that is, sympathizers of the leader of the FN, Jean-Marie Le Pen), claiming Dewinter's group had abandoned the Flemish question in favor of the immigration issue.[11] Ultimately, the party made a clear choice in favor of the more electorally-rewarding platform, but embedded the issue of immigration in some of the old nationalist rhetoric.[12] Nonetheless, a number of key members left the Vlaams Blok in response.[13]

Following the Vlaams Blok's breakthrough in the Antwerp council elections of 1988, plans for a *cordon sanitaire* to exclude the Vlaams Blok were launched at the instigation of Jos Geysels of the Flemish Green Party, Agalev. The heads of all other Flemish parties with representatives in the federal Parliament agreed to refuse, as the text of the political protocol put it:

> any political agreement or negotiations with the Vlaams Blok, be it in the context of democratically elected bodies on the local, provincial, regional, national and European levels, or in the context of elections for these bodies.[14]

151

According to the signatories, the alleged repudiation of fundamental democratic principles and the rejection of human rights by the Vlaams Blok formed the basis of the agreement.

This development of a *cordon sanitaire* had important consequences for the Vlaams Blok, as the party would now need an absolute majority for enacting their policies. However, the party leader, Karel Dillen was accustomed to describe the *cordon sanitaire* as an *insurance policy* for an anti-establishment party like the Vlaams Blok, as it guaranteed a considerable proportion of the oppositional vote:

I was basically very happy with its existence. There was something a bit too much about it: everybody against us. If the sense is that there is a hunt out for us, then this will only drive people to take the side of the outlaw.[15]

Playing it hard between (early 1990s – mid 1990s)

In the aftermath of the party's national breakthrough on 24 November 1991 – when the Vlaams Blok gained more than 10 per cent of the Flemish votes in an election day that later came to be called *Black Sunday* – Dewinter and Dillen published a policy pamphlet on foreigners, the so-called *70-point Programme* – a name strongly redolent of Le Pen's *Fifty Measures to Help Manage the Problem of Immigrants*. The plan comprised of the Vlaams Blok's manual for solving the 'foreigner problem', calling *inter alia* for the complete closure of the borders to non-European immigrants and the application of an 'own people first' principle in all areas of policy. Moreover, it included a plan for the gradual repatriation of non-European foreigners to their countries of origin. Those who were without work, had large families to maintain or lived in social housing would be the first affected. Dewinter argued that, for the protection of the Flemish identity and the application of the principle of serving one's own people first, a halt to immigration, an accelerated repatriation of foreigners and stiffer regulations against illegal immigrants were needed.[16] Along similar lines, the Vlaams Blok campaigned in the 1991 elections with the slogan 'Out of Self-Defense'. In his campaign speeches, such as that on the Vlaams Blok's *Family Day* (1 May 1991), Dewinter used aggressive and deliberately insulting rhetoric; for example: 'Only prostitutes leave their doors open. We don't want to transform Flanders into a public brothel open to any foreigner from Africa or Asia'.[17] This radical rhetoric was accompanied by the use of symbols such as a broom and boxing gloves, promising a thorough cleanup of society and a tough crackdown on crime and illegality, on the campaign materials of the Vlaams Blok.

From an electoral point of view, the decision by the Vlaams Blok to prioritize the immigration issue and to adopt a 'hard' approach was highly successful. In the federal elections of 1991, it had managed to triple its electoral results of 1987, and during the federal elections of 1995 and 1999, it continued to grow. In the municipal elections of 1994, the Vlaams Blok even became the biggest party in Antwerp, Belgium's second biggest city. Due to the *cordon sanitaire*, however, the party remained excluded from power.

The softening of the party's discourse (mid 1990s – mid 2000s)

In 1996, the 70-point programme was revised, and a new version softened the party's radical stance by raising the possibility of assimilating, rather than expelling, non-European immigrants.[18] By 2000, the Vlaams Blok had discarded its 70-point plan. Although the party made no proposals that distanced it completely from its content, the Vlaams Blok saw disavowing the plan as a means to soften its image, so as to put an end to the *cordon sanitaire* and to appeal to supporters of the Flemish Liberal-Democrats (Vlaamse Liberalen en Democraten, VLD) and the Flemish Christian Democrats (Christen-Democratisch en Vlaams, CD&V).[19] On the issue of immigration, the emphasis was now placed upon the assimilation of foreigners 'who wish to tie their lot to that of our own people's community'.[20]

In an interview with the newspaper *De Standaard*, Dewinter argued that:

the 70-point programme suited our strategy at the time, a hit and run strategy of creating tension. We were a young party which needed to break through and which had to make limpid proposals. We are now a few years down the road, and society has evolved. We too have evolved.[21]

In the same interview, Dewinter indicated that he wanted to smooth out political bumps in the road:

the Vlaams Blok is a tanker changing course. That happens slowly, steadily and cautiously [...] We will round off any sharp edges, and slide somewhat to the centre-right. But not too much, since our unique selling proposition remains a clear position on immigration, security and Flemish independence.[22]

Dewinter acknowledged that the electoral strategy of the party had become more mild. Significantly, the former election gimmicks were replaced with a family portrait. As Dewinter saw it, previous campaigns, such as those featuring brooms and boxing gloves, gave the party too radical an image.

This moderation of the Vlaams Blok message may be seen as a vote-maximizing strategy. Indeed, in the second half of the 1990s, the Vlaams Blok gradually transformed from an anti-establishment party to an office-seeking party, one with ambitions to participate in policy-making and government. The term 'platform party' was used with ever-greater frequency during this time, meaning that the Vlaams Blok presented itself now as more than a one-issue party or a whip party.[23] The electoral success of 1999 came to be understood by the party in this context as well, with Dewinter claiming that 'the Vlaams Blok has succeeded in profiling itself as a party with a full platform, ready to offer a real alternative to the fussing and fiddling of the traditional parties'.[24]

In the following years, there was increasing discussion regarding the possibility of sharing power. The leading functionaries of the Vlaams Blok saw their party evolve from an opposition party to a governing party. To that end, the party sidelined its founder Dillen, who had always seen the greatest danger to the Vlaams Blok in the aforementioned temptation by the fleshpots of political power. The new generation (Dewinter, Annemans and Vanhecke) that had by now come to completely control the party saw Dillen as too much of a hardliner and thus a hindrance to the key evolution of the Vlaams Blok from a radical right party to a right-conservative party.

In the run-up to the local council elections of 2000, Dewinter persuaded his supporters that the Vlaams Blok had, in fact, evolved into a platform party:

the Vlaams Blok is ready to assume the reins of power, if the voter wishes it. The Vlaams Blok is not the perpetual opposition party the media and the traditional parties take us for. No, the Vlaams Blok is prepared to tackle in earnest the problems which face us: we are ready![25]

The brochure *10 Preconceptions about the Vlaams Blok* (1998), put out to combat perceived prejudices against the party, included a chapter on assuming political responsibility. This key chapter made it clear that the party was, under certain conditions, prepared to enter into a coalition. Although the leaders of the Vlaams Blok continued to describe the ongoing *cordon sanitaire* as proof that the other parties in Belgium were the real anti-democrats and prejudicial politicians, they appeared increasingly uncomfortable with this barrier to their political aspirations. With the *cordon sanitaire* in place and thus without hope of a coalition government, the bar for electoral success remained at an unreachable 50 per cent of the vote. Therefore, the Vlaams Blok was faced with a choice: either react to the existence of the *cordon sanitaire* by further watering down its message or stick with its old message and remain on the sidelines. The party chose the first option. Significantly, Vanhecke immediately corrected a news anchor referring to him as the chairman of a radical right party during the campaign for the 2003 federal elections responding that the Vlaams Blok was, instead, a right-conservative party.

However, the constraints of Belgium's *cordon sanitaire* were not the only motivation for the Vlaams Blok to adjust its message. Since 1994, the French-speaking socialist party, Parti Socialiste (PS), had been trying to cancel state funding for the Vlaams Blok with the argument that the measure of forced repatriation of foreigners, as it was formulated in the party's 70-point program, violated the European Treaty on Human Rights.[26] In order to block such attempts, the party program was altered in 2001 in order to make it fully compatible with the European Treaty on Human Rights. Furthermore, in October 2000 the Belgian Centre for Equal Opportunity and Combatting Racism, together with the League of Human Rights, registered a complaint with the Correctional Court against three non-profit organizations related to the Vlaams Blok, claiming these had violated the Belgian anti-racism laws of 1981. The accusers referred to several of the Vlaams Blok's publications, such as the election agenda for 1999 and the party platform from 1997, where the Vlaams

Blok was – according to the complainants – endorsing discrimination. The challenged passages were those in which the party called for a separate educational system for children of non-European immigrants; a tax on employers who employed non-European immigrants; and a restriction of unemployment benefits and child allowances for such immigrants. After a long and difficult process, including many transfers of the case to various courts, the Court of Cassation in November 2004 finally imposed fines upon the Vlaams Blok's non-profit bodies for infractions against the anti-racism law.

From Vlaams Blok to Vlaams Belang (mid 2000s)

Only a week after the Court of Cassation's ruling, the Vlaams Blok re-christened itself the Vlaams Belang. This decisive judgment had left the way open for the prosecution of individual Vlaams Blok candidates and could have led to the withdrawal of political rights or the Vlaams Blok vanishing from Parliament. Moreover, the ruling could have served as a crowbar to pry away any form of state subsidy from the party. As a result, the Vlaams Blok felt obliged to change its name. Although the change was a reaction to an external stimulus rather than a consequence of an internal party strategy it fit nicely with the party's strategy to evolve into a mainstream, right-conservative people's party.

The way in which the party handled questions on non-European immigrants exemplifies this evolution. In the early 1990s, the party was crystal clear on the matter:

the guest workers will not integrate on their own [...] The Vlaams Blok calls for a humane but firm policy of return to the countries of origin for the vast majority of non-European foreigners residing here.[27]

In 2004, however, the Vlaams Belang's *Statement of Principles* held that immigrants would be simply expected to:

respect the laws [and] conform to our culture, our norms and values, our way of life and to principles such as the separation of church and state, democracy, freedom of expression, and the equality of men and women.

Only those 'immigrants who refuse, deny or oppose this, a policy of return needs to be developed'.[28] As the change in these two passages highlights, the possibility of assimilation was accentuated while radical right aspects were watered down. Although the *cordon sanitaire* continued to exist in political terms, the media that up-to-then had isolated the party began to treat Vlaams Belang members as mainstream politicians, inviting them onto talk shows and to do interviews.[29]

With this new statement of principles and diluted platform, the Vlaams Belang aimed to finally sever ties with its radical right past and become a solidly conservative party with nationalism, immigration and law-and-order policies as its driving points, thus leaving the door open to possible participation in the government. This transformation was reflected in the more extensive range of topics addressed within the party, as can be seen by the organization of its first conference on economic policy.[30] In those years, the Vlaams Belang also managed to attract several new members with a more moderate profile, including well-known media figures such as the successful manager Freddy Van Gaever, radio and television presenter Jurgen Verstrepen, ex-Miss Belgium Anke Vandermeersch and ex-Miss Flanders Marie-Rose Morel. This new strategy made the party more popular than ever; in the 2004 Flemish regional elections, for example, it received the votes from almost a quarter of the Flemish electorate and became the largest party in the Flemish Parliament.

Competition from new right-conservative parties and renewed radicalization

The year 2007 was a turning point in the electoral results of the Vlaams Blok / Vlaams Belang. For the first time in its history, the party no longer grew electorally. In the federal elections of that year, the party lost some 220,000 votes when compared with the Flemish elections of 2004. This began a destructive period – exacerbated in subsequent federal and regional elections, and accompanied by numerous internal struggles – between different party factions. These quarrels culminated in July 2011, with the decision by a large group of members to leave the party – including heavyweights such as former party leader Vanhecke; and Koen Dillen, the son of the party founder, Karel Dillen. An important reason for the decline in the Vlaams Belang's popularity was the success of two new right-conservative parties, the Lijst Dedecker (Dedecker List, LDD) and, most notably, the Nieuw-Vlaamse Alliantie (New Flemish Alliance, N-VA). These new parties not only represented meaningful competition on the conservative right side of the political spectrum but also offered effective chances to influence policy – unlike the Vlaams Belang, which remained isolated on account of the *cordon sanitaire*.

The LDD was founded in 2007 by Jean-Marie Dedecker, a former Judo coach who entered politics in 1999 with the liberal-democratic party VLD, but had been expelled in 2006 after a series of critical statements about influential VLD politicians. He responded by founding his own party, which focused upon strict immigration rules and law-and-order measures, while carefully avoiding statements that might be considered racist. Like the Vlaams Belang, Dedecker's LDD had a strong populist discourse, including one-liners such as 'if they hit you on your left cheek, you should hit them back with your right fist', 'the problem with the media is that almost all journalists are left-wing' or 'the reason why I became right-wing is the lack of free speech in left-wing parties'.[31] Dedecker claimed to bring the *common sense of people* – which became the party's slogan – back into politics. In the federal elections of 2007, the LDD surprised friends and foes alike by surpassing the five per cent election threshold, correspondingly receiving one seat in the Senate and five in the Chamber. Yet Dedecker's hope of developing the LDD into a broad, right-wing people's party ultimately failed. In the 2010 federal elections, the LDD suffered dramatic losses and only retained one seat in the Chamber. This electoral defeat was mainly the result of internal quarrels within the party and of the remarkable growth of another new conservative party: the N-VA.

Similar to the Vlaams Belang, the N-VA has its roots in the Flemish nationalist party Volksunie [VU]. By the end of the twentieth century, friction between conservative and progressive members had led to the dissolution of the VU. While attempts to form a progressive nationalist party ended in failure, conservative nationalists successfully launched the N-VA in 2001. Like the Vlaams Belang, the N-VA has ambitions for making Flanders an independent republic. Yet unlike other parties, the N-VA had ambitions for making Flanders an independent republic. However unlike the Vlaams Belang, the N-VA supports and does not exclude the possibility of making political deals with the Vlaams Belang. However, unlike the Vlaams Belang, the N-VA supports the European Union and, despite promoting a stricter approach to immigration policies, it avoids stereotyping, generalizations and the scapegoating of immigrants and asylum seekers. Unlike other parties the N-VA refuses to align with the *cordon sanitaire.*

Since the leadership of the N-VA did not consider the party strong enough to achieve the five per cent election threshold, they initially campaigned in alliance with the Flemish Christian Democrats [CD&V]. Given its alliance with the N-VA, the CD&V needed to heighten its Flemish profile in the run up to the 2007 federal elections, which they won. However, once in government, the CD&V failed to deliver the promised state reform necessary to provide Flanders with greater political autonomy. As a result, N-VA broke the alliance and decided to campaign on its own in subsequent elections. This risky decision paid off. Disappointed by the fact that the CD&V had been unable to fulfil its promises, Flemish voters turned massively to N-VA in the 2010 federal elections, making it the largest party in Flanders with 28 per cent of the vote.

While substantial support for the N-VA came from disillusioned CD&V voters, many former Vlaams Belang voters also switched to the N-VA.[32] Like the mainstream political parties in Flanders, the Vlaams Belang was surprised by the quick and unexpected rise in popularity of the N-VA. While the Vlaams Belang had for a long time been immune to internal quarrels, the steady success of the N-VA combined with the Vlaams Belang's own loss of voters caused friction within the party.[33] Several factions developed and turned against each other, each suggesting different strategies in dealing with the party's new competitor. Even the election of businessman Bruno Valkeniers as the new party leader in 2008 did not put an end to this internal quarrelling.

Given that the Vlaams Belang had once found success with aggressive anti-immigrant rhetoric – only later softening it in order to broaden its constituency – Dewinter pushed for a return to earlier rhetoric to stem the loss of voters to the N-VA. Other factions close to former party leader Vanhecke opposed a return to the aggressive rhetoric of former times, but were pushed to the side and eventually left the party. Under Dewinter's guidance, the Vlaams Belang's 'old wine in new bottles' is to deploy aggressive rhetoric combined with attempts to debunk the moderate conservative views of the N-VA as naïve.[34]

Significantly, Dewinter tried to heighten the Vlaams Belang's profile by linking Flemish Independence more closely to the party's traditional anti-immigration perspective.[35] Dewinter accused the N-VA of being naïve and cowardly by focusing exclusively upon Flemish Independence while overlooking the importance of preserving the authenticity of Flemish identity; one put at risk by 'hordes of immigrants'.[36] While the N-VA primarily associates Flemish nationality with language in the respected tradition of the Flemish Movement, the Vlaams Belang has broadened its focus to include other identity markers such as religion, Flemish traditions and clothing. Thus, even when born in Flanders and speaking Dutch, a Muslim girl wearing a headscarf cannot be considered Flemish. With the metaphor 'a cat born in a fish-shop is still a cat and not a fish', Dewinter insisted that it was not enough to be born in Flanders and to speak Dutch in order to be considered Flemish.[37] According to Dewinter, debates about nationalism in Belgium and Flanders necessarily involve a discussion of multiculturalism as well. Using the slogan 'This is Our Country!' Dewinter argued that 'multi-cultural equals multi-conflict', for a society can only function properly and peacefully in the long term if people share a *Leitkultur* (common culture).[38] As multiculturalism stands against a genuine *Leitkultur*, such a policy inevitably leads to a fractured society suffering constant conflict. In this new phase of more explicit radicalism, Dewinter went as far as to warn that: 'the Judeo-Christian European civilization faces extinction because of [...] multiculturalism'.[39]

Even more so than immigrants in general, Muslims became the central focal point in the new discourse of the Vlaams Belang; exemplified by the 2007 campaign 'No Jihad-Streets in Flanders!' Any attempt to change Flemish traditions in order to incorporate immigrants was now labeled by the Vlaams Belang as an assault upon an authentic Flemish identity. The decision by the (socialist) Antwerp City Council to rename the traditional Christmas market 'Winter Feast Market' to stimulate participation by the city's large Muslim population was met with fierce opposition by Dewinter who, tellingly, called it a first step towards 'the Islamization of Flanders'.[40] Building upon widespread fears in Flemish society about the effects of an aging population on the social security system, one of the Vlaams Belang's 2009 party slogans was: 'Where is the money for your pension? In the pocket of Mohammed!'[41] Following the Swiss ban on minarets, the Vlaams Belang also tried to recover some of its former momentum by organizing protest marches against the construction of new mosques on Flemish territory, arguing that minarets were part of a 'master plan to introduce Islamic rule in Europe'.[42] Similar conspiratorial and aggressive rhetoric about Islam as a 'predator' that attacks 'weak prey'[43] – which used to be common in the early days of the party but was later abandoned during its outwardly moderate years – is prominent again in Dewinter's most recent speeches. Significantly, while older symbols reflecting the fighting spirit of the Vlaams Blok – the broom and, most notably, the boxing gloves – had been abandoned in the 1990s and replaced by far more peaceful family pictures, Dewinter launched a new campaign in May 2011 – with the symbol of the pocket knife.

Remarkably, the Vlaams Belang became so radical in its anti-immigrant and anti-Islam discourse in recent years that it has sacrificed some of its former standpoints and political goals in order to be more consistent in its criticism of Islam. For example, while the party used to be skeptical on gay rights – styling itself as a defender of traditional gender roles and family values (for example, in 1996, it was the only party to oppose the liberalization of abortion and the adoption of same-sex marriage in Belgium)[44] – the Vlaams Belang has recently championed both women's rights and those of same-sex couples as part of its resistance against what it labels as 'the Islamization of our society'.[45] Vlaams Belang also used to be a staunch defender of the amnesty for Flemish nationalists who had been condemned for collaboration with the Nazis after the Second World War, even in cases when this collaboration involved the persecution of Jews.[46] Today, however, the Vlaams Belang no longer wishes to be reminded of its former standpoint on collaboration. It even searches for alliances with conservative forces in Israel as potential allies in its struggle against Islam.[47] According to Dewinter, the Vlaams Belang has 'learned from mistakes in the past. We no longer wish to have anything to do with that dark history. We want to be a modern party that has nothing to do with anti-Semitism'.[48]

Yet recent opinion polls indicate that Dewinter's decision to again radicalize the party and to return to a less veiled rhetoric does not seem to have the desired electoral effect. The Vlaams Belang's internal quarrels continue and the tough stance of the N-VA in negotiations over a new federal coalition government in Belgium has only increased the popularity of the Vlaams Belang's main rival. Instead of supporting Dewinter's new strategy, dozens of former Vlaams Belang-politicians all over Flanders have defected to the N-VA in the run-up to the municipal elections of October 2012. Remarkably, at a time when different radical right parties have recorded electoral growth across Western Europe, the Vlaams Belang – once amongst Europe's most successful radical right parties – continues to lose support.

Conclusion

The focus of this chapter has been in examining the changing discourse of the Vlaams Belang, as well as its electoral and political context. We have shown how moderation in the rhetoric of the Vlaams Blok/Vlaams Belang, from its founding in 1978 until the beginning of the 2010s, is closely related to its political and electoral context and, perhaps most importantly, the *cordon sanitaire* imposed by the other Flemish political parties. This is of course not to say that the Vlaams Belang has reacted solely or blindly to external pressures. For example, changes in the party's leadership, such as the replacement of party founder Karel Dillen by a younger generation led by Filip Dewinter, has had a clear impact on the party's electoral trajectory.

By tailoring its message from radical to more moderate and back to radical, the Vlaams Belang has swiftly reacted to the changing political climate in Flanders. At the end of the eighties, the party filled a gap in the Flemish political system by introducing a radical anti-immigrant discourse. To further broaden its electoral appeal as well as to increase the chances of political decision-making at the regional and national level, the Vlaams Blok softened its discourse by the 1990s. This new strategy was reinforced by the condemnation of the party due to its violation of the 1981 law against racism, which also resulted in the party changing its name to the Vlaams Belang.[49] The recent return to a more aggressive far right rhetoric – with its center focus upon a radical anti-Muslim rhetoric that, in its aggressiveness, even exceeds the tone of the early days – can be seen as an attempt to distinguish itself from its recently ascendant opponent on the conservative right side of the political spectrum: the Flemish-nationalist N-VA. In response, the Vlaams Belang has abandoned their focus on becoming more populist and moderate, replacing the softer tone of the 1990s with a return to a far more radical rhetoric.

The return to a more familiar radical right rhetoric has so far been ineffective. At a time when different radical right parties are making headway all over Western Europe, the party that was once considered a model of success in radical right-wing circles faces substantial electoral decreases. Predictions concerning the conclusion of Flanders' premier radical right party seem premature, however, especially in times when the electoral behavior of the constituency has become highly unpredictable and volatile. Nevertheless, it remains to be seen whether the Vlaams Belang will be able to recover its former momentum. It will also be interesting to observe which strategic decision – particularly with respect to its rhetoric on foreigners, and especially Muslims – the party will take as a result of future changes to its political and electoral milieu. The electoral fortunes of the N-VA, as well as how the Vlaams Belang continues to respond to the success of its current main competitor, will surely be revealing in regard of the party leaders' capabilities to revive a party that many already have declared obsolete.

ENDNOTES

[1] Alexandre Dézé, 'Between Adaptation, Differentiation and Distinction: Extreme Right-Wing Parties within Democratic Political Systems', in R. Eatwell and Cas Mudde eds., *Western Democracies and the New Extreme Right Challenge* (London/New York: Routledge, 2004), p. 20.

[2] Cas Mudde, *Populist Radical Right Parties in Europe* (Cambridge: Cambridge University Press, 2007).

[3] Kris Deschouwer, *The Politics of Belgium: Governing a Divided Society* (Basingstoke: Palgrave Macmillan, 2009), p. 28.

[4] Lode Wils, *Van de Belgische naar de Vlaamse natie. Een geschiedenis van de Vlaamse beweging* (Leuven: Acco, 2009).

[5] Patrick Hossay, *Contentions of Nationhood: Nationalist Movements, Political Conflict, and Social Change in Flanders, Scotland, and French Canada* (Lanham: Lexington Books, 2002), p. 148.

[6] Jeroen Dewulf, 'The Flemish Movement: On the Intersection of Language and Politics in the Dutch-Speaking Part of Belgium', *Georgetown Journal of International Affairs* 13/1 (Winter/Spring 2012), pp. 23 – 33.

[7] Pieter Jan Verstraete, *Karel Dillen. Portret van een rebel* (Bornem: Aksent, 1992).

[8] Ibid., p. 128.

[9] Chris Husbands, 'Belgium: Flemish Legions on the March', in Paul Hainsworth ed., *The Extreme Right in Europe and the U.S.A.* (London: Printer Publishers, 1992), pp. 126 – 150.

[10] J. Jaspers, *De uitdaging moet nationalistisch zijn* (Antwerp: Universiteit Antwerpen, 2003).

[11] Cas Mudde, 'One Against All, All Against One!: A Portrait of the Vlaams Blok', *Patterns of Prejudice* 29 (1995), pp. 5 – 28.

[12] Jo Buelens and Kris Deschouwer, *De verboden vleespotten. De partijorganisatie van het Vlaams Belang tussen oppositie en machtsdeelname* (Brussels: VUB Press, 2002).

[13] Mark Deweerdt, 'Overzicht van het Belgische politieke gebeuren in 1988', *Res Publica Politiek Jaarboek 1988* 31 (1989), pp. 236 – 301.

[14] Sofie Damen, 'Strategieën tegen extreem rechts. Het cordon sanitaire onder de loep',

Tijdschrift voor Sociologie 22 (2001), pp. 89 – 110.

[15] Verstraete, *Karel Dillen*, p. 151.

[16] Marc Spruyt, *Wat het Vlaams Blok verzwijgt* (Leuven: Van Halewyck, 2000).

[17] Jérôme Jamin, 'The Extreme Right in Europe: Fascist or Mainstream?', *The Public Eye* 19/1. Available at: http://www.publiceye.org/magazine/v19n1/jamin_extreme.html (accessed 13/04/2012).

[18] Cas Mudde, *The Ideology of the Extreme Right* (Manchester: Manchester University Press, 2000).

[19] Mark Deweerdt, 'Overzicht van het Belgische politieke gebeuren in 2001', *Res Publica Politiek Jaarboek 2000* 44 (2000), pp. 155 – 255.

[20] Filip Dewinter, *Immigratie: de tijdbom tikt* (Brussels: Vlaams Blok, 1996).

[21] Bart Brinckman and Bart Dobbelaere, 'Het goudhaantje van het Vlaams Blok wil de scherpe kantjes eraf. Interview met Filip Dewinter', *De Standaard*, 25 October 2003.

[22] Ibid.

[23] Buelens and Deschouwer, *De verboden vleespotten*.

[24] Filip Dewinter, *Kaderblad Vlaams Blok* (Brussels: Vlaams Blok, 1999), p. 74.

[25] Ibid., p. 76.

[26] Spruyt, *Wat het Vlaams Blok verzwijgt*, pp. 72 – 75.

[27] See *Uit zelfverdediging. Verkiezingsprogramma 1991* (Brussels: Vlaams Blok, 1991), p. 45.

[28] See *Waarom Vlaams Belang? Beginselverklaring* (Brussels: Vlaams Belang, 2004), p. 2.

[29] Tom Cochez, *Eigen belang eerst. De vuile oorlog binnen het Vlaams Belang* (Leuven: Van Halewyck, 2010).

[30] Hilde Coffé, '(Small) Entrepreneurs First! Analysis of the Economic Discourse of the Vlaams Belang', *Journal of Language and Politics* 7 (2008), pp. 31 – 52.

[31] See interview with Jean-Marie Dedecker in 'Humo sprak met Jean-Marie Dedecker', *Humo* (28 October 2008). Available at: http://www.humo.be/humo-archief/21416/humo-sprak-met-jean-marie-dedecker (accessed 13/05/2012).

[32] Teun Pauwels, 'Explaining the Strange Decline of the Populist Radical Right Vlaams Belang in Belgium: The Impact of Permanent Opposition', *Acta Politica* 46 (2011), pp. 60 – 82.

[33] Lieven De Winter, 'The Vlaams Blok: The Electorally Best Performing Right-Extremist Party in Western Europe', in Xavier Casals ed., *Political Survival on the Extreme Right: European Movements Between the Inherited Past and the Need to Adapt to the Future* (Barcelona: Int. de Ciencias Poltiques I Socials, 2005), pp. 95 – 125.

[34] Bart Brinckman, 'De softies kunnen beschikken. Ergernissen bij Vlaams Belang', *De Standaard* (2 April 2011).

[35] Peter De Lobel, 'Vlaams Belang scherpt migratiestandpunt aan', *De Standaard* (11 April 2011).

[36] Raf Liekens, 'De Wever is te laf. Interview met Filip Dewinter', *P-magazine* (8 December 2010).

[37] Joël De Ceulaer, 'Baas onder eigen hoofddoek', *Knack* (15 July 2009).

[38] See 'Geen supermoskee in Lier', posted by Filip Dewinter on 5 June 2011 on his blog: http://www.filipdewinter.be/betoging-geen-supermoskee-in-lier-toespraak-en-fotoverslag (accessed 13/04/2012).

[39] See 'The Colonization of Europe: How Europe Could Become Eurabia', posted by Filip Dewinter on 9 February 2011 on his blog: http://www.filipdewinter.be/filip-dewinter-op-bezoek-in-amerika-toespraak-fotoverslag (accessed 13/04/2012).

[40] See speech by Filip Dewinter on 10 April 2011 entitled "Kordaat immigratiebeleid werkt", posted on the Vlaams Belang website at: http://www.vlaamsbelang.org/files/201104

10congres.pdf (accessed 13/04/2012).

[41] For more on the context of this provocative statement in Dewinter's speech, see 'In de pocket van Mohammed-uitspraak was afgesproken met Bruno Valkeniers' at: http://aff.skynetblogs.be/archive/2009/11/04/in-de-pocket-van-mohammed-uitspraak-was-afgesproken-met-bru.html (accessed 13/05/2012).

[42] See Dewinter, 'Geen supermoskee in Lier'.

[43] See Dewinter, 'The Colonization of Europe'.

[44] Spruyt, *Wat het Vlaams Blok verzwijgt*, pp. 183 – 95.

[45] Marc Joris, 'Islamofobie is een plicht voor iedereen! Interview met Filip Dewinter', *Gazet van Antwerpen* (28 February 2009).

[46] Marc Spruyt, *Wat u moet weten over het Vlaams Belang* (Berchem: EPO, 2006), pp. 77 – 162.

[47] In December 2010, Filip Dewinter participated at an international conference in Ash-kelon, Israel, entitled 'The Lawfulness of Legitimate Defense Applied by a State Against Fundamentalist Islamic Terror Attacks'. A Dutch translation of Dewinter's presentation at the conference can be found at: http://www.filipdewinter.be/toespraak-filip-dewinter-colloquium-%C2%AB-de-strijd-tegen-radicale-islam-en-moslimterrorisme-een-kwestie-van-zelfverdediging-%C2%BB (accessed 13/05/2012).

[48] Interview Filip Dewinter with *Elsevier* Magazine entitled 'Liever wolf in het bos dan ge-ketende hond', published by Dewinter on his blog on 19 July 2010. See: http://www.filipdewinter.be/liever-wolf-in-het-bos-dan-geketende-hond (accessed 13/05/2012).

[49] Jan Erk, 'From Vlaams Blok to Vlaams Belang: Belgian Far-Right Renames Itself', *West European Politics* 28 (2005), pp. 493 – 502.

DEFENDING DUTCH FREEDOM:
THE FAR RIGHT IN THE NETHERLANDS, 1932 – 2012

Koen Vossen

Unlike many other Western-European countries, such as Belgium, Germany, France and Austria, the Netherlands does not have a strong tradition of nationalism, populism and xenophobia. In addition, Dutch democracy has never been seriously challenged by anti-system parties of the right or the left. The lack of a far right tradition is often explained as a result of the social structure of Dutch society. The Netherlands is historically a nation of sailors and merchants, and has never had a powerful landowning nobility, peasantry or military class.[1] Moreover, the Netherlands has not faced problems with minorities, either within its borders or with Dutch minorities outside its borders. 'As a nation we are after all satisfait, and it is our duty to remain so', wrote the great Dutch historian Johan Huizinga in 1934.[2] Of course, being 'satisfait' is not the right state of mind for political projects that seek to overthrow the existing order. Moreover, Dutch society was for most of the twentieth century divided into different segments or 'pillars'; a Protestant, a Catholic and a secular pillar. The secular pillar was divided between a socialist working-class and liberal middle and upper classes.[3] These subdivisions all had their own schools, universities, associations, unions and political parties. As a result, certainly until the 1960s and 1970s, it was very difficult for new parties to enter the Dutch electoral market. For far right parties this was even more difficult because of the trauma of the German Occupation and the role of the Dutch National-Socialist Movement (NSB).

However, since the turn of the century the Dutch political landscape has radically changed. Once a rather dull haven of political stability and societal harmony, in which foreign media showed little interest, the Netherlands has now made headlines abroad with political assassinations in 2002 (the maverick politician Pim Fortuyn) and again in 2004 (the controversial film-maker Theo van Gogh). This was followed by a vote against a new constitution for the European Union in 2005, and the spectacular rise of parties that are often labeled as far right or populist.[4] These parties are the Lijst Pim Fortuyn (LPF), which attained 17 per cent of the vote in 2002 and the Partij voor de Vrijheid (Freedom Party or PVV) which received 15.5 per cent of the vote in 2010. After the last elections the PVV, led by Geert Wilders, emerged as an important player in the coalition formation. After rather complicated deliberations, a minority government was formed between the liberals and Christian-Democrats, which was 'tolerated' by the PVV in parliament in exchange for influence on governmental policy. One of the main outcomes of this relationship was the implementation of a stricter immigration and asylum policy.

This chapter will not attempt to explain exactly why, after 2002, these new parties have become more successful in the Netherlands. This would require much more extensive research than has been undertaken here. The goal of this chapter is to analyze the rhetoric of the Dutch far right parties of the twentieth and twenty-first centuries and to determine whether this rhetoric has hidden other political projects. In the Netherlands in particular, Jaap van Donselaar has argued that, especially in the case of far right parties, there is a distinction between front-stage and backstage performances.[5] The front-stage political program and rhetoric is often little more than a mask, behind which a more radical face is hiding. Political scientists therefore should not only focus on the political program and parliamentary behavior, but also on the debates within the party and on the political track record of the militants. Van Donselaar's front-stage / backstage approach has been fiercely criticized by others, including Meindert Fennema. According to Fennema, 'the front-stage, backstage tends to have an essentialist conception of the extreme right and runs the risk of infinite regression. How do we know that behind the backstage there is not yet another face hiding away?'[6]

Indeed, Fennema's objections offer some advice to prevent us from over-simplifying. However, as Fennema also admits, in countries where strong nationalist, xenophobic and authoritarian rhetoric has become a taboo after the Second World War, and where far right parties could suffer from political or legal repression, the study of backstage activities is highly relevant. After 1945, the Netherlands was without any doubt a country in which nationalist, authoritarian and xenophobic rhetoric was taboo for a very long time. To understand why this was the case, it is necessary to examine the main National Socialist party in the Netherlands in the 1930s, the Nationaal Socialistische

Beweging (NSB).[7] Moreover, as recent studies have proven, within the NSB one can also make a distinction between a front-stage and a backstage rhetoric. Whether this is also true for the most successful post war far right parties of the twentieth century, the Boerenpartij (Farmer's Party) and the Centre Democrats, will thereafter be scrutinized. In the final section, the rhetoric of Pim Fortuyn (LPF) and Geert Wilders (PVV) will be analyzed.

The Nationaal Socialistische Beweging

The first far right movement that had some electoral success in the Netherlands was the Nationaal Socialistische Beweging (NSB: National Socialist Movement) that attained 8 per cent of the vote in the 1935 provincial elections.[8] Because of its role during the German Occupation, the NSB has become by far the most infamous of all Dutch political parties, making far right party formation after 1945 very difficult.

The history of the NSB is a striking example of a party that radicalized as a result of growing societal isolation and the influence of militants within the party. The sudden rise of the NSB in 1933 coincided with the transfer of power to Hitler and his National Socialist Party in Germany. This triggered an excitement in Germany that proved to be contagious in the Netherlands too. For those who saw Hitler's revolution as the cure for Dutch 'diseases', the NSB seemed to be the most obvious party to support. However, the impression that the Dutch NSB was identical to the German NSDAP was to a large extent misunderstood. The NSB had indeed copied the NSDAP programme, but it left out the essential paragraphs on racial theory and the *Führerprinzip*. Furthermore, the NSB was initially also not an anti-Semitic movement; indeed, it even had some Jewish members. Of all the variants of interwar fascism, the leader of the NSB, the engineer Anton Mussert and most of the original members, preferred Italian Fascism above Hitler's National Socialism, which was considered to be too radical for Dutch standards. Mussert, however, had chosen the adjective 'national socialist' because fascism had a bad reputation in the Netherlands as a result of the presence of a dozen vulgar fascist movements whose main activity seemed to be forming splinter movements with pompous names.[9] Besides, Mussert thought that the epithet 'national socialism' was a proper description of his idea of nationalism for the masses.[10] His main goal was a unified Dutch nation in which the old 'pillars' – Catholic, Protestant and socialist – would be dissolved while the malfunctioning democracy would be abolished in favor of a more technocratic regime. Backstage, many militants held more extreme racist and anti-Semitic viewpoints. Because of their numbers, these new members who wanted a strong orientation on the German example became ever more able to determine the course of the party.[11] The party's adversaries could easily accuse the NSB of being unpatriotic because of its affinity with German National Socialism. By 1936 / 1937 the NSB had become an ideological copy of the German NSDAP, making the party the perfect partner for the German occupying force between 1940 and 1945.

The role of the NSB during the Occupation made far right party formation after 1945 very difficult. Already in 1943, the Dutch government in exile had introduced a law in which any party formation on national socialist or fascist ideologies was prohibited. After the war, many of the members of the NSB were arrested and Mussert and a few other leading NSB figures were executed. Most active NSB members lost their political rights (both passive and active suffrage) for some time.[12] Moreover, the memory of the Second World War – which was the first war and Occupation experienced by the Netherlands since the Napoleonic period – became the cornerstone of post-war Dutch identity. The NSB symbolized the 'wrong' in what was called 'the right-wrong-scheme' which dominated the image of the Occupation period. As various recent studies have shown, even children of former members of the NSB suffered from their parents' political choices during and before the war.[13] It is often suggested that guilt over the large percentage of deported Dutch Jews (the highest percentage in western Europe) led to vigilant antifascism and a projection of all evils on the NSB (and Germany). It is indeed remarkable that, unlike countries such as Belgium, France or Italy, the Netherlands did not have a vivid far right subculture of former collaborators. New parties, especially those on the 'right' of the political spectrum, were always suspected of having personal or ideological ties with the NSB.[14] For electoral success, it was therefore necessary for far right parties to share the vigilant anti-fascism. Even in the current debates on right-wing populism and anti-immigration sentiments, one can find simplistic comparisons that are made with the NSB, leading to fierce debates gravitating around demonization and the misuse of history.

The Boerenpartij

After the Second World War, the pre-war political landscape was more or less restored. Only a few new parties emerged in the Netherlands. Among them were some minor far right parties populated by former members of the NSB and frustrated returnees from the Dutch East-Indies. None of them attained more than 0.5 per cent of the vote. In the 1960s a new far right party emerged which was more successful. The Farmers' Party was founded in 1958 by Hendrik Koekoek, who was also the leader and founder of the Free Farmers. The Free Farmers were a protest movement against the strong governmental intervention in agricultural affairs and the strong influence of the corporatist agricultural organizations. Their battle against governmental interference was framed as a battle against totalitarian systems such as communism and fascism.[15] Following Isaiah Berlin, one could perceive the freedom the Free Farmers and the Farmers' Party demanded as a negative liberty, a freedom from interference.[16]

Inspired by the success of Pierre Poujade in France, Koekoek hoped to form a broader party of protest against the established parties and the traditional divisions in Dutch society. Besides farmers his target group consisted of small tradesmen, artisans and rightist nationalists. In 1963, the Farmers' Party gained a rather unexpected 2.13 per cent of the vote, which equated to 3 seats. In the months before, the party had gained a great deal of attention as a result of some conflicts between the police and Free Farmers who had refused to pay their taxes. In the media and on television, Koekoek acted as a spokesperson for these farmers. He gained popularity due to his farmer's accent and peasant wisdoms. Especially in *De Telegraaf*, the largest newspaper in the Netherlands, Koekoek became something of a cult-figure, a man 'who dared to say it like it is'. In 1966 the Farmer's Party attained its best result in municipal and provincial elections with almost 7 per cent of the vote. Perhaps the most striking results were those in cities such as Amsterdam (9.4 per cent), Utrecht (9.2 per cent) and Haarlem (10.3 per cent). Koekoek had become the figurehead for a wave of rightist dissatisfaction with the established parties and with the paternalistic political culture.[17] Again freedom from interference was the key message, together with comparisons between the resistance against fascism and communism and the party's resistance against the mainstream or the three 'pillar-dictatorship' – that is the three 'pillars' of Catholicism, Protestantism and socialism.

Following what were, by Dutch standards, spectacular results, the party was troubled by internal conflicts and bad publicity. Various chosen delegates appeared to have been collaborators during the war, among them one senator who had been a member of a more radical and more anti-Semitic offshoot of the NSB. Koekoek was rather reluctant to apostatize these candidates and started to make wild accusations of the alleged 'wrong' behavior of other politicians during the war.[18] Various members left the Farmers' Party and founded an 'emergency council' to purify the Farmers' Party from the outside.[19] *De Telegraaf* now withdrew its albeit unofficial support. During the 1967 national elections, the Farmers' Party lost almost half of its 1966 constituencies. In the following years the party witnessed various new offshoots, and in 1971 the party attained a mere 1 per cent of the vote.

When concentrating on the front-stage (i.e. the party programs and rhetoric in campaigns and in parliament), the Farmers' Party could best be labeled as conservative in social and cultural affairs and almost libertarian in economic affairs. Its fierce criticism of the established parties and the political elite of the country, together with its celebration of the honesty and simplicity of the farmer, were reminiscent of populist agrarian parties in the United States (the People's Party), Canada (Social Credit) and France (the Poujade movement).[20] Nevertheless the Farmers' Party is often considered as a far right party. This is in part due to the NSB past of some candidates, but also due to an early, neo-Marxist study by sociologist A. T. J. Nooij on the connection between authoritarian personality-structure (measured by Adorno's so-called f-scale) and sympathy for the Farmers' Party.[21] However, there are no internal party documents or archival records in which the party showed an uglier, more extreme right face. The evidence for more radical viewpoints backstage remains therefore rather circumstantial.

The Centre Parties: Centrumpartij and the Centrum-Democraten

In the 1980s and the 1990s, the Centrumpartij (CP) and its successor the Centrum Democraten (CD) could be regarded as the Dutch version of far right anti-immigration parties such as the Front National and the Vlaams

Blok.[22] Yet unlike their French and Flemish counterparts the CP and CD were not very successful. In 1982, the CP entered parliament with one seat (0.8 per cent of the vote). After some internal conflicts, the leader of the CP, Hans Janmaat, broke away and founded the CD. In 1994 the CD won three seats in parliament (2.5 per cent), but in 1998 all seats were lost and the CD disappeared from the political stage.

The rise of the Centre Parties coincided with a new wave of immigration to the Netherlands in the 1970s and 1980s. Most immigrants were guest workers and their families from Turkey and Morocco or inhabitants of former colonies such as Suriname and Antilles. As Lucardie noted, the distribution of CD and CP voters around the country showed similarities with the spatial distribution of minorities.[23] This was especially the case in the impoverished districts of the urban centers (Amsterdam, Rotterdam, The Hague, and Utrecht) where a high concentration of immigrants attracted a relatively strong support for both the CP and the CD. Both for voters and for party members, resistance against multicultural society and immigration were the essence of the Centre Parties. The populist demands for direct democracy, the stress on conservative values and the pleas for tax reduction were of less importance. At the same time the parties' viewpoints on immigration and multicultural society led to complete political and societal isolation. Janmaat and his followers were generally considered racists or even fascists who had to be excluded from Dutch political life. As David Art has noted, this repression went far beyond the existence of a *cordon sanitaire*, which was announced the moment the CD won its parliamentary seat and was enforced by every political party at every political level. It also involved significant pressure from employers, anti-fascist groups, the media and the state's internal security services.[24] In March 1986 anti-fascist militants even set fire to a hotel where the CD had a meeting. The party secretary (Janmaat's wife) had to jump from the second store of the burning building and lost her leg. In the Dutch media the assault was not condemned but rather trivialized.[25]

Because of this highly repressive environment, there were suspicions that the Centre Parties were developing a more moderate front-stage to avoid legal persecution. To determine whether the viewpoints of the party were more radical backstage than they were front-stage, various journalists joined the party undercover. In 1994, three undercover journalists had gained entrance to the CD at the same time. All journalists portrayed the CD as 'a bunch of fascists, criminals and scum' who often made highly racist comments. Some members even glorified Hitler's achievements and saluted violence against foreigners.[26] The conclusion of most journalists and political scientists was that the CD had a more radical backstage than front-stage. As David Art has shown, backstage radicalism and vulgarity was also a consequence of the highly repressive political climate. As he puts it:

> The CD attracted only those who welcomed confrontation with antifascist activists, those who calculated that the potential financial compensation of a council seat was worth risking their job for, those who participated in criminal activities, and those whose political convictions outweighed all of the negative repercussions.[27]

After 1998 the CD broke down, as the CP'86 (a more radical offshoot) was ruled illegal by an Amsterdam court in 1998.

The Lijst Pim Fortuyn

The Lijst Pim Fortuyn is without any doubt the most spectacular 'flash-party' the Netherlands has ever witnessed. Founded in February 2002, the party attained 17 per cent of the vote in the national elections on 17 May 2002. The elections were held only nine days after the assassination of Pim Fortuyn, the leader and founder of the LPF. The LPF entered a government coalition but this government fell only six months later. In the national elections of January 2003 the LPF lost more than two thirds of its constituencies. In 2006 the party was dissolved.

There is some discussion as to whether the LPF can accurately be described as a far right party. In the campaign for the 2002 elections some of Fortuyn's political opponents placed him in the same category as Jörg Haider and Jean Marie Le-Pen because of his provocative statements on immigration ('The Netherlands are full'), integration of minorities ('a complete failure') and Islam ('a cold war against Islam is needed'). Moreover, as various political scientists have argued, most of Fortuyn's voters voted for the LPF because of the issue of immigration.[28] However, it is difficult to recognize traditional far right viewpoints in the party program or in Fortuyn's books.[29] The LPF had various candidates of non-Dutch origin (for example a female Muslim and a black Cape Verdean business-man) and even delegated a junior-minister of Surinamese origin, who was the first black junior-minister in Dutch history. Also, two days before his death Fortuyn pleaded for a general pardon for a large group of ex-asylum seekers in the Netherlands. Finally, on a more personal level, Fortuyn was very open about his nightly adventures in gay bars, and his preference for young Moroccan boys. As various authors have argued, his homosexuality and flamboyance enabled Fortuyn to put the sensitive issue of immigration and Islam on the agenda. It shielded him and his voters from charges of narrow-mindedness or petit-bourgeois xenophobia, which is essential in a nation that is often generally considered open minded and progressive.[30]

One could argue that Fortuyn introduced into Dutch political discourse a new repertoire, which made it possible to be considered progressive yet criticize immigration and a fully multicultural society. The essential ingredient connecting progressiveness and antagonism against full multiculturalism was their stance on Islam. Following Samuel Huntington's Clash of Civilization theory, Fortuyn portrayed Islam as a strong, homogeneous culture with 'backward' values and ideas.[31] The rise of Islam therefore directly threatened western liberties and achievements such as the separation of the State and the Church, women's emancipation and the acceptance of homosexuality. To defend Dutch liberties and progressiveness, it was therefore necessary to oppose what Fortuyn called the 'Islamization of our culture', which was allowed by the naïve left-wing multiculturalism. By making a taboo every debate on cultural standards, national identity and immigration policy, it was claimed the left-wing multiculturalists had surrendered to 'cultural relativism', and a refusal to acknowledge that modern Dutch (or Western) culture was far superior to Islamic culture. With this new message that was appealing to a wider audience, did LPF hide a more radical backstage politics? There is very little evidence for this claim. Backstage rhetoric, which could be labeled racist, xenophobic or authoritarian appear to be absent. The LPF did attract some former members of far right parties, but their number is low.[32] Most members did not have a political track record of any sort, and their only common feature was their support for Fortuyn. After Fortuyn's death the LPF had to form a policy and strategy based on Fortuyn's writings and statements: but what exactly did Fortuyn mean when he talked of a cold war against Islam? Did he really propose a general pardon for former asylum seekers? Of course, these questions led to all kinds of conflicts worsened by the absence of a successor leader who could dominate the party.[33] The most tangible result of all conflicts on interpretation was the election program of 2003. In the election program of 2003, on subjects such as Islam, immigration and especially law and order, one can see some movement further to the right but not enough to use the label far right. Arguably the most radical proposal was to forbid the wearing of headscarves by civil servants, which was justified as a consequence of the separation between the Church and the State.

The Party for Freedom

Since Fortuyn's death and the disintegration of his party in the following months, various new parties have attempted to step into what has often been perceived as a political 'vacuum'. By 2006 Geert Wilders and his Party for Freedom (PVV) proved the most promising candidate to fill this vacuum. After the PVV had made a modest electoral debut in the 2006 national elections (5.9 per cent), Wilders succeeded in attracting an enormous amount of national and international media attention by offering a whole range of spectacular storylines and events. These included the release of his anti-Islam movie Fitna (March 2008) and his detainment at Heathrow Airport as a consequence of the UK Home Secretary's ban on him entering the country in February 2009. In the 2010 national elections the PVV more than doubled its constituency, gaining 15.5 per cent of the vote, making it a serious contender for coalition formation.

The attempt to classify the PVV in ideological terms has puzzled many observers both in the Netherlands and abroad.[34] Should the party be considered as a populist, a nationalist or even a fascist one? Or is Wilders a genuine radical liberal who is defending Dutch freedom against the rise of Islam? In the Netherlands, the attempts to ascribe Wilders to an ideological category became a national debate in which journalists, politicians, intellectuals and even television celebrities have engaged. Whereas before 2002 commentators were sometimes too eager to classify such new parties as extreme right, there is now a remarkable reluctance to use such labels for the PVV. Without any doubt, this reluctance is a result of the assassination of Pim Fortuyn by a political activist, which some considered to be a direct result of a campaign of 'demonizing Fortuyn' by the left-wing parties and press: 'the bullet came from the left', as LPF politician Peter Langendam stated.[35] After the assassination of filmmaker Theo van Gogh by a radical Islamist, Geert Wilders has been living under permanent police protection.

Moreover, there are some remarkable programmatic differences between the PVV and other far right parties in Europe. First of all, Wilders seeks his main political allies not in Europe, but in Israel and the United States. In Israel he feels connected to both Avigdor Lieberman and his Israel Beiteinu party and Ariyeh Eldad's Ha Tikvah-Party, which both oppose a two state solution. In the United States, Wilders has an expanding network of fellow Islam fighters with their own small organizations and blogs, such as Pamela Geller (Atlas Shrugs, Stop Islamization of America), Robert Spencer (JihadWatch), David Horowitz (Freedom Centre) and Daniel Pipes (Middle East Forum and Campus Watch).[36] This strong focus on the United States and Israel was quite unusual within the European far right family, which has not been known for its love of either the United States or Israel. Another remarkable aberration is Wilders' libertarian opinions on ethical issues, which resemble those of the LPF. The PVV advocates for rights on abortion, euthanasia and embryo selection, presenting itself as a fierce defender of women and gay emancipation in the face of the advance of an 'intolerant and backward Islam'.[37] It is hard to imagine another far right politician offering a resolution in parliament to allow homosexual soldiers to wear their military uniform in the Gay Pride parade!

One could consider both peculiarities. The ethical / libertarian aspect, and the orientation towards the USA and Israel, are necessary ingredients to make a far right program in the Netherlands acceptable. The focus on the United States and Israel distances Wilders from simplistic associations with fascism, the Holocaust and the Second World War. By stressing his role as the protector of Dutch modernity and freedom against a caricatured portrayal of Islam and progressive naivety, Wilders presented himself as the main heir of Pim Fortuyn. However, with regard to Islam, Wilders has developed a more polarizing discourse compared to Fortuyn, as demonstrated by his proposals to ban the Koran, to introduce a 'head-rag tax' and to expel non-integrated

Muslims. In his speeches and in interviews, Wilders increasingly showed a more radical form of Islamophobia, based on apocalyptic conspiracy theories focused on the supposed forthcoming Islamification of Europe. Following Bat Ye'or's infamous Eurabia theory and Sam Solomon and E. Al Maqdisi's Al Hijra-theory, Wilders has regularly tried to 'unmask' the immigration of Muslims as an integral part of a deliberate strategy of Islamification (an old strategy supposedly known in Islam as 'al Hijra', according to Wilders), which was permitted by left-wing political parties hoping to gain a new, loyal constituency after the loss of their old support base.[38] Referring to the Islamic dogma Taqqia, which would give Muslims living in non-Muslim countries the right to hide their true beliefs, Wilders increasingly began to doubt the sincerity of Muslims who seemed willing to assimilate.[39]

One could argue that Wilders considers Islam more dangerous to western civilization than Fortuyn, and therefore calls for more radical measures to protect democracy. Whether Wilders is really, as he claims, fighting Islam to protect Dutch freedom and democracy is disputed. According to some Dutch commentators, Wilders and his close allies are 'archetypical modern fascists' who are only interested in gaining power and destroying democracy.[40] The fact that the internal organization of the PVV is extremely hierarchical, is often considered an indication of Wilders' anti-democratic attitude, with his Islamophobia compared to National Socialist anti-Semitism. Both accusations are based on the assumption that the PVV is more radical backstage than front-stage. Little however is known about the internal workings and discussions of the PVV, as access to the party is tightly controlled. Unlike the CD, we can note that a journalist who had infiltrated the party did not meet fanatic militants with neo-Nazi agendas, but rather encountered political professionals, who mainly criticized the narrow-mindedness of the left-wing parties and press.[41] There is also some evidence that backstage some of the PVV militants complain about Wilders' radical Islamophobia and the lack of party organization and internal democracy.[42] One could thus argue that the PVV's backstage is rather more moderate than its front-stage, and not the other way around. The same applies for many of its voters who support the PVV because of its broad anti-immigration-stance but reject Wilders' proposals for a 'head-rag tax'.[43]

Defending Dutch Freedom

After 1945 the political opportunity structure in the Netherlands for far right parties was not very favourable. The trauma of German Occupation and the role of the NSB during the war had made all far right and right wing party formation highly suspect. New rightist parties had to invent a new framework to connect their mostly nationalist and conservative rightist messages with the anti-fascist ideology, which had become fundamental to the post-war Dutch consensus. Thus, the Farmers' Party framed its battle against the interventionist government and patronizing elites as a battle of free people against the 'dictatorship of the pillars' (the organized segments in Dutch society that gravitated around Catholicism, Protestantism and socialism). Because of the presence of former NSB members in the party this specific framework lost its power. Their presence suggested a distinction between a more respectable front-stage and a more (neo-) Nazi backstage. Due to a lack of archival records, however, we cannot be certain whether neo-Nazi viewpoints were held behind the respectable front-stage.

From the very start, the Centre Parties lacked a new anti-fascist framework for their anti-immigration stance. The party was therefore immediately accused of fascist and racist tendencies. These accusations were substantiated by some undercover research behind the scenes. However, in 2002 Pim Fortuyn succeeded in putting the immigration issue on the agenda by stressing that modern western values and Islam were incompatible. A strict immigration and integration policy now became a necessity in order to defend the unique Dutch modernity against a perceived new totalitarian threat, which Fortuyn compared to fascism and communism. By claiming to fight in the name of Dutch tolerance, freedom and progressiveness, Fortuyn now used the language of left-wing anti-fascism. It was one of the reasons why left-wing parties had trouble in responding to this new challenge. Geert Wilders also used Fortuyn's frame of a clash between 'free' western and 'totalitarian' Islamic civilization, but went further in his proposals and especially in his rhetoric. For Wilders, Dutch freedom could only be protected with radical means such as the ban on the Koran, a tax on headscarves and even expelling non-integrated Muslims. By presenting Islam as the new fascism, Wilders is able to present himself as the new Churchill who the world needs in times of war and his op-

179

ponents as the new Chamberlain, whose naivety almost led to the destruction of the West. The radicalism of Wilders' rhetoric and proposals demonstrate the sheer power of this new frame in which Islam is the new fascism.

ENDNOTES

[1] Ernst Heinrich Kossmann, *The Low Countries 1780 – 1940* (Oxford: Oxford University Press, 1978).

[2] Johan Huizinga, *Nederland's Geestesmerk* (Amsterdam: 1935).

[3] Arend Lijphart, *The Politics of Accommodation. Pluralism and Democracy in the Netherlands*. (Berkeley: University of California Press, 1968).

[4] Concerning the classification of new parties: Koen Vossen, 'Classifying Wilders. The Ideological Development of Geert Wilders and his Party for Freedom'. *Politics*, 31/3 (2011), pp. 179 – 189.

[5] Jaap van Donselaar, 'Post-War Fascism in the Netherlands'. *Crime, Law and Social Change* no. 19 (1993), pp. 87 – 100. See also: Cas Mudde, *The Ideology of the Extreme Right* (Manchester: Manchester University Press, 2000).

[6] Meindert Fennema, 'Some conceptual Issues and Problems in the Comparison of Anti-Immigrant Parties in Western-Europe', *Party Politics* 3 (1997), pp. 473 – 492, 487.

[7] Especially Robin te Slaa and Edwin Klij, *De NSB. Ontstaan en opkomst van de Nationaal-Socialistische Bewegung* (Amsterdam: Boom, 2009).

[8] Te Slaa and Klij, *De NSB*. Koen Vossen, *Vrij vissen in het Vondelpark. Kleine politieke partijen in Nederland 1918 – 1940* (Amsterdam: Wereldbibliotheek, 2003); Jan Meijers, *Mussert. Een politiek leven* (Amsterdam: Boom, 1984).

[9] Examples are the so-called Oranje-Fascisten (Orange Fascists), het Verbond voor National Herstel (The Alliance for National Recovery) and het Verbond van Actualisten (the Alliance of Actualists).

[10] Meijers, *Mussert.*

[11] Te Slaa and Klijn, *De NSB.*

[12] Jaap van Donselaar, *Fout na de oorlog. fascistische en racistische organisaties in Nederland. 1950 – 1990* (Amsterdam: Bert Bakker, 1991).

[13] Bas Kromhout, *Fout geboren. Het verhaal van kinderen van foute ouders* (Amsterdam: Uitveverij Contact, 2004); Ismee Tames, *Besmette jeugd. De kinderen van NSBers* (Amsterdam: Uitgeverij Balans, 2009).

[14] Hans Wansink, *De erfenis van Fortuyn. De Nederlandse democratie na de opstand van de kiezers*. (Amsterdam: Uitgeverij Meulenhoff, 2004).

[15] Koen Vossen, 'De andere jaren zestig. De opkomst van de Boerenpartij'. *Jaarboek Documentatiecentrum Nederlandse Politieke Partijen* (2004), pp. 112 – 132.

[16] Isaiah Berlin, *Liberty* (Oxford: Oxford University Press, 2004).

[17] Vossen, 'De andere jaren zestig'.

[18] Donselaar, *Fout na de oorlog.*

[19] Ibid.

[20] Paul Taggart, *Populism* (Philadelphia: Open University Press, 2000).

[21] Adrianus T. Nooij, *De Boerenpartij. Desoriëntatie en radikalisme onder boeren* (Amsterdam: Boom, 1969).

[22] Cas Mudde, *The Ideology of the Extreme Right* (Manchester: Manchester University Press, 2000).

[23] Paul Lucardie, 'The Netherlands. The Extremist Centre Parties'. Hans-Georg Betz and

Stefan Immerfall, *The New Politics of the Right. Neo-Populist Parties and Movements in Established Democracies* (New York: Palgrave MacMillan, 1998), pp. 111 – 124.

[24] David Art, *Inside the Radical Right. The Development of Anti-Immigrant Parties in Western Europe* (Cambridge: Cambridge University Press, 2011).

[25] Wansink, 'De erfenis van Fortuyn.' p. 122.

[26] Lucardie, 'The Netherlands'.

[27] David Art, *Inside the Radical Right* (Cambridge: Cambridge University Press, 2011).

[28] Wouter van der Brug, 'How the LPF Fuelled Discontent: Empirical Tests on Explanations of LPF Support', *Acta Politica* 38/1. pp. 98 – 106.

[29] Tsjitske Akkermans, 'Anti-Immigration Parties and the Defence of Liberal Values: The Exceptional Case of the Lijst Pim Fortuyn' *Journal of Political Ideologies* 10/3 (October 2005), pp. 337 – 354; Cas Mudde, 'The Pink Populist. Pim Fortuyn for Beginners', *E-Extreme* 3/2 (2002); Dick Pels, *De geest van Pim. Het gedachtegoed van een politieke dandy* (Amsterdam: Anthos, 2003).

[30] James Kennedy, 'De laatste der moderne Mohikanen'. *Nieuwste Tijd* 8 (2003). Art, *Inside the Radical Right*, p. 180.

[31] Pim Fortuyn, *Tegen de islamisering van onze cultuur* (Speaker's Academy, 1997).

[32] Jaap van Donselaar en Peter R. Rodrigues, *Monitor racisme en extreem-rechts: vijfde rapportage* (Amsterdam: Anne Frank Stichting / Universiteit Leiden, 2002).

[33] Art, *Inside the Radical Right*, pp. 180 – 182.

[34] Koen Vossen, 'Classifying Wilders'; Meindert Fennema, *Geert Wilders. De tovenaarsleerling* (Bert Bakker, 2010); Paul Lucardie, 'Rechts-extremisme, populisme of democratisch patriottisme? Opmerkingen over de politieke plaatsbepaling van de Partij voor de Vrijheid en Trots op Nederland', *Jaarboek Documentatiecentrum Nederlandse Politieke Partijen* (2007), pp. 176 – 190.

[35] *Het Parool*, pp. 13 – 5. 2002.

[36] Vossen, 'Classifying Wilders'.

[37] Election Programme PVV: *De agenda van hoop en optimisme. Een tijd om te kiezen. PVV 2010-2015.*

[38] Bat Ye'or, *Eurabia. The Euro-Arab Axis* (New York: Associated University Press, 2005). Sam Solomon and E. Al Maqdisi, *Modern Day Trojan Horse, Al Hijra: The Islamic Doctrine of Migration* (ANM Press, 2009).

[39] Martin Bosma, *De schijn-élite van de valse munters* (Amsterdam: Uitgeverij Bert Bakker, 2010); Vossen, 'Classifying Wilders'.

[40] Thomas von der Dunk, *Het nieuwe taboe op de oorlog* (Amsterdam: Van Gennep, 2011); Anton Zijderveld, *Populisme als politiek drijfzand* (Hilversum: Cossee, 2009); Rob Riemen, *De eeuwige terugkeer van het fascisme* (Tilburg: Nexus Instituut, 2010).

[41] Karen Geurtsen and Boudewijn Geels, *Undercover bij de PVV. Achter de schermen bij de partij van Geert Wilders* (Amsterdam: Mm boeken, 2009).

[42] *De Volkskrant* 20/12/2011; *De Telegraaf* 18/01/2012; *NRC Handelsblad* 18/01/2012.

[43] *NRC Handelsblad* 25/09/2009.

FAR RIGHT RHETORIC IN THE UNITED STATES:
A CARNIVAL OF BUNCOMBE

Leonard Weinberg

The rhetoric of far right groups and organizations in the United States has undergone significant change since World War II. These rhetorical changes, in turn, reflect long-term transformations in public sentiment about racial and religious minorities and the role of the United States in the world. One way of illustrating these changes is to point out that, in the 1920s, the Ku Klux Klan (KKK) attracted hundreds of thousands of followers throughout the South and other parts of the country. In these regions candidates for public office would often claim membership in, or an affinity with, the KKK, its doctrine of racial supremacy and its anti-Semitic and anti-Catholic rhetoric. Today, of course, Barak Obama is the President of the United States and Klan rallies, when they occur, are typically met by counter-demonstrations. Often the police need to be called in order to protect the Klansmen from their infuriated opponents.

Technology for disseminating radical right ideas has also undergone dramatic changes. During the 1920s and 1930s advocates of radical right ideas had to communicate them in newspapers (for example: Henry Ford's *Dearborn Independent*) and by radio broadcasts (for example: Father Charles Coughlin's *Christian Front* Sunday evening broadcasts on NBC). Today, of course, not only do the mass media offer limited opportunities for expression, particularly 'talk radio' and the cable television channels, but thanks to the new social media, radical activists can circumvent the rules governing the former and present themselves via interactive websites (for example: White Aryan Resistance, Stormfront) for multiple purposes. These long-standing websites were created by Tom Metzger and Don Black respectively. Both Metzger and Black, former Klansman's, have been active in the American radical right for many years.

The best way to begin this account is by first defining our terms: what is the far right and what does it encompass? Second, what did the American far

183

right look like in the years leading up to World War II? Third, how and why has the radical right changed in the three quarters of a century since the end of that conflict? Finally, we seek to understand how the rhetoric has changed to adjust to the new realities. In order to do this we will have to specify what we have in mind by political rhetoric.

In one of the major studies of far right activity in the United States, Lipset and Raab suggest that its defining attributes include what they refer to as 'monism': the view that there is only one right answer to any question and that competing ones are inherently illegitimate.[1] They also refer to 'moralism', according to which the world is divided into the good and the bad, light and dark, and attempts to achieve a compromise between the two is sinful. Further, events do not occur by accident; a malevolent conspiracy controls, or is attempting to control, all aspects of public life in the United States. A small group of powerful men (almost always men) really determine what goes on in Washington, Wall Street or the world more generally. Average people (what the late Robert Mathews, head of the Silent Brotherhood, referred to as 'sheeple') need to be made aware of who is really running things – hence the importance of rhetorical presentations.

Lipset and Raab describe these attributes as 'procedural extremism', meaning those groups on the far-left may display them as well. For example, American admirers of Leon Trotsky or Mao would be procedural extremists. In the American context, what constitutes far right? The answer: a commitment to what they label 'preservatism', a desire to preserve or restore an America that either no longer exists or is in grave danger of becoming extinct. Typically, what needs to be preserved or restored is a United States governed by Lockean liberal ideas – individualism, private enterprise, and personal responsibility.[2] Or, to be less kind, we might also include nineteenth century social Darwinism as an important component.

In thinking about the political rhetoric of the far right, Murray Edelman's work on *The Symbolic Uses of Politics* is worth quoting: 'The employment of language to sanctify action is exactly what makes politics different from other methods of allocating values'.[3] Some political language, as Edelman points out, is intended to promote quiescence, to reassure recipients that all is well. Some political rhetoric is also intended to express solidarity. Patriotic speeches on the Fourth of July are obvious examples. These are not the qualities of far right rhetoric, however. Instead the latter is typically challenging and divisive. It is often intended to arouse resentment against various targets and separate the 'us' from the 'them'. Exactly who or what the 'them' is has varied between earlier and newer forms of far right rhetoric. To see this more clearly it is worth turning to the American far right in the 1930s.

Lipset and Raab divide far right groups during the Depression era into three impulses: nativist, fascist and conservative.[4] By nativist they have in mind the KKK, plus the Defenders of the Christian Faith of the Reverend Gerald Winrod and William Dudley Pelley's Silver Shirt organizations. Those dominated by the fascist impulse include Senator Huey Long's Share Our Wealth Movement and Father Charles Coughlin's National Union for Social Justice. The conservative impulse was dominated, again according to Lipset and Raab, by the business-focused National Liberty League.

In the case of the Liberty League, which ran a candidate for president in 1936 – Congressman William 'Liberty Bell' Lemke – this was an organization that attacked the Roosevelt New Deal for reasons having to do with the role of government in the economy. This business-backed organization was preservatist on economic grounds. It advocated the return to an era in which the free market alone determined the allocation of resources. Free enterprise would right the ship, not government interference. There appeared to be little expression of racial or religious bigotry in the Liberty League's presentation of itself. This was not the case, however, with most of the other groups encompassing the 1930s far right.

During the 1930s, what the nativist groups wished to preserve was white Protestant supremacy. To do this they borrowed, ironically, from the thriving European fascist movements. Reverend Gerald Winrod from Wichita Kansas (aka 'The Jayhawk Nazi') visited Germany in 1934 and returned to his native state expressing admiration for Hitler's achievements. He established a magazine *The Defender*, (which achieved a circulation of approximately 40,000 at the height of the Depression), and an organization, Defenders of the Christian Faith, which provided him with an opportunity to spread his message. The message was that a truly Christian America was being undermined by the un-American manipulation of Jews, the embodiment of the Anti-Christ. Winrod had few kind words for the papacy either. Both the latter and the international Jewish conspiracy were bent on undermining the American Republic. Tellingly, amongst Winrod's key lieutenants was one James True, the inventor of a type of billy club (a device used to bash heads), whose nickname was 'The Kike Killer'.[5]

William Dudley Pelley was another figure committed to the latter enterprise. An ex-Hollywood screenwriter, magazine journalist and novelist, Pelley formed the Silver Shirt Legion. Active in Los Angeles and the West Coast, his Silver Shirts were intended, he said, to save native-born Protestant America in the same way the Black Shirts had saved Italy and the Brown Shirts had saved Germany. For Pelley, salvation meant freeing the country from the grip of the 'New Deal': not only was Roosevelt himself secretly Jewish but the whole New Deal was the creation of a Jewish/Communist conspiracy. Pelley warned that 'The Jew's racial philosophy, flagellated by rabbinical instruction, is the exact antithesis of the American doctrine of freedom'.[6]

Winrod and Pelley's groups were not alone, just the most prominent. David Wyman, Leonard Dinnerstein and others estimate there were about 100 anti-Semitic groups active during the Depression.[7] These groups included fascist bands such as Joe McWilliams and his Christian Mobilizers, who specialized in attacking Jews on the streets of Boston; and ones like George Deatherage's Knights of the White Camellia ('We're for Christ and the Constitution'), who confined themselves to flyers and pamphlets.[8] The medium may have been different, but their message was the same.

The 1930s was not a decade during which the KKK thrived. Its leadership suffered a series of embarrassing financial and sexual scandals at the end of the 1920s. (At one point during the 1920s the journalist H. L. Mencken had referred to the millions of southern supporters from the Klan as 'the secular wing of the Methodist church in the South').[9] Membership dwindled and by the end of the Depression it was only a shell of its former self. Its spokesmen even toned down the group's anti-Catholic rhetoric. In contrast, the fascist impulse during the Depression, according to Lipset and Raab, was best represented by two groups: Louisiana Senator Huey 'Kingfish' Long's Share Our Wealth movement, and Father Charles Coughlin's National Union for Social Justice (later the Christian Front). Lipset and Raab have some difficulty fitting these movements into their ideas about the Preservatist character of fascist groups. The same difficulty has confronted analysts of European fascism over the years: is it left, right or something else? And if it is neither what is it?[10]

186

Long, who was assassinated before he could challenge Roosevelt for the presidency in 1936, was less interested in preserving the U.S. Constitution than in ending the Depression. His economic schemes involved the government awarding low-income families $5000. The money necessary to make these gifts would come from enforced taxation of the wealthy. Above a certain level, the bank accounts of millionaires would be confiscated by federal authorities, whatever the limits imposed by the rule of law. In fact, Long was contemptuous of laws and law-makers. A spell-binding orator, he sought to develop a direct rapport with Americans by proclaiming 'every man a king!', and creating Share our Wealth clubs throughout the country. Conspicuously missing from Long's rhetoric was any expression of religious or racial bigotry.

This was not the case, however, with another popular demagogue of the 1930s, the radio priest Father Charles Coughlin. A Canadian by birth, Father Coughlin was assigned a church in a Detroit suburb, one with a small number of worshippers. To attract more people to attend mass he hit on the idea of delivering his sermons over the radio. With the coming of the Depression, Coughlin's radio talks – by all accounts he was an exceptionally gifted orator – went national. At this point, his appeals for social justice were based on the papal encyclicals *Rerum Novaram* and *Quadragiesmo Anno*, with their concerns about the exploitation of the poor. The target of his animus was that of an economic elite that was largely responsible for the Depression.

Coughlin was an early supporter of Roosevelt and the New Deal. He mobilized a National Union composed largely of Catholics to support New Deal projects. By 1936 however, he had changed his mind about Roosevelt's reforms. After a visit to Italy he began to celebrate Mussolini's achievements. Hitler also received kind words. By the late 1930s the National Union was reorganized as the Christian Front, a nationwide organization that sought to fight Jewish / Communist control over Washington. 'The Jews' and the 'Jew Deal' increasingly replaced the religiously neutral reference to an economic elite as responsible for the country's woes. Leonard Dinnerstein captures the atmosphere at Christian Front rallies:

Christian Fronters were called on to 'liquidate the Jews in America' [...] Jews were assailed as communists, international bankers, and war mongers. Speakers referred to the President of the United States as 'Rosen-

187

felt' or 'Rosenvelt', praised Franco as that 'great Christian general who drove the reds out of Spain', and championed Hitler as 'the saviour of Europe'.[11]

Coughlin's talks drew a mass radio audience with listeners numbering in the millions. These talks, sponsored by the Ford Motor Company, continued unabated until the attack on Pearl Harbor in December 1941, after which Coughlin was silenced by the Church. Before retiring, the 'radio Priest' delivered multiple sermons on the importance of keeping the United States out of World War II – a conflict into which he believed that American Jews were committed to dragging the country.

In this regard, another group that warrants comment is the German American Bund.[12] Composed largely of recent German immigrants to the United States, the Bund was formed in 1933 as the Friends of the New Germany, changing its name in 1936 at the organization's national convention. The Bund was headed by a Führer, the best known of whom was Fritz Kuhn. The Bund leadership divided the United States, at least in their minds, into *Gaus* – the same way in which the Nazis had divided Germany – and appointed a *Gauleiter* for each region. On the one hand, Bund members paraded in Nazi-like uniforms and engaged in paramilitary training. On the other hand, the Bund also sought to present itself as a patriotic organization committed to preventing the U.S. from entering the war on the side of Britain. Accordingly, it held a rally at Madison Square Garden in New York in 1939, at which pictures of George Washington ('no entangling alliances') were prominently displayed and where, almost needless to say, Jews were accused of unpatriotic war-mongering.

During these years, public opinion firms such as Gallup and Roper began polling Americans about important public issues. As for the threat and then the reality of war in Europe were concerned, these surveys suggested Americans were not as isolationist as many have been lead to believe. When given a choice of either helping Britain and France or staying out of the war, the former option grew in support steadily from slightly over 35 per cent in May 1940 to slightly under 70 per cent in the month before Pearl Harbor.[13] The various far right groups, though noisy, were clearly losing the argument.

The same cannot be said about attitudes towards Jews during the 1930s and throughout the war years. Never before or after has the level of anti-Semitic attitudes been so high. Public opinions about Jews were probed repeatedly by Gallup and Roper from the mid-1930s through to 1945 (these surveys were supported by the American Jewish Committee and the Anti-Defamation League out of fear that Hitler's genocidal policies would be taken up by Americans). These attitudes did not abate during the war. In fact, they mounted and reached a high in the months leading up to D-Day in June 1944. In addition to widespread conventional stereotypes about greed and dishonesty, surveys taken during the war years added allegations of Jewish draft-dodging and war profiteering on the black market.[14]

Perhaps reflecting heightened social tensions, repeated physical attacks on Jews occurred in Boston, New York and a few other cities. Further race riots broke out in Detroit, New York and Los Angeles. The latter involved attacks by Navy personnel on zoot-suiters, (Mexican-American youths thought to be mistreating their girlfriends). Despite the heightened bigotry, the far right groups were unable to exploit this. The U.S. Justice Department pursued cases against Pelley, Winrod and their cohorts on grounds of sedition once the US entered WWII. Groups and individuals suspected of pro-Axis sympathies were depicted in the press as not only unpatriotic but un-American subversives as well.

Post-war changes

In the case of the far right in the decades following the end of the war, we should bear in mind that the time period is much longer and the number of groups belonging to this sector of political life much larger. We also need to bear in mind changes in economic, social and international circumstances. To put matters as succinctly as possible, the Depression and the War were replaced by an era of prosperity that extended into the 1970s. Against this background, public opinion surveys pointed to a long-term decline in anti-Semitism, racial and religious bigotry, a development likely related to increasing levels of education.[15] In terms of its role in the world, America shifted from isolationism to a global 'super-power' committed to a struggle against communism, the Soviet Union and the People's Republic of China. What consequences did these long-term changes have on the far right?

189

The best way of explaining the impact of these changes involves dividing the far right into two broad categories: right-wing populists and far right radicals.[16] The two sets of groups share the aforementioned characteristics Lipset and Raab identified and consequently belong to the same family. However, especially in terms of their popular support and rhetoric, these two groups differ from one another in meaningful ways.

Like much of the far right rhetoric in the United States during the 1930s, anti-communism became the dominant motif for right-wing populists from the beginning of the Cold War in the late 1940s almost to the collapse of the Soviet Union itself. What distinguished the right-wing populists from other anti-communist groups was their view that the threat to the US came not from the USSR or the Warsaw Pact, but from domestic 'Communists' who, they alleged, could be found in all areas of public life. The goal was to expose and root-out subversive elements wherever they could be found. Opponents referred to this process as a 'witch hunt'; for example, the playwright Arthur Miller wrote *The Crucible* in the 1950s in which he drew a parallel between the Salem witch trials of the seventeenth century and the McCarthy era.

Senator Joe McCarthy of Wisconsin created a mass movement and a climate of fear in the early 1950s from his position as the chairman of a Senate investigating committee. At his hearings, McCarthy and his chief counsel, Roy Cohen, interviewed various witnesses seeking to uncover their communist backgrounds and persuade them to 'name names'; that is, to identify friends and acquaintances who may have had some link to communist and communist 'front' organizations in the past.[17] Until his formal censure by his colleagues in the Senate in 1954, McCarthy's investigations achieved widespread popular support to a point where some considered him a contender for the Republican presidential nomination.

McCarthy's search for communists was non-sectarian. His rhetoric was free of anti-Semitism and group bigotry more generally. If anything, he tended to point out pillars of the Protestant establishment in the State Department as drawn, or allegedly drawn, to the communist enterprise: Alger Hiss, Dean Acheson, Owen Lattimore, William Remington, and American diplomats in China in the 1940s at the time of Mao's Revolution. Yet McCarthy was simply one figure, although an important one, in the anti-Communist crusades of the 1940s and 1950s. There were a host of groups and organizations committed to warning Americans of a virtually non-existent domestic communist danger, few of whom blamed Jews, Catholics, recent immigrants or blacks for placing the country in peril.

The John Birch Society was among the most prominent of these groups. The Society was founded in 1958 by Robert Welch, a retired candy manufacturer, and named after a Baptist missionary in China who had been killed by Communist insurgents in 1946. Welch published his *Blue Book* in 1961, which described the threat facing America:

> the truth I bring you is simple, incontrovertible, and deadly. It is that unless we can reverse those who now seem inexorable in their movement, you have only a few more years until the country in which you live will become four separate provinces in a world-wide Communist dominion ruled by police-state methods from the Kremlin.[18]

What drew attention to the group was Welch's allegation that President Dwight Eisenhower and Secretary of State John Foster Dulles were part of the Communist conspiracy.

To fight this imminent threat, Welch's society created chapters in several states and they, in turn, opened American Opinion bookstores containing material warning of this purported danger. (If the threat was as imminent as Welch imagined, you would think it would have taken more than bookstores to block the communist advance). Among the publications the bookstores sold was a two-volume collection, *The Biographical Dictionary of the American Left*. As with McCarthy's subversives, these volumes named names. But those names were typically members of the American establishment, and quite often Republicans – including the likes of Angier Biddle Duke, Eugene Black, Henry Ford II, and Milton Eisenhower.[19]

There were a handful of Jews included in the volumes, yet their inclusion seemed to be based on what they did – or allegedly did – rather than who they were. Thus, for example, Sol Linowitz, the founder of Xerox, was included clearly because he had served as an Ambassador in the Kennedy administration, rather than because of his religious background. In fact, the John Birch Society went out of its way to stress its non-sectarian character. Welch even expelled Revilo P. Oliver, an anti-Semitic college professor because of his anti-Jewish writings.

The same absence of venom directed against American Jews was characteristic of two prominent anti-Communist crusaders of the 1950s and early 1960s. On apparent behalf of their evangelical principals, Reverends Billy James Hargis and Dr. Fred Schwarz launched Christian anti-Communist crusades to warn Americans of the Communist threat. Their crusades, largely focused on fund-raising were free of anti-Catholic, anti-Semitic and racist sentiments. It was sufficient if one was aware of the communist threat irrespective of social background.

Far right perceptions of a domestic communist threat did not disappear as the 1960s progressed. Rather it tended to merge with, and be supplanted by, the struggle over racial equality and reactions against anti-Vietnam War protests. A key figure in the right-wing populist reactions to these developments was Governor George Wallace of Alabama. Wallace rose to national prominence in 1964 (when he entered the Democratic presidential primaries) based on his opposition to racial integration. His serious run on the presidency occurred in 1968 when he ran as the candidate of the miniscule Independent American Party. The atmosphere during that year was electric. Major race riots had followed the assassination of Martin Luther King, Jnr. At the country's major universities there were massive protests against the War. A new counter-culture of 'flower-children' and hippies had emerged.

In this context, Wallace's third party run on the presidency attracted close to 13 per cent of the national vote. Was this a racist backlash, particularly in the South, where Wallace did best? Perhaps, but over the course of his campaign he rarely mentioned race. Instead Wallace built his campaign around the demand for a restoration of 'law and order'. Mass protests and urban rioting needed to be quelled. It was best, Wallace said repeatedly, to let the 'police handle it'. Those individuals Wallace both condemned and derided were 'bearded, beatnik bureaucrats' who wanted to tell people how to live their lives. The real culprits were pointy-headed intellectuals and Berkeley professors, who were not smart enough to lean a bicycle against a wall without assistance. By contrast, Wallace defined himself as the champion of ordinary Americans – barbers, beauticians, firemen – in the struggle against those who would disrupt their lives and tell them what to do. In short, Wallace campaigned as a right-wing populist, speaking for the people rather than as a race-baiter.[20]

Wallace's career was cut short when he was the target of an assassination attempt while campaigning once again for the presidency, in 1972. The attack left him paralyzed and, eventually, repentant for his racist sins. The end of Wallace was not, however, the end of right-wing populism. New forces emerged in the 1970s and 1980s.

By the end of the 1970s, a powerful new entry had become a centre of public attention and political life. This was the Christian Right. Its rise to prominence was associated with the appearance of 'televangelists'. Preachers as Pat Robertson, Jerry Fallwell, James Dobson, and Jimmy Swaggart developed mass audiences, numbering in the millions, on cable television stations throughout the country, but especially in the southern 'Bible Belt'.

Fallwell and Dobson respectively created the organizations 'Moral Majority' and 'Focus on the Family' to 'fight for a restoration of a strong role for Christianity in the public arena' (for example, prayer in public schools). They, and the other televangelists, condemned abortion and homosexuality. Who or what prevented a return to the high moral standards for which these fundamentalists stood? Their answer was a philosophy: 'secular humanism'. America had fallen into decay, they asserted, because of what were essentially the ideas of the Enlightenment.[21]

Rather than claiming 'the Jews' were responsible for the country's woes, the Christian Right tended to be philo-Semitic, at least to the extent of supporting Israel and, especially, the Jewish state's control of Jerusalem. Later, spokesmen for various Zionist causes began appearing in evangelical churches. Despite the televangelists' sources of support in the South, African-Americans were not targets of abuse either. The Christian Right had strong ties during the Reagan era with what came to be known as, the New Right. The latter was well-funded by the Coors family and other wealthy individuals, in order to create a web of organizations to support right-wing Republican candidates for public office. The rhetoric may have been populist, but the reality was that the New Right was supported by a relative handful of multi-millionaires.

The key figures in the New Right were Richard Viguerie, Paul Weyrich, Howard Phillips and Terry Dolan. All these figures had entered politics via Young Americans for Freedom (YAF), a Republican Party youth group. With the exception of Phillips, who was Jewish, the other leaders were Catholic. What these individuals had in common was hostility to the country's liberal

'Eastern Establishment' as exemplified by Nelson Rockefeller. Their goal was to push the Republican Party in a rightward direction. In particular, these new rightists stood for high defense spending in support of the anti-Communist struggle; American individualism; a limited role for the government in the economy; and the moral principles of the Christian Right. To that end, the New Right sought to harness the Christian Right's energy to promote this agenda. By using a combination of direct mail appeals (which Viguerie pioneered) and political action committees, New Right groups promoted the candidacy of office-seekers at congressional and local levels who were committed to dismantling the New Deal reforms of the 1930s and Lyndon Johnson's Great Society programs of the 1960s.[22]

The end of the Cold War and the dissolution of the Soviet Union seemed to leave the New and Christian right without a plausible foreign enemy. A new foe though was not long to emerge. In the aftermath of the American-led effort to expel Iraqi forces from Kuwait (1990 – 1991), President George Walker Bush referred to the emergence of a 'New World Order'. He meant that the end of the Cold War was going to produce a unipolar world, one with the U.S. as the dominant force. However, Pat Robertson and a long list of other rightists construed the New World Order in conspiratorial terms – Bush and his establishment cohorts intended to replace American sovereignty with the United Nations or some smaller aggregation of international bankers and power brokers.

Paranoid fears mounted, with some observers noticing mysterious unmarked trains, or trains marked with UN symbols and black helicopters passing through or flying over various sections of the country in preparation for a New World Order seizure of power.[23] It was believed that the first goal of the New World Order was to disarm patriotic Americans so that the country would be left helpless when invading forces (likely Chinese) crossed the border from Canada.[24] These fears contributed to the formation of the militia or patriot movement, the dominant form of right-wing populism during the 1990s. Other concerns that helped stimulate its formation included worries that new gun control legislation would lead to the confiscation of what members regarded as a constitutionally protected right. Particularly in rural areas, especially ones hard-hit by farm foreclosures, 'sovereign citizens' expressed bitter resentment against the federal government's excessive regulations, claiming immunity from the latter. In some cases, those drawn to the movement, refused to recognize any legal entity above the level of the county.

The result was the appearance of paramilitary groups in many of the 50 states, prepared to do battle against the imaginary New World Order and authentic law enforcement agencies. Most leaders of these state militias repeatedly explained that their bands recruited militiamen (and a few women) without regard to race, religion or ethnicity. In reality, the founders and early leaders of the Militias of Montana (MOM), John, Randy and David Trochmann and Michigan's, Norman Olsen, had backgrounds in white supremacist groups. Following the disclosure that Timothy McVeigh, the Oklahoma City bomber, had been a militia member, or at least on its fringes, the movement lost its momentum and a significant number of its gun-toting participants.[25]

In recent years however, the militia movement has made something of a comeback. The election of Barak Obama to the presidency in 2008, coupled with growing fears about border security and illegal immigrants have contributed to this resurgence.[26] One group, the Hutaree Militia, active in Michigan, Ohio and Indiana was accused by federal authorities of seditious conspiracy involving a plot to murder policemen ('foot soldiers of the New World Order') as a way of setting off an armed conflict to topple the government in Washington.

Far right radicals

Thus far it has been shown that a key feature of right-wing populism in the post-war decades was the replacement of hate speech directed at racial, religious and ethnic minorities with abstract, non-sectarian enemies against whom all Americans could struggle. If you believed correctly, you could participate in the fight against communism, the United Nations, the New World Order and so on, irrespective of racial or religious background. Although a segment of the American right did not follow this pattern. Here we refer to groups that two-leading watchdog organizations, the Southern Poverty Law Centre (SPLC) and the Anti-Defamation League (ADL), label 'hate groups'.

At present (2012), the SPLC estimates that there are over 1,000 such 'hate groups' active in the United States.[27] Since the election of President Barack Obama in 2008, their numbers have swelled. Some consist of no more than a handful of members or followers, typically with their own websites. In addition, far right radicalism has been plagued for many years by fragmentation and disputes among aspiring leaders. For instance, following the 2004 death of the long-time Aryan Nations' leader, Richard Girnt Butler, there was a fight to replace him that has still not been resolved. Not only are there clashes of egos, but there are often serious mutual suspicions, with different far rightists accusing each other of secretly being FBI agents or, even worse, Jewish.

There is also the temptation to believe many far rightists are not all that bright. The following incident involving George Lincoln Rockwell, founder of the American Nazi Party, provides a reason for the temptation:

Roy Frankhauser, a veteran of the ultra-right scene in the United States, had a memorable encounter with Rockwell during his first visit to 'Hate-Monger Hill', as the American Nazi Party headquarters was known. The obese, chain-smoking Frankhauser telephoned for an appointment for himself and a few friends, but Rockwell heavily bandaged from recent oral surgery, had trouble pronouncing his words. As a result Frankhauser and company, dressed in Nazi outfits and armed to the teeth, went to the wrong address, only to be chased away by an old woman brandishing a broomstick. When they finally arrived at Rockwell's domicile, Frankhauser and the others were ushered into a waiting room with a very low ceiling, their rifles in hand. Surprised by these motley interlopers, one of Rockwell's bodyguards reached for his gun and accidently squeezed the trigger, shooting a hole through his pants and scalding his thigh. Moments later, Rockwell barged in to see what all the ruckus was about. Frankhauser and company immediately snapped to attention and hoisted their bayonets straight into the ceiling, while the injured bodyguard hopped around on one leg cursing. 'Who the [expletive deleted] are you?' Rockwell screamed. 'We're Nazi soldiers', Frankhauser responded earnestly.[28]

Despite its various problems and the slap-stick comedy noted above, it is all too easy to dismiss right-wing radicals as not worth much attention. For no other reason, we should pay attention, because of the volume of violent acts committed by members of these hate groups over the years. Bearing this out, Christopher Hewitt reports that close to one third of terrorist incidents in the United States between 1954 and 2000 involved white racists/far rightists. They also accounted for more than half of the fatalities involved (the latter figure included the 161 people killed in the April 1995 Oklahoma City bombing at the Murrah Federal Building).[29] Since McVeigh's bombing, the SPLC has calculated that radical right groups were involved in 75 terrorist plots, conspiracies and acts.[30] These terrorist acts involved the deaths of some 28 law enforcement officers, suggesting that this is not a phenomenon to be easily dismissed.

The SPLC divides their extensive compilation of contemporary 'hate groups' into the following categories: KKK, Neo-Nazi, White Nationalist, Racist Skinhead and Christian Identity. The groups falling under each category have their own identities, themes and peculiarities. For example, the KKK groups these days stress 'White Power!' rather than their former stock-in-trade, explicit anti-black racism. In keeping with this more 'positive' rhetoric, some KKK figures have sought to convey a more moderate image. Former Louisiana legislator David Duke embodies this new approach.[31] There are, however, certain common features that overlap. It is not uncommon these days for National Socialists and Klansmen to hold joint rallies and for racist skinheads to chant 'White Power! White Pride!' at their own gatherings. In short, we are dealing with what the English anthropologist Colin Campbell refers to, as a 'cultic milieu'.[32] This milieu consists of groups and followers of beliefs and practices rejected by the general population. In our case, we are dealing with a milieu of religious and political ideas, which most would regard as fanciful. And believers are usually able to switch from one category of group to another without much difficulty. It makes sense then to examine the fundamental views of those caught up in this milieu. In other words, what are the common denominators of far right rhetoric in the contemporary US?

Religion

The principal religious denominations of right-wing radicals are Christian Identity, Odinism, and Creativity. They appear to have surfaced as mainstream Christian denominations, especially fundamentalist ones, yet have come to abandon long-standing racist, xenophobic and anti-Semitic precepts. Christian

197

Identity is a religion devised in Southern California in the years following World War II.[33] Its founders, John Wesley Swift, William Potter Gale and a handful of others synthesized theories of white racial supremacy with aspects of Christian belief. The result was a theology that asserted a dual creation: God's first effort at creating human beings failed. This failure produced a race(s) of 'mud people', incapable of achieving a high level of civilization, on a second occasion God succeeded in creating Adam and Eve, the first Aryans.

According to this racist 'theology', trouble arose in Eden when Eve had sexual relations with the Devil, disguised as a snake. The result of that union was the first Jew – literally the 'seed of Satan'.[34] The United States was intended by God to be the land of the Aryans. Instead the country's major cities have been overrun by 'mud people' – or in other words, people of 'color'. This infestation has been the work of the Jews whose diabolical scheme is to control the U.S. and eventually the rest of the world. For some members of the radical right milieu Identity is tainted because of its Christian roots. This taint is based on the Jewish origins of many Christian beliefs.

Instead, some radical rightists seek to worship the pre-Christian gods of Northern Europe.[35] For 'Aryans' there is a natural affinity between this type of paganism and their blood-determined racial characteristics. The affinity between the worship of Odin (or Wotan) and the Norse or Teutonic pantheon and the German National Socialism of Heinrich Himmler's pantheistic variety is apparent:

> The origins of Odinism as a self-conscious reconstruction of Teutonic beliefs lie in nineteenth century Germany. Against a background of burgeoning nationalism, *volkish* writers speculated on the Germans' spiritual resources in resisting Rome's conquest and their recalcitrant conversion to Christianity under Charlemagne.[36]

Creativity, or the Church of the Creator, represents another effort to instill white racial pride, in an increasingly diverse America. Creativity was itself the creation of Ben Klassen, a Ukrainian immigrant, Florida state legislator, and successful businessman. Klassen rejected all ideas about the supernatural as 'spooks in the sky'. In place of the 'spooks' Klassen asserted 'our race is our religion', which became Creativity's slogan. Among its sixteen commandments are, 'It is the avowed duty and holy responsibility of each generation to assure and secure for all time the existence of the White Race upon the face of this planet' (its first commandment); and 'Remember that the inferior colored races are our deadly enemies, and the most dangerous of all is the Jewish race. It is our immediate objective to relentlessly expand the White Race, and keep shrinking our enemies' (its third commandment).[37]

Soon thereafter, Klassen proclaimed himself the church's 'Pontifex Maximus'! and called on his followers to prepare themselves for a racial holy war – often shorthanded as the racist code 'RaHoWa!'– that would restore white racial supremacy. Since his incitement, the goal of most radical right groups has been to ignite a racial holy war. Their random terrorist attacks on African-Americans are often intended to raise tensions in the hope that a race war will result (see below). After Klassen's suicide in 1993, there was a struggle to succeed him. Eventually this struggle was won by Matt Hale, a law-school graduate from Peoria, Illinois. Hale managed to re-invigorate the group, renaming it the World Church of the Creator. The name change proved to be Hale's undoing. He sued another group using the same name for copyright infringement. The judge in the case ruled against Hale, who then threatened the judge. The result was a criminal prosecution, Hale's conviction and long-term prison sentence.

Political beliefs

Right-wing populists believe in the wisdom of 'The People', uncorrupted by political parties and other intermediaries. Right-wing radicals typically do not. Their rhetoric is restorational in tone, in that they hope to restore white racial supremacy in the United States and, indeed, on a worldwide basis. Although they do not regard ordinary white people as smart enough to figure out, much less implement, a racial holy war. It would take an elite or white vanguard to lead the way and ignite a racial revolution. The appeal of the late William Pierce's novels, *The Turner Diaries* and *Hunter*, was their depiction of ways by which a small band of revolutionaries (or in the case of *Hunter's* 'lone-wolf' protagonist, a single individual) can lead the way and provoke a racial holy war in which threatened whites will need to defend themselves.

Many right-wing radicals are not nationalists or patriots, at least in a conventional sense. 'Freemen' or 'sovereign citizens' do not regard as legitimate any government institution above the level of the country. They are consequently under no obligation to obey the laws, including, and especially ones concerning, income taxes and land foreclosures.

For many on the radical right the basic attachment is to race, not country. For them, the white or Aryan race is an endangered species. The natural habitat of the white race is to be found in North America, Europe, Australia, New Zealand and, to a lesser extent, South Africa. The rest of the earth is inhabited by inferior races; populations incapable of meaningful cultural or significant achievements. These inferior races have invaded the Aryan's habitat and threaten it with elimination and, unless something is done (i.e. a racial revolution), the sole source of human creativity will face extinction. Right-wing radicals pull few punches when it comes to identifying the enemy. The United States, and through it much of the world, is under the control of ZOG, a Zionist Occupation Government, or JOG, a Jewish Occupation Government. Jews constitute a satanic conspiracy that has already surreptitiously taken control of the mass media and America's major government institutions. ZOG promotes race-mixing, abortion, mass immigration and homosexuality in its unceasing attempt to destroy the Aryan race and plunge the world into darkness.

Yet if this racist rhetoric is unmistakable, perhaps surprisingly, radical rightists have mixed views concerning the Holocaust. Some publicists have mounted a campaign of Holocaust denial, suggesting the Jews have concocted tales of Nazi mass murder as a way of winning sympathy, for themselves and especially the state of Israel. On the other hand, other radical rightists believe that Hitler was too lenient. Jews then and now need to be exterminated for the sake of human survival. The principal Holocaust denial institution in the United States has been the Institute for Historical Review, founded in 1978 by Willis Carto, the publisher of The Spotlight, a radical right weekly. The Institute publishes a Journal devoted to publishing 'scholarly' articles based on 'scientific' evidence, demonstrating that the genocide never occurred.[38] Prominent neo-Nazi figures from George Lincoln Rockwell onwards have expressed support for the Holocaust, often lamenting that Hitler had not been able to finish the job – though a certain ambivalence can be detected. Sometimes the same individual will deny the Holocaust while a little later applaud its results.

Radical right rhetoric in the United States tends to be freer in tone and substance than similar speech in Western Europe. In Germany and elsewhere there are rules aimed at controlling 'hate speech' that are largely missing in the U.S. Thanks to First Amendment protections the Holocaust denial, for example, has become something of a growth industry. Little restrains neo-Nazis and racist skinheads from displaying the Swastika and other symbols of the Hitler dictatorship at rallies and other public gatherings. Some regard for popular opinion does serve to restrain more murderous expressions.

It is also worth mentioning that original Nazi rhetoric was affected by the language of the German bureaucracy. Terms like 'Final Solution', 'resettlement', 'special tasks' and so on were really the applications of bureaucratic speech for Nazi purposes used in order to obfuscate what they were doing. In the United States, on the other hand, the radical right characteristically hates the government and its various institutions and has little interest in borrowing its vocabulary.

Conclusions

The underlying problem with the contemporary radical right in the U.S. is that its rhetoric does not match its reality. The rhetoric, religious and secular, has long been devised to warn of ZOG. Essentially this rhetoric is an up-dated version of Nazi and other European ideas about the threat posed by Jews to Aryans, ideas modified to suit American circumstances. Current reality, though, points the base of the radical right in a different direction. Today, 'rarely has the United States seen a more reckless and bare-knuckled campaign to vilify a distinct class of people and compromise their fundamental civil and human rights'. The writer refers, of course, to American Muslims.[39] Since 9/11, American Muslims have been the targets of a substantial volume of violence, ranging from street-corner attacks to the burning of mosques and other Islamic structures. Rabble-rousers have come forward to denounce Sharia Law and the designs of Muslims to impose it throughout the country. In Florida, a fundamentalist preacher burnt the Koran in public. State legislators have considered measures to outlaw Sharia in response to a non-existent threat.

These developments provide radical right organizations such as the White Aryan Resistance, Storm Front and the National Alliance, with a potential for expanding their base of social support. Replacing anti-Semitic with anti-Muslim rhetoric would certainly make sense for these groups. Given the radical right's history though, it finds it difficult to make the necessary adjustments.[40] Right-wing populist groups also confront a serious problem, though not as serious as that faced by the radical right. In the present, more than five decades since the end of World War II, right-wing populists have sought, with considerable success, to avoid the kind of nativism and xenophobia that characterized its pre-war predecessors.

Today though, we are witnessing the 'return of the native' (*pace* Thomas Hardy). Hispanics represent the fastest growing element in the U.S. population. There are popular concerns in some parts of the country that Spanish is more commonly spoken than English. In many areas, election ballots are printed in both English and Spanish. Popular fears have also been mounted over the presence of illegal immigrants taking jobs away and draining resources from the native-born. In short, we appear to have the basis for a large-scale restoration campaign available to right-wing populists throughout the country. The KKK and other nativist groups seem to have an opportunity for a revival. Whether they are able to take advantage of the opportunity remains to be seen.

ENDNOTES

[1] Seymour Lipset and Earl Raab, *The Politics of Unreason* (New York: Harper and Row, 1970), pp. 3 – 33.
[2] Ibid.
[3] Murray Edelman, *The Symbolic Uses of Politics* (Urbana Ill: University of Illinois Press, 1964), p. 114.
[4] Lipset and Raab, p. 150.
[5] David Bennett, *The Party of Fear* (Chapel Hill, NC: University of North Carolina Press, 1988), pp. 244 – 245.
[6] Bennett, p. 246.
[7] David Wyman, *The Abandonment of the Jews* (New York: Pantheon Books, 1984), p. 9; Leonard Dinnerstein, *Anti-Semitism in America* (New York: Oxford University Press, 1994), p. 112.
[8] David Bennett, *The Party of Fear* (New York: Vintage Books, 1995), p. 247.
[9] H. L. Mencken, *On Politics: A Carnival of Buncombe* (Baltimore MD: The John Hopkins University Press, 1956), p. 167.
[10] See for example, Zeev Sternhell, *Neither Left nor Right: Fascist Ideology in France* (Princeton NJ: Princeton University Press, 1996).
[11] Dinnerstein, p. 121.
[12] O. John Rogge, *The Official German Report* (New York: Thomas Yoseloff, 1961), pp. 113 – 129; it bears noting that there was a small Russian Fascist movement headquartered in Connecticut and that Mussolini had considerable support among mem-

bers of the Sons of Italy among immigrants throughout the country.

[13] Adam Berinsky *et al.*, 'Revisiting Public Opinion in the 1930s and 1940s', *PS* 44/3 (July 2011), pp. 518 – 519.

[14] Charles Stember, *Jews in the Minds of Americans* (New York: Basic Books, 1966), pp. 81 – 85.

[15] Seymour Lipset and Earl Raab, *Jews and the New American Scene* (Cambridge: Harvard University Press, 1995), pp. 95 – 100.

[16] Chip Berlet and Matthew N Lyons define Populism as a movement that celebrates the 'People' and expresses anti-elitist sentiments, *Right-Wing Populism: Too Close for Comfort?* (New York: Guilford Press, 2000), pp. 4 – 5.

[17] For an interpretation see, Daniel Bell ed., *The Radical Right* (New York: Doubleday, 1962), pp. 39 – 86.

[18] Robert Welch, *The Blue Book of the John Birch Society* (Belmont MA: Western Islands, 1961), p. 1.

[19] Francis X. Gannon, *Biographical Dictionary of the Left* (Belmont MA: American Opinion, 1968).

[20] See Marshall Frady, *Wallace* (New York: World Publishing, 1968), pp. 179 – 245.

[21] For a general discussion see *The Religious Right* (New York: The Anti-Defamation League, 1994).

[22] Richard Viguerie, *The New Right: We're Ready to Lead* (Falls Church VA: The Viguerie Company, 1981), pp. 8 – 16.

[23] See, for example, Jim Keith, *Black Helicopters over America: Strike Force for the New World Order* (Lilburn GA: IllumNet Press, 1995).

[24] For an expression of these views, see Richard Hobbs, *You and the New World Order* (Sparks NV: ColDoc Publishing, 1995).

[25] For a concise account see Mark Potok, 'The American Radical Right', in Roger Eatwell and Cas Mudde eds., *Western Democracies and the New Extreme Right Challenge* (London: Routledge, 2004), pp. 41 – 61.

[26] Heidi Beirich, 'Midwifing the militias', *SPLC Intelligence Report*, 137 (Spring 2010), pp. 30 – 35.

[27] Mark Potok, 'The Year in Hate and Extremism', *Intelligence Report*, 141 (Spring 2011).

[28] Quoted in Martin Lee, *The Beast Reawakans* (New York: Little Brown, 1997), p. 161.

[29] Christopher Hewitt, *Understanding Terrorism in America* (London: Routledge, 2003), p. 15.

[30] *Terror from the Right* (Montgomery AL: SPLC, 2009).

[31] See Douglas Rose ed., *The Emergence of David Duke* (Chapel Hill NC: University of North Carolina Press, 1992).

[32] Colin Campbell, 'The Cult, the Cultic Milieu and Secularization', in Jeffrey Kaplan and Heléne Lööw eds., *The Cultic Milieu* (Walnut Creek: Alta Mira Press, 2002), pp. 12 – 25.

[33] Michael Barkun, *Religion and the Racist Right* (Chapel Hill NC: University of North Carolina Press, 1994), pp. 3 – 47.

[34] Michael Barkun, *A Culture of Conspiracy* (Berkeley CA: University of California Press, 2003), pp. 119 – 120.

[35] Mattias Gardell, *Gods of the Blood* (Durham NC: Duke University Press, 2003), pp. 33 – 89.

[36] Nicholas Goodrick-Clarke, *Black Sun: Aryan Cults, Esoteric Nazism and the Politics of Identity* (New York: New York University Press, 2002), p. 257.

[37] Jeffrey Kaplan, 'Right-Wing Violence in North America', in Tore Bjørrgo ed., *Terror from the Extreme Right* (London: Frank Cass, 1995), p. 64.

[38] Michael Shermer and Alex Grobman, *Denying History* (Berkeley CA: University of California Press, 2000), pp. 453 – 544.

[39] Robert Steinback, 'Jihad Against Islam', *Intelligence Report*, 142 (Summer 2011), p. 15.

[40] One of the curiosities of the current situation is that right-wing radicals and Islamists share a common hatred for Jews. Sometimes disguised or sanitized as 'anti-Zionism' the latter also perceive ZOG as in control of the United States.

PART 3

CENTRAL, SOUTHERN AND EASTERN EUROPE

A CASE STUDY OF ANTI-SEMITISM IN THE LANGUAGE AND POLITICS OF THE CONTEMPORARY FAR RIGHT IN GERMANY

Gideon Botsch and Christoph Kopke

Anti-Semitism is, today too, one of the central ideological elements within the extreme right-wing, whereby the enemy actually implied is frequently concealed behind various agitation topics such as 'globalization', 'criticism of the system', 'foreign infiltration', 'criticism of Israel', 'the Middle East conflict' and 'coming to terms with the past'. Here, historical continuities can be discerned between these ideas and earlier anti-Semitic forms and contents but also more recent points of reference to contemporary discourses and topics.[1]

Racism and anti-Semitism were not only central ideological motifs of historical German fascism – of which the exemplar remains National Socialism – and its 'völkisch' (i.e., racial nationalist) precursors, but remains ideological mainstay in the worldview of the German radical right today. Individual factions differ, however, in the extent to which they emphasize these ideas, and the manner in which they articulate such themes. A consideration of these different factions in post-war and contemporary Germany is the focus of this chapter, which uses the changing language of anti-Semitism as a case study to explore elements of 'doublespeak' amongst far right rhetoric in German politics. In doing so, the following questions will be analyzed: how, when, and in what forms does anti-Semitism appear in the political semantics, rhetoric, ideology and argumentation in Germany's far right scene?

Far right ideology embraces a wide number of concepts of inequality. Anti-Semitism performs the special function of integrating these elements and seemingly mediating between the contradictions that exist. For the far right, the Jews are to an extent still the common denominator linking all of their basic ideological precepts. As such, the assessment by an independent think tank – which submitted a report, commissioned by the German Federal government in 2011 – is basically correct in claiming 'Anti-Semitism is, today too, one of the central ideological elements within the extreme right-wing'.[2]

The changed context

In the context of Federal German democracy, modes of anti-Semitic thought and expression have clearly shifted and become less obvious since the end of World War Two. Bergmann and Erb identified 'communication latency' [*Kommunikationslatenz*] as a characteristic feature of anti-Semitism within contemporary German democracy:

The concept of communication latency assumes that there are anti-Semitic attitudes within the population that are articulated in suitable situations during private communication among individuals who are on close terms. On the other hand, a prejudice-repressing mechanism is also at work, i.e., the climate of public opinion repels public expression of anti-Semitism [...] As long as there is consensus among the political and cultural elites to maintain this pressure of opinion [...], this repression of prejudice is capable of effectively banning anti-Semitism from public communication, and in the long run [...] helps weaken the tradition of anti-Jewish stereotypes.[3]

However, in Germany, as well as in other European countries, 'the boundaries of what is viewed as [...] acceptable in the public sphere are changing and eroding, and with it the latency of anti-Semitism'.[4] In the context of a number of discourses – such as that concerning 'German victims', or the generalization of genocidal tendencies in the twentieth century, or the Middle East conflict – anti-Semitic expression is becoming more apparent. Nonetheless, on the whole this constitutes no more than shifts within a field that continues to be characterized by the phenomenon of 'communication latency'. Against that background, the far right hopes to find sympathies at least amongst some parts of the German public when mobilizing the issues of 'German-Jewish relations', an ostensible 'civil religion of guilt' imposed on the

German people by the 'vengeful Jews', or the role of the 'Jewish state' Israel in the Middle East conflict. In general terms, though, the role anti-Semitism plays in the far right can be described thus:

> Although all relevant extreme right parties and factions work with anti-Semitic stereotypes, and anti-Jewish feeling is always present, no [post-war] organization has hitherto placed the central focus of their propaganda on anti-Semitism. Recently, however, the use of anti-Semitic stereotypes has increased. Putative taboo-breakers could (unintentionally) break the 'communication latency' down.[5]

Irrespective of the questions of when and to what extent anti-Semitism is placed at the 'center of their propaganda', hostility towards Jews clearly remains a central point on the political agenda of the far right. Compelled to present their anti-Jewish tendencies in such a way that they conform to democratic language, the contemporary German far right has developed its own euphemistic language in response.

Crucially, the unintentional users of most forms of latent or manifest anti-Semitism in Germany today are frequently not conscious of it, but the euphemistic language of the anti-Semitic far right is used quite deliberately. To circumvent the law or avoid other obstacles, they articulate themselves in such a way that veils or encodes anti-Semitic content. A few examples of the German far right's turn to encoded language in this century will be highlighted and analyzed below.

Primary and secondary forms of anti-Semitism

Anti-Semitism and hostility towards Jews has undergone a striking process of transformation since the end of the Second World War. Anti-Semitism nevertheless continues to be a point of identification for all parties and factions of the German far right today – one considered an indispensable feature of German right-wing extremism, or as an 'essential ideological element of the far right'.[6] Anti-Semitism performs a number of functions for the far right and essentially remains 'within the camp, a central – inalienable, even – ideological element'.[7]

Among the far right in Germany today, forms of hostility towards Jews which can be described as 'primary anti-Semitism' remain consistently in evidence. This type of anti-Semitism attempts to take up the popular clichés and antagonisms of traditional nineteenth century anti-Semitism or to mobilize and revitalize the racist anti-Semitism of German Nazism.[8] While most old stereotypes and antagonisms concerning Jews continue to exist, new ones have also been added. More recent accusations against Jews sometimes update older themes, such as the motif of a Jewish collaboration spanning the entire world – a 'Jewish global conspiracy' as expounded in the *Protocols of the Elders of Zion* – or the assumption that Jews are especially avaricious and 'work-shy', as well as particularly cold-hearted or cruel.

Additionally, there are motifs and claims that may collectively be described as 'secondary anti-Semitism';[9] that of 'resisting memory and guilt' or 'exonerative anti-Semitism', which is based mainly on the reversal of the victim and perpetrator roles. Thus, 'secondary anti-Semitism' is 'driven by the impulse to reject or downplay the memory of the Shoah' and 'motivated by the perception that Jews, the victims and their children, embody the painful history of Nazi genocide'.[10] Collectively, the Jews are hereby accused, among other things, of drawing financial gain in the form of compensation and restitution from the persecution and murder committed by the Nazis. Contrary to well-established facts, it is even frequently claimed that the Holocaust never happened but was invented by the Jews in order to morally blackmail and financially exploit the Germans.[11] Yet even when the Nazis' policy of destruction is not openly denied, attempts are made to diminish its gravity: sometimes by claiming that the victims' death toll is exaggerated; sometimes by referring to other forms of mass murder, ethnic cleansing or genocide by way of diminishing the enormity of Nazism's 'Final Solution of the Jewish Question'. In 1940s Germany, for instance, reciprocal Allied bombings, expulsion and deportation of German minorities from the countries of central and Eastern Europe, and the political purges carried out by the Allies after 1945 have all been cited in this specifically German form of evasive 'revisionism'.[12]

Elements of anti-Jewish stereotypes, scenarios and claims are altered and re-asserted again and again in varying combinations. It bears noting that the contemporary anti-Semite does not adhere to the neat boundaries drawn by the academic discourse on anti-Semitism,[13] that seeks to neatly separate forms of primary and secondary anti-Semitism. However, different factions may be observed to place different emphases upon each of these discourses, perhaps in order to create tactical variances.

'White Power', neo-Nazis and the National Democratic Party

Open anti-Semitism – that is, accusing Jews of operating as a force in the background, still working deliberately against the German people – can be found right across the political spectrum of non-party-affiliated neo-Nazis, especially in the 'comradeships' (*Kameradschaften*) and the 'free forces' (*freie Kräfte*). An ideological channel feeding the far right youth scene is provided by the songs of sub-cultural 'White Power' music, which has been communicating the whole historical range of anti-Semitic motifs, prejudices and fantasies since the 1990s. Within the extreme right-wing spectrum, music bands are often the most outspoken voices – and their corresponding anti-Semitism is usually unambiguous and very aggressive. Since many bands do not expect to be legally able to sell their CDs in Germany, they exercise no restraint, even that of avoiding criminalization; sometimes even openly advocating the abuse, humiliation and murder of Jews, the destruction of Israel and the entire Jewish race; or by declaring their support for Nazism and the Holocaust.[14] Consequently, some songs deny the Holocaust while others glorify it, or even call for its repetition.[15] Anti-Semitic illustrations are widely used on CD covers, in fanzines, on stickers and websites, so much so that the far right can be said to make use of an 'anti-Semitic pictographic language'.[16] This often adopts images, caricatures and slogans from the Nazis' biological anti-Semitism or borrows from them in altered forms.

The National Democratic Party (*Nationaldemokratische Partei* or NPD) works in alliance with the self-styled 'free forces' cited above. The NPD is the most significant party-political grouping of Germany's far right.[17] Founded in 1964 as an assemblage of different parties and groupings, it formulated in its early years a comparatively moderate, yet still radical nationalist platform. Beginning with the Bavarian elections of 1965, it gathered mass support at the ballots in several of the federal states, but failed to win the necessary 5 per cent to get access to the national parliament, *Deutscher Bundestag*, in the elections of 1969. Even though the early NPD tried to distance itself from Na-

tional Socialism, and publicly pledged its allegiance to the democratic constitution, several contributions to the party press and public, or semi-public,
speeches of its leading activists showed that in the party, a deep-rooted anti-
Semitic bias was still present. In the 1970s, when it became merely one of
several splinter parties and action groups in a fractured 'national opposition', it
radicalized its ideology, but still avoided a too openly anti-Semitic language.
However, the party and its youth organization Young National Democrats
(*Junge Nationaldemokraten*) kept in close touch with the developing neo-Nazi-
gangs and nationalist paramilitary training groups (*Wehrsportgruppen*), which
showed a growing tendency to articulate open anti-Semitism in its leaflets and
magazines, and even in violent and terrorist attacks. For example, in 1979 the
Austrian authorities arrested a German fugitive and neo-Nazi terrorist who had
prepared a series of bomb attacks on Jewish citizens. In the same year, an activist from the NPD youth organization blasted transmitter masts in south-west
Germany and, thus prevented the broadcasting of the American TV series
'Holocaust' in some regions of the Rheinland-Palatinate. Neo-Nazi violence
reached its climax with the bomb attack on the *Oktoberfest* in Munich in the autumn of 1980. At the same time, an activist of the banned (Bavarian)
Wehrsportgruppe Hoffmann, assassinated a Jewish publisher and his spouse
in Erlangen. Militia leader Hoffmann himself had made his way, with a core
group of followers, to a Palestinian refugee camp in Lebanon, where he and
his followers were trained and probably also took part in combat with the Israeli
Defense Force. A split-off group of this *Wehrsportgruppe Libanon* later put
bombs underneath cars with U.S. license plates in Frankfurt/Main, the location
of the U. S. Army headquarters in Germany. This particular group also maintained a close relation to East Germany's secret service, as well as to Palestinian terrorist groups. When the German state started to prohibit some violent
groups and arrest some of their prominent leaders, the NPD had to distance
themselves from this open anti-Semitic and neo-Nazi-circle. At this time, it
started its xenophobic anti-immigrant-campaign. With the perception of immigration as a planned and organized plot against the national identity of the
Germans – conceptualized as 'over-foreignerization' (*Überfremdung*) – this
campaign was framed by an unexpressed anti-Semitic bias.[18]

The NPD was then marginalized in the late 1980s and early 1990s by
more moderate far right competitors in the electoral field, on the one hand,

and by the agile neo-Nazi-groups and violent far right youth subcultures, on the other. Only in the late 1990s, did its popularity rise anew, to the point that it became – and is currently – represented in several local councils and even two East German regional parliaments.[19] This success was largely the result of its increased cooperation and links with a broad neo-Nazi spectrum of activists across Germany. Together, they regard themselves as the 'national opposition' and 'national resistance'. This cooperation is evident in party campaigns and, above all, at demonstrations.

'Stop Zionist World Rule': marches and demonstrations

Anti-Semitic motifs are a constant feature of these so-called marches, but the NPD – and also most of the comradeships – seldom put anti-Semitism as the focus of its campaigns. In 2000, however, the NPD organized a march at the Brandenburg Gate – the same place where, 67 years before, the Nazi storm troopers cheered to their leader when he was appointed German Reich Chancellor – to protest against the erection of a Holocaust monument in Berlin. Two years later the NPD protested in Potsdam with the slogan 'Stop mass immigration of Russian Zionists – Germany for us Germans'.[20] Additionally in 2004, when other far right groups focused on protests against the erection of mosques and Muslim congregation buildings, two attempts by the NPD in Bochum to protest against a planned new synagogue where banned. In June, finally, the local NPD succeeded and organized what it called the 'first demonstration against the erection of a synagogue in the Federal Republic of Germany'.[21]

Moreover, for the NPD it seemed much more attractive to focus their protests on Israel and the Middle East conflict.[22] In 2001 and 2002, the NPD successfully organized joint demonstrations with the 'free forces' in Jena and Berlin 'in solidarity with Palestine' (and Iraq). Anti-Israel-campaigns were in most cases organized by the neo-Nazi comradeships until 2005. Now the NPD forces of the Rhineland organized marches in Essen, Bochum and Dortmund in 'solidarity with Palestine' and against 'solidarity with Israel', and 'Zionist world rule'. But when in January 2009 they campaigned to 'Stop the Israeli Holocaust in the Gaza strip', the march was banned, (although some minor action happened the following day).

This example shows that there is still a certain red line the NPD are not

allowed to cross without provoking serious reactions by the state and civil society. The reminder of the Holocaust, in combination with the chosen place
and date (close to the Holocaust memorial and the Brandenburg Gate, a few
days before the date of the Nazi takeover, which is traditionally celebrated by
German neo-Nazis), took it one step too far. On the 'solidarity' marches of
2005 and 2006, when the NPD protested against Israel's policy in the Palestinian territories, it was in most cases allowed to march. Only in July 2006,
when the demonstrators called for the destruction of the Jewish state, were a
larger group of activists – amongst them Udo Voigt, then chairman of the
NPD – arrested by the police.

Solidarity activities for Palestine – often in the context of campaigns for
peace, or left wing, anti-imperialistic campaigns – are quite common. We
cannot discuss here to what extent those activities are also motivated by anti-
Semitic biases. The German far right's criticism of Israel is definitely not motivated by humanistic or pacifist sentiments. For them, Israel is the 'collective
Jew': an imagined ideal of unrestrained Jewishness; and moreover, the centre of the supposed Jewish global power and finance capital, and so forth.[23]
Social scientist Fabian Virchow has researched the strategy of responding to
far right demonstrations in Federal Germany through an analysis of the content of their appearances, rallies and marches:

> This anti-Semitism, sometimes declared to be anti-Zionism, has a long
> tradition in the German far right and, in the form of the victim/perpetrator
> reversal, serves among other things to relativize the Shoah.[24]

Party programme

However, is this anti-Semitism actually anchored in the NPD's party program? In contrast to the NSDAP, the NPD's official party program contains no
open support of anti-Semitism. Taking further programmatic material into consideration, however, it soon becomes clear that anti-Semitism pervades the
worldview of the NPD on every level. The 'Jew' envisioned by NPD's functionaries, supporters and voters, is the conspirator who is rotten to the core
and ultimately at the root of all evil. This is also shown in many NPD documents. An internal party advisory paper of June 2006 clearly manifests the

anti-Semitic and ethnic-nationalist grounding of the NPD.[25] Thus, under the heading 'Is the NPD an "anti-Semitic" party?' this document states:

> What is meant by anti-Semitism? The criticism of Jewish interest groups? Of course we reserve the right to criticize the big-mouthed comments and never-ending financial demands of the Central Council of Jews in Germany. There is no ban on criticizing Jews. Sixty years after the end of the war, we will not be morally blackmailed, politically subordinated and financially bled dry by the Holocaust industry, to use the Jew Norman Finkelstein's term [...] So anti-Semitism means the criticism of Jews? Of course Jews can be criticized too. No German has to put up with the Jewish-driven cult of guilt of the last sixty years and the never-ending topic of Jewish victims. The psychological warfare conducted by Jewish power groups against our people must finally stop. After all, it is clear that the Holocaust industry just intends to continue squeezing the Germans financially under moral pretexts.[26]

In the above exemplar of contemporary 'doublespeak' by the NPD, a clear range of anti-Semitic stereotypes are repeated and Jews are singled out as not belonging amongst 'the Germans'. In similar statements by far right parties and factions, members of the Jewish minority are regularly denied a place among the German nation.[27] However, in its current party program, the NPD chooses its words more carefully. Under 'Point 13: End the cult of guilt', for example, it says:

> For the sake of its future, Germany needs a national view of history that places the central focus on the continuity of the lives of our people. We National Democrats reject the state-decreed cult of guilt, which not least serves foreign financial interests and promotes German self-hatred, especially among the young. We resist the moral self-destruction of our nation that is brought about by the one-sided assignment of historical guilt on Germany, by the praise of acts of treason and the glorification of Allied war criminals. To preserve the honour of the German people, the biased treatment of the past must end and there must be freedom of research and instruction.[28]

215

Although Jews are not explicitly mentioned, anti-Semitic motifs are clearly apparent. For instance, in the contrast between 'our people' and 'foreign financial interests'. Finally, the demand for 'freedom of research and instruction' in this context refers quite clearly to the legalization and legitimization of a pseudo-academic denial of Nazi mass crimes.

Globalization as 'globalism'

A related area is the specifically far right focus on the topic of 'globalization', which forms an important campaign issue. The NPD quickly recognized the usefulness of this topic,[29] denouncing so-called globalization in its party program as early as 1996. From 2001, this catchword increasingly became a central focus of the NPD's propaganda. In January 2002, Party chairman Udo Voigt drew up a political strategy document for the party executive, delineating the socio-political thrust of the party. He declared 'globalism / globalization' to be the central issue of that year (one in which federal elections were scheduled). Globalism, as defined by Voigt, is one aspect of economic imperialism, [its] defining feature [the] erosion of state executive authority in favor of corporate rule [and its] methods [the] limiting of government mechanisms to control domestic markets, euphemistically called free trade. Globalization is, by this definition, the term used to denote the process of globalism, the consequences of which include 'poverty, unemployment, cuts in social services and the devastation of nature'.[30] At least in part, this anti-globalization campaign was designed to target voters of the Party of Democratic Socialism (*Partei des demokratischen Sozialismus* or PDS), the successor of East Germany's former Communist Party and later renamed The Left (*Die Linke*), and attract some supporters of the environmentalist and global justice movements in Germany. Yet in its advisory paper cited above, the NPD further argues:

Globalization is the planetary outgrowth of the capitalist mode of economy under the direction of big business. Although by nature, Jewish-nomadic and siteless, its main political and military headquarters are the East Coast of the USA. That is why globalization is a flagrant imperialist strategy of the USA to force the American Way of Life – or rather, the American Way of Death – exploitable by the major US companies, on to the whole world. [...] The cultural Americanization promoted by modern communication technologies and mass media weakens the organically grown identities of the nations and works towards a consumerist-conditioned global standard.

According to this conception, the global world order is shaped by the influence of a 'supranational' imperial power lying *behind* the major market forces and working towards maximizing profits, destabilizing nations and alienating their peoples. Albeit not explicitly named, these Jewish forces are supposedly based above all in the USA and in Israel – often shortened to 'USrael' on the scene – and formerly also in other political centers (especially the Soviet Union). Their main goals include weakening Germany as well as destabilizing and controlling the Middle East.

The NPD's aggressive agitation against 'brutal interest-capitalism' refers to classical and central motifs of right-wing extremist economic and social programs: it is against the 'financial', more precisely 'loan capital', and agitates to 'break the bonds of "Interest Slavery"'. A critique of capitalism from the right traditionally begins with the sphere of circulation and tends to systematically overestimate the role of financial capital. The admittedly increased influence of this sector throughout the twentieth century, however, certainly spurs such ideas. Indeed, the fatal consequences of individual financial transactions as well as the structural problems resulting from the changes in the global capital markets are easily absorbed and mobilized. One should not conclude from this, however, that concern about these actual tendencies is the driving motivation, because beyond all thematic actuality a high level of programmatic continuity can be seen in this area as well.

But such anti-Semitic motivation is not pushed into the forefront in all texts by NPD authors. Thus a text about the 'foundations of a national democratic macro-economic doctrine' mentions the speculative maneuvers of the investment banker George Soros and its consequences – perhaps exaggerating them, but it refrains from mentioning his Jewish origins.[31] In the party programs, and in some other arenas, the explicit mention of Jews is avoided, while the propaganda works with stereotypes, which are coded sometimes less obviously than others, but at least in the closer circle of addressees are easily decodable.

As this suggests, the NPD has a tenor which prejudices can tap into: the

217

widespread disapproval of the state of Israel; criticism of the USA and its policies (upon which supposedly Jewish lobbyists have too strong an influence);
the enduring stereotype of the 'rich Jew'; and lastly, the 'exonerative anti-
Semitism' mentioned above, which seeks to conclude the critical examination
of the German past and accuses the Jews of making money out of the Holocaust. But even if anti-Semitism is not used to attract voters to the NPD, the
party needs its concept of the nefarious 'Jews'. Only in this way can it offer a
neat explanation of the world and integrate it within the anachronistic, contradictory worldview of the far right.

It may be, in conclusion, that such encoded hostility towards Jews might
not even be deciphered at the grass roots of the NPD. But in fact, precisely
here, simple key terms and catchphrases are enough, especially since far
right audiences are by now used to this form of doublespeak. In its publications, the NPD continues to use an array of ciphers and codes which are not
immediately obvious to the newcomer but which make it clear to activists
what is meant by 'the Israelis', 'the American East Coast' or the 'global no-
madic finance capital', to name just a few. If one deciphers these codes, the
rhetoric of a Jewish-based power conspiratorially working against German interests becomes clearly apparent in the basic political precepts and discourse
of the NPD and similar far right groups operating today.

ENDNOTES

[1] Bundesministerium des Innern, *Antisemitismus in Deutschland. Erscheinungsformen,
Bedingungen, Präventionsansätze. Bericht des unabhängigen Expertenkreises Antisemitismus* (Berlin: BMI, 2011), p. 24.

[2] Ibid.

[3] Werner Bergmann and Wilhelm Heitmeyer, 'Communicating Anti-Semitism. Are the
"Boundaries of the Speakable" Shifting?', *Tel Aviver Jahrbuch für deutsche Geschich-
te*, 33 (2005), pp. 70 – 89, 72; see Werner Bergmann and Rainer Erb, 'Kommunikationslatenz, Moral und öffentliche Meinung. Theoretische Überlegungen zum Antisemitismus in der Bundesrepublik Deutschland', *Kölner Zeitschrift für Soziologie und So-
zialpsychologie*, 38 (1986), pp. 223 – 246; Werner Bergmann and Rainer Erb, *Anti-
Semitism in Germany. The Post-Nazi Epoch since 1945* (New Brunswick: Transaction
Publications, 1997); Werner Bergmann, 'Is there a New "European Antisemitism?"
Public Opinion and Comparative Empirical Research in Europe', in Lars Rensmann
and Julius H. Schoeps eds., *Politics and Resentment. Antisemitism and Counter-
Cosmopolitanism in the European Union* (Leiden: Brill, 2010), pp. 83 – 116.

[4] Lars Rensmann and Julius H. Schoeps, 'Politics and Resentment: Examining Antisemitism and Counter-Cosmopolitanism in the European Union and Beyond', in Rensmann and Schoeps eds., *Politics and Resentment*, pp. 3 – 80, 12; see Lars Rens-

mann, *Demokratie und Judenbild. Antisemitismus in der politischen Kultur der Bundesrepublik Deutschland* (Wiesbaden: VS, 2004); Bergmann and Heitmeyer, 'Communicating Anti-Semitism'; Samuel Salzborn, *Antisemitismus als negative Leitidee der Moderne. Sozialwissenschaftliche Theorien im Vergleich* (Frankfurt/New York: Campus, 2010); Monika Schwarz-Friesel, Evyatar Friesel and Jehuda Reinharz eds., *Aktueller Antisemitismus – ein Phänomen der Mitte* (Berlin/New York: de Gruyter, 2010).

[5] Bundesamt für Verfassungsschutz ed., *Die Bedeutung des Antisemitismus im aktuellen deutschen Rechtsextremismus* (Köln: BfV 2002), p. 38.

[6] Ibid., p. 3; see also Juliane Wetzel, 'Antisemitismus im internationalen Rechtsextremismus', in Herbert Strauss, Werner Bergmann and Christhard Hoffmann eds., *Der Antisemitismus der Gegenwart* (Frankfurt/Main / New York: Campus 1990), pp. 101 – 123; Juliane Wetzel, 'Antisemitismus als Element rechtsextremer Ideologie und Propaganda', in Wolfgang Benz, Wolfgang ed., *Antisemitismus in Deutschland. Zur Aktualität eines Vorurteils* (Munich: dtv 1995). It remains to be discussed whether this statement also applies to those forces which have reoriented their strategy towards taking an anti-Islamic stance. We believe that their demonstrative support of Israel by no means necessarily indicates abandonment of basic anti-Semitic sentiments. It seems to merely constitute an attempt to employ Israel as a supposed ally in the 'fight against Islam' and suggest that the extreme right anti-Semitism has been superseded by anti-Muslim prejudice.

[7] 'Bundesministerium des Inneren', *Antisemitismus in Deutschland*, p. 21.

[8] Julius H. Schoeps and Joachim Schlör eds., *Antisemitismus. Vorurteile und Mythen* (Munich: Zweitausendeins, 1995); Jüdisches Museum Wien ed., *Die Macht der Bilder. Antisemitische Vorurteile und Mythen* (Vienna: Picus, 1995); Wolfgang Benz, *Bilder vom Juden. Studien zum alltäglichen Antisemitismus* (Munich: Beck, 2001).

[9] See Rensmann, *Demokratie und Judenbild*; Benz, *Bilder vom Juden.*

[10] Rensmann and Schoeps eds., *Politics and Resentment*, p. 474; see also Rensmann, *Demokratie und Judenbild.*

[11] Brigitte Bailer-Galanda, Wolfgang Benz and Wolfgang Neugebauer eds., *Die Auschwitzleugner. 'Revisionistische' Geschichtslüge und historische Wahrheit* (Berlin: Elefanten Press, 1996); Elke Mayer Verfälschte Vergangenheit, *Zur Entstehung der Holocaust-Leugnung in der Bundesrepublik Deutschland unter besonderer Berücksichtigung rechtsextremer Publizistik von 1945 bis 1970* (Frankfurt: Peter Lang, 2003).

[12] See Regina Wamper, *Das Kreuz mit der Nation. Christlicher Antisemitismus in der Jungen Freiheit* (Münster: Unrast, 2008).

[13] See Lars Rensmann, *Kritische Theorie über den Antisemitismus. Studien zu Struktur, Erklärungspotential und Aktualität* (Berlin/Hamburg: Argument, 1998); Rensmann, *Demokratie und Judenbild*; Salzborn, *Antisemitismus als negative Leitidee der Moderne.*

[14] Certain comments glorifying the Nazis or using symbols of banned organizations, approving of or denying their crimes, or inciting violence against minorities are in certain circumstances excluded from the right to freedom of opinion in Germany and have been made a punishable offence under criminal law. In addition, a state agency, the *Bundesprüfstelle für Jugendgefährdende Medien* (Federal Department for Media Harmful to Young Persons), can put – according to the Youth Protection Law – a legal ban on the distribution of objects it considers to be 'harmful or dangerous to minors', which is the case if the material tends to 'endanger their process of developing a so-

cially responsible and self-reliant personality. In general, this applies to objects that contain indecent, extremely violent, crime-inducing, anti-Semitic or otherwise racist material', cit. http://www.bundespruefstelle.de/bpjm/information-in-english.html (accessed 18/05/2012). Anti-Semitism is *nota bene* explicitly mentioned here.

[15] Rainer Erb, 'Antisemitismus in der rechten Jugendszene', in Werner Bergmann and Rainer Erb eds., *Neonazismus und rechte Subkultur* (Berlin: Metropol, 1994), pp. 31 – 76; Rainer Erb, 'Er ist kein Mensch, er ist ein Jud. Antisemitismus im Rechtsrock', in Dieter Baacke, Klaus Farin and Jürgen Lauffer eds., *Rock von Rechts II. Milieus, Hintergründe und Materialien* (Bielefeld: GMK, 1999); Gideon Botsch, 'Gewalt, Profit und Propaganda. Konturen des rechtsextremen Musiknetzwerkes', in *Blätter für deutsche und internationale Politik* 46 (2001), pp. 335 – 344; Christian Dornbusch and Jan Raabe eds., *RechtsRock, Bestandsaufnahme und Gegenstrategien* (Münster: Unrast, 2002).

[16] Rainer Erb, 'Der ewige Jude. Die Bildersprache des Antisemitismus in der rechtsextremen Szene', in Archiv der Jugendkulturen ed., *Reaktionäre Rebellen. Rechtsextreme Musik in Deutschland* (Berlin: Tilsner, 2001).

[17] For the following historical overview, see Gideon Botsch, *Die extreme Rechte in der Bundesrepublik Deutschland 1949 bis Heute* (Darmstadt: WBG, 2012).

[18] We still miss a profound study of the unexpressed anti-Semitic content which functions as an ideological framework for the racist and xenophobic concepts of 'Überfremdung' or 'Volkstod' (Death of the Nation). Cf. Rensmann, *Demokratie und Judenbild*.

[19] On the NPD see, inter alia, Uwe Hoffmann, *Die NPD. Entwicklung, Ideologie und Struktur* (Frankfurt: Peter Lang, 1999); Uwe Backes and Henrik Steglich eds., *Die NPD. Erfolgsbedingungen einer rechtsextremistischen Partei* (Baden-Baden: Nomos, 2007); Gideon Botsch and Christoph Kopke, *Die NPD und ihr Milieu. Studien und Berichte* (Münster/Ulm: Klemm und Oelschläger, 2009).

[20] See Fabian Virchow, 'Demonstrativer Antisemitismus. Wie die extreme Rechte den Antisemitismus auf die Straße trägt', in Gideon Botsch et al., (eds.,) '...und handle mit Vernunft'. Beiträge zur europäisch-jüdischen Beziehungsgeschichte (Hildesheim: Olms, 2012), pp. 398 – 417, 403.

[21] Ibid., p. 411.

[22] Ibid., p. 405.

[23] Lars Rensmann, Der Nahost-Konflikt in der Perzeption des Rechts- und Linksextremismus', in Klas Faber, Julius H. Schoeps and Sacha Stawski eds., *Neu-alter Judenhass. Antisemitismus, arabisch-israelischer Konflikt und europäische Politik* (Potsdam: VBB, 2006), pp. 33 – 48, 34 – 36.

[24] Virchow, *Demonstrativer Antisemitismus*, p. 404.

[25] Rainer Erb and Michael Kohlstruck, 'Die Funktionen von Antisemitismus und Fremdenfeindlichkeit für die rechtsextreme Bewegung', in Stephan Braun, Alexander Geisler and Martin Gerster eds., *Strategien der extremen Rechten. Hintergründe – Analysen – Antworten* (Wiesbaden: VS, 2009), pp. 419 – 439, 427; Fabian Virchow, *Argumente für Kandidaten und Funktionsträger demokratischer Parteien und Wählervereinigungen 2008 – Eine Entgegnung auf ein Schulungsmaterial der NPD* (Potsdam: TB, 2008).

[26] NPD-Parteivorstand – Amt für Öffentlichkeitsarbeit ed., *Argumente für Kandidaten und Funktionsträger. Eine Handreichung für die öffentliche Auseinandersetzung* (Berlin: NPD 2006), p. 10; see Virchow, *Argumente*.

[27] Cf. Report on Anti-Semitism 2011: p. 15.

[28] NPD ed., *Arbeit. Familie. Vaterland. Das Parteiprogramm der Nationaldemokratischen Partei Deutschland (NPD). Beschlossen auf dem Bundesparteitag am 4. / 5. 6. 2010 in Bamberg* (Berlin: NPD, 2010), p. 14.

[29] For a detailed analysis of this phenomenon see: Gideon Botsch and Christoph Kopke, 'National Solidarity – No to Globalization. The Economic and Sociopolitical Platform of the National Democratic Party of Germany (NPD)', in Sabine v. Mering and Timothy W. McCarty eds., *Right-Wing Radicalism Today. Perspectives from Europe and the USA* (London/New York: Routledge, 2013, p. 37 – 59).

[30] NPD-Parteivorstand ed., *Strategische Leitlinien zur politischen Arbeit der NPD. Positionspapier des Parteivorstandes* (Berlin: NPD, 2002).

[31] NPD-Parteivorstand ed., *Grundlagen einer nationaldemokratischen Volkswirtschaftslehre. Raumorientierte Volkswirtschaft statt Basar-Ökonomie. Positionspapier des Arbeitskreises Wirtschaftspolitik beim NPD-Parteivorstand* (Berlin: NPD, 2006), p. 23.

'FASCISM FOR THE THIRD MILLENNIUM': AN OVERVIEW OF LANGUAGE AND IDEOLOGY IN ITALY'S CASAPOUND MOVEMENT

Anna Castriota and Matthew Feldman[1]

> We want to become protagonists of our times and not just some extras in a show whose script has already been written, giving us the part of being evil, subversives, fanatical. We will please our enemies if we would behave like this. We are not going to hide in the basements to conspire in the shadow. Commander D'Annunzio, accused of a plot against the regime, of which he was a fierce adversary, answered: 'I dare, not conspire'. This is also our motto.

Introduction: 'Set keel to breakers, forth on the godly sea'[2]

At first sight, CasaPound seems a raft of contradictions. On the one hand, this is an Italian far right movement whose loosely affiliated supporters, according to the first Anglophone report on their online profile, are more likely to advocate violence than any other 'populist group' in contemporary Europe.[3] On the other hand, this still-predominately social movement blossomed via traditionally left-wing housing occupations; and moreover, owes its name to the (in)famous American poet, Ezra Pound. Hardly traditional fare for the notoriously influential far right in postwar Italy. Furthermore, CasaPound openly praises Mussolini and advocates a return to Italian Fascism, yet at the same time disseminates its message and organizes its activities chiefly through new media technologies. So just what gives with CasaPound?

This lack of clarity typically extends to the few commentators who have thus far tried to explain CasaPound. According to the Swiss historian Aram Mattioli, for instance, CasaPound should be considered within the context of flourishing far right groups in Italy following the collapse of the Soviet Union and the end of the Italian First Republic in the first half of the 1990s.[4] To be sure, the demise of communism and the Italian political scandal dubbed 'Mani Pulite [Clean Hands]' created a completely new scenario in the country, doubtless contributing to the rise of a populist far right in Italy over the last generation.[5] In stark contrast, sociologists Daniele di Nunzio and Emilio Toscano note the originality of CasaPound with respect to Italian far right groups of this century: 'From the sociological analysis here, the distance of CasaPound from the cultural references, political and social composition of the Italian radical right emerges clearly, by their proposing a new interpretation of fascism aimed to overcome the dichotomy right-left'.[6] So which is it? Or can it be both: that CasaPound is part and parcel of Italy's well-entrenched far right; *and* that the movement's 'originality' marks it out as something different from Italian rightist movements like the Northern League (Lega Nord, LN), the National Alliance (Alleanza Nazionale, AN which before 1995 took the form of the influential 'post-fascist' MSI, or Movimento Sociale Italiano); and most recently, the far-right Tricolored Flame (Movimento Sociale-Fiamma Tricolore, MS-FT)?[7]

As perhaps Italy's most recent and novel group in a rash of post-, neo- and unashamedly fascist movements since 1945 – itself concluding nearly 23 years of political domination by Benito Mussolini's Italian Fascists (Partito Nazionale Fascista, or PNF) – CasaPound first 'officially' appeared in 2003 under the leadership of the long-time far right activist and musician, Gianluca Iannone, a self-styled 'fascist of the third millennium'. For all the movement's socio-political attempts to 'Make it New', to use Ezra Pound's celebrated advice for modernist cultural production, twentieth century precursors and influences are clearly apparent over the first decade of CasaPound's development. In this respect, it is worth noting that Ezra Pound's catchphrase was itself adapted from a sixth century Chinese inscription: 'Make it new day by day make it new'.[8] So too with CasaPound's relationship with fascism in Italy, both before and after the watershed year of 1945: there is little of ideological substance that is new here under the Italian sun.

As suggested by the above, this chapter provides a thematic overview of the CasaPound movement, paying especial attention to its use of language along the way – particularly that of Iannone, undeniably the movement's 'charismatic personality'. That a canonical poet-turned-fascist is 'name-checked' in the movement's very title, moreover, suggests the utility of this discursive approach.[9] That the role of language (since time immemorial a reservoir for poets and writers), was key to Pound himself is announced, for instance, in his 'Addendum for C' notes for his self-defined 'epic poem including history', *The Cantos*:

> A pity that poets have used symbol and metaphor
> and no man learned anything from them
> for their speaking in figures.[10]

Pound composed this during WWII, when his support of fascism facilitated thousands of pro-Axis radio items; in turn leading to his indictment for treason by the US government. This was not, of course, lost on CasaPound's founder, who said in an interview:

> Ezra Pound was a poet, an economist and an artist. Ezra Pound was a revolutionary and a fascist. Ezra Pound had to suffer for his ideas, he was sent to jail for ten years to make him stop speaking. We see in Ezra Pound a free man that paid for his ideas; he is a symbol of the 'democratic views' of the winners.[11]

These 'ideas' included advocating a spiritual and economic vision of fascist ideology, while without doubt – in keeping with Axis wartime propaganda – anti-Semitism was a major part of Pound's rhetoric at this time. Revealingly, the symbol referred to in the 1941 fragment cited above was *'neschek'* – 'the crawling evil / slime, the corrupter of all things' – an ancient Hebrew word for usury; which by that time closely connected in both Pound's poetry and wartime broadcasts, with the latter bringing about treason charges in July 1943. Considering the prominence of the 'Pound Case' during these years and, indeed, since, scholars have exhaustively analyzed the depths and drivers of Pound's often-scurrilous anti-Semitism.[12] To cite but three excerpts published as long ago as 1976 – taken from literally scores contained in Pound's 1,516 page FBI file – in his shortwave broadcasts from Radio Rome to the US and UK, Pound announced:

Nothing can save you, save a purge. Nothing can save you, save an affirmation that you are English. Hore-Belisha is not. Isaacs is not. No Sassoon is an Englishman racially. No Rothschild is English, no Streiker is English, no Roosevelt is English, no Baruch, Morgenthau, Cohen, Lehman, Warburg, Kuhn, Kahn, Schiff, Sieff or Solomon was ever yet born Anglo-Saxon. And it is for this filth that you fight. (15 March 1942)

Don't start a pogrom. That is, not an old style killing of small Jews. That system is no good, whatever. Of course, if some man had a stroke of genius, and could start a pogrom at the top. (30 April 1942)

Just which of you are free from Jewish influence? Just which political and business groups are free from Jew influence, from Jew control? Who holds the mortgage, who is the dominating director? (19 March 1943)[13]

Obviously, Pound's anti-Semitism was neither a debatable case like, say, T.S. Eliot's; nor a purely literary one as with J.F. Céline. Instead, this became Nazi-style anti-Semitism, enthusiastically undertaken for Axis ends throughout the period of the Holocaust. Nonetheless, in the aforementioned interview with the founder of CasaPound, Iannone made this remarkable claim about Pound's anti-Semitism:

To associate Ezra Pound and anti-Semitism is an absolute twist. It is the same for CasaPound, it has no sense. It is true that we are against Israel['s] politics towards Palestinians, against the bombing of civilians, and the embargo on international help. To say so does not mean to be anti-Semitic, it means analyzing facts.[14]

As this single example highlights, then, language can be used as much to conceal as clarify. In keeping with many Italian far right movements since the watershed of 1945, this is of particular relevance to CasaPound – even if its online presence and the social movement aspects of its organization clearly mark it out as a manifestation of the European 'new far right'[15] – indeed, more specifically as a kind of 'Fascism for the third millennium'. Before moving on to a closer examination of CasaPound, however, a brief consideration of this term is in order.

In twenty-first century Italy there remain several 'fascist', 'neo-fascist' and even 'post-fascist' political movements. This spectrum is broad enough to range from legitimate, *democratic* political parties sitting in Parliament, to far more *revolutionary* expressions of fascist ideology. This may seem to the observer to be a kind of *contradictio in terminis*, or may at least signify a failure in the process of de-fascistization that the country went through after WWII.[16] This is borne out by an interview with the far right journalist, Marcello Veneziani, in response to one of the authors' questions about how it was possible to have an openly xenophobic party like Lega Nord sitting in the Italian parliament. In response, Veneziani replied that they were 'post-fascists' or 'fascists of the third millennium', who believed in an inclusive form of democracy rather than an exclusive one.[17] Similarly, there are other 'post-fascist' movements in Italy that similarly propose a new version of Fascist ideas in an attempt not to simply re-affirm their shared ideology, but, rather, to revitalize – in a different format and context – the same ideological core; sometimes expressed as a 'return to the future'.[18]

In much the same way, CasaPound reveals key elements of continuity with the past *as well as* updating core fascist concepts and forms of self-representation. Especially relevant in terms of the latter is the prominent use of new media (notably the internet), not only for organizational messages and discussions but for the cultural dissemination of the arts, music and so on. Yet whatever its audio-visual effectiveness, even a cursory analysis of the movement reveals a strong impulse to openly declare their radical ideological and political inclinations. This too is correspondingly borne out in another interview with Iannone from late 2011:

CasaPound is based around four principles: culture, solidarity, sport and (obviously) politics. These four domains can be seen as social actions in one way or another. CPI organize book presentations, plays, concerts, debates about movies and has a monthly publication (*Occidentale*) [...] We try to communicate in a radical mode and renew our dream. We want to launch it and give it a new spin. It could be through music or art.[19]

CasaPound Italia: 'Noi ci facciam scannar per Mussolini'

'CasaPound Italia', to give the movement its full name (often abbreviated as CPI, as above), is an association of recent formation. In fact, the movement's 'unofficial' birth occurred on 12 July 2002, when a group of well-known far right activists occupied a public building that had been empty for several years, in order to house some of those unable to rent or own a property. As is usually reported in media accounts of CasaPound, this type of squatting is generally regarded as 'socialist', and has long been the preserve of left-wing groups.[20] The occupied building in Rome was renamed 'CasaMontag' – after Guy Montag, the protagonist of Ray Bradbury's science fiction novel *Fahrenheit 451* – giving rise to what were called ONCs (Occupazioni Non Conformi, or Non-conformist occupations). On 26 December 2003, the same group then occupied a building on the Via Napoleone in Rome and renamed it the 'CasaPound Italia'. Interestingly, in providing their own account of the movement's origins on its website, the illegal occupation of derelict buildings are referred to as 'mine vaganti' (loose cannon) operations. Here too, stress is placed upon the voluntarism of the movement and its 'non-conformist' stance. In this sense, CasaPound is clearly different from the more party-political tendencies within the Italian far right. In fact, Iannone and the movement largely refuse any association with established far right groups, claiming to operate on a different level:

> Q: What kind of relationship does CasaPound have with the other parties of the so-called 'Radical Right'?
> A: CPI is external and autonomous to any party. Being independent means that we can dialogue and cooperate with any party that is willing to have an honest confrontation, whether this party would be internal or external to the 'Radical Right'.[21]

Here again, language plays its part in casting the movement as 'independent'. In reinforcing this sense of a seemingly amorphous political grouping, another interview by Iannone responds directly to the charge that Casa-Pound is a far right organization:

First of all, linking CP to the right-wing is a bit restrictive. CasaPound Italia is a political movement organized as an association for social promotion. It starts from the right and goes through the entire political panorama. Right or Left are two old visions of politics; we need to give birth to a new synthesis.[22]

In making such declarations of political and ideological neutrality, the group's 'front-stage' rhetoric aims to portray an openness towards those with different ideas and perspectives. Yet in also signaling to a more hard-core 'backstage', the attentive reader can detect in Iannone's characterization of CasaPound a transcendence of the right and left, a hallmark of fascism's self-representation, identified by the late George Mosse, as 'a revolution attempting to find a 'Third Way' between Marxism and capitalism'.[23] These ideas were clearly delineated in Benito Mussolini and Giovanni Gentile's widely-circulated 1932 *Enciclopedia Italiana* entry for 'The Doctrine of Fascism':

> Fascism is totalitarian, and the Fascist State, the synthesis and unity of all values interprets, develops, and gives strength to the whole life of the people... Therefore Fascism is opposed to Socialism, which confines the movement of history within the class struggle [...] Fascism is opposed to Democracy, which equates the nation to the majority.[24]

Correspondingly, and as proclaimed by CasaPound's official website, the idea of a movement approaching political action like the post-war Italian left was conceived still earlier, in the late 1990s, when a group of far right activists frequenting the neo-fascist pub 'The Cutty Sark' in Rome, decided to create a more structured political identity for their meetings. The hagiographical account on CasaPound's website further announces that, far from being a rag-tag collection of neo-Nazis or skinheads, these activists were instead a 'group of rebel souls'.[25] CasaPound's opaque use of the expression 'rebel souls' discursively appears non-political – simply referring to those rejecting the perceived socio-political conformity of contemporary Italy. Moreover, from their own, sanitized history of the movement it seems that the expression 'rebels' is an overture towards a broader section of 'non-conformist' society rather than just those defining themselves as 'fascists' or far right supporters. The expression 'rebel souls' additionally recalls the enthusiasm and energy surrounding the Italian avant-garde movement in the years leading up to the Great War. Here too, another not-so-concealed fascist element may be identified. Published in 1909 by Filippo T. Marinetti, the first *Futurist Manifesto* advances strikingly similar views of 'freedom' and 'rebellion' found in Casa-Pound's official declarations.

Correspondingly, two groups stemming from the main movement of CasaPound bear close resemblance to Italian Futurism; an avant-garde movement that was, in some respects, the midwife of Mussolini's subsequent *Fascismo*. The first is called 'Turbodinamismo' (Turbodynamism), a group whose link appears on CasaPound's official webpage. Without mincing words, the *Manifesto del Turbodinamismo* proclaims that 'Turbodynamism is the glorification of the gratuitous, violent and inconsiderate gesture'.[26] In fact, the very choice of the group's name recalls central elements of the Futurist message: 'Except in struggle, there is no more beauty. No work without an aggressive character can be a masterpiece. Poetry must be conceived as a violent attack on unknown forces, to reduce and prostrate them before man'.[27] Both Italian manifestos, moreover, emphatically praise recourse to violent action as the privileged means of self-affirmation.

The second, artistic sub-group deriving from CasaPound is named 'Artisti per CasaPound' (Artists for CasaPound). Once more, there is a thread connecting Italian Fascism and Futurism: 'This group is a group of artists who express in the arts projects devoted to the idea of beauty and freedom; they can only find such freedom of expression in the non-conformist culture always promoted by CP'.[28] A similar aim of creating a 'new man', who is able to rise above the constrictions of middle-class mediocrity, is another commonplace in fascist ideology; long ago articulated as the *homo fascistus,* so dear to Mussolini. Fascist Party Secretary Achille Starace – who declared in November 1933 that the title 'Duce' could only be spelled in capitals – phrased this myth of the *uomo nuovo* succinctly in a laudatory speech just before the outbreak of World War Two: 'The creation of the man, of Mussolini's new Italian, capable of believing, of obeying, of fighting, has been our constant objective, towards which the Party has channeled all of its forces'.[29]

Yet another key continuity with Mussolini's Italy, updated by CasaPound, is the importance of youth – the very name of Mussolini's Fascist Anthem ('*Giovinezza*'). Writing as Party Secretary for Mussolini's PNF in 1931, Giovanni Giurati stressed: 'It is among the young that all the great movements in history have found their prophets, their soldiers, their martyrs. It is well known that the more life is held in contempt, the more value it acquires, and the young, since they are more prepared to embrace a faith are precisely for this reason more prepared to pay the final sacrifice for it'.[30] Accordingly, it is important to note that the average age of a CasaPound member is between 18 and 30. This owes much to the movement's active promotion of social and cultural events, especially sport:

> CPI works on everything that concerns the life of our nation: from sport to solidarity, culture and of course politics. For sports, we have a soccer team and academy, we do hockey, rugby, skydiving, boxing, Brazilian jiu-jitsu, scuba diving, hiking groups, caving, and climbing. For solidarity, we have first aid teams, we do fundraising activities for the Karen people, and we provide help to orphans and single-mums. A phone line called 'Dillo to CasaPound' (tell it to CasaPound) is active 24/7 to give free advice on legal and tax issues. On the cultural ground, we host authors and organize book presentations; we have an artist club, a theatre school, free guitar, bass guitar and drum lessons, we created an artistic trend called Turbodinamismo, we have a publishing company, dozens of bookshops and websites. Politically we propose various laws like the Mutuo sociale (social mortgage), Tempo di essere Madri (Time to be a mother) or against water privatization and so many more. Speaking about CPI is never easy because all these things are CASAPOUND. All of these represent our challenges and projects for now and for the millennium.[31]

Furthermore, Iannone is only in his mid-forties, and cultivates the image of youth as the lead singer in the movement's 'house band'. Indeed, one of the first acts in the movement's 'pre-history' was the 1997 formation of the punk band Zetazeroalfa. Given that, like sport, music is typically regarded as a privileged tool of communication among young people, the presence of a populist rock band has undoubtedly contributed to the resonance of Casa-Pound's political message.

This valorization of youth, moreover, is a constant trait. One of Casa-Pound's favoured slogans is 'ho 17 anni per sempre' (I am seventeen forever), underscoring the ideological role of youth for the movement. Violently bearing this out is another practice – as revealing as it is now notorious – '*Cinghiamattanza*' (literally 'belt-fighting'). Iannone's band, Zetazeroalfa, plays a song aimed at whipping up frenetic energy in 'mosh pits' with the following lyrics:

> One, I take off the belt, Two, the dance will start, Three, I will get to choose my target, Four, Cinghiamattanza! [...] Here there is the whip, the room is on fire, the life of the Ardito is burning, you will yell Cinghiamattanza![32]

This practice has become a trademark for CasaPound's image, and even has an associated blogspot, declaring that 'Cinghiamattanza is a macabre dance that we have among camerati [sic], a physical expression of style and force. Cinghiamattanza is honor, is street fighting but with an ethics of its own; constructive confusion, sweat and will. Ultimately, Cinghiamattanza is an act of love'. After music performances or even belt-fighting tournaments, the less-than-tender injuries thus obtained are often exhibited online as quasi-'war' wounds (particularly evident through social networking sites, as well as on YouTube and on a range of dedicated webpages).[33] On occasion, Casa-Pound's leadership tries to play down the culture of Cinghiamattanza, claiming it is merely a way for youths to channel their natural force and vitality. Yet whatever the front-stage presentation, in practice, Cinghiamattanza is also employed when members of CasaPound are involved in clashes with political opponents.

Other characteristics, revealing 'updated continuities' with the historical experience of Fascism in Italy, are voluntarism and the cult of action. A similar impulse to radically effect change leads CasaPound's website to proclaim: 'To us politics is action, direct and popular participation is the most simple way to solve conflicts and social injustices'.[34] This stress upon politics as action re-calls another core principle of Italian Fascism. This too can be traced to Iannone's band Zetazeroalfa; for instance, in the lyrics of the '*Nel Dubbio, Mena*' (When In doubt, just fight):

> When in doubt, fight! I miss the synopsis, I miss the photocopy, I miss the pain of living, I miss the sunshine of the future, I miss what is right, I miss our world, I miss a new fridge and everything else, I miss also the hair-

dryer with whom I don't do a fuck, I please myself and then I am not longer embarrassed. No, don't be worried! In doubt, fight and you will see that you will live longer! No, don't be worried! In doubt fight and you will see that you will live longer, longer, longer!!!![35]

The lyrics express a *malaise de vivre* of youth and the failure of socialism (referred to as the 'sunshine of the future') and the bourgeois assumptions of capitalism (symbolized by the fridge and the hairdryer). This homage to youth – to whom the song is clearly addressed – is not one of despair but instead an encouragement to activism. Correspondingly, the conclusive verses of the song quite simply glorify violence; fighting is valorized in order to feel more alive, to live longer. In other words, the song is a hymn to the use of violence as an expression of a vitalistic, youthful force, one that is considered a positive response to socio-political issues of the day. It is not quite Mussolini's favored slogan *'Libro e moschetto – fascista perfetto'* (Book and rifle – perfect fascist), but the similarities are palpable.

More generally, CasaPound refers to Zetazeroalfa as a 'challenge to the world of the equals', the cornerstone of liberal democracy.[36] This objection is no mere anachronism of the movement, but is better understood in light of Mussolini's well-known criticism of democracy – advanced in the 1932 'Doctrine of Fascism', notes John Pollard,

in the clearest terms, a rejection of the liberal-democratic doctrine of individual, imprescriptible human rights: The principle that society exists solely for the well-being and liberty of the individuals who compose it does not seem to fit with the laws of nature, laws which only take the species into consideration and sacrifice the individual.[37]

Understood in this sense, equality becomes little more than a 'false impression' provided by liberalism. Nor is the connection fanciful: Gianluca Iannone is among those creating an honor squad to stand continuously outside Mussolini's tomb in his birth place, the small town of Predappio.

The documents from the Fascist era most frequently invoked by Casa-Pound are the *Carta del Lavoro* (*Labour Charter*, 1927) and the *Discorso di Verona* (*Verona Manifesto* for the Saló Republic, 1943). These two texts exemplify Fascism's 'third way' attempts at socialism for the nation and, despite being written sixteen years apart and in quite different historical circumstances, are nevertheless attempts to balance continuing social injustices in the Italian system. The 1927 *Carta*, for instance, represents an answer to the socialist and communist trade unions that had recently been banned. The *Carta* thus superseded all prior laws used to regulate labor questions in Italy. The document is simple, containing an introduction and 18 points detailing the economic matters to be regulated. The *Verona Manifesto*, for its part, was proclaimed under Nazi occupation in Autumn 1943; it is in this respect less 'third way' than 'radical right'. More generally, in comparing the *Carta* and Mussolini's 1943 *Verona Manifesto* with the CasaPound political program, a number of interesting parallels arise. The latter declares: 'Because of its history and its destiny, Italy has to again be a forerunner within a Europe that has to be united, independent, sovereign, at peace and peaceful'.[38] Interestingly enough, this is directly evocative of the *Verona Manifesto's* endorsement of 'the creation of a "European community" through the federation of all nations'.[39] Fascism's advocacy for a pan-European federation is an important aspect of CasaPound's vision – and a decidedly anti-EU one. The movement's official website correspondingly offers the following explanation of CasaPound's monthly magazine, *L'Occidentale*:

The West (Occidente) etymology means *sol occidens*, the setting sun. It is historically and geopolitically that land born as a result of hate for Europe and that has infused the old continent with bombs, imposing upon the world a regime made of arrogance, robbery and homogenization.[40]

Revealingly, *L'Occidentale* resumed publication under CasaPound but, before its lapse, remained a journal with strong ties to Italian neo-fascism.[41]

By contrast, more difficult to pinpoint is the degree of xenophobia and racism – the hallmark of far right movements in Europe for literally decades – advocated by CasaPound. The movement advances the notion that they are not racists at all. A good example highlighted online is a 'mission' undertaken by CasaPound members to the Serbian enclaves in Kosovo in order to bring food, medicines and general relief. Importantly, the aid was addressed to the Christian Serbs and not, for instance, to Muslim Albanians in Kosovo. This is needed,

CasaPound declares, because '[Serbian] villages, homes, schools, hospitals are "hostages" of an Albanian electricity company which manages the distribution of electricity in the area'.[42] CasaPound's relief mission may thus be interpreted as an attempted defense of a white, Christian minority within an area of Muslim majority – a trend strikingly in keeping with the contemporary far right across Europe. When challenged on controversial topics like religious tolerance or xenophobia, CasaPound's front-stage answer seems one of openness to diversity. Yet here too, careful reading suggests a language used to signal key 'backstage' fascist traits:

> Q: Is CasaPound a xenophobic movement?
> A: Absolutely not. Phobias are by their own definitions for all those of weak intellects and fearful hearts. CPI wants to do an analysis [of the problem immigration] and provide solutions not feed obsessions. We want radical analysis and non-conformist solutions without looking for the simplest solution, to look for scape goats [sic]. We are not interested in a war between paupers, and the fears of the bourgeoisie. That said, this does not mean that our condemnation of mass migration, of the multi-racist society is less strong.[43]

What is interesting to notice in the above passage is a conciliatory tone at the start, quickly followed by an affirmation of xenophobia. Use of the term 'multi-racist' rather than 'multi-racial' is not accidental, for 'multi-racist' underlines the notion that human groups can be neatly divided into 'races', which are ultimately better off remaining 'pure' rather than 'mixed'. This interpretation is supported by CasaPound's position on immigration, as set out in their political program:

> The infernal migratory mechanism is one of the main elements of loss of identity and social, cultural and existentialist impoverishment of all the populations involved in it whether hosts or guests. In this system designed to kill peoples, do not exist winners but only an elite of few private groups with their own ideological prejudices and an anti-national group with its own economic interests.[44]

Thus, the anti-immigration element is concealed by apparent compassion towards those migrating. Migration is therefore perceived as an impoverishment for different ethnic groups coming together. The associations or groups that tend to protect or insert the immigrants into the local culture simply labeled as 'anti-national' (itself, arguably, another coded anti-Semitic reference). CasaPound's diagnosis of the problem of migration, no less than its solution, is simple:

Against the infernal machine of the multi-racist society we propose the problems created by migration through: the blockage of the migratory waves; cooperation with the economic areas outside Europe thus to create their development and liberation from the yoke of the multi-nationals; support to all those extra-European independent movements so to create the conditions for a settlement of the autochthonous populations.[45]

The movement's program continues in much the same vein in recommending suspension of the Schengen agreement (allowing for the free circulation of European citizens). In reference to the recent immigration wave from Western Europe by recent EU accession states from Central and Eastern Europe, the program declares: 'An "internal Third World" cannot exist in Europe, which would export slaves and delinquents towards the most economic advanced areas of the continent'.[46] Once again, here the message appears encoded for – with a superficial reading – it looks like CasaPound takes a largely supportive attitude towards immigrants. Yet whatever the linguistic obfuscation, the 'help' on offer is towards repatriation of migrants to their native countries of origin, further underscoring CasaPound's views regarding the separation of peoples. It is not for nothing that the movement's symbol is a turtle: a creature always bringing its own home with it.

In this respect, CasaPound's endorsement of so-called 'ethnodifferentialism' is right out of the New Right's playbook. Summarizing this recent development in far right propaganda, Steve Bastow notes that this view is 'presented as an anti-racist recognition of cultural difference. True racism, as the ND [Nouvelle Droite in France] also argues, is the attempt to integrate immigrants, undermining both cultures: that of host and of immigrant'.[47] In this sense, as Pierre-André Taguieff has impressively shown, racism is thus turned on its head, with those advocating multiculturalism branded racists for diluting the cultural – not racial – homogeneity of otherwise 'pure' ethnic blocs (for example: Europe, Africa).[48] While the same ends of racial separation are served as more 'unreconstructed' forms of ethnic prejudice and the recommendations are notorious far right fare – repatriation, closing borders, banning 'foreign' religious symbols, and so on – the discourse is starkly different. This form of 'right-wing Gramscism', Roger Griffin argues, seeks:

> to undermine the intellectual legitimacy of liberalism by attacking aspects of actual existing liberal democracy: materialism, individualism, the universality of human rights, egalitarianism, multi-culturalism, and so on. 'Metapolitical fascism' did so not on the basis of an aggressive ultra-nationalism and axiomatic racial superiority, but in the name of a Europe restored to the (essentially mythic) homogeneity of its component primordial cultures, and by the application of a 'differentialist' ideal which seeks to put an end to rampant 'vulgarization' and ethnic miscegenation that they see endemic to modern societies.

In what sounds like a template for CasaPound's hybrid form of fascism, Griffin continues:

> Later versions of the extraordinarily prolific, logorrheic New Right have placed increasing stress on the need to transcend the division between Left and Right in a broad anti-global front. In short, the metapolitical perpetuation of inter-war fascism's crusade against liberal decadence advocates in its varied factions the inauguration of a new global order that would preserve or restore (through policies and measures never specified) unique ethnic and cultural identities (first and foremost European/Indo-European ones) allegedly threatened by globalization.[49]

If, by 'metapolitical', Griffin understands a *tout court* rejection of democratic elections then this, too, only partly characterizes CasaPound. For instance, some members of the group have participated in the Rome local elections within the ranks and file of La Destra, a populist right-wing party founded by one-time neo-fascist, Francesco Storace; the openly radical right party Tricolored Flame, created by the well-known neo-fascist activist and politician, Pino Rauti; and even a handful standing under Berlusconi's PDL (Partito delle Libertà; the Party of Liberty).[50] Even in terms of more indirect political engagement, CasaPound's political connections are unusual, if nevertheless perceptible. Thus, Pino Rauti's son-in-law Gianni Alemanno – who at the time of writing Mayor of Rome – attempted to 'donate' CasaPound's squatted headquarters via an €11.5 million purchase from Rome's municipal treasury.[51] But this must be counted against far more visible, unconventional CasaPound centers now dotted across Italy, reputedly housing 5,000 members; an active student group called 'Blocco Studentesco' (Student's Bloc) which, tellingly, employs the BUF's encircled lighting flash as their logo; the aforementioned cultural groups (Artisti per CasaPound and Turbodinamismo), in addition to 15 bookshops, 20 pubs, 8 sport associations, and a web radio station; the (in)famous *Radio Bandiera Nera* (*Black Banner Radio*) – where the use of the color 'black' is a clear reference to Italian Fascism (in particular, the reference here is to the 'Black Shirts'). Similar to the undertakings of Alain de Benoist's GRECE – creator of this 'metapolitical' approach[52] – CasaPound has held more than 150 conferences around Italy and, as noted above, continues a monthly publication of *L'Occidentale* and remains involved in the aforementioned non-profit organization, *Solidarite Identites*, which promotes aid to developing countries like Kosovo.

As noted at the outset, perhaps the most idiosyncratic aspect of Casa-Pound's hybridization of 'neo-fascism and the third way'[53] tradition of Italian Fascism is most conspicuously evident in CasaPound's approach to social housing and poverty relief – hardly the stuff of European far right stereotypes since 1945. In fact, CasaPound's occupation of unused buildings to provide shelter for those otherwise unable to afford it doubtless carries real overtones of social justice. This initiative is part of their program of 'social mortgage' (mutuo sociale), in which they propose that the family occupying a given building can acquire an apartment, paying only the costs of construction.[54] Although traditionally associated with left-wing groups, these occupations are nevertheless closely related to their core ideology. For example, there are certain rules to respect to be accepted to live in one of the CasaPound buildings: no drugs, guns or prostitution; and in striking contrast to these behavioral codes, having Italian citizenship. Furthermore, the association is committed to voluntary work. CasaPound has also organized squads to help the recent victims of floods striking northern Italy (2011) and in April 2009, furthermore, these same volunteer squads later assisted in relieving the Abruzzi region after a major earthquake.

Once more, seeming contradictions arise. How are images of volunteers in natural catastrophes reconciled with activists loyal to Fascist ideology? Quite easily, actually, in light of the 'new consensus' on fascism. Attempts to regenerate the 'national community' through voluntary social initiatives – in this case, housing the homeless, or organizing volunteer squads for natural disasters – in no way precludes radical right ideology. To this end, consider Roger Griffin's definition of the 'broadly congruent' understanding of fascist ideology over the last generation:

> fascism is a genus of modern, revolutionary, 'mass' politics which, while extremely heterogeneous in its social support and in the specific ideology promoted by its many permutations, draws its internal cohesion and driving force from a core myth that a period of perceived national decline and decadence is giving way to one of rebirth and renewal in a post-liberal new order.[55]

That CasaPound activists would recognize such a harmony between social welfare and fascist praxis, and indeed even endorse a perspective like Griffin's, is borne out by numerous interviews with leading figures in the movement. In the words of the online broadcaster for CasaPound's *Black Banner Radio*: 'We are an organization of social advancement that aims to use the power of volunteering to defend its social visions [...] What we love of fascism is the attention to justice, the great social and administrative achievements in the interest of the entire national community', Cristiano Coccanari declares, 'and the work done to render Italy a destined community from the Alps to Sicily, and not a mere geographic expression'.[56] More recently, and in a similar vein, an interview with CasaPound's official spokesperson maintains: 'Q: What is the main concern of CasaPound? A: Politics. Namely, we are concerned of the good with the polis. In other words, to give hope, dignity, strength, will, to a population that has been exhausted and tired'.[57] This willingness to help the polis through voluntary organizations finds its roots in any number of Fascist declarations; perhaps most prominently, from the final clause in the aforementioned *Verona Manifesto* from 1943, often cited by CasaPound activists:

> With this preamble to the Constituent Assembly, the Party shows not only that it is going to the people, but that it stands by the people. For its part, the Italian people must realize that there is only one way for it to defend its conquests of yesterday, today, and tomorrow, namely to repel the enslaving invasion of Anglo-American plutocracies, which have given a thousand signs of their desire to increase the distress and misery of Italian life. There is only one way to achieve all its social goals: fight, work, win.[58]

In this way, the putatively 'leftist' actions and fascist ideology of Casa-Pound are not only compatible; they are inextricable.

Conclusion: 'I tried to make a paradiso terrestre'

Perhaps on account of its recent vintage, it has been journalism rather than academic scholarship that has, to date, best squared the perceived circle presented by CasaPound's iconoclastic ideology. In charting CasaPound's development, Tom Kington's analysis seamlessly merges the historic ('Mussolini') and the contemporary (new) far right:

> CasaPound's approach to economics is pure Mussolini 'We would like to see communications, transport, energy and health renationalized and the state constructing houses which it then sells at cost to families', said Di Stefano. On immigration, the stance is typical of the far right. 'We want to stop it,' says Di Stefano. 'Low-cost immigrant workers mean Italians are unable to negotiate wages, while the immigrants are exploited'.[59]

So too with CasaPound's discourse and ideology generally: this is – quite self-consciously – 'fascism of the third millennium'. As shown above, this example of a twenty-first century European far right movement advocates a revolutionary, socialist and 'ethno-differentialist' form of fascism. Examination of CasaPound's politics thus reveals an engagement with Italian interwar Fascism, of the *fasci di combattimento* and even the Saló Republic. Yet, as underscored by the use of a global, multilingual blog, 'metapolitical' website and online merchandising, CasaPound is not merely nostalgic.[60] This is not simply a re-run of the (ignominious) past, but is instead a 'return to the future'; a contemporary version of fascist ideology.

Correspondingly, CasaPound cannot be easily explained as just another 'neo-fascist' group *sic et simpliciter.* In researching this chapter, for instance, the authors contacted a CasaPound member for a background interview, who rejected the label 'neo-fascist': 'I am a fascist' he said. There was no need to add anything else. In much the same way, CasaPound's adoption of political tactics typical of the postwar left – such as disaster relief or creating 'centri sociali' (community centers) – is no paradox; instead, it is an attempted application of Fascism's 'third way' to contemporary Italian realities. As Casa-Pound activists know only too well, it was the original 'daring ones', the Arditi under D'Annunzio, who occupied Fiume after World War One; while in Milan in 1919, their principal inspiration, Mussolini, launched his first Fascist manifesto from an occupied building in the Piazza San Sepolcro.

Finally, that words have consequences was borne out by Mussolini's bid to 'regenerate' Italy: 'the Fascist regime's seizure of power, repression and wars left a "body count" of an estimated one million dead'.[61] Yet one need only look to fascism's more recent history in Italy to draw a similar conclusion. Here too, CasaPound's Italia is at the forefront of developments. That language matters was not lost on Italy's Foreign Ministry, for instance, upon finding that its Consul-General in Japan, Mario Vattani, was filmed giving a Fascist salute and praising the Saló Republic while performing at a CasaPound event with his band 'Sotto Fascia Semplice' (Under a Simple Fascist Banner).[62] Nor was this lesson lost upon Ezra Pound's daughter, Mary de Rachewiltz, who recently undertook legal action in Italy to force the movement to change its name. Her efforts were redoubled, she declared, upon learning of the shooting rampage by a CasaPound member in December 2011.[63] Before killing himself, the author and accountant, Gianluca Casseri, murdered two street vendors in Florence and paralyzed a third.[64] For all CasaPound's doublespeak about non-racist 'ethno-differentialism' and for all their attempts to portray a 'friendly fascism' through welfare voluntarism, Casseri targeted only black African migrants. That he had been, at least to some degree, radicalized by CasaPound's tireless calls to action and violence is but

241

a further reminder that language – in particular far right language, however sanitized and 'reconstructed' – is all too often a spur to action. Cutting through CasaPound's ideological sophistry and pointing this out was one of the Senegalese street traders who was victimized by this all-too-familiar fascism of the third millennium: 'Don't tell us he was a madman, [...] because if he was he would have killed whites as well as blacks'.[65]

ENDNOTES

[1] Matthew Feldman would like to thank the Cantemir Institute, History Faculty, University of Oxford, for a Senior Research Fellowship facilitating the completion of this text.

[2] This chapter's epigraph is taken from an interview on CasaPound's official website, available online at: http://www.casapounditalia.org/ (accessed 28/05/2012). All Italian translations by Anna Castriota. Finally, each of the three section titles are taken from Ezra Pound, *The Cantos* (London: Faber and Faber, 1998), p. 3 (Canto I); 202 (Canto XLI); 816 [Notes for CXVII and so on], respectively.

[3] Jamie Bartlett, Jonathan Birdwell and Mark Littler, *'The rise of populism in Europe can be traced through online behaviour...': The New Face of Digital Populism* (London: Demos, 2011), pp. 96 – 98. Alongside this report, a bespoke study of CasaPound's online profile is also available online at: http://www.demos.co.uk/projects/populismineurope (accessed 28/05/2012).

[4] See Aram Mattioli, *'Viva Mussolini': Die Aufwertung des Faschismus im Italien Berlusconis* (Paderborn: Ferdinand Schöningh Verlag, 2010).

[5] Following the 'Mani Pulite' scandal in 1994, 77.6 per cent of the Italian electorate supported 'Anti-Political Establishment Parties' according to Amir Abedi, *Anti-Political Establishment Parties: A Comparative analysis* (London: Routledge, 2004), pp. 52 – 55, 53.

[6] Daniele Di Nunzio, Emanuele Toscano, 'Can We Still Speak about Extreme Right Movements? CasaPound in Italy between Community and Subjectivation Drives', presented at the XVII Congress of the International Sociological Association, Gothenburg, Sweden, 11 – 17 July 2010.

[7] For effective Anglophone studies of each of these movements, see Anna Cento Bull and Mark Gilbert, *The Lega Nord and the Northern Question in Italian Politics* (Basingstoke: Palgrave, 2001); and Antonio Carioti, 'From the Ghetto to Palazzo Chigi: The Ascent of the National Alliance', in Roger Griffin with Matthew Feldman eds., *Fascism: Critical Concepts*, vol. V (London: Routledge, 2004), pp. 57 – 78. On the MSI, see Piero Ignazi, *Extreme Right Parties in Western Europe* (Oxford: Oxford University Press, 2003), pp. 35 – 44. More recent comparative studies include Jonathan Hopkin and Piero Ignazi, 'Newly Governing Parties in Italy: Comparing PDSI/DS, Lega Nord and Forza Italia', in *New Parties in Government*, Kris Deschouwer ed., (Abingdon: Routledge, 2008), pp. 45 – 64; Marco Tarchi, 'Recalcitrant Allies: The Conflicting Foreign Policy Agenda of the *Alleanza Nazionale* and the *Lega Nord*', in *Europe for the Europeans: The Foreign and Security Policy of the Populist Radical Right*, ed., Christina Schori Liang (Aldershot: Ashgate, 2007), pp. 187 – 207. On the Tricolored Flame, see Anna Cento Bull, 'Casting a Long Shadow: The Legacy of *stragismo* for the Italian Extreme Right', in *The Italianist* 25 (2005), pp. 260 – 279, esp. 272 – 274.

[8] Cited in the most recent biography by Alec Marsh, *Ezra Pound: Critical Lives* (London: Reaktion Books, 2011), p. 47, which continues: 'In this sense modernism is really about *re-*

newal; its innovation is meant to renovate the world. Modernism is about beginning again. From the beginning, Pound always looked to reprise the Renaissance'.

[9] For three recent discussions of Pound and fascism, see Serenella Zanotti, 'Fascism', in Ezra Pound in Context, ed., Ira B. Nadel, (Cambridge: Cambridge University Press, 2011), pp. 376 – 390; Matthew Feldman, 'The "Pound Case" in Historical Perspective: An Archival Overview', in the Journal of Modern Literature 35/2 (2012), pp. 83 – 97; and Leon Surrette's Dreams of a Totalitarian Utopia: Literary Modernism and Politics (Montreal: McGill-Queen's University Press, 2011), pp. 220 – 250.

[10] Ezra Pound, 'Addendum for C', in The Cantos, p. 813. For a discussion of this 'epic' poem, see, for example, Lawrence Rainey, ed., A Poem Containing History: Textual Studies in The Cantos (Michigan: University of Michigan Press, 1997).

[11] See 'An Interview with Gianluca Iannoe', posted at Folkadvance on 6 Febuary 2012, available online at: http://folkadvance.org/ italy/gianluca-iannone-interview (accessed 28/05/2012).

[12] Pound, 'Addendum for C', 812 – 813. For academic accounts of Pound's anti-Semitism, see Flory's uncompromising view that Pound's anti-Semitism was born after a mental breakdown around 1935 in her 'Pound and Anti-Semitism', in the Cambridge Companion to Ezra Pound, ed., Ira B. Nadel (Cambridge: Cambridge University Press, 1999), pp. 284 – 300. For more general, empirically substantiated accounts of Pound's unmistakeable anti-Jewish vitriol, see the general accounts by Robert Casillo, The Genealogy of Demons: Anti-Semitism, Fascism and the Myths of Ezra Pound (Evanston, IL: Northwestern University Press, 1988); and rather more charitably, Leon Surette, Pound in Purgatory: From Economic Radicalism to Anti-Semitism (Urbana, IL: University of Illinois Press, 1999). Finally, Ezra Pound's radio broadcasts for Fascist Italy have been widely circulated and, more than four decades ago, culminated in the full publication of 120 radio broadcast scripts under the title 'Ezra Pound Speaking': Radio Speeches of WWII, ed., Leonard Doob (Westport, CN: Greenwood Press, 1978).

[13] These excerpts, and many others, were reproduced long ago in C. David Heymann's unflinching account of Pound's politics, Ezra Pound: The Last Rower (New York: Viking Press, 1976), pp. 116 – 122. Following his release from St Elizabeth's sanatorium in 1958, Pound returned to Italy, where he resumed contact with a number of far right ideologues including Valerio Borghese, Vanni Teodorani and Ugo Dadone. Of the latter, revealingly, one of Pound's biographers has noted that, in Spring 1961, Pound stayed with Dadone, who 'was involved with the neo-Fascist Movimento Sociale Italiano and regularly wrote articles about them in right-wing journals. They held a May Day parade, wearing jack-boots and black armbands, displaying the swastika, shouting anti-Semitic slogans, and goose-stepping. Among those photographed at the head of the parade was Ezra'. See Humphrey Carpenter, Ezra Pound: A Serious Character (London: Faber and Faber, 1988), pp. 873 – 874.

[14] See: http://folkadvance.org/category/casapound (accessed 28/05/2012).

[15] For a brief overview of the term 'new far right', see Paul Jackson et al., The EDL: Britain's 'New Far Right Social Movement' (Northampton: RNM Publications, 2011), pp. 7 – 11, available online at: www.radicalism-new-media.org/?page_id=599 (accessed 28/05/2012).

[16] Although now slightly dated, the best Anglophone account of the development of the Italian far right since 1945 remains Franco Ferraresi's excellent Threats to Democracy (Princeton: Princeton University Press, 1996). esp. chapters 1, 4, 6 and 7.

[17] Marcello Veneziani, unpublished interview with Anna Castriota, August 2007.

[18] See, for example, Marco Tarchi, 'Italy: A Country of Many Populisms', in Daniele Albertazzi

and Duncan McDonnell eds., *Twenty First Century Populism* (Basingstoke: Palgrave, 2008), pp. 84 – 99; and for a more focused view of revolutionary youth activism, see Stéphanie Dechezelles, 'The Cultural Basis of Youth Involvement in Italian Extreme Right-Wing Organizations', in *Journal of Contemporary European Studies* 16/3 (2008), pp. 363 – 375.

[19] 'Retake Everything!', an interview with Gianluca Iannone posted at *Open Revolt!* on 15 December 2011. Available online at: http://openrevolt.info/2011/12/15/casa-pound/ (accessed 28/05/2012).

[20] See, for example, 'CasaPound and the New Radical Right in Italy', posted at *libcom.org* on 28 June 2011. Available online at: http://libcom.org/library/casa-pound-new-radical-right-italy#footnote2_2kk6qu4 (accessed 28/05/2012).

[21] See 'Le FAQ di CPI' [Frequently Asked Questions] on CasaPound's official website, available online at: www.casapounditalia.org/index.php?option=com_content&view=category&id=40&Itemid=66 (accessed 28/05/2012). For a similar interview with CPI's founder Gianluca Iannone on the subject of Italian fascism, see Alessandro di Capriccioli, 'Roma, CasaPound spiazza tutti', *l'Espresso*, 8 February 2012. Available online at: http://espresso.repubblica.it/dettaglio/roma-casapound-spiazza-tutti/2173 562 (accessed 28/05/2012). Tellingly, this interview was translated and cross-posted on the leading 'White Pride World Wide' website, *Stormfront* (available online at: www.stormfront.org/forum/t866233/): '...at that time [under Mussolini] there was more freedom of expression than there is now. Anyway, we claim the freedom to say that fascism did many good things, and we want to speak about those things. We live in a country where fascism lasted twenty years and anti-Fascism lasted sixty-six. There is the consolidation of power positions behind the word "anti-fascism". They mute you, your demonstrations and activities are prohibited, even when there is a flood in Genova and your militants go to help out, even when you spend your forces on volunteering'.

[22] Interview with Gianluca Iannone, posted on *Tumblr*, available online at: www.tumblr.com/tagged/ iannone (accessed 28/05/2012).

[23] For an overview of front-stage / back-stage discourse, see Cas Mudde, *The Ideology of the Extreme Right* (Manchester: Manchester University Press, 2000), p. 20ff; and for a succinct characterization of fascism as a 'Third Way', see George Mosse, cited in Roger Griffin, ed., *Fascism* (Oxford: Oxford University Press, 1995), pp. 303 – 304.

[24] Benito Mussolini and Giovanni Gentile, 'The Doctrine of Fascism', partially reprinted in John Whittam, *Fascist Italy* (Manchester: Manchester University Press, 1995). cited p. 156.

[25] See *CasaPound*, 'La Storia', available online at: http://www.casapounditalia.org/index.php?option=com_content&view=category&id=36&Itemid=61 (accessed 28/05/2012).

[26] 'The Manifesto of Turbodynamism', available online at: http://www.ideodromocasapoun d.org/?p=690 (accessed 28/05/2012).

[27] Filippo Tommaso Marinetti, 'The Founding and Manifesto of Futurism', in Umbro Apollonio, ed., *Futurist Manifestos* (New York: Viking Press, 1973), pp. 19 – 24, 21.

[28] See 'Artisti per CasaPound', available online at: www.artistipercasapound.org/ (accessed 28/05/2012).

[29] Cited in Emilio Gentile, *The Struggle for Modernity: Nationalism, Futurism and Fascism* (Westport, CN: Praeger, 2003). Also cited in ibid., (p. 84), for instance, Mussolini claimed: 'We must scrape and pulverize, in the character and mentality of the Italians [...] It is an immense labour. The Risorgimento was but the beginning, because it was the work of tiny minorities; the world war, instead, was profoundly educational. Now it is a matter of continuing, day by day, this remaking of the national character of the Italians'.

[30] Giovanni Giurati, 'The Young and the Party', translated and reprinted in Roger Griffin, ed., *Fascism*, cited p. 68.

[31] See: www.folkadvance.org/category/casapound (accessed 28/05/2012).

[32] Lyrics from the song 'Cinghiamattanza', taken from CasaPound's official website (accessed 28/05/2012).

[33] See, for example: www.cinghiamattanza.blogspot.com (accessed 28/05/2012).

[34] Communication on CasaPound's official website, 18 October 2009. Available online at: www.casapounditalia.org (accessed 28/05/2012).

[35] Lyrics from the song 'Nel Dubbio Mena' taken from CasaPound's official website.

[36] See: 'Le FAQ di CPI', www.casapounditalia.org/index.php?option=com_content&view= category &id=36&Itemid=61 (accessed 28/05/2012).

[37] See John Pollard, *The Fascist Experience in Italy* (London: Routledge, 1998). cited p. 126.

[38] See 'Il Programma' on CasaPound's official website, titled 'Una Nazione [A Nation]', cited pp. 1 – 2. Available online at: http://www.casapounditalia.org/images/unanazione. pdf (accessed 28/05/2012).

[39] 'The Verona Manifesto of the Republican Fascist Party', partially translated and reprinted in Griffin, *Fascism*, ed., p. 87.

[40] See 'Chi Siamo' on CasaPound's official website, available online at: www.casapounditalia.org/index.php?option=com_content&view=category&id=35&Ite mid=60 (accessed 28/05/2012).

[41] On the origins of the periodical 'Occidentale' see: Enrico Sartori on www.novopress/cultura/22-04-2005. Novopress.info., on: http://it.novopress.info (accessed 28/05/2012).

[42] On: www.casapounditalia.org/attivita', link to: www.solidarite-identite (accessed 28/05/2012).

[43] See: www.casapounditalia.org/index.php?option=com_content&view=category&id=40& Itemid=66 (accessed 28/05/2012).

[44] 'Il Programma', p. 4.

[45] Ibid., p. 4.

[46] Ibid.

[47] Steve Bastow, 'A Neo-Fascist Third Way: The Discourse of Ethno-Differentialist Revolutionary Nationalism', reprinted in Griffin with Feldman, eds., *Fascism*, vol. V, cited p. 77.

[48] In Christopher Flood's impressive summary, '[h]aving tracked de Benoist's theoretical trajectory from white-supremacist biological racism to ethno-differentialism, Taguieff came to the view that de Benoist's positions in this and other areas had evolved to such a degree that he could no longer be classed straightforwardly as a thinker of the extreme right or even be conveniently pigeonholed in conventional left-right terms at all.' 'Pierre-André Taguieff and the Dilemmas of Antiracism', in *l'esprit créateur* 37/2 (1997), pp. 68 – 78, cited p. 69.

[49] Roger Griffin, 'Fascism's New Faces (and New Facelessness) in the "Post-Fascist" Epoch', reprinted in Matthew Feldman, ed., *A Fascist Century* (Basingstoke: Palgrave, 2008). cited pp. 195 – 196.

[50] Some CasaPound activists participated as candidates in the local elections held in 2008; for a general overview, see: www.casapounditalia.org/politica (accessed 28/05/2012).

[51]'Il Campidoglio acquista sede Casapound Il Pd insorge: è una vergogna', as reported in *Il Messaggero Roma* on 25 April 2012. Available online at:

http://www.ilmessaggero.it/articolo.php?id=192603 &sez=HOME_ROMA (accessed 28/05/2012). The authors are grateful to Andrea Rinaldi for drawing this development to their attention. Gianni Alemanno's apparent attempt to purchase the building for CasaPound activists was recently struck down by the Italian Audit Court; see, 'La Corte dei conti boccia i bilanci del Comune' in *La Repubblica Roma*, 25 Maggio 2012. Available online at: http://roma.repubblica.it/cronaca/2012/05/25/news/la_corte_ dei_conti_boccia_i_bilanci_del_comune-35865319/ (accessed 28/05/2012).

[52] For a detailed analysis of De Benoist's pedigree and intellectual trajectory, see Pierre-André Taguieff, 'The New Cultural Racism in France', in *Telos* 83 (1990), pp. 109 – 122; and Pierre-André Taguieff, 'From Race to Culture: The New Right's View of European Identity', in *Telos* 98/99 (1993), pp. 99 – 125.

[53] For an excellent overview, see the chapter by this name in Steve Bastow and James Martin, *Third Way Discourse: European Ideology in the Twentieth Century* (Edinburgh: Edinburgh University Press, 2003). chapter. 4.

[54] See 'Il Programma', p. 10.

[55] Roger Griffin ed., *International Fascism: Theories, Causes and the New Consensus* (London: Arnold, 1998). cited p. 14; italics in original.

[56] Cristiano Coccanari, cited in 'Casa Pound Italia: Neo-Fascism on the Rise', posted at *cafebabel.com* on 23 March 2010. Available online at: http://www.cafebabel.co.uk/art icle/33321/casa-pound-italia-fascism-neo-fascism-duce.html (accessed 28/05/2012).

[57] See: 'Le FAQ di CPI'.

[58] Griffin, ed., *Fascism*, p. 87.

[59] Tom Kington, 'Italy's Fascists Stay True to Mussolini's Legacy', *The Guardian* 6 November 2011. Available online at: http://www.guardian.co.uk/world/2011/nov/06/italy-fascists-true-mussolini-ideology ?INTCMP=SRCH (accessed 28/05/2012).

[60] See, respectively: http://zentropa.info/; http://www.ideodromocasapound.org/; and www.zazzle.co.uk/casapound+gifts (all accessed 28/05/2012).

[61] Michael R. Ebner, *Ordinary Violence in Mussolini's Italy* (Cambridge: Cambridge University Press, 2010). cited p. 11.

[62] 'Italy's Osaka Consul Recalled Over Fascist Rock Band Links', *The Telegraph*, 24 January 2012. Available online at: www.telegraph.co.uk/news/worldnews/europe/italy/903 4972/Italys-Osaka-consul-recalled-over-fascist-rock-band-links.html (accessed 28/05/ 2012).

[63] Tom Kington, 'Ezra Pound's Daughter Aims to Stop Italian Fascist Group Using Father's Name', *The Guardian*, 23 December 2011. Available online at: http://www.guardian.c o.uk/world/2011/dec/23/ezra-pound-daughter-italian-fascist (accessed 28/05/2012).

[64] See, for example, 'CasaPound Runs Riot in Foreign Market', *Sch News*, 16 December 2011. Available online at: http://www.schnews.org.uk/stories/CASAPOUND-RUNS-RIOT-IN-FOREIGN-MARKET/ (accessed 28/05/2012).

[65] Tom Kington, 'Florence Gunman Shoots Senegalese Street Vendors Dead', *The Guardian*, 13 December 2011. Available online at: http://www.guardian.co.uk/world/2011/de c/13/florence-gunman-shoots-street-vendors (accessed 28/05/2012).

ANTI-SEMITISM ON THE CURRICULUM: MAUP – THE INTERREGIONAL ACADEMY FOR PERSONNEL MANAGEMENT

Per Anders Rudling[1]

The Interregional Academy for Personnel Management, better known under its Ukrainian acronym MAUP (*Mizhrehional'na Akademiia Upravlinnia Personalom*) is unique among universities in the former Soviet Union.[2] As the largest private institution of higher education in Ukraine, MAUP has the credentials of a university, and issues academic degrees up to the Ph.D. level. In English, it is therefore often referred to as a university. However, a more precise translation of the Ukrainian *nederzhavnyi uchobovyi zaklad* would be 'private educational establishment': an accredited institution whose university degrees are accepted internationally. MAUP claims to have 'educated more government officials, diplomats and administrators than any other university and has the highest academic accreditation Ukraine provides, as well as recognition from UNESCO'.[3] The tens of thousands of MAUP graduates include deputy ministers, members of parliament, mayors, diplomats, military commanders, businessmen, heads of schools and universities as well as senior members of the administration of former president Viktor Yushchenko.[4] For several years during the first decade of the twenty first century, MAUP was assisted by powerful interests, and its connections and influence have reached the very highest echelons of the Ukrainian government, linked to several Ukrainian top political figures, including two Ukrainian presidents. Until 2005, Viktor Yushchenko, the third president of Ukraine, served on MAUP's board of directors and on the supervisory board of MAUP's journal *Personal*, whilst also heading up one of their institutes.[5] Until November that year, so did his Foreign Minister Boris Tarasiuk.[6]

Leonid Kravchuk, the first elected president of Ukraine, took part in the establishment of MAUP in the early 1990s. He was a long-term member of MAUP's Board of Trustees, a regular participant at MAUP events, and even has a MAUP institute named in his honor.[7] All three politicians received honorary doctorates from MAUP.[8] They share this honour with David Duke, the former

247

Grand Wizard of the Ku Klux Klan.[9] The MAUP leadership was preoccupied, obsessed, some would say, with Jews, aggressively promoting a radical form of anti-Semitism, more overt and aggressive than the more refined and polished 'doublespeak' which characterizes much of the Western European far right.

Through Duke, MAUP is connected with white supremacy groups in the United States. On 9 September 2005, Duke was awarded a 'real' Ph.D. in history after having successfully defended a thesis entitled 'Zionism as a Form of Ethnic Supremacism', unanimously approved by the 10 member examining committee. Between 2005 and 2008, Duke taught classes in history and international relations at MAUP.[10]

David Duke, in his Ph.D. ceremonial graduation gown together with Rector Mykola Holovatii.

Using Soviet-era terminology, MAUP prefers words such as 'Zionists' and 'cosmopolitans' when referring to Jews. MAUP presents itself as 'the only Ukrainian institution of science and higher education, dedicated to the studies of the thankless themes of the theory and practice of Zionism in the modern world'.[11]

Its publications are sold by street vendors and by in major bookstore chains.[12] In addition to domestic hate literature, MAUP also publishes Ukrainian and Russian translations of anti-Semitic literature from around the world; from Werner Sombart's *Die Juden und das Wirtschaftsleben*, Middle Eastern tracts on blood libel, US and Western European Holocaust denial, to the tsarist forgery *The Protocol of the Elders of Zion*.[13] Reflecting the political nature of MAUP, textbooks in supposedly apolitical subjects such as anthropology often have anti-communist and anti-Semitic content.[14]

From left to right: Jürgen Graf, *The Great Lie of the 20th Century*; Natalia Lapikura and Valeri Lapikura, *Do not Revive old Horrors: A Chronicle of the Struggle Against Judeo-Nazism* and Herohii Shchokin, *The Organizers of Bolshevism: Their National and Personal Background*.

MAUP was founded in 1989 and privatized after the collapse of the Soviet Union in 1991.[15] During its first years of existence, until February 1994, MAUP went under the name *Vsesoiuznyi zaochnii universitet unpravleniia personalom* (The All-Union Correspondence University of Personnel Management).[16] MAUP is headed by Heorhii Shchokin, who has been its rector since 1990.[17]

In addition to being the president and founder of MAUP, Shchokin was a co-founder of the far right Ukrainian Conservative Party, (*Ukrains'ka konservatyvna partiia*). The party calls for the reintroduction of the Soviet-era 'nationality' clause into Ukrainian passports, demands that all Ukrainian bodies of power should consist of at least 80 per cent ethnic Ukrainians, only ethnic Ukrainians should be eligible to become head of state, and that Jewish rights be strictly curtailed.[18] Shchokin's connections to the Middle East are extensive; the MAUP President has addressed three conferences in Saudi Arabia, and at least one 'anti-Zionist' conference in the United Arab Emirates, in October 2002.[19] He made headlines in the Ukrainian press when he claimed that Osama Bin Laden was really a Jew by the name of Benya Landau.[20]

MAUP captured a large section of the anti-Semitic publishing sector; by the end of 2005 its academic publishers produced 85 per cent of all of the anti-Semitic materials sold in Ukraine.[21] Up to 57,000 students are studying at MAUP's 55 affiliates and seven regional institutions across Ukraine, and its student body almost doubled between 2004 and 2006. Curiously, there are hardly any Jews left in Ukraine. According to the 2001 Ukrainian census, there are only 103,000 Jews in Ukraine, or 0.2 per cent of the population.[22] In fact, the editions of MAUP's anti-Semitic publications are considerably larger than the entire Jewish population in Ukraine.

MAUP's growth appears to have been at least partly made possible by external funding. The institution is partly funded by governments in the Middle East, particularly Saudi Arabia and Iran,[23] but also, in the mid-2000s, Libya and Palestine.[24] The ultra-nationalist publicist Anatolii Shcherbatiuk, formerly an employee at MAUP's newspaper *Personal Plius,* claimed that MAUP also receives money from the Russian security service, the FSB.[25]

The MAUP leadership argues that Ukrainian and Persian culture share common roots and have established a special department for Iranian studies. In March 2006, the ambassador of the Islamic Republic of Iran visited MAUP and Shchokin, to discuss the establishment of a Ukrainian cultural centre in Iran and to negotiate a formalized exchange programme between MAUP and Iranian universities.

MAUP also has strong links to Azerbaijan. Its Institute of Social Sciences is named in honour of Heidar Aliev, a Brezhnev-era Politburo member-turned-founding-father of independent Azerbaijan and an authoritarian dynastic ruler in the former Soviet republic. In March 2006 Ambassador Taliat Aliev led a delegation from the Azerbaijani parliament to MAUP.[26] Similarly, in 2006, representatives from Libya delivered lectures on Muammar al-Gaddafi's political theories, and seminars on the former Libyan dictator's so-called *Green Book.*[27] MAUP already has hundreds of students from the Middle East, many of whom cite the 'anti-Zionist' activities of MAUP as their primary reason for attending the institution.[28] As a result of the presence of 'anti-Zionists' from all across the Middle East, MAUP has an extensive network of alumni and supporters in 60 countries.[29]

In order to enlighten the public about the 'practice of Zionism in the modern world' MAUP has arranged a number of 'scientific' conferences. In November 2002 at an 'All-Ukrainian scientific conference devoted to the memory of millions of people who perished from the famine in 1932 – 1933'[30] the MAUP leadership argued that 'Jewish publicists are suppressing the facts on who organized the Ukrainian Holocaust of 1933'.[31] Present at the conference were academics, ambassadors and politicians, including the first President of Ukraine, Leonid Kravchuk, who chaired MAUP's Board of Trustees.[32]

MAUP has retained close connections to several important political figures on the political right. One such figure is Levko Luk"ianenko, a former prisoner of conscience, presidential candidate, former member of the *Verkhovna Rada* for the Iuliia Tymoshenko bloc and former ambassador to Canada. A holder of a MAUP honorary doctorate, Luk"ianenko is one of the most high-profile anti-Semites in Ukraine.[33] Luk"ianenko blames the Ukrainian famine on a 'satanical' Stalinist government,[34] in which, he claims, 'the most important administrative positions in the commissariats, the Communist Party and the punitive organs almost 450, or 80%, were held by Jews'.[35]

As director of the Association of Researchers of Ukrainian *Holodomors*,[36] Luk"ianenko argues for the need of a second Nuremberg process against the organizers of Soviet communism, 95 per cent of which he claims were Jewish.[37] 'In order for Ukrainians to become themselves and to start developing, they should get rid of Judeo-Zionist Communism and accept in their souls the Ukrainian national idea', Luk"ianenko argues.[38] He provided a list of the perpetrators of the 1932 – 1933 famine, organized in such a way that nearly all names on the list were Jews. The most prominent name being Josef Stalin, '(his full, real name, Iosip David Vissarionovych Dzhuhashvili – Koba). Georgian Jew,' and 'V. Lenin – Blank. Jew on the maternal line, Calmuck on the paternal'.[39] Other MAUP scholars rely on the *Protocols of the Elders of Zion* as an authoritative primary source, spelling out the ambitions of 'Bolshevik Zionist animals' to achieve world domination through hypocrisy and fraud.[40]

At a June 2005 MAUP conference, titled 'A Dialogue of Civilizations: Zionism as the Biggest Threat to Contemporary Civilization?' David Duke was guest of honour.[41] Other foreign guests included the ambassadors of Iran, Syria and Palestine.[42] Delegates at the conference called for the deportation of Jews from Ukraine.[43] Luk"ianenko stood up to give Duke a standing ovation.[44]

Luk"ianenko singled Jews out as responsible for Stalin's terror, alleging that they reject physical labour, that 'Zionists' are traditionally opposed to Ukrainianhood, and that 'the Jewish puppet masters who control mass media use their blood money to install love for the beautiful and soulless life in order

251

to cultivate the animal instincts of our young'. Luk"ianenko concluded by adding that there is no anti-Semitism in Ukraine.[45] In April 2005, President Yushchenko awarded Luk"ianenko the most prestigious order of the republic, *Hero of Ukraine*, in recognition of his 'civic valour and his selfless dedication in championing the ideals of freedom and democracy'.[46] Shchokin and MAUP interpreted this award as recognition of their activities.[47] Then Prime Minister Yuliia Tymoshenko, herself a holder of a MAUP honorary doctorate,[48] ignored calls to distance herself from Luk"ianenko,[49] her bloc re-nominating him as a leading candidate in its list for the March 2006 elections.[50]

As an academic institution, MAUP grossly violates academic freedom. It is permeated with the political views of its leadership and is intimately linked with Shchokin's Conservative Party. The websites of the two organizations are linked, and they are led by roughly the same group of people. Faculty members are strongly encouraged to join the party and their presence at party congresses and other political events is required.[51] All former and current students are forced to sign up for a subscription to the anti-Semitic journal *Personal Plius* (*Personnel Plus*), as well as other anti-Semitic journals such as *Za Vil'nu Ukraïnu Plius* (*For a Free Ukraine Plus*) and *Ukrïns'ka Hazeta Plius* (*The Ukrainian Herald Plus*).[52] Refusal to subscribe means a fail is given in exams and no graduation.[53] Students and staff at MAUP have been coerced to sign up for party membership; people who refused have been physically threatened. In June 2005 the Kharkiv branch of MAUP, led by its rector, supported student demands not to be signed up for membership in the Conservative Party. In response, Shchokin went to Kharkiv together with 'a group of skinheads who threatened the Kharkiv rector with violence and firing'.[54] Freshmen have been forced to fill out detailed forms on language and background, to be filed with MAUP. They are divided into three groups: 'commanding the Ukrainian language, and using it in daily life'; 'in command of Ukrainian, but not speaking it'; and 'Russian-speaking'.[55] In 2005, a number of senior regional administrators at MAUP sent the Ukrainian Prosecutor General Sviatoslav Piskun an open letter, expressing concerns that 'the recent replacement of several directors at MAUP regional institutes is directly associated with their ethnicity'.[56]

Anti-Semitism and esoteric, racial mysticism permeates the UKP. Until 2008 nearly all articles, statements and books by Shchokin or other leading MAUP /

UKP representatives dwelled on the 'Jewish question,' promoting a Manichean worldview, and world history as a struggle between good and evil. In their version of history, all evil stems from the Jews, who in turn are the children of the Devil. Christianity and Islam, on the other hand, represent good, in eternal opposition to the 'Satanic Zionist Jews'. Race also plays an important role, and Ukrainians are depicted as the most glorious of races. According to the UKP, the origins of Ukrainian history are found in 'the Tripilian civilization that began 7,514 years ago. Ukraine itself became the '*ur*-fatherland of the greatest and the most glorious family of the contemporary world – the Indoeuropean'.[57] At the same time, Conservative Party advocates a Ukraine based upon Christian and Orthodox values. Shchokin appears to be struggling with the Jewish origins of Christianity, and has sought to disprove the Jewish origins of Christ: 'Jesus Christ [...] was never a Jew. The only Jew among the twelve apostles was Judas, who betrayed him'.[58] According to Shchokin, in this epic struggle between good and evil, Christians need to join with Muslims against Jewish vice. 'Antichrist, who rules the Jewish kingdom based in Jerusalem, the third temple of Jehovah, i.e. in contemporary Israel' is the incarnation of evil.[59] Therefore, he maintains, Ukraine needs to establish an 'ethnocracy,' which would be a basis for a strong Hetmanate, or Cossack State: 'God created the people differently, and nationalism is a natural feeling, given to us by God himself. Therefore, it must become the state ideology. Without it as the basic ideology, a strong state cannot be developed'. Such a Ukrainian state, 'the geopolitical and spiritual centre of Europe', would need both a strong Cossack army and to regain nuclear weapons. Jews should have their nationality spelled out in their passports,[60] and the size of the ethnic Ukrainian population dramatically increased in order to compensate for the twentieth century Judeo-Bolshevik and Judeo-Liberal 'kuchmist'[61] 'genocides' against the Ukrainian nation. In addition, Shchokin argues, the diaspora needs to be repatriated to Ukraine.[62] At the turn of the century, he claims, there were 80 million ethnic Ukrainians. Since 1991, Ukraine has lost five million people in a Jewish-administered genocide, and this is, according to Shchokin, bound to continue. Claiming to rely on numbers from UN experts, Shchokin asserts that 'in 2050 the total number of Ukrainians will be 23 million people, in other words an extermination of the titular nation in Ukraine by some 500,000 people a year [...] [B]y 2070, according to most leading population experts, this will have led to the total destruction of Ukrainianhood – one of the oldest nations of the world'.[63] According to Shchokin, there are three leading ideologies in the world today: communo-socialism, Judeo-liberalism and national conservatism. Shchokin's party claim to represent the third trend, while 'The first two have common origins, as it is obvious that the initiator of Judeo-Bolshevist Marxism-Leninism was Moses Hess, from which both Zionism as well as "scientific" socialism stems'.[64]

In 2003 MAUP Professor Vasyl' Iaremenko published an essay titled *Jews in Ukraine Today: Reality without Myths*. The article has since been re-published in a book by the same name. Iaremenko is a specialist on the history of Ukrainian journalism, who has taught classes at the University of Bratislava, Slovakia, and the University of Alberta, Canada.[65] In his book, Iaremenko dismisses Ukrainian anti-Semitism as a myth spread by the Jewish-controlled mass media,[66] while asserting that Bolshevism is a creation by international Jewry. In his rendering of history, this conspiracy is aimed particularly against ethnic Ukrainians. 'Today, Zionists [...] are the largest and most dangerous threat to Ukraine, to the rights, dignity, moral, spiritual and economic sovereignty of the Ukrainian people'.[67] Iaremenko describes the Jewish minority in Ukraine as, 'an alien political force, which de facto controls international trade, national capital, mass media, and the sphere of book publishing in Ukraine and it must [therefore] be restrained and regulated by strict government and state control'.[68] Unsupported by facts, he alleged that 'there are 136 (158 according to other sources) deputies of Jewish nationality in the Verkhovna Rada,' and that '90 per cent of Ukrainian banks are run by "managers" of Jewish nationality'.[69]

Like MAUP rector Shchokin, Iaremenko claims that the removal of the nationality category from Ukrainian passports enabled a 'Jewish lobby' to operate within Ukraine, and demands its reintroduction.[70] 'Ukrainian Jewry lives by their own laws. When these collide with Ukrainian laws, the Jews win out', Iaremenko complains.[71] An example of this, according to Iaremenko, is the 1932 – 1933 man-made famine, the blame of which he attributes to the Jews.

To these charges he adds Stalin's political terror from 1935 – 1939, claiming that the Ukrainian government, the NKVD and all Punitive Organs were up to 90 per cent controlled by Jews[72] – a number, Iaremenko maintains, which increased to 99 per cent at the time of the 1937 – 1938 terror.[73] Revealingly, he describes Stalinist rule as a 'Jewish Holocaust of Ukrainians 1921 – 1922,

1932 – 1933 and 1937 – 1938'.[74] To this, Iaremenko adds the curious accusation that Jews were the architects of the Holocaust. Not only did the Jews finance the Nazis: they also made up the majority of the SS. Iaremenko claims that Ukraine was 'invaded by German fascists along with a 400,000-strong horde of Jewish SS men'.[75] The logic here is that given their past behaviour, the Ukrainian Jews only have themselves to blame for the pogroms.[76]

Without listing sources for his extraordinary claims, Iaremenko claims that it was not the Ukrainian auxiliary police that murdered the Jews at Babi Yar, but the Jews themselves. 'If we are to be honest, the Ukrainian police stood back, while the Jewish *Polizei* were brought to Babi Yar. And there were 15,000 of them! That is also a truth that the Zionists want to conceal'.[77] In addition to the 1932 – 1933 famine, the Stalinist terror and the Holocaust, Iaremenko holds the Jews responsible for organizing slavery and the international sex trade through the centuries.[78] Iaremenko alleges that 'Jewish oligarchs, funded by international Zionist centres' prevented a renaissance of Ukrainian culture, and instead flooded the Ukrainian TV channels with pornography, murder and drugs.[79] *Personal Plius* claims that 'ever since the Jews arrived from Germany in the late 1800s they have saturated the market of "erotic literature"'. Since then, they have allegedly spread their pornography over the world.[80]

MAUP 'researchers,' scholars, and politicians often refer to the tsarist forgery *The Protocol of the Elders of Zion*. In 2005, MAUP published a new, annotated Ukrainian edition in commemoration of the centennial issue of its original publication.[81] Not only do the MAUP 'researchers' regard the protocols as authentic; the introduction explains how the twentieth century unfolded according to the outlines in the *Protocols*, and how its ideas were 'very popular among Jewish Bolsheviks and the supreme leadership of the Red Army, which predominantly consisted of Jews,' but also with US politicians such as Allen Dulles, Henry Kissinger, and Zbigniew Brzezinski and the leadership of the CIA, all of whom would supposedly be linked together by 'Judeo-masonic' organizations.[82]

For some time, MAUP maintained close contacts with the Ukrainian diaspora. In the summer of 2004, the OUN(b)-dominated Ukrainian Congress Committee of America (UCCA) Executive Director Tamara Gallo Olexy and the Kyiv Bureau Director of the UCCA Viktoria Hubska, visited the MAUP campus, to discuss UCCA participation in MAUP conferences on the *Holodomor*.[83]

Journalists who scrutinized MAUP's activities were violently attacked in late 2005 and early 2006.[84] On 21 December 2005, the Pechersky district court of Kyiv ruled that two newspapers, *Stolichnye Novosti* and *Stolichka,* had published 'negative and non-factual' reports on MAUP. They were temporarily closed, and forced to pay MAUP $10,000, and Shchokin personally $5,000 in damages. Some analysts interpreted this as an attempt by the government to silence media voices that were critical of anti-Semitism in Ukraine.[85] Emboldened by this ruling, MAUP decided to sue a number of well-established historians who had signed a petition accusing MAUP of xenophobia and causing 'moral damage' to the reputation of Ukrainian academia.[86] Between 2002 and 2008 MAUP issued a constant stream of statements and official declarations addressed to Kofi Annan of the United Nations, then-President Yushchenko, his Prime Minister Yekhanurov and others, making a number of radical anti-Semitic demands.

On 4 November 2005, Shchokin and the MAUP leadership issued, in broken English, a statement of solidarity with the Iranian President Ahmadinejad's threat to wipe Israel off the map, referring to Israel as an 'artificially created state (classic totalitarian type)', and announcing that its 'inevitable death' was near. MAUP 'makes a decisive protest against the large-scale campaign, organized by Zionists, against the Islamic Republic of Iran and its President Mahmud Ahmadi Nedzhad (sic) [...] where he quoted the words of the Iranian spiritual leader Aiatoli Homeni (sic) about the future death of Israel and the USA'. According to the MAUP leadership, the 'Zionist leaders of the USA and England' and 'other almost fully Zionistic countries of Western Europe' are at the first stages of the Third world war. The present premier of Israel, Ariel Sharon, the world-wide war criminal, declared in public about a willingness to begin this war in 1982 [...] There is nothing more than sacrilege and an ill-intentioned treachery of all humanity by the small group of 'devil's children' and their Satanic comrade-in-arms, who are covered up by the light flag of Christianity.[87]

As MAUP started to generate significant international attention, it became a liability to Ukraine's reputation. Poland announced that it would no longer recognize MAUP degrees, due to the political nature of the institution.[88] *Personal Plius* responded by declaring that Aleksandr Kwasniewski was Jewish.[89] As international pressure was increasing towards Yushchenko's government, it began to distance itself from Shchokin's circle.[90] Tarasiuk finally cut his ties with MAUP in November 2005. Reportedly this happened after pressure from Yushchenko, who had distanced himself from MAUP only a few months earlier. On 6 December 2005, Yushchenko condemned MAUP for the first time,[91] and on 23 January 2006, a similar condemnation followed from Tarasiuk, 'I think that all positive forces in Ukraine must evaluate the activities of MAUP. There is no place for anti-Semitism and xenophobia in Ukraine'.[92] The picture was ambiguous; at the same time, Tymoshenko presented her list of candidates for the March 2006 elections to the Rada. Once again, Luk"ianenko was nominated as one of her Bloc's top candidates.[93]

The MAUP leadership has lashed out against the organizations that most actively pressured Yushchenko's government to distance themselves from MAUP. Thus, MAUP decried B'nai Brith as a 'Judeo-Nazi' international 'Judeo-Masonic organization', and the Anti-Defamation League as a 'Jewish Gestapo', claiming that 'organized Jewry' intends to carry out a further genocide against the Ukrainian nation.[94] MAUP detected satanic Jewish plots behind many headline stories, even asserting a conspiracy behind the death of former Yugoslav president Slobodan Milošević's death while in custody at the Hague, demanding criminal proceedings against 'Mrs. M. Olbright' (*sic*) and others for Milošević's 'tardy medical treatment'. 'The [MAUP] Presidium states that the Hague Tribunal made a mistake during the investigation of crimes against Yugoslav people committed in 1999. Real criminals whose actions resulted in sustained losses of civilians, destruction of houses and industrial buildings should be punished'.[95] Similarly, MAUP linked the publication of a set of provocative cartoons, some of which depicted the Muslim prophet Muhammad, in the provincial Danish daily *Jyllands-Posten,* to a 'Zionist' conspiracy. In an open letter to Kofi Annan, the MAUP leadership stated that:

> This may show that the provocative action, aimed at kindling international and religious dissention in the spirit of a notorious 'clash of civilizations' concept, has been prearranged. The presidium of the Academy is asking the UN to investigate thoroughly who actually owns printings that create hostility among religions since it is known that approximately 70% of world mass media is possessed or controlled by representatives of the

Jewish Diaspora with its ruling centres – World Jewish Congress, World Zionist Organization and so on.[96]

During the spring of 2006, MAUP publications ran stories of blood libel and allegations of the systematic Jewish ritual murder of Christian children.[97] When the Ukrainian government announced that they had invited the president of Israel to an international forum on the memory of the Holocaust on 27 September 2006, to commemorate the sixty-fifth anniversary of Babi Yar, *Personal Plius* published an article accusing Jews of the mass murder, alleging that Adolf Hitler, Eva Braun, Rudolf Hess, Heinrich Himmler, Reinhard Heydrich, Alfred Rosenberg, Hans Frank, Robert Ley and Adolf Eichmann were themselves Jewish:

[The above mentioned Nazis] were degenerates, and blamed this degeneration on their own Jewish blood. That is the reason why they exterminated other Jews. This is the same story as the one behind the Spanish inquisition.

Particularly offensive to Ukrainian Jewish organizations was a MAUP kiosk which, until it was closed by the authorities in May 2007, sold anti-Semitic literature at the site of the Babi Yar massacre.[98]

From the perspective of 2013, it appears that political successes for the Ukrainian Conservative Party were limited. A planned joint ultra-nationalist bloc with Yurii Shukhevych's far right paramilitary UNA-UNSO, called The National Liberation Bloc of Shukhevych and Shchokin, 'God and Ukraine Above All!' failed and the UKP performed dismally in the March 2006 polls.[99] The MAUP press responded by claiming that the elections had been 'totally falsified'. After the break with Yushchenko, MAUP lashed out at their former associate:

We will add here that the President of Ukraine, who was elected with violations of current legislation as a result of an additional third round of elections. Forming of such an illegitimate power is the basis for the establishment of an illegal future dictatorship with a criminally-totalitarian manner, which can be defined as bandocracy.[100]

At the same time, *Personal Plius* printed enthusiastic reports on the fair and free elections in neighbouring Belarus, where Lukashenka had been re-elected with 83 per cent of the popular vote in an election which the EU, OSCE and the US described as 'fundamentally flawed'.[101] MAUP started to orient itself away from their former allies in the Yushchenko camp, increasingly soliciting support from authoritarian CIS governments, but also from ultra-nationalists elsewhere. At the end of April 2006, MAUP awarded an honorary doctorate to the Polish Deputy Prime Minister Andrzej Lepper, leader of the populist *Samoobrona* (Self-defence) Party, a junior partner within the arch-conservative government of Jarosław Kaczyński.[102] Human Rights groups, such as the Anti-Defamation League called on Lepper to renounce any links with MAUP, something he refused to do.[103] In the winter of 2006, a list of prominent Ukrainian and diaspora intellectuals signed an open letter in support of the academics facing litigation, and condemning MAUP's anti-Semitism 'as an affront to academic ethics'.[104] After 2006, courting the diaspora, an important priority for MAUP and the Conservative Party, became increasingly difficult. In November 2007 the Ukrainian Ministry of Foreign Affairs appointed an Ambassador at Large to Combat Xenophobia, Racism, and Discrimination. On November 30, the US ambassador met with him to discuss MAUPs activities. He acknowledged the problem of hate crime and that these incidents were damaging Ukraine's international reputation. The US embassy reported to Washington that the Ukrainian Ambassador 'opined that xenophobia can be tied to low living standards and Ukraine's history of anti-Semitism,' and that the SBU, the Ukrainian security service, 'needed to do more to investigate MAUP's funding, especially from external sources that Horin called "significant".'[105]

Since the fall of 2007, MAUP has sharply curtailed its anti-Semitic activities. It is not clear why. Rabbi Ianel Bleich argues that this shows 'that MAUP was a pawn of Muslims, extremists or Russian nationalists'.[106] In any case, in 2009, MAUP's share of the hate literature in Ukraine had fallen to 50 per cent.[107] However, in late 2011 MAUP literature was still being sold in academic bookstores across Ukraine. Anti-Semitic literature is sold openly, including in the central squares of Kyiv and Lviv.[108] The MAUP university book store in Kyiv were selling the *Protocols of the Elders of Zion*, David Duke's *The Jewish Question Through the Eyes of an American*,[109] Swiss Holocaust denier Jürgen Graf's *The Great Lie of the 20th Century*,[110] books like *Ritual Murder:*

259

Historical Evidence,[111] *The Jewish Mafia and its Cult,*[112] and *The Matzoh of Zion,* by former Syrian Deputy Prime Minister Mustafa Tlass.[113] Established Ukrainian historians have cited MAUP's translation of David Duke as an un-exceptional source.[114] Following Yushchenko's rehabilitation of the most significant interwar Ukrainian fascist movement, the Organization of Ukrainian Nationalists (OUN), MAUP has taken part in the promotion of their legacy: in 2011, MAUP organized an international conference on the leading ideologue of the OUN, Dmytro Dontsov, a passionate, organic anti-Semite.[115]

Like the UNO-UNSA, the UKP failed to gain mass support. Following the demise of Yushchenko and his *Nasha Ukraina* in 2010, the most successful Ukrainian extreme right party is Oleh Tiahnybok's *Svoboda.* Based primarily in Western Ukraine, it combines populist rhetoric, historical revisionism and ultra-nationalist symbolism, presenting itself as the intellectual heir of the OUN. With 10.44 per cent of the popular vote *Svoboda* had a break-through in the October 2012 parliamentary elections.[116]

Conclusion

MAUP's conspiratorial narrative shows many similarities with that of Russian nationalists and Stalinists. The people associated with MAUP are a heterogeneous crowd: it includes Lukashenka supporters and people nostalgic for the Soviet era, as well as former dissidents, such as Luk"ianenko and Yurii Shukhevych, who spent many years in Soviet prisons. Shchokin positions himself somewhere in the middle between the Western Ukrainian anti-Soviet and the 'Eurasian' anti-Western traditions. He aimed at using anti-Semitism, under the Soviet 'anti-Zionist' label as a common denominator to unite disparate political figures and interests. MAUP was an ambitious attempt at turning conspiracy theories, half-truths and hate speech into academic discourse and political capital. It aimed at legitimizing White supremacists by conferring them scholarly credentials and coordinating them with Middle Eastern 'anti-Zionists'.

In MAUP's discourse we recognize patterns of National Socialist as well as Soviet anti-Semitic traditions: the Jew as a pimp and sexual predator was a staple in *Der Stürmer,* the linking of Zionism to Nazism a frequent theme in Soviet 'anti-Zionist' propaganda. The idea that Moscow had a master plan to kill off the

Ukrainian people in order to re-populate Ukraine with Russians, or 'Muscovites' ('*moskali*') is not new, but was a staple in émigré OUN(b) ideology.[117]

The hysterical tone and the grossly inaccurate claims made by MAUP are unique in Europe in that they are presented as academic discourse. Yet MAUP's high profile anti-Semitism, while crude and extreme, does not differ much from the official rhetoric of its sponsors Iran, Syria, and colonel Gaddafi's now-deposed regime in Libya. The al-Assad clan turned Holocaust denial into official Syrian government policy, their Iranian sponsors maintain a similar line. MAUP's attempts to transplant a discourse, prevalent in the Middle East to a post-Soviet environment may have been a lucrative business; funding from Middle Eastern dictatorships appears to have been significant. Many questions remain unanswered. A deliberate operation to discredit Yushchenko, either from opponents within Ukraine, or in Russia, as some observers have alleged, cannot be excluded.

MAUP's radical anti-Semitic discourse may appear farcical, but in a notoriously corrupt society with a limited democratic tradition, conspiratorial explanations do find a receptive audience in at least some sections of society. Furthermore, anti-Semitism is on the rise in Ukraine, and it is not stigmatized in the same way as it is in Western Europe and North America.[118] Recent studies show that a fourth of Ukrainians do not want to accept Jews as citizens of Ukraine, and less than 3 per cent would be willing to accept a Jew as a family member.[119] The rise in anti-Semitic attitudes among young people was particularly strong. According to a 2006 poll 45 per cent of Ukrainians between the age of 18 and 20 would like to see no Jews living in Ukraine.[120]

Parts of Luk"ianenko's narrative became government policy under Yushchenko: in July 2008, the Ukrainian Security Forces (SBU), which Yushchenko had assigned propaganda duties, organized a public hearing on the 1932 – 1933 famine, in which it presented a list of nineteen perpetrators of the 'famine-genocide', of which eight people (40 per cent) were Jews.[121] The fortunes of the activists associated with MAUP have differed. Shchokin and Iaremenko continue to run their apparently lucrative private university, albeit with a lower profile, Luk"ianenko and Shukhevych their nationalist activism. David Duke has been banned from entering Ukraine. Andrzej Lepper was disgraced by a sex scandal; he and his party fell out of the Sejm, Lepper himself committed suicide in August, 2011.[122] The 'Arab spring' swept Gaddafi

261

from power. In the moment of writing, the Syrian government is facing an open rebellion and its fate appears uncertain.

ENDNOTES

[1] The author wishes to thank Oleksandr Burakovs'kyi for suggestions and constructive criticism and Taras Kuzio for generously sharing materials and references with him.

[2] Per Anders Rudling, 'Organized Anti-Semitism in Contemporary Ukraine: Structure, Influence and Ideology', *Canadian Slavonic Papers/Revue canadienne des slavistes* XLVIII / 1 – 2 (March – June 2006), pp. 81 – 118; idem. 'Anti-Semitism and the Extreme Right in Contemporary Ukraine', in Andrea Mammone, Emmanuel Godin, and Brian Jenkins (eds.), *Mapping the Extreme Right in Contemporary Europe: From Local to Transnational* (London and New York: Routledge, 2012), pp. 189 – 205.

[3] See White Supremacist and MAUP Professor David Duke's site: www.davidduke.com 'ADL Seeks Closure of Largest University in Ukraine and the imprisonment of hundreds of Academics', at: http://www.davidduke.com/?p=468#more-468 (accessed 06/12/2005) and the Anti-Defamation League's site 'Ukraine University Schooling in Anti-Semitism' at: www.adl.org/main_Anti_Semitism_International/maup_ukraine.htm (accessed 09/12/2005).

[4] 'NCSJ Backgrounder'.

[5] See the Anti-Defamation League's site 'Ukraine University Schooling in Anti-Semitism', at: http://www.adl.org/main_Anti_Semitism_International/maup_ukraine.htm (accessed 09/12/2005); and E. Morgan Williams ed., 'Ukraine President Yushchenko Criticizes Magazine over "Anti-Semitism"', *The Action Ukraine Report – AUR*, Number 612, 6 December 2005. Mar'iana Oleinik, 'Chelovek, mnogo povidavshii", *Stolichnye Novosti*, No. 33 (181), 11 – 17 September 2001, at: http://cn.com.ua/N181/politics/firsthands/firsthands.html (accessed 16/05/2006).

[6] Matveyev and Ruby, 'Anti-Semitism in Ukrainian Media Up, and its Acceptance is Worrying Jews', NCSJ, Advocates on behalf of Jews in Russia, Ukraine, the Baltic States and Eurasia, 21 September 2004. Tarasiuk's involvement with MAUP went back a number of years. From February 2001 he was the Director of Social Studies and International Relations at MAUP, where he had close relations with Shchokin and his deputies. Oleinik, 'Chelovek...' (2001) Tarasiuk and Yushchenko were not the only politicians working at MAUP. So were Boris Oliinyk, Viktor Pinzenyk and Gennadii Udovenko. Mar'iana Oleinik, 'Vzriraia na litsa' *Stolichnye Novosti*, No. 37 (185). 9 – 15 October 2001, at: http://cn.com.ua/N185/po litics/firsthands/firsthands.html (accessed 16/05/2006).

[7] Oleksandr Burakovs'kyi, *Evrei i ukraintsy, 1986 – 2006: istoriia i analiz evreisko-ukrainskikh otnoshenii* (New York: IRSA Publishers, 2007), p. 308. Kravchuk's relation with MAUP is enigmatic. On one hand, he has attended several MAUP conferences and had articles and papers published in the MAUP press. He also serves on the board of MAUP. On the other hand, his political party, the 'united' Social Democratic Party of Ukraine, or SDPU(o), is often viciously attacked by MAUP, and Kravchuk himself appears as a co-editor of a SDPU(o) publication, highly critical of MAUP and their 'xenophobic-racist Sabbath'. See L. M. Kravchuk *et al.*, eds., *Narushenie prav cheloveka i politicheskie repressii v Ukraine, Ion'*, 2005 (Kyiv: Dovira, 2005), p. 45. *Zolota Knyha Ukraïns'koi Elity: Informatsiino – imidhevskyi al'manalk u 6 tomakh/Golden Book of Ukrainian Elite: Information and Image Anthology in 6 Volumes. Vol. 6* (Kyïv: Kompaniia IEvroimidzh, 2001), p. 175. *Holodomor 1932-1933 rokiv iak velichezna trahediia ukraïns'koho harodu: Mater.*

Vseukr. Nauk. Konf. Kyïv, 15 listop. 2002 r. (Kyïv: MAUP, 2003), pp. 7 – 9.

[8] Vladimir Matveyev, 'Earning Reputation for Anti-Semitism, University asks U.N. to "Close" Israel', *Jewish Telegraphic Agency* 6 December 2005, at: http://www.ncsj.orh/AuxPa ges/120105MAUP.shtml (accessed 07/05/2006).

[9] See: 'David Duke Achieves Doctorate in Ukraine' at: http://www.davidduke.com/index.ph p?p=394; also see the Anti-Defamation League's site at: http://www.adl.org/main_An ti_Semitism_International/maup_ukraine.htm (both accessed 20/10/2005).

[10] Ibid.

[11] Vasyl' Iaremenko, *Ievreï v Ukraïni s'ohodni: real'nist' bez mifiv* [*Jews in Ukraine Today: Reality without Myths*] (Kyïv: MAUP, 2003). 52.

[12] Eduard Doks, 'Babii Iar – eto zhidovskaia legenda', *AEN, Agenstvo Evreiskikh Novostei*, 7 May 2006, at: http://www.aen.ru/anti-semitism/story-id=628/ (accessed 23/05/2006).

[13] For a survey of the persistent fascination with the works of Werner Sombart in the For-mer Soviet Union, see Joachim Zweynert and Damiel Riniker, *Werner Sombart in Rußland. Ein vergessenes Kapitel seiner Lebens- und Wirkungsgeschichte.* (Mar-burg: Metropolis, 2004). See also the review by Lars Fischer in *East European Jewish Affairs* 35/1 (June 2005), p. 133.

[14] See for instance Iurii Alekseevich Shilov, *Istoki slavianskoi tsivilizatsii* (Kyiv: MAUP, 2004), pp. 13 – 17, 633 – 636.

[15] 'NCSJ Backgrounder: The Inter-Regional Academy of Personnel Management (MAUP, IAPM)', *NCSJ, Advocates on Behalf of Jews in Russia, Ukraine, the Baltic States and Eurasia*, 1 December 2005, at: http://www.ncsj.org/AuxPages/120105MAUP.shtml#MA3 (accessed 07/05/2006).

[16] 'Shchokin, Heorii Vasyl'ovych', in Iurii Marchenko and Oleksander Telemko eds., *Kto ie kto v Ukraïni* (Kyïv: K.I.S., 2004), p. 969.

[17] The English-language so-called *Golden Book of Ukrainian Elite*, listing the most influen-tial people in Ukraine, provides the following account of its rector: 'The Interregional Academy of personnel management owes its numerous accomplishments to George V. Shcokin, [sic] institutional founder and top manager, famous scientist, gifted ad-ministrator, and outstanding idea man [...] The International Who's Who Centre acknowledged George Shcokin as an outstanding person of the 20th century, while the American Who's Who Institute enlisted his name to the 500 world's most influen-tial leaders'. *Zolota Knyha Ukraïns'koi Elity*, vol. 6, p. 175.

[18] Rainer Rupp, 'Nationalheld entpuppt sich als Antisemit: Ukraine: Auf Konferenz wird gegen Juden gehetzt – in Anwesenheit von Neonazis und ranghohen Politikern', *Junge Welt*, 10 June 2005, at: http://www.jungewelt.de/2005/06-10/011.php; Anatoly Podolsky, 'Once More About the Banality of Evil', *Ukraïns'kyi tsentr vyvchennya istoriï Holokostu*, at: http://www.holocaust.kiev.ua/eng/research/researchm.htm. Oleg Var-folomeyev, 'Xenophobes to Contest Seats in Ukrainian Parliament', *Eurasia Daily Monitor*, 9 January 2006.

[19] Matveyev and Ruby, 'Anti-Semitism'. His anti-Semitic speeches were later published as Heo-rihii Shchokin, *Kyl'turnoe raznoobrazie mira: puti i prepiatstviia* (Kyiv: MAUP, 2003).

[20] Alexander Muratov, 'Jewish Question', *Jewish Observer*, 15/58 (August 2003).

[21] 'Ukrainian Jews Worried About New Party', *Jerusalem Post*, 6 April 2005. See also The Religious Information Service of Ukraine, 24 August 2005, at: http://www.risu.org.ua/eng/news/article;6978/ 'NCSJ Backgrounder: The Inter-Regional Academy of Personnel Management (MAUP, IAPM)' NCSJ, Advocates on Behalf of Jews in Russia, Ukraine, the Baltic States and Eurasia, 1 December 2005,

at: http://www.ncsj.org/AuxPages/120105MAUP.shtml#NCSJ (both accessed 06/12/2005).

[22] Rudling, 'Organized Anti-Semitism", p. 83.

[23] Anatoly Podolsky, 'Once More About the Banality of Evil', *Ukraïns'kyi tsentr vyvchennia istoriï Holokostu*, at: http://www.holocaust.kiev.ua/eng/research/researchm.htm (accessed 20/09/2005). See also the Testimony of Mark B. Levin, Executive Director NCSJ: Advocates on Behalf of Jews in Russia, Ukraine, the Baltic States and Eurasia Before the United States House of Representatives Committee on International Relations, 6 October 2004, at: http://www.house.gov/international_relations/108/lev100604.htm (accessed 20/09/2005); and Matveyev, 'Earning reputation'.

[24] See 'US Department of State: Ukraine: International Religious Freedom Report, 2005, Released by the Bureau of Democracy, Human Rights, and Labour'. Released 8 November 2005, at: http://www.state.gov/g/drl/rls/irf/2005/51588.htm (accessed 07/12/2005).

[25] 'MAUP is a provocative organization, hostile to the Ukrainian state, which is funded by "Arab and Russian money", and through means of deliberately disseminating anti-Semitic propaganda [...] and thus discrediting the Ukrainian domestic policy in the eyes of the world – as xenophobic and chauvinist. The aim is to keep Ukraine out of the EU and bring them closer to Russia with the aim of fusing the two and Ukraine losing its independence'. Anatolii Shcherbatiuk, 'FSB okopalas' v MAUP: Informatsiia do rozdumiv', open letter to the head of Sluzhba Bezpeki and the Ukrainian Ministry of Internal Affairs, 27 March 2006, at: http://ord.com.ua/categ_1/article_50630.html (accessed 29/04/2006). However, Shcherbatiuk is a questionable source of information. A fanatical anti-Semite, Shcherbatiuk's style of writing is similar to that of his employer Shchokin. 'Our Muscovites (moskali) and yids (zhydy) can live and multiply only in a neglected and weakened social organism. They do not multiply according to traditional sociological norms, nor do they follow general moral rules. They rather operate on the basis of the particular biological principles, mastered by parasites. After all, we cannot expect a different behaviour and relation of that material [...] Are we to keep humiliating ourselves in the eyes of the surrounding peoples, by our constant dependence on a people, which the Germans in disgust inject with phenol?' Shcherbatiuk extols the purity of the blood of the Ukrainian nation, while advocating the ruthless and immediate destruction of Russian and Jewish parasites. For this purpose, Shcherbatiuk proposes 'cleansing units' modeled after the *Einsatzgruppen* to operate in Ukraine and in territories to which extreme Ukrainian nationalists lay claim. Anatolii Shcherbatiuk, 'Osnovy sanatsii', *Neskorena natsiia*, 16 November 1993 and Bohdan Bozniuk, 'Ukraina: Perelovka istorii. Palachei v geroi hatsii?', *Morskaia Gazeta*, No. 19. 16 February 2002. On Shcherbatiuk, see Oleksandr Burakovs'kyi, *Istoriia rady natsional'nostei Narodnoho Rukhu Ukrainy, 1989 – 1993* (New York: IRSA Publishing, 2007), pp. 153 – 160; 'Heorhii Shchokin zustrivsia z tymchasovym povirenym Islamskoï Respubliki Iran v Ukraïni panom Saied Akhmed Musavi Maleki'. MAUP Official News Site, 24 March 2006, at: http://www.maup.com.ua/news/news.php?idn=359 (accessed 05/05/2006).

[26] 'Vizit do Ukraïny delehatsiï u skladi deputativ Meli-medzhlisu (azerbaidhans'koho parlamentu)', MAUP Official news site, 24 March 2006, at: http://www.maup.com.ua/news/news.php?idn=358 (accessed 05/05/2006).

[27] 'Studenty-mizhnarodnyky Akademiï zaniomliat'sia z "Zelenuiu Knyhoiu", MAUP official news, 7 October 2006, at: http://www.maup.com.ua/news/news.php?idn=225 (accessed 05/05/2006).

[28] Matveyev, 'Earning reputation'.

[29] Ibid.

[30] *Holodomor* 1932 – 1933, p. 278.

[31] Iaremenko, p. 96. In this Ukrainian Holocaust, Iaremenko maintains, 'Not a single Jew died of hunger in 1933', p. 97.

[32] *Zolota Knyha Ukraïns'koi Elity*, pp. 175 – 176.

[33] Luk"ianenko, *Zlochynna sut'*, p. 130 (back cover).

[34] Levko Luk"ianenko, 'U lystopadovi zhalobni dni', in *Komu buv vyhidnyi holodomor?: Statti* (Kyiv: MAUP, 2004), p. 44.

[35] Ibid.

[36] *Holodomor* is the term used for the Ukrainian famine of 1932 – 1933. It is predominantly used by those who endorse the interpretation that the 1932 – 1933 man-made famine in the Soviet Union constituted genocide. The term appeared in the Ukrainian diaspora in the 1980s and was re-exported to Ukraine at the conclusion of that decade. It is also used to distinguish the famine in predominantly Ukrainian-speaking lands from that of other parts of the USSR, such as the Volga region, the Northern Caucasus, and Kazakhstan, which also suffered enormous population losses in the famine. Luk"ianenko's organization refers to *Holodomors* in the plural to denote the inclusion of the famines of 1921 and 1946 – 1947 in Ukraine. On Luk"ianenko's association, see Johan Dietsch, *Making Sense of Suffering: Holocaust and Holodomor in Ukrainian Historical Culture* (Lund: Department of History, Lund University, 2006), pp. 208 – 209.

[37] Levko Luk"ianenko, *Zlochynna sut' KPRS-KPU: Niurnberh – 2* (Kyiv: MAUP, 2005), pp. 42 – 44.

[38] Luk"ianenko, *Zlochynna sut'*, p. 123.

[39] Luk"ianenko, 'U lystopadovi zhalobni dni', p. 44.

[40] Ihor Khyzhniak, 'Natsional'nyi vymir u peredumovi vynyknennia holodomoru 1932 – 1933 rokiv v Ukraini: Dopovid' na Vseukrains'kii naukovii konferentsii "Holodomor 1932 – 1933 rokiv iak velychezna trahediia ukrains'koho narodu, 15 lystopada 2002 roku", in M. A. Drozdets'ka ed., *Komu buv vyhidnyi holodomor?: Statti* (Kyiv: MAUP, 2004), pp. 55 – 62.

[41] Matveyev and Ruby.

[42] 'Sionizm – Zahroza Svoitoviy tsivilizatsiï: U MAUP vidbulasia IV Vsesvitnia naukova konferentsiia "Dialoh tsivilizatsiy"' *Personal Plius* No. 23 (122), 8 – 14 June 2005. pp. 5 – 8.

[43] 'Tymoshenko: Toss out Luk"ianenko', Editorial, *Kyiv Post*, 9 June 2005, at: http://www.kyivpost.com/opinion/editorial/22803/ (accessed 27/08/2005).

[44] The Religious Information Service of Ukraine, 24 August 2005, at: http://www.risu.org.ua/eng/news/article;6978/ (accessed 27/08/2005).

[45] Levko Luk"ianenko, 'Do evreis'koho pytannia, abo Chy isnuie Ukraïni anti-Semitism?' *Personal Plius*, No. 26 (73), 2004. pp. 4 – 5.
Incidentally, MAUP Professor Vasyl' Iaremenko singles out the editor of the English language newspaper *Kyiv Post* as one of its enemies. Iaremenko knows to inform us about the reason for *Kyiv Post's* sensitivity to open racism: they are part of the conspiracy against Ukraine. '[W]e are consuming the information and spiritual productions of the Jewish ideological kitchen. Today we need to raise the question about creating a Ukrainian TV, which instead of supporting the politics, ideology, cultural disinformation or information of Zionist Jewish centres in the US, would promote our Ukrainian [culture]'. As an example of this un-Ukrainian media outlet Iaremenko lists 'Jed Sandes, American Zionist Jew, Citizen of the United States, Publishing the Papers *Korrespondent* and *Kyiv-Post* in Kyiv'. Iaremenko, pp. 83 – 84.

[46] 'Levko Luk"ianenko: "Hero of Ukraine"', *Den'*, 26 April 2005, at:

http://www.day.kiev.ua/136386/ (accessed 10/10/2005); Rudling, 'Anti-Semitism and the Extreme Right in Contemporary Ukraine', p. 196.

[47] H. V. Shchokin, 'Zirka heroia – bortsiu za derzhavnist', *Personal Plius*, no. 17 (115), 27 April – 3 May 2005. p. 1. 'Levko Luk"ianenko – Heroi Ukraïny',] *Personal: zhurnal intellektualnoï elity* 5 (2005), pp. 3 – 4.

[48] Burakovs'kyi, *Evrei i ukraintsy, 1986 – 2006*. p. 308.

[49] 'Tymoshenko: Toss out Luk"ianenko', Editorial, *Kyiv Post*, 9 June 2005. For Luk"ianenko's credentials, see Iuliia Tymoshenko's official site: http://ww2.tymoshenko.com.ua/eng/elections/partners/ (accessed 15//2005).

[50] Oleg Varfolomeyev 'Tymoshenko Comes Up With Election Strategy', *Eurasia Daily Monitor*, 12 December 2005, and JM, 'Former Ukrainian Premier's Bloc Drafts Parliamentary Election List' *RFE/RL Newsline* 8 December 2005. Vol. 9, No. 228.

[51] Sergei Kostunenko, 'Prikaz po MAUP: Chitat' rasistskie bredni!', *Stolichnye Novosti, elektronnaia versia*, No. 23 (360), 22 June – 4 July 2005, at: http://www.cn.com.ua/N360/resonance/scandal/scandal.html (accessed 09/05/2006).

[52] Vladimir Matveyev, 'Kiev University to UN: "Close" Israel', *Jewish Times*, 7 December 2005, at: http://www.jewishtimes.com/News/5231.stm (accessed 07/12/2005).

[53] Kostunenko.

[54] 'David Duke and Ukrainian MP Attend Anti-Semitic Conference in Kiev', UCSJ: Union of Councils for Jews in the Former Soviet Union, 10 June 2005, at: http://www.fsumonitor.com/stories/061005Ukraine.shtml (accessed 27/08/2005).

[55] Kostunenko.

[56] Kravchuk *et al.*, ed., pp. 44 – 45. It should be emphasized that this bulletin was published by the United Social Democratic Party of Ukraine, headed by former president Leonid Kuchma's chief of staff Victor Medvedchuk, who was decidedly opposed to the Orange Revolution. Medvedchuk is one of the people most often demonized as a 'Jew', 'Zionist' and 'Bundist' in MAUP's publications.

[57] Heorhii Shchokin, 'Z viroiu v ukraïns'ku Ukraïnu!', MAUP News Online, 23 January 2006.

[58] Ibid.

[59] Ibid.

[60] Vasyl Iaremenko, 'Zaiava Federatsiï patriotychnykh vydan' Ukraïni Ministru iustitsiï Ukraïny R. Zvarychu', *MAUP News online*, 7 April 2005, at: http://www.maup.com.ua/news/news.php?idn=139 (accessed 20/10/2005).

[61] A derivative with reference to Leonid Kuchma, the second President of Ukraine, 1994 – 2005.

[62] Ibid.

[63] Heorhii Shchokin, 'Suchasnyi politychnyi stan v Ukraïni ta perspektyvy palaments'kykh perehoniv (dopovid' na z'ïzdi Ukraïnskoï Konservativnoï partiï 14 zhovtnia 2005 roku) Kyïv, 2005', MAUP News Online, at: http://www.maup.com.ua/news/news.php?idn=234 (accessed 01/05/2006); Heorhii Shchokin, 'Z viroiu v ukraïns'ku Ukraïnu!', *MAUP News Online*, 23 January 2006, at: http://www.maup.com.ua/news/news.php?idn=320 (accessed 01/05/2006).

[64] Ibid.

[65] Iaremenko taught the history of Ukrainian pre-revolutionary journalism and publishing for over 30 years and has a fairly impressive number of publications behind him. Iaremenko (2003) back cover, pp. 27, 55, 106.

[66] Ibid., p. 17.

[67] Ibid., p. 4.

[68] Ibid., pp. 12 – 13.

[69] Ibid., p. 15, p. 33.

[70] Ibid., p. 24.

[71] Ibid., p. 18.

[72] Ibid., p. 15, pp. 23 – 24.

[73] Ibid., p. 109.

[74] Ibid., p. 55, p. 109.

[75] Ibid., p. 111.

[76] Ibid., pp. 19 – 20.

[77] Ibid., p. 106. Ironically, in the recent past, other extreme Ukrainian nationalists have publicly found the Ukrainian participation in the mass murder at Babi Yar a source of pride. For instance, in the Rivne city *Rada* in 1995 the extreme nationalist Shkuratiuk stated: 'I am proud of the fact that among 1,500 *Polizei* executioners in Babi Yar there were 1,200 OUN men but only 300 Germans'. Myrs'kii, Naiman, 46, citing the nationalist newspaper *Neskorena natsiia* 5 (1995).

[78] Iaremenko, pp. 22 – 23. See also pp. 85 – 87.

[79] Ibid., p. 64.

[80] 'Ievreï zdiisnyly seksual'nu revolutsiiu v Amerytsi i zapravliaiut' pornuindustiieiu', *Personal Plius*, No. 19 (170), 10 – 16 May, 2006, at: http://www.personal-plus.net/article.php?ida=678 (accessed 16/05/2006).

[81] V. D. Bondar (ed.,), *Sions'ki protokoly: dzherela i dokumenty* (Kyiv: MAUP, 2005).

[82] 'Vid vydavnytsva', *Sions'ki protokoly*, p. 7.

[83] 'Ukraïntsi ameryky vidvidali akademiiu', *Personal Plius*, No. 27 (74), 19 – 25 July 2004. p. 11. Less than a year later, UCCA attempted to distance themselves from MAUP, claiming that 'The Government of Ukraine has taken appropriate measures against the xenophobic/anti-Semitic activities and propaganda of Inter-regional Academy of Personnel Management (MAUP). The Ministry of Education has been entrusted with this responsibility. The Ukrainian Congress Committee of America is distressed by the on-going activities of MAUP. In June 2005, the UCCA issued a statement condemning the institution's practices of anti-Semitic programmes and propaganda and has denounced their conferences predicated on religious and national hatred. We believe such programmes and defamatory statements of the academy's rector have no place within Ukraine's democratic society'. Michael Sawkiw Jr., through his secretary Marie Duplak 'UCCA Statement on Protection of Minority Rights', at: http://ucca.org/uccanews/story/121 9051701.shtml (accessed 09/05/2006). The UCCA is affiliated with the Bandera wing of the Organization of Ukrainian Nationalists. On the OUN's attitudes to Jews, see Marco Carynnyk, 'Foes of our Rebirth: Ukrainian Nationalist Discussions about Jews, 1929 – 1947', *Nationalities Papers* 39/3 (2011), pp. 315 – 352.

[84] 'JTA correspondent beaten', *JTA Daily Briefing*, 14 December 2005; 'Newspaper Editor Beaten Up', *Kyiv Post*, 13 April 2006.

[85] 'Kiev Court Shuts Down Newspapers for Reporting on Anti- Semitism', *UCSJ: Union of Councils for Jews in the Former Soviet Union*, 23 December 2005.

[86] The academics sued were Myroslav Popovych, Iaroslav Iatskiv, Nataliia Iakovenko, Stanislav Kul'chytskyi, Oleksandr Mayboroda and Iurii Shapoval. 'MAUP podala do sudu na akademikiv Natsional'noï akademiï nauk', *5 Kanal*, at: http://5tv.com.ua/newsline/184/0/20564/ (accessed 20/04/2006).

[87] 'Stop world Zionism offensive to the speech and thought freedom: Statement of the Presidium of the International Personnel Academy', *MAUP News Online*, 4 November 2005 (accessed 01/05/2006).

[88] Matveyev, 'Earning Reputation', 'Pol'sha ne priznaet diplomy MAUP!', *MIGNews* (Media International Group), 16 December 2005, at: http://mignews.com.ua/articles/1 89248.html (accessed 09/05/2006).

[89] For this information, *Persona Plius* cites G. Klimov, 'Protokoly sovetskikh mudrevtsov' (Krasnodar, 2001), p. 350. Klimov is 'an American author with Russian origins', who in turn cites a 'book, recently published in Switzerland' by a certain Khenneke Kardel. The title of the book is given as *Hitler – sozdatel' Izrailia*, [Hitler, the Founder of Israel], (Geneva, 1987). The article is signed Antinaklepnits'ka Liha Ukraïny, often poorly translated as 'Antislanderous League of Ukraine'. The references to the Anti-Defamation League are hard to miss. This Anti-Semitic MAUP-associated organization is headed by M. Senchenko, a prominent MAUP leader. 'Khto buv hospadarem Babinoho Iaru?' *Personal Plius*, No. 17 (168) 26 April – 2 May 2006, at: http://www.personal-plus.net/print.php?ida=645 (accessed 07/05/2006).

[90] Varfolomeyev 'Tymoshenko'; 'Levko Luk''ianenko: "Hero of Ukraine"', *Den'*, 26 April 2005, at: http://www.day.kiev.ua/136386/ (accessed 03/10/2005).

[91] Matveyev, 'Earning Reputation'.

[92] 'Ukrainian Ministers Condemn "Anti-Semitic" University', *European Jewish Congress*, 27 January 2006. Varfolomeyev, 'Xenophobes'.

[93] 'Former Ukrainian Premier's Block Drafts Parliamentary Election List' At: www.rferl.org/newsline/2005/12/08/081205.aps (accessed 09/12/2005).

[94] Shchokin, Iaremenko, Holovatyi *et al.*, 'Prypynyty zlochynni diï orhanizovanoho ievreist-va', *Personal Plius*, No. 15 (113) 14 – 19 April 2005, at: http://personal-plus.net/print.php?ida=120 (accessed 01/05/2006).

[95] 'Statement of the Presidium of the International Personnel Academy', *MAUP News Online*, 20 March 2006, at: http://www.maup.com.ua/news/news.php?idn=349 (accessed 01/05/2006).

[96] Heorhii Shchokin, 'Address of the International Personnel Academy Concerning Offensive Caricatures in European Publications', *MAUP News Online*, 2 February 2006, at: http://www.maup.com.ua/news/news.php?idn=327 (accessed 01/05/2006).

[97] 'Ubyvstvo v Kyievi: Chi ne ritual'ne?', *Personal Plius*, No. 16 (167), 19 – 25 April, 2006, at: http://www.personal-plus.net/print.php?ida=616 (accessed 01/05/2006).

[98] Rudling, 'Anti-Semitism and the Extreme Right in Contemporary Ukraine', p. 197.

[99] Ibid., p. 196.

[100] 'Appeal of Political and Public Organizations to the International Community in Relation to the Election of 2006 in Ukraine', *MAUP News Online*, 18 April 2006, at: http://www.maup/com.ua/news/news.php?idn=372 (accessed 01/05/2006).

[101] Maryna L'vova, 'Pro revoliutsiiu, vybory ta batsku...', *Personal Plius*, No. 16 (167), 19 – 25 April, 2006, at: http://personal-plus.net/print.php?ida=621 (accessed 05/05/2006).

[102] 'Pochesnyi doctor MKA – vitse-prem'ier Pol'shchi', *Personal Plius*, No. 19 (170), 10 – 16 May 2006, at: http://www.personal-plus.net/article.php?ida=669 (accessed 16/05/2006). As with the people at MAUP, Lepper denies being an anti-Semite, despite his support of Jean-Marie Le Pen and previous praise for Hitler's economic policies. Lepper, who had a background as a pig farmer and communist, shared some of MAUP's enthusiasm for the Belarussian President Aliaksandr Lukashenka. In 2004, Lepper expressed his support for changes in the Belarussian constitution so that Lukashenka could run for a third term as President, expressing his hope that Lukashenka would remain President 'till he dies'. Lily Galili, 'I'm no fascist' Haaretz.com, 6 May 2006, at: http://www.haaretz.com/hasen/pa ges/ShArt.jhtml (accessed 08/05/2006). Simon Araloff, 'Poland's Elections: Andrzej Zbig-

new Lepper – Peasantry's Iron Fist (8-10%)', *Global Challenges Research, AIA – Axis Information and Analysis*, 3 October 2005, at: http://www.axisglobe.com/article.as p?article=410 (accessed 08/05/2006). See also *The Beetroot: Politics and Current Affairs of Poland, Central Europe and the EU from a British Journalist in Warsaw*, at: http://beetroot.blogspot.com/2005/10/presidential-candidate-andrzej-lepper.html (accessed 08/05/2006).

[103] Piotr Gillert, 'Niech odda doktorat: Organizacje żydowskie o Lepperze', *Rzeczpospolita*, 2 May 2006. 'Human Rights Group concerned about "Extremist" Parties in Poland's New Coalition', *Kyiv Post*, 2 May 2006, at: http://www.kyivpost.com/bn/24381/print/ (accessed 08/05/2006).

[104] 'Proty ksenofobiï, za evropeis'ku Ukraïnu: borot'ba trivae', *Svoboda* No. 6, 10 February 2006. pp. 9 – 10. 'CIUS expresses Solidarity with Scholars who oppose Anti-Semitism', *Ukrainian Weekly*, Vol. LXXIX, No. 4, 22 February 2006. p. 6.

[105] American Embassy Kyiv to Secretary of State, Washington DC, Confidential US embassy cable 10 December 2007, reference ID 07KYIV3034, 'Ukraine: MOI and MFA discuss plans to fight xenophobic attacks: 12(c), Ambassador meets with MFA Ambassador at Large on Xenophobia' *Wikileaks*, http://wikileaks.org/cable/2007/1 2/07KYIV3034.html# (accessed 26/09/2012).

[106] Nadine Epstein, 'The Mysterious Tale of a Ukrainian University's Anti-Semitic Crusade', *Moment Magazine*, (November/December 2009), p. 70.

[107] Epstein, 'The Mysterious Tale', p. 71.

[108] Rudling, "Organized Anti-Semitism", p. 85; Jared McBride, 'Euro 2012: Maiden of Hate?', *Kyiv Post*, 21 December 2011, at: http://www.kyivpost.com/news/opinion/le tters/detail/119367/ (accessed 23/05/2012).

[109] Deivid Diuk [David Duke], *Evreiskii vopros glazami amerikantsa: moe issledovanie sionizma* (Kyiv: MAUP, 2002).

[110] Jurgen Graf [Jürgen Graf], *Velikaia lozh' XX veka: Mif o genotside evreev v period II Mirovoi voiny* (Kyiv: MAUP, 2005). Original title *Der Holocaust-Schwindel* (Basel: Gideon Burg Verlag, 1993).

[111] Monakh Neofit, I. Dal', T.I. Butkevich, *Istoricheskie svidetel'stva ritual'nykh ubiistv* (Kyiv: MAUP, 2004).

[112] V. D. Bondar ed., *Evreis'ka mafiia ta ii kul't* (Kyiv: MAUP, 2006).

[113] Mustafa Tlass, *Matsa Sionu* (Kyiv: MAUP, 2004). Original title *Matzo of Zion* (Damascus: Dar Tlass, 1991).

[114] For instance, historian Ivan Patryliak relies on David Duke to show the Jewish predominance over the Soviet Communist party. Ivan Patryliak, *Viis'kova dial'nist' OUN(B) u 1940 – 1942 rokakh*, (Kyiv: Kyivs'kyi natsional'nyi universytet imeni Taras Shevchenka, Instytut istrii Ukrainy NAN Ukrainy, 2004), p. 326, citing Deivid Diuk, *Evreiskii vopros glazami amerikantsa: moe issledovanie sionizma* (Kyiv: MAUP, 2002), pp. 39, 49.

[115] Mizhrehional'na Akademiia upravlinnia personalom, Ukrains'ko-Azerbaidzhans'kyi Instytut sotsial'nykh nauk i samovriaduvannia im. H. A. Aliieva, Naukovo-ideolohichnyi tsentr imeni Dmytra Dontsova. '7 zhovtnia 2011 roku vidbudet'sia Mizhnarodna naukovo-praktychna konferentsiia "Spadshchyna Dmytra Dontsova: actual'nist" filosofs'ko-politychnykh ta literaturnnykh vizii', Call for papers. Thanks to Evgenia Sakal for this reference.

[116] Tadeusz A. Olszański, 'Svoboda Party – the New Phenomenon on the Ukrainian Right-Wing Scene', *Centre for Eastern Studies*, 5 July 2011, at: http://www.osw.waw.pl/en/publikacje/osw-commentary/2011-07-05/svoboda-party-new-

phenomenon-ukrainian-rightwing-scene (accessed 05/11/2011); Andreas Umland, 'Ukraine's Right-Wing Politics: Is the Genie out of the Bottle?' *Open Democracy Russia, Post-Soviet World*, at: http://www.opendemocracy.net/od-russia/andreas-umland/ukra ine-right-wing-politics-is-genie-out-of-bottle (accessed 11/11/2011), and Per Anders Rudling, "The Return of the Ukrainian Far Right: The Case of VO Svoboda," in Ruth Wodak and John E. Richardson (eds.), *Analyzing Fascist Discourse: European Fascism in Talk and Text* (London and New York: Routledge, 2013), pp. 228 – 255.

[117] See, for instance: 'The 1932 – 1933 Holocaust in Perspective', *Ukrainian Echo: A Monthly English Language Supply to "Homin Ukrainy"*, 1 June 1983. p. 1.

[118] Volodymyr Paniotto, 'Dynamics of Anti-Semitism in Ukraine (1994 – 2006)', Paper presented at the ASN 12th Annual World Convention, New York, Columbia University, 12 – 14 April, 2007 pp. 19 – 20; Rudling, 'Anti-Semitism and the Extreme Right', pp. 189 – 205; Jeffrey Burds, 'Ukraine: The Meaning of Persecution', *Transitions Online*, at: http://www.history.neu.edu/fac/burds/Burds-Transitions.pdf (accessed 03/05/2006).

[119] Rudol'f Ia. Myrs'kyi, Oleksandr Ia. Naiman, *Iudofobiya proty Ukrainy: stari zaborony i moderni vyhadky*. Vydannya druhe (Kyiv: Akademiia istorii ta kul'tury ievreiv Ukrainy im. Shimona Dubnova, 2000). 75; Natalia V. Panina and Evhen I. Golovakha, *Tendencies in the Development of the Ukrainian Society (1994 – 1998). Sociological Indicators (Tables, Illustrations and Commentaries)*. (Kiev: National Academy of Sciences of Ukraine, Institute of Sociology, 1999), pp. 90 – 93; Nikolai Butkevich, 'Chronicle of anti-Semitism in Ukraine: 2002 – 2004' (Washington, DC: UCSJ—Union of Councils for Jews in the Former Soviet Union, December 2004). 5, at: http://www.fsumonitor.com/stories/12140 4ChronicleinUkraine.pdf (accessed 07/12/2005).

[120] The European Commission against Racism and Intolerance, *Third report on Ukraine*, CRI, 2008(4). Adopted on 29 June 2007 (Strasbourg: Council of Europe, 2008), 25 at: http://hudoc.ecri.coe.int/XMLEcri/ENGLISH/Cycle_03/03_CbC_eng/UKR-CbC-III-2008-4-ENG.pdf (accessed 15/03/2008).

[121] Per Anders Rudling, *The OUN, the UPA, and the Holocaust: A Study in the Manufacturing of Historical Myths* (Pittsburgh: The Centre for Russian and East European Studies, 2011), p. 30.

[122] Epstein, 'The Mysterious Tale'; 'Andrzej Lepper nie żyje. Powiesił się w biurze Samoobrony', 5 August 2011, *Portal Informacyjny Tokfm.pl*, at: http://www.tokfm.pl/Tokfm/1,102433,10071519,Andrzej_Lepper_nie_zyje__Powiesil_ sie_w_biurze_Samoobrony.html (accessed 27/08/2011).

LANGUAGE OF AUTHORITIES AND RADICAL NATIONALISTS

Alexander Verkhovsky

One of the constantly discussed topics in Russian society can be described as 'the threat of Russian nationalism'. It is often assumed that a society, brought up in the spirit of 'Soviet internationalism', along with the authorities, sharing the same worldview, find themselves in opposition to nationalists, who incite enmity between ethnic communities. Almost everything in this picture is misconstrued; in particular, the very opposition between 'good society' and 'bad nationalists' is a fake. In reality, estimates and proposals that emanate from various political groups in society, including different factions of the ruling bureaucracy, represent a continuous spectrum of opinion, where drawing a clear line is quite difficult. The language of the nationalist opposition mimics the mainstream discourse, while many mouthpieces of the said mainstream media discourse often mimic the nationalist language for one reason or another. Within the realm of ethno-political discourse there is a shifting area of 'doublespeak'.

This chapter, written ahead of December 2011, starts with examining the relationship between the nationalist opposition and the authorities, as it has developed during the reigns of Vladimir Putin and Dmitry Medvedev. Next, I move to the official reaction, primarily discursive, to the Moscow riots of December 2010, which have drastically raised the profile of nationalism as a public threat. The response to the same December events from other social forces is also worthy of attention; the same is true for the subsequent counter-reaction of nationalists to the official reaction. The discursive games, played by all these parties, have created not just the doublespeak effect, but an illusion of a broad consensus in the field of ethnic politics throughout the entire spectrum from the state leaders to at least some nationalists.

The 2000s: nationalists and the authorities

The 2000s are characterized by an increasingly heated debate regarding the kind of social problems that can be considered ethnic (and are definitely interpreted as such in today's Russia) and those that cannot. However, prior to analyzing current discursive trends, it is necessary to say a few words regarding the overall political landscape, upon which they unfold. The past decade began with a sharp increase in mass ethnic xenophobia,[1] and the level reached in 2000 has remained virtually unchanged ever since. In the early years of the decade the theme of racist violence entered public consciousness due to a string of pogroms on street markets. At the same time radical nationalist groups, together with the mass media, concentrated their attention on the subject of migration (both immigration and internal 'non-Slavic' migration).[2] This rhetoric was immediately influential to Vladimir Zhirinovsky's Liberal Democratic Party of Russia (*Liberal'no Demokraticheskaya Partiya Rossii*, LDPR) and then by the Motherland (*Rodina*) parliamentary bloc. Anti-immigration themes and the political mobilization of ethnic nationalists have subsequently made significant advances, in spite of fairly strict limitations from above. The entire decade was marked by competition between two main trends in Russian nationalism – the imperialist variety (*impertsy*) and the ethno-nationalist one, which currently shows far greater success and mobility.[3]

Over the years, popular plotlines of nationalist propaganda and various ways to adapt it to the existing legal requirements were rehearsed to the point of automatism, and, by the beginning of the second decade of the century, they gradually emerged into two rhetorically related themes – 'ethnic crime' and 'the problem of the Caucasus' – the latter denoting not so much the problem of the North Caucasus as a region, but the problem created by immigrants from the Caucasus in other parts of Russia. The nationalist opposition, ever more insistent in recent years, has infused this discourse with harsh criticism of the authorities, styling them as corrupt, anti-national or even anti-Russian and serving the 'foreign-born'.[4]

It is difficult to say whether the nationalists have narrowed down their agenda intuitively – sensing the mood of wider society – or, conversely, whether this mass sentiment came into existence largely as a result of nationalist agitation. However, there is no doubt that in the early 2010s, public opinion has simply become a more amorphous replica of Russian ethno-nationalist propaganda. This is manifested in a high level of grass-roots ethnic xenophobia,[5] particularly among the youth, and most pronounced in the two capitals (which is of high political significance in itself); in its focus on people from the North Caucasus; and on 'illegal immigrants from the CIS [Commonwealth of Independent States] countries', i.e. from the Caucasus and Central Asia.[6] Notably, the anti-Caucasus sentiment begins to outweigh anti-migrant sentiment, especially among the youth.[7] An even more important manifestation of ethno-nationalist influences is evident in the choice of issues people cite as causing the most tension. Generally about half of the respondents do not appear to be able to name any specific reasons for their dislike of migrants, and only a minority of the remaining respondents point to such causes as the threat of terrorism or job competition. Meanwhile, the majority complain about the difference in standards of conduct, 'the lack of respect for the customs', and similar themes.[8] These views were even more clearly expressed by 'the experts' – who, in fact, were just groups of socially active citizens, recruited by Polytekh in several regions. A survey of these experts revealed that attitudes towards ethnic groups correlate, in fact, only with peculiarities of their behavior.[9] Focusing on 'cultural differences' implies that the 'problem of the foreign-born' is inherently unsolvable, indicating, in practice, that 'they' have a choice of either acting just like 'us' (the idea behind the 'code of Muscovite', much-discussed in 2010 – 2011),[10] or leaving.

Nevertheless, the problem of the North Caucasus is real and so severe that there are serious doubts as to whether it can be resolved at all. One is not just talking about frequently discussed issues such as terrorism, the rise of radical Islam, the excessive level of regional criminalization and corruption, or the staggering unemployment rate. It seems that the region, instead of becoming closer to the rest of Russian society in its social structure, has actually moved in the opposite direction. The region, especially Dagestan and Chechnya, is governed in such a distinct manner that it hardly seems to belong to the same country as the rest of the Russian Federation; indeed, in many ways these republics resemble problematic colonies. Apparently federal government policies have not been effective in breaking the regional trend of disintegration. Most people, of course, do not think in terms of integration. As mentioned above, their concerns focus on terrorism and the perceived 'bad behavior' of migrants from the Caucasus who have settled elsewhere in the country. It came to the point, that in the above-mentioned Polytekh Survey, 26 per cent of young people were in favor of the separation of the Caucasus from Russia, even when an interviewer clearly warned them that this choice could lead to Russia's disintegration. Of the undecided, 14 per cent tended to justify their position by mentioning the futility of territorial separation, given that migrants from the Caucasus would still remain in Russia.[11]

Russian nationalists have long and largely sympathetically discussed the topic of territorial separation with the Northern Caucasus. However, their leaders realize that this idea presents many practical problems, and it has never gained broad support. Instead of separation, they advance an almost unanimously supported slogan 'No more feeding the Caucasus', essentially demanding an end to the direct and indirect support of the region from the federal budget.[12] Nationalists extensively used this slogan when attempting to attract the attention of xenophobically-inclined ordinary citizens, who incidentally show them no support at the moment.

A rather diverse group of authors have put together a report, published as a brochure entitled *The Caucasus 2011: The Russian View*,[13] which appears quite moderate in its tone. The authors of the brochure present separating the Caucasus as a backup option, in case the region refuses to assimilate. The report was initiated by the Russian Platform (*Russkaia Platforma*), a coalition of small organizations who position themselves as the moderate Russian nationalists. This includes, among others, the Russian Social Movement (*Russkoe obshchestvennoe dvizhenie*, ROD), led by Konstantin Krylov and Vladimir Thor; the Russian Citizens Union (*Russkii grazhdanskii soiuz*, RGS) led by Anton Susov and Aleksandr Khramov; and the Moscow Defense League (*Liga oborony Moskvy*), under the leadership of Daniel Konstantinov. However, 'for internal use' on the streets, the slogan 'No more feeding the Caucasus' transforms into the more explicit: 'The Caucasus will starve!' (*Kavkaz budet golodat!*) – a version overheard by the author during a nationalist rally on 11 June 2011. This is just one example of the Russian Platform leaders addressing the audience with moderate speeches, and some of their audience subsequently attacking passers-by of 'non-Slavic' appearance on the street.[14]

The leaders of 'The Russians' movement – created in May 2011 from the Movement Against Illegal Immigration (*Dvizhenie protiv nelegalnoj immigratsii*, DPNI), Slavic Strength (*Slavianskaia Sila*, SS, formerly the Slavic Union (*Slavianskii Soiuz*) renamed after the ban), the National Socialist Initiative (*Natsional-sotsialisticheskaia Initsiativa*) and several smaller organizations –

also spoke against territorial separation. In July 2011, these leaders even paid an official visit to Chechnya, where the republic's leader, Ramzan Kadyrov, received them. Both parties certainly viewed negotiations as successful in consolidating their 'ethnic leadership role', which is extremely important to them. Alexander Belov and Dmitry Demushkin declared after the trip that they were highly impressed by Kadyrov's management of the republic, and that the region's separation could not solve the existing problems.[15]

Throughout the 2000s, the authorities reacted in various ways to nationalist activity and to the increasingly pronounced turn of public opinion, towards viewing ethnic issues as problematic. From 2003 to 2006 the government conducted an experiment with the Motherland bloc, attempting to bring xenophobic sentiments, and a significant part of nationalist activity under the control of the Kremlin. The experiment failed and was abandoned. Later, from 2007 to 2009, it was repeated on a smaller scale with pro-Kremlin youth movements who copied the rhetoric and some practices from the DPNI and other publicly active ethno-nationalists. Simultaneously, efforts were made to split such nationalists into varying levels of radical factions. However, these experiments were, once again, halted in the second half of 2009, since they had failed to keep the ultra-right movement under control.[16] In the meantime, starting mid-decade, the authorities had to undertake a more pronounced fight against racist violence. This action reached its peak in 2010, when about 300 people were convicted for such crimes.[17]

Throughout the entire period under discussion, the official discourse included two components. The first of these components focused on counteracting extremism. Further discussion of this discourse – which is based on defending the authorities and on suppressing opposition of any kind, and closely connected to the corresponding legislation and its highly problematic practical implications[18] – is outside the scope of this chapter. The second component, inherited from the Soviet era, is often referred to as 'interethnic conflict resolution' (*razreshenie mezhnatsional'nykh konfliktov*, literally: the resolution of conflicts between nationalities).[19] In addition to the problematic use of the word nationality here – which in both Soviet and modern Russian political parlance denotes ethnic community – the very notion of such a conflict implies that its antagonists are organized along ethnic lines. Thus, typical hate crimes, i.e. situations where several ideologically-motivated racists at-

275

tack one or two passers-by are instantly elevated to a higher status, implicitly implying the need for negotiation between their respective 'ethnic parties'. The public often regards such negotiations as a problem-solving mechanism; in some instances they can even materialize in the form of meetings between the leaders of so-called 'ethnic diasporas' and the leaders of Russian ethno-nationalist organizations. The negotiations between the authorities of Kyrgyzstan with the neo-Nazi Slavic Union, *Slavyanskii soiuz*, SS, where, among other issues, the parties discussed the SS pledge not to attack the Kyrgyz, represent the most extreme example.[20]

Since the theme of the 'dominance of migrants' has become one of the central ethno-nationalist propaganda issues, it is natural to expect an official response to such fierce criticism. Besides episodic statements on the economic necessity of migration, and pleas to obey the law, the authorities responded primarily by introducing regional labor migration quotas. These quotas in no way reflect economic reality, thus clearly indicating that the measures have a propaganda purpose (bribes, resulting from the introduction of quotas, line the pockets of local and regional officials, rather than federal ones, so simple corruption interests cannot serve as the explanation for the federal quota policy).

So-called 'ethnic crime', namely the allegedly high level of criminal activity among ethnic minorities, is the other key ethno-nationalist theme, (here we could reasonably expect to find some evidence to clarify the issue from the law enforcement agencies). However, the police keep no official statistics on ethnicity, so such an answer remains elusive. Nevertheless, they keep citizenship data that generally contradicts the nationalists' claims, and approximately 4 per cent of the apprehended criminals are non-citizens,[21] roughly corresponding to their population share in the country.[22] Yet this is a statistic that is almost never mentioned. Meanwhile, even senior law enforcement leaders occasionally comment that labor migrants contribute to the worsening crime situation. In all fairness, journalists contribute significantly to this misperception too, by presenting statements and especially statistical data in such a way as to create the most disturbing impression. A common misrepresentation, whether intentional or not, is to intersperse data on immigrants with data on 'non-locals'.[23] Although the above-mentioned statements from public officials are not that frequent, they happen to be the ones repeated most often and thus reach the widest audience. Moreover, it seems that such statements meet the expectations of most journalists who cover these issues. Possibly, the situation is exacerbated by the absence of clear, official explanations that could elucidate why migrants do not present a critical crime risk, accompanied by data analysis of types of criminal activity, distribution within the regions, and so forth.

Thus, on the topic of 'migration as a problem', the government demonstrates no visible opposition to ethnic nationalists. The public perceives this unexpected consensus as a dead end. The problem is stated and repeated multiple times, but no solution has ever been offered, despite the sense that these are being proposed. On one side, we see proponents of mass deportation, closed borders, an introduction of a visa barrier for Former Soviet Union countries, and so on. However, these voices are relatively quiet, due to their marginal political status and their limited media access. On the other side, there are proponents of integration programs and comprehensive anti-discrimination measures, who have even less public resonance. Meanwhile, the suggestions from government officials of various positions are repeated from one year to another, with no practical activity to accompany them, so they are thus ignored, or met with sarcastic comments. As a result, the media genre of hopelessly ruminating upon the deadlock of the so-called 'policy on nationalities' (*natsional'naia politika*), becomes ever more pervasive.[24]

Public reaction to riots on Manezhnaya Square

December 2010 became a seminal month for the development of Russian nationalism and its role in the larger society. On 6 December, soccer hooligan Yegor Sviridov was killed in a brawl with migrants from Russia's North Caucasus region. Soccer hooligans, whose disappointment with the criminal investigation process was carefully cultivated by the ultra-right, came out for the mass rally on December 11 on Manezhnaya Square under the Kremlin walls. About three thousand people chanted racist slogans, beat up about 40 people (on the street and later in the metro), and quite successfully confronted riot police units (OMON).

The riots, organized by radical nationalists on Manezhnaya Square, and other related events of December 2010,[25] dramatically raised the profile and degree of emotion for all ethnicity-related discussions. This topic has rapidly attained increasing importance in 2011, which implies its relevance during the federal elections, both parliamentary and presidential. However, Russia's current political system allows no open debate within 'big politics', (such as the Government, the parliamentary parties, even semi-official public organizations) unless sanctioned by the Kremlin. Since nationalist parties have been explicitly excluded from big politics since 2006 (and subsequently disappeared), the debates around racism, migration, and similar issues have become distorted. There is a sharp contrast between the extent of popular demand on this issue, and the absence of any meaningful discussion.

Not just the political system in general, but the nationalist movement itself is equally distorted. In the eyes of budding activists, their inability to participate in electoral politics and the elections' quality, simply lower the value of political activism per se. Meanwhile, this is largely a youth movement that is quickly adding younger age cohorts. These young people either quickly become disillusioned and return to their private lives, or turn to violence as the most easily available option (although the ultra-right circles actively discuss the fact that this latter course of action is also problematic). However, it must be noted that, even in the absence of pressure from the authorities, the Russian nationalist movement is experiencing an extreme deficit of non-violent members. It is close to impossible to find a nationalist willing to condemn so-called direct action.[26] Specific to Russia, this problem greatly reduces the nationalist movement's ability to influence public debate.

Instead of nationalists, whose more intellectual representatives are quite coherent in expressing their vision and formulating proposals, these same ideas are broadcast to the public through other figures not always directly related to nationalists. Certain journalists who specialize in 'protecting Russians' play a special role in the process. They interpret numerous conflicts and problems as essentially 'interethnic', and deliver this interpretation to a wider audience. Particularly in the wake of a major news item, where ethnic factors have played an important role, the journalists try to identify similar events. Thus any conflict involving different ethnic groups becomes perceived as an essentially interethnic conflict. This perception seems to have become accepted almost universally.

The most significant recent example is the media coverage of a conflict in the village of Sagra in the Sverdlovsk Region. The narrative is fairly straightforward. Several villagers came into conflict with a local drug dealer, and then he called gangsters to his aid. On 1 July 2011 the armed gangsters drove into the village in several cars, where they were met by the villagers who put up an armed resistance. One gangster was killed in a shootout and subsequently an investigation was opened, but not actively pursued. There was even an attempt to pin the blame on the peasants, rather than the gangsters. However, the coverage of the conflict was clearly ethnically tinged from the very start, the author of widely circulated reports Yevgeny Roizman – the head of the City without Drugs organization (*Gorod bez narkotikov*), and notorious not only for his extreme 'treatment' methods for addicts, but also for his frequent racist remarks – stressed that the drug dealer was a Roma, the peasants were Russian and the gangsters were Azeri. Roizman's colleague and the original source, Evgeniy Malenkin, directly called the gangsters 'animals' (*zver'ki*), an ethnic slur.[27] The overwhelming majority of subsequent texts that mention Sagra view the events as a case of interethnic conflict, with varying degrees of criticism directed at the police. Meanwhile, even the initial report from the City Without Drugs organization contained no indication whatsoever that the conflict was in any way motivated by ethnic hatred. It was simply described as a gang attack on the village. Such a unanimous interpretation of the Sagra story is even more remarkable when compared with analysis of the events on Manezhnaya Square. In the latter case, despite the fact that the participants clearly expressed ethnic hatred, many commentators have sought to downplay the ethnic theme.[28]

On occasion, journalists deliver keynote articles in an openly nationalist vein. In a popular periodical such a move always attracts attention. For example, after the events on Manezhnaya Square, one well-known journalist, Dmitry Sokolov-Mitrich, published an article,[29] remarkably, calling not for protection of the ethnic Russian interests, but for the protection of 'atomized' urbanites from the wild Caucasus natives who supposedly live according to different laws and gradually, little by little, were taking power in Russian cities. The author proposed to embark on 'legal terrorism' against people from the Caucasus, punishing them for any infraction to the fullest extent of the law, in order to instil respect for general civil standards of behavior. Notably, the author expressed no misgivings regarding the racial selectivity of the proposed measures, while the editors of one of the country's top newspapers apparently felt no misgivings either. Moreover, he seemed to be convinced that the 'zero tolerance' policy in New York was guided by the exact same approach, and that such a policy reflected the wishes of the majority of citizens, who support the slogan of 'Fuck the Caucasus! Fuck!'

Many notable public figures actively support such 'ethnic conflict' rhetoric, whether consciously or by inertia. In this regard, it is important to mention leaders of the major religious organizations. Traditionally, religious and ethnic identities in Russia are poorly differentiated, but this lack of distinction is institutionalized. For example, only the so-called 'traditional religions' (Orthodoxy, Islam, Buddhism and Judaism) are represented in the Interreligious Council of Russia, and yet they differ from almost all others precisely because they can point to their 'ethnic area', which does not intersect with the ideal ethnic areas of their Council partners. This notion of 'area' separation does not just reflect reality (exceptions do exist but are few in number), but is also constantly reinforced by the religious leaders. After the events on Manezhnaya Square, Archpriest Vsevolod Chaplin, the Russian Orthodox Church representative, proposed the creation of interfaith committees to address so-called 'interethnic conflicts'.[30] This proposal is extremely unrealistic (it is hard to imagine what a priest and a mufti would have done on Manezhnaya Square on December 11, 2010, or, rather, what would have been done to them). Yet, surprisingly, President Medvedev approved Father Vsevolod's proposal during the State Council session on 11 February 2011.[31]

In addition to being implicitly based on the 'ethnic conflict' concept, this approach to peacekeeping elevates the status of participants in past or future riots above hooligans, or even criminals (to whom the government and the society can show a degree of leniency depending on the circumstances), to legitimate representatives of their 'people'.[32] Deacon Andrei Kuraev, a rather moderate figure and one of the most audible voices of the Russian Orthodox Church, expressed this idea quite openly. On the subject of the Manezhnaya Square riots he said, 'The pogrom has always been the reaction of the defenceless, who are tired of hoping for official protection'.[33]

Not to be outdone, parliamentary parties cannot ignore the public demand to address the topic of nationalism. The ruling United Russia Party is in the best position to shirk social demands, and in previous elections it trailed its opponents in the amount of 'hate speech' during the campaign.[34] The Liberal Democratic Party (*Liberal'no-Demokraticheskaia Partiia Rossii*, LDPR), which initially positioned itself as nationalist (although the party and its leader Vladimir Zhirinovsky have demonstrated no continuity or adherence to principles on most issues),[35] is of course, always eager to pick up the xenophobic rhetoric. Nevertheless, during the 2011 parliamentary election season, the Liberal Democratic Party was unusually outspoken. It did not merely limit itself to cooperating with selected radical nationalist groups on the periphery, but it created an affiliated 'Russian Committee', which included the leaders of leading, publicly active organizations of radical Russian ethno-nationalists.

Cooperation of other registered parties with radical nationalists, even if it has increased, still remains a peripheral phenomenon. However, while avoiding politically risky (and for many people, morally unacceptable) collaborations with the radicals, party leaders actively utilize certain elements of their rhetoric. As an example, one can cite the case of Boris Nadezhdin, the leader of the Just Cause (*Pravoe delo*) liberal party organization in the Moscow Region, who was wrongly accused of recruiting skinheads into his organization.[36] There is no doubt that Nadezhdin, a self-identified Russian liberal, ever recruited anyone more radical then Viktor Militarev, a moderately nationalist activist and political strategist. However, Nadezhdin stepped forth with the slogan 'The Moscow Region – the Russian Land' (*Podmoskov'e – Russkaia Zemlia*) and clarified its meaning as follows:

> if, hypothetically speaking, you came here, no matter if you are originally Chinese, the Caucasus native, Japanese, whatever, and you plan to live here and want your children and grandchildren to live here, you need to become Russian, if not by the colour of your skin, then by your culture, traditions, and customs. Because this is how people have lived here from time immemorial.[37]

Next, Nadezhdin declared that Europe had practiced multiculturalism for the past 20 years, while the United States had practiced a 'melting pot' strategy. Only the latter, Nadezhdin insisted, was the correct way. This strategy is understood as complete assimilation, including giving Russian names to one's children, although he never went as far as to suggest mandatory baptizing, otherwise the Hindus in their villages 'will drop their dead into the Oka

281

river, and so on', Of course, 'the soil' concept pertains not just to immigrants. If the Moscow Region has been, and must remain 'the heartland for the Russian people', then Nadezhdin has to add:

I respect the desire of the Chechen people that it [i.e. the Chechen land] should be the heartland of the Chechen people, with the mosques in Grozny, and Kadyrov ruling there for all eternity, and so on. I don't go in there to impose my rules.

It is also remarkable, that Nadezhdin insisted that people with non-Russian last names (such as Roizman or Pletosu) could not possibly be Russian nationalists. Thus, Nadezhdin's rhetoric is aimed at assimilation, but actually works to divide the population, including citizens, on the basis of their ethnic and, separately, ethno-territorial identity. We see how even moderately liberal Nadezhdin legitimizes Roizman, who is inclined towards racist interpretations. Meanwhile, Roizman has collaborated with obvious ethno-nationalists, with whom Nadezhdin would have refused to associate. This becomes possible due to the phenomenon of doublespeak linking the chain. No less significant is the desire of mainstream politicians to reach the untapped segments of the electorate.

Finally, we should not expect the so-called 'outside' – that is to say with no chances for admission to the parliament – democratic, opposition to be immune to these tendencies. For example, Vladimir Milov's group, expelled from the Solidarity movement (or according to other interpretations, having left on their own accord) for their nationalist inclinations, continued its activities under a new name, Democratic Choice (*Demokraticheskii Vybor*). In this capacity, they have entered a liberal democratic coalition, with the People's Freedom Party (*Partiia Narodnoi Svobody*, PARNAS). In its preliminary program, Democratic Choice proposed such measures as limiting the ability of the North Caucasus natives to travel to other regions of the country.[38] Moreover, lacking mass support, and aware of its own weakness, the democratic opposition has no adequate expulsion mechanism, even for radical-nationalist elements. For example, defenders of the Khimki forest were joined by the fairly radical ultra-right activists in their full regalia, but no protests from the movement's leadership have ensued.[39]

From 2010 to 2011, the economist and publicist Michael Delyagin, whose work all of the major opposition Democratic periodical readily publish, attempted to create a nationalist-populist party Motherland – Common Sense (*Rodina – Zdravyi Smysl*), in partnership with another well-known journalist, Maxim Kalashnikov, who directly calls himself a National Socialist.[40] Even this connection seems to have had no effect on Delyagin's respectability. Delyagin does not consider himself to be a nationalist, but he understands the situation in the country as follows:

> what is now officially considered 'nationalism' and 'extremism' is, in essence nothing but an unconscionably late and incredibly weak manifestation of the self-preservation instinct of the Russian people and the Russian civilization as a whole in the face of monstrous ethnic aggression.

He clearly indicates the source and shape of this aggression – 'the growing terror from the Caucasus' – and furthermore, insists that this aggression 'as far as we can judge, is supported by the authorities'.[41] The readiness of the 'outside' democratic opposition to tolerate doublespeak, even partially accept it, is obviously related to the opposition's weakness (in addition to all the considerations outlined above in reference to Boris Nadezhdin); one's perceived weakness leads to a sharp drop in selection criteria towards one's potential allies.

Government attempts to correct its course in ethnic politics after December 2010

The events of December 2010 clearly indicate that the country's leadership needs not only to provide an immediate response, but also to correct the course of its so-called 'ethnic policies'. After several days of complete confusion, the response contained no surprises. Both members of the 'ruling tandem' (a standard Russian term denoting the Putin-Medvedev regime during Medvedev's presidency) spoke in favor of tough and indiscriminate (in the ethnic sense) measures in order to maintain the rule of law. The situation, indeed, called for such statements, but this was obviously not enough.

Vladimir Putin was the first leader to make any meaningful statements

283

regarding potential policy corrections, thus he is the first person to be discussed in our analysis of the ruling tandem. Only a few days after the riots he
met with the leaders of the soccer hooligans – a completely useless step,
given that in December these leaders demonstrated their inability to control
many fans, especially the youngest ones. He also visited the grave of Yegor
Sviridov, whose murder in a street brawl precipitated the unrest. Such a step
would have deserved a heartfelt approval, had it not been such an extraordinary exception to Putin's usual practise; it was the only time he had ever visited a grave of a hate crime victim. By late December, Putin even called for a
more stringent regulation of residential registration, including possible criminal
liability for violators.[42] However, the latter populist statement had no real impact. Overall, his explicit attempts to flirt with potential supporters of ethno-
nationalists ended there, probably because the credible threat of further unrest had already passed.

At the same meeting, where Putin spoke about the tightening of residential registration rules, he also advocated the idea of uniting the political nation,
although he never actually used that term. The concept of the political nation
has been a sensitive issue both in the USSR and in post-Soviet Russia, since
the term 'nation' (natsiia) traditionally stands for an ethnic group, and all of
these ethnic nations are thought to have realized their national sovereignty in
such a way as to form the 'multi-national people', first within the framework of
the Soviet Union, and then within Russia. The transfer of the term 'nation' to
the general civic level undermines the existing political significance of ethnic
groups, in particular, the significance of ethnically-based administrative institutions and elites. Therefore, the notion of civic unity still does not sit well with
Russian politicians; it is unable to compete with an established notion of people as the union of ethnic nations.[43] Recognizing that building a political nation requires a unifying basis (as an example he used the ideological unity of
the Soviet people), Putin proposed to develop 'pan-Russian patriotism' (an
obvious tautology).

Putin's statements generally remained within the paradigm of 'interethnic
conflict resolution'.[44] This paradigm manifests itself through Putin's reliance
on time-tested formulas, such as 'interethnic harmony'. Nevertheless, we
have to admit that the Prime Minister does not avoid specific, sensitive issues
(such as the targeted recruitment of students from the North Caucasus),[45]

even when he knows that the audience will be displeased. For example, he spoke of the inevitability of further labor immigration to the activists of the Independent Trade Unions of Russia.[46] Putin pays great attention to ethnic tolerance education, but instead of approaching it through civic solidarity or equality, he interprets it traditionally, i.e. ethnographically 'We must always remember that ethnic conflict is sometimes caused by ignorance, a lack of education, a lack of knowledge about one's own culture and the culture of one's neighbors'.[47] Naturally, he says nothing about the practical strategies of migrant integration, and never uses the word 'discrimination' at all – indeed, he is far from unique in this respect.

In his educational message, the Prime Minister emphasizes the very same attitude towards ethnicity as the above-mentioned Boris Nadezhdin. That is to say, the approach that the media usually associates with the folk proverb 'When in Rome, do as the Romans do', sometimes expressed in Russia as 'don't come to the strange monastery with your own set of rules'. Putin has stated repeatedly that people should adapt their ethno-cultural traditions to reflect those associated with their current place of residence, whether that be permanent or temporary. Moreover, the 'culture of interethnic communication' is defined as 'if someone moves to a non-traditional residence territory, he must respect the culture, the language and the customs of the people, among whom he chooses to live'.[48] The question arises as to what form this 'respect' should take, but it is impossible to get an answer here, not only from Putin but even from far more approachable officials. However, Putin has given us at least some idea. While meeting with representatives of the North Caucasus youth organizations, recalling the debate in Europe about the wearing of veils, he stated that if the host 'people' (meaning ethnicity, not a political nation) perceives certain behavior (for example, veiling) 'as religious and cultural aggression, if it causes rejection, then one needs to treat this with understanding, and not impose one's own rules'. Putin added: 'I fully admit that some people have extremely radical views, but then they should go and live in a place where these radical views are the norm'.[49]

In the spirit of 'interethnic conflict resolution', Putin spoke about the need for interaction between ethnic organizations, and even addressed them directly during a special meeting in July 2011. He specifically highlighted the role of religious organizations with a traditional lack of distinction between religion and ethnicity. The then Prime Minister even indulged in rather strange pseudo-theological speculations: 'You know that we have Eastern Christianity – Orthodoxy. And some theorists of Christianity say that in many ways it is closer to Islam than, say, to Catholicism'.[50]

Moving on, Dmitry Medvedev's views regarding possible ethnic policy changes were markedly different from Putin's, not least because of their rapid evolution. As recently as late December 2011, the President talked only about the restoration of 'ethnic harmony', demonstrating almost no populist gimmicks, except when he thought necessary to mention the need to 'be more stringent in blocking illegal immigration channels'. Strikingly, he never repeated Putin's words about civic unity.[51] However, in January 2012 he delivered a keynote speech to the Federal Assembly leadership. Insisting that Russian ethno-cultural traditions represented unity in diversity, he singled out the special role of Russian culture, not only as the largest quantitatively, but also as 'the basis, the developmental core of our entire multi-national culture'. Medvedev paid particular attention to Orthodoxy, even including such statements (somewhat unexpected in this context) as 'over the past few years Russia has built new churches, museums, and pilgrim hotels in the Holy Land. These actions undoubtedly strengthen Russian traditions'. In this context, it is important to bear in mind that Dmitry Medvedev has a much greater reason to be called 'the Orthodox president' than Vladimir Putin. It was during Medvedev's presidency that the steps, which were unsuccessfully advocated by the ROC during Yeltsin's and Putin's presidency, were finally implemented: teaching religion in schools and having official military priests in the army.[52]

There is nothing new about the concept of an alliance of ethnic cultures under the Russian culture's leadership. The President went on to say that the notion of culture was not limited to mere traditions, but also included that modern culture needed a more intentional development: 'We need to support modern Russian folklore, contemporary music and literature, and the traditions that emerge in our lifetimes'. Medvedev finished his speech on a high note: 'this is the only way to develop synthetic national values'.[53] Perhaps the former President was really counting on the fact that modern cultural trends, much more open in terms of 'intercultural communication', could facilitate the process of national integration. Of course, cultural practices by themselves cannot ensure such an outcome, but at least this speech made a substantive argument regarding the unity-building process among Russian citizens.

During the specially convened meeting of the State Council, *On Measures to Strengthen Interethnic Harmony* on 11 February 2011,[54] Medvedev gave a similar speech, albeit with some corrections. He spent less time talking about the dominant role of Russian culture, except for reiterating the requirement that immigrants must be able to speak Russian (and that the government was working on appropriate measures). Meanwhile, he emphasized that Western leaders' speeches about 'the failure of multiculturalist policies' have no relevance for Russia. Instead, Medvedev insisted on Russia's inherently multicultural nature. However, he said nothing specific about the policy of multiculturalism, typifying the trend for politicians and bureaucrats in Russia to confuse the meaning of 'multiculturalism' as a policy, with the fact that Russian society includes multiple cultures. At the same time, Medvedev openly declared the need 'to create a full-fledged Russian nation while preserving the identity of all peoples in our country', but only in his closing remarks, after several participants of the meeting had expressed their support for such an idea.

The President's practical proposals centered primarily on education – that of the young, officials and citizenry in general – and were either abstract or somewhat lightweight. Public service announcement videos, for example, were discussed at length. Once again, the role of religious leaders received special attention. However, Medvedev also touched upon the very real issue of ethnic discrimination when forming regional governments. It was suggested that the government and the President's representatives in federal districts should submit their proposals for 'eliminating these imbalances'.

Thus, Medvedev never actually expanded on the proposals he put forward in December. In general, he acted quite cautiously. Notably he made no further statements of any significance in the following spring and summer months. His circumspect behavior can be explained by the fact that the higher echelons of bureaucracy still show no signs of agreeing on a single appropriate strategy. Significantly, despite the fact that the Concept of Russian State Policy on Nationalities (*Kontseptsiia gosudarstvennoi natsional'noi politiki*), adopted in 1996, is almost unanimously considered obsolete, there has been no progress in developing and adopting a new one.

Overall, Medvedev's February speech was based on a report 'On measures to strengthen interethnic harmony', prepared by the Ministry of Regional Development and distributed to the participants of the February meeting.[55] However, after consulting the actual text of the report, it becomes evident that the President never fully articulated the report's position, apparently wary of its unambiguous wording, although everything he managed to say stems from that very concept briefly summarized below. The report urges the government:

> to undertake systematic measures aimed at strengthening civic unity of Russians, while addressing the issue of ethnic and cultural well-being of the Russian majority and preserving the ethnic and cultural diversity of the Russian nation.[56]

The report also repeatedly refers to the concept of the 'majority'. For example 'the unique features of Russia and the Russian civilization' are 'multiple ethnicities, religious confessions and lifestyles, with ethnic (Russian) and religious (Orthodoxy) majorities'. Current world trends are thought to include, along with mass migrations, the clash between secular and religious paradigms, 'the search within democratic societies for the legislative solution to their absolutization of the minority rights while neglecting the rights of the majority'.[57] The report, with a perhaps unique honesty among official documents, opens its list of problems inherited from the Soviet Union, with the 'territorial-administrative division based on ethnic principles'.[58] With regard to Russia the text deliberately uses the term 'Russian civilization', borrowing from the rich tradition of 'civilizational nationalism'.[59] Modern Russian nationalism views this tradition as an alternative to ethnic nationalism; the report also opposes the latter, explicitly stating so in its text.

The report's approach and proposals are best illustrated by its list of 'key issues in the sphere of interethnic relations'. It has to be quoted in its entirety, since the choice of words and order of importance effectively illustrate the position of the report's authors:

- weak Russia-wide civic identity, namely for the youth from the North Caucasus, along with increasing significance of ethnic and religious identity;
- ethnic and religious political radicalism and extremism, particularly among the youth;
- problematic socio-cultural self-perception of the Russian people, the absence of fulfilment in their ethno-cultural needs with a background of growing migration and mobilization of other ethnic communities;
- growth of nationalist sentiments among Russian youth;
- a low activity of non-governmental organizations;
- a lack of public consensus on the basic values of the Russian society, the continued lack of significance of traditional values (including family and religious values) in the life of a modern Russian citizen, against the background of increased activity of religious organizations, both traditional and new;
- attempts to undertake a series of geo-political projects in the territory of the Russian Federation in the interests of certain foreign governments, ethnic or religious communities, aimed at destabilizing the social and political situation in Russia to the point of its collapse along ethnic or religious lines.[60]

As such, the report clearly and unequivocally supports forming a precedence of civic identity over ethnicity, specifically via the educational system. Data from the surveys, conducted by the Russian Public Opinion Research Centre (*Vserossiskii tsentr izucheniia obshestvennogo mneniia*, VCIOM), confirms that such a change in priorities is indeed possible. The surveys indicate that the Russian population views ethnic and especially religious differences as increasingly less important.[61]

The report also comments on the historical equivalence of two concepts: Russian (*Russkii* i.e. ethnic Russian,) and Russian citizen (*Rossiyanin*). It is worth mentioning that the report's key quote belongs to Petr Struve, one of the most important liberal nationalists of the early twentieth century. In today's environment, strengthening the role of the Russian language is seen as a key priority.

Finally, with regard to minorities, the report even mentions the problem of discrimination and the need for social adaptation by immigrants. A goal of state policy is formulated as 'overcoming corruption in state government and law enforcement agencies that fosters public discontent and impunity of some members of ethnic communities'.[62] We have to admit that the report chose the most politically correct formula to address the popular social theme of 'ethnic crime'.

Reaction of officials and society to the ruling tandem's course correction

A striking difference between the clear wording of the above-mentioned report – which leaves no room for different interpretations – and the obvious evasiveness of the President's speeches is hard to ignore. No less important is the response among the top levels of bureaucracy to the conceptual approach, manifested by both of these sources. A variety of responses were observed at the State Council Presidium meeting in February, despite the fact that such gatherings tend to fully agree with a given position suggested by the President or the Prime Minister.

Even the Rostov Region Governor, Vassilii Golubev, who presented the report of the State Council working group, departed somewhat from the report's message in his presentation. For example, when discussing the origins of current problems, he only cited historical or external reasons, but not current policy deficiencies. 'Ethnic self-perception' was emphasized to a far greater extent than in the report; it was even said that 'at the moment we don't have enough public organizations that develop and propagate Russian culture, folklore, traditions, after all, the Russian language'.[63] When speaking about the overarching goal of forming a state-wide civic identity, Golubev suggested that 'special attention should be paid to the peace-promoting social potential of ethno-cultural associations, religious organizations, fellowships and communities'.

Golubev accurately identified two interconnected problems, 'First, we need to agree on terminology and establish basic implementation approaches to the state policy on nationalities; then agree on the unifying ideas we are trying to promote'. Yet he and the other speakers during that meeting, or later, failed to accomplish not just the latter task (which is objectively quite difficult), but even the former one. This was a point noted by leading anthropologists and sociologists, who gathered to discuss the same set of issues a month later.[64]

Regional leaders supported the idea of forming a nation-wide civil identity, and the idea of Russian cultural domination (first and foremost the key role of the Russian language) in this process. Even the Presidents of national republics (Yakutia-Sakha and Dagestan) made statements to this effect, although the President of Bashkortostan, Rustem Khamitov, still insisted on maintaining bilingualism. Medvedev received even more radical support from the President of Kabardino-Balkaria, Arsen Kanokov: 'in my opinion, the leading role in this process of the Russian people, their language and culture, should be encoded in our legislation'.[65] He also pointed out the importance of strengthening traditional moral and religious values of the country's various peoples. Valentina Matvienko also suggested 'writing into law the content basis of the nation-state idea of modern Russia'.

Because of such disparate responses, and given their lack of clarity on the subject matter, there is no reason to have any confidence in the ability of the political elite to carry out a conceptually coherent state policy. Moreover, the country's top executives do not properly encourage the highest quality of existing official documents, namely the aforementioned report 'On measures to strengthen interethnic harmony'. Though it can and should be criticized, we cannot expect the state apparatus to produce something of better quality at this time, as the discussion at the level of senior officials is practically non-existent.

The public reaction to the Presidential policy statements of January-February 2011, meanwhile, was exceptionally weak. For the most part, the non-governmental media reaction was limited to ironic paraphrases, with an emphasis on the term '*Rossiyanin*' (literally 'of Russia'), which does not have a high reputation in today's Russian language, and on analogies with the notion of 'the Soviet people'. Sociologists, Emil Panin and Vladimir Mukomel, offered some substantial criticism of the President's initiative, correctly pointing out that such a super-ethnic unity needs to be implemented via the concept of a civic nation. For the latter to emerge, Russia would need an active civil society and the corresponding civic consciousness of its citizens, both of which are rather weak in today's Russia.[66] One has to add that the existing political regime has no interest in strengthening these civic virtues. It is indicative that neither Putin nor Medvedev have ever used the term civic nation. Possibly, the Russian leaders looked to too many political nations of Europe and Latin America in their authoritarian periods as examples.

The reaction of some Russian ethnic nationalists is also worth noting. Certain others, Pavel Svyatenkov for example, chose to ignore new official ideological initiatives.[67] Konstantin Krylov, who usually writes about every-thing under the sun, also kept silent. Meanwhile, Mikhail Remizov, one of the most moderate authors among ethno-nationalists, almost agreed with Medvedev. He had no objection to the civic nation concept, which he used precisely because its formation implied powerful unification, expressed not through a language or common ethnographic features, but instead through the 'homogeneity of political culture and civic consciousness'. Remizov wrote that if the government achieved such uniformity from everyone, including the Caucasus natives, the Russians would be quite satisfied by the outcome: 'the main quest of Manezhnaya Square can well be interpreted as the quest for a civic nation'.[68]

However, the claim within the State Council Report that '*Rossiyane*' (Rus-sian citizens) and Russians are historically the same can be twisted to serve the cause of the opposition. This was immediately done by the more radically inclined authors, albeit figures far removed from street radicals, Boris Vinogra-dov and Andrei Saveliev. They have criticized Medvedev for trying to build a '*Rossianic*' nation at the expense of the Russian nation, 'From our point of view, Russia has already formed a nation that exists as a phenomenon of Rus-sian political culture'. Then they repeated a common nationalist complaint, 'the bureaucracy and the ethnocracy formed an alliance against the Russians' – in other words, the charge of ethnocracy applies to anyone but the Russians. No-tably, however, the authors never insist on some kind of cultural 'Russification', they claim that 'all issues of nationality (ethnicity) and religious affiliation should be left to the private citizen's discretion, and the state must adhere to a strict "unifying role"'. They also stress that all nationalities must 'assimilate into the Russian civic nation, while retaining their ethnographic features and their faith'. Here, the preferred analogy is the 'melting pot' of the United States with the WASPs (White Anglo-Saxon Protestants) at its nucleus.[69]

Thus Saveliev,[70] who firmly believes in a racial approach, stands today on the same ground as Dmitry Sokolov-Mitrich, a typical frightened urbanite, and liberal Boris Nadezhdin. The same views can be deduced from the thicket of contradictory rhetoric coming from the President. We would like to point out this example of rare harmony between these dissimilar figures. While Nadezhdin's legitimation of Saveliev's language has been unintentional, the same cannot be said for sure in the case of Sokolov-Mitrich. Without going into further examples, we can state that doublespeak as a legitimation instrument for the most radical movements can be used with a differing degree of awareness.

Meanwhile, Konstantin Krylov, one of the most original and compelling advocates for Russian ethno-nationalism, certainly does not agree with the President. For him, the current government is alien (*inorodcheskii*) and anti-Russian and therefore, by definition, cannot be a source of any constructive nation-building. Krylov also cannot accept the formation of any identity more important than the existing Russian people, understood as the blood-related kinship community.[71] He is far from alone in espousing this interpretation.

The government very gently offers the public a gradual transition from the current ethnic policy to a new one, in the spirit of the aforementioned general agreement. The current policy can be characterized in two ways. First, it is practically absent, and never formulated clearly. Second, it is based on the priorities of 'maintaining peace between nationalities' via maintaining a balance between various sides in these 'interethnic relations' (*mezhnatsion-al'nye otnosheniia*): whether these are leftovers from the Soviet era (for example territorial ethnic elites); random (for example the so-called 'national ethnic diasporas'); or even have no actual structure at all ('youth from the Caucasus'). This policy requires only a repetition of the thesis that multi-ethnicity is to the country's advantage, and needs no further informative statements.

The new policy is expected to become one of a greater unification of the country, both in the area of written law and regular law. This process is likely to also be accompanied by the promotion of patriotic sentiment, and the underscoring of the significance of the Russian and Orthodox core of the emerging political nation. From the country leaders' current statements and actions we cannot draw any conclusions regarding the pace of this process, or the extent to which the intended integration of immigrants and ethnic minorities will resemble cultural assimilation. In fact, it is impossible to judge whether this process of designing the melting pot will ever begin at all.

It is already obvious, however, that the reaction from various social groups to a possible change in the political course is inconsistent, if visible at all. In these conditions the change in strategy might happen only in the wake of a noticeable wave of unrest on the scale no smaller than the one in December 2010.

Thus, the lack of coherent official strategy for counteracting ethnic nationalism is expected to strengthen the ultra-right position even further. Even if we disregard additional legitimization, acquired by the ultra-right as a result of participation in the protest movement of the winter and spring of 2011 – 2012, we can still conclude that the legitimization of the ultra-right associations leads to further entrenchment of their outlook and terminology in the mainstream public discourse. In response to this process, the authorities and many groups within society will continue to adopt elements of the ultra-right language, thus supporting the peculiar 'racism legitimization spiral' in Russia.

ENDNOTES

[1] Lev Gudkov, 'Rossiia dlia russkikh: ksenofobiia i anti-immigrantskie nastroeniia v Rossii' (Russia for Russians: Xenophobia and Anti-Immigrant Sentiment in Russia), in *Nuzhny li immigranty rossiiskomu obshestvu?* (Does Russian Society Need Immigrants?) (Moscow: Fond Liberal'naya Missiya (Liberal Mission Foundation), 2006), pp. 31 – 78.

[2] Ibid. See also Alexander Verkhovsky and Galina Kozhevnikova, *Etnicheskaia i religioznaia intolerantnost v rossiiskikh SMI: rezultaty monitoringa 2001 – 2004 gg.* (Ethnic and Religious Intolerance in Russian Mass Media: Results of Monitoring 2001 – 2004) (Stuttgart: *ibidem*-Verlag, 2005).

[3] This topic certainly merits more detailed attention. See Verkhovsky, 'Evolutsiia postsovetskogo dvizheniia russkikh natsionalistov' (Evolution of Post-Soviet Movement of Russian Nationalists), *Vestnik Obshestvennogo Mneniia* (The Russian Public Opinion Herald) 1/107 (2011), pp. 11 – 35.

[4] For example, see the following headline on the DPNI site: 'Praviashie national-predateli gotoviat novyi antirusskii zakon' (Ruling National-Traitors Prepare a New Anti-Russian Law) at: http://www.dpni.org/articles/kommentari/10230/ (accessed 29/06/2012). The government is sometimes directly labelled 'anti-Russian'. See '13go Marta Prikhodi na Izbiratel'nyi uchastok. Vyrazi svoe otnosheniie k partii zhulikov i vorov' (On March 13 Go To the Elections! Express your opinion about the party of thieves and crooks), ibid., 9 March 2011. See: http://dpni.org/articles/novosti_dp/21023/ (accessed 29/06/2012).

[5] See for example 'Natsionalizm v Rossii' (Nationalism in Russia) at: http://www.levada.ru/26-09-2011/natsionalizm-v-rossii (accessed 29/06/2012).

[6] See the results of opinion polls conducted by the All-Russian Public Opinion Research Centre (Vserossiiskii Tsentr Issledovaniia Obshestvennogo Mneniia, VCIOM) in the report of the Ministry of Regional Development 'O merah po ukrepleniiu mezhnatsional'nogo soglasiia v rossiiskom obshestve' (On Measures to Strengthen Inter-Ethnic Harmony in the Russian Society) at: http://www.minregion.ru/activities/interethnic_relat

ions/national_policy/505/902.html (accessed 29/06/2012) (hereinafter, 'Report of the Ministry of Regional Development'), pp. 15 – 17.

[7] In a survey of young urbanites, 39 per cent expressed their dislike of migrants from the Caucasus (even worse results than police officers, who are disliked by 27 per cent of the respondents), and 20 per cent expressed their dislike of foreign workers. This data was collected by the Polytekh agency, in a survey commissioned by the Public Chamber of Russia. See: 'Mezhnatsional'naia neterpimost' v gorodskoi molodezhnoi srede' (po sledam sobytii na Manezhnoi) (Ethnic intolerance in urban youth (in the wake of the events on Manezhnaya Square)) at: http://www.oprf.ru/files/oprosmol odezh.pdf (accessed 29/06/2012) (hereinafter, 'Polytekh Survey'), pp. 48 – 49.

[8] Ibid., p.17.

[9] Ibid., pp. 21 – 30.

[10] The following interview by a Moscow official started the discussion: Liubov Pyatiletova, 'Moskvichi pyati morei' (Muscovites of the Five Seas). Michael Solomentsev: 'Stavku nuzhno delat' na to, chto ob'ediniaet zhitelei stolitsy' (Place Your Bets on What Unites the Capital's Residents), *Rossiyskaya Gazeta*, 16 June 2010.

[11] Polytekh Survey, pp. 52 – 54.

[12] The North Caucasus republics are currently among those most dependent on federal subsidies, although still trailing the regions of the Far East.

[13] The text is available on the site of a journal published by the moderate wing of Russian ethnic nationalists *Kavkaz 2011: Russkii vzgliad* (The Caucasus 2011: The Russian View), *Voprosy Natsionalizma* (Issues of Nationalism) at: http://vnatio.org/arhiv-nomerov/node82/ (accessed 29/06/2012).

[14] See the examples: 'V Moskve proshli aktsii natsionalistov' (Nationalist Actions Took Place in Moscow) at: http://www.sova-center.ru/racism-xenophobia/news/racism-nationalism/2011/10/d22681/ (accessed 14/05/2012).

[15] Alexander Belov, 'Davaite vosstanavlivat' Rossiiu!' (Let Us Restore Russia!) at: http://www.apn.ru/opinions/article24469.htm (accessed 29/06/2012).

[16] Galina Kozhevnikova, 'Ultra-pravye tendentsii v prokremlevskikh molodezhnykh dvizhe-niiahk' (The Ultra-Right Tendencies in the Pro-Kremlin Youth Movements), in *Russkii natsionalism mezhdu vlast'u i oppozitsiei* (Russian Nationalism Between Government and Opposition) (Moskva: Panorama Centre, 2010), pp. 4 – 17.

[17] Relevant statistics can generally be found on the SOVA Centre website at: http://sova-center.ru/database (accessed 06/29/2012), as well as in the appendix to the most recent report on the manifestations of radical xenophobia, also available on the SOVA Centre website. For hard copies see the appendices to *Xenophobia, Freedom of Conscience and Anti-Extremism in Russia in 2010* (Moskva: SOVA Centre, 2012).

[18] The latest annual report: Maria Rozalskaya, 'Nepravomernoe primenenie anti-extremistskogo zakonodatel'stva' (Misuse of Anti-Extremist Legislation in Russia in 2010), ibid., pp. 66 – 87. News and reports on this topic can also be found on the SOVA Centre website in the section on 'Inappropriate Anti-extremism' at: http://sova-center.ru/misuse (accessed 29/06/2012).

[19] Alexander Osipov wrote: 'In the Soviet period, the main ideological cliché denoting the direction of public policy in this area was the "friendship of peoples". In the late 80s – early 90s the emphasis has shifted markedly, and the above thesis started to be expressed via negation, as conflict prevention and resolution. This formula carries no particular content, but provides the basis for a variety of rhetorical tricks to justify social engineering of a varying nature and direction'. Alexander Osipov, 'Konstruiro-

vanie etnicheskogo konflicta i rasistskii diskurs' (Constructing ethnic conflict and racist discourse), in *Racism v yazyke sotsial'nykh nauk* (Racism in the Language of Social Sciences) (St. Petersburg: 'Aletheia', 2002), pp. 45 – 69.

[20] 'Ne vesti peregovorov s neo-natsistami' (No Negotiations with the Neo-Nazi) at: http://www.sova-center.ru/racism-xenophobia/publications/2009/01/d15173/ (accessed 29/06/2012).

[21] According to official statistics of the Ministry of the Interior of the Russian Federation. See, for example, the crime data for January-December 2010 at: http://www.mvd.ru/pressce nter/statistics/reports/show_88233/ (accessed 29/06/2012).

[22] In the summer of 2011, Vladimir Putin said: 'According to various sources, somewhere between 7 million to 10 million immigrants now live here in Russia', see: 'Predsedatel Pravitelstva Rossijskoj Federatsii V.V.Putin vstretilsya s predstavitelyami konfessij I natsionalno-kulturnykh obshestvennyh oprganizatsij' at: http://premier.gov.ru/even ts/news/15972/ (accessed 29/06/2012). If we assume that Putin's numbers excluded those who had already obtained citizenship, and then take the smallest figure in his range, we have to conclude that non-citizens commit somewhat fewer crimes than citizens. The balance would likely be re-established if we take the unsolved crimes into account.

[23] The above was described, using a speech by the Chairman of the Investigative Committee Alexander Bastrykin, as an example, in Aleksei Bessudnov, 'Zachem prokuratura pripisyvaet inostrantsam lishnie prestupleniia' (Why Does the Prosecutor's Office Attribute Extra Crime to Foreigners) at: http://slon.ru/articles/35786/ (accessed 29/06/2012). For the text of Bastrykin's speech (not the only example available, but a very illustrative one), see Vystiplenie Predsedatelya Sledstvennogo komiteta pri Generalnoj prokurature Rossijskoj Federatsii Bastrykina A.I. na mezhvedomstvennom soveschanii po voprosam protivodejstviya prestupnosti migrantov i sovershenstvovanii form i metodov immigratsionnoj politiki (Speech by Bastrykin A. I., Chairman of the Investigative Committee of the Prosecutor of the Russian Federation at the inter-ministerial meeting on fighting migrant crime and improving forms and methods of migration policy) at: http://www.sledcom.ru/actual/4637 (accessed 29/06/2012).

[24] A striking example among many: Vadim Rechkalov, 'Poka ya dobryi' (While I'm Still Nice), *Moskovsky Komsomolets*, 4 August 2011.

[25] They are described in more detail in Galina Kozhevnikova, Alexander Verkhovsky, 'The Phantom of Manezhnaya Square: Radical Nationalism in Russia and Efforts to Counteract it in 2010', in *Xenophobia, Freedom of Conscience and Anti-Extremism in Russia in 2010* (Moskva: SOVA Centre, 2011), pp. 5 – 41.

[26] I covered this in more detail in Alexander Verkhovsky, 'Evolution of Post-Soviet Movement of Russian Nationalists'.

[27] Initial information in LiveJournal: 'Zveri Zabludilis' (Animals Got Lost) at: http://malenkin.l ivejournal.com/190699.html (accessed 29/06/2012); 'S'ezdili' (Took a Trip) at: http://roizman.livejournal.com/1197298.html (accessed 29/06/2012).

[28] See for example the Polytekh Survey.

[29] Dmitry Sokolov-Mitrich, 'Manezhnoe Pravosudie' (Manezh Justice), *Komsomolskaya Pravda*, 13 December 2010.

[30] Rekommendatsii soveschaniya predstavitelej sinodalnogo Otdela po vzaimootnosheni-yam Tserkvi i obschestva i molodezhnykh obschestvennykh objedinenij (Recommendations of the Meeting of Representatives from the Synodal Department for Church and Society Relations and Youth Organizations) at: http://www.interfax-religion.ru/?act=documents&div=1077 (accessed 29/06/2012).

[31] Zasedanie prezidiuma Gossoveta o merakh po ukrepleniyu mezhnatsionalnogo soglasiya (The State Council Presidium meeting on measures to strengthen interethnic harmony) at: http://news.kremlin.ru/news/10312/print (accessed 29/06/2012).

[32] See: Rekommendatsii soveschaniya predstavitelej sinodalnogo Otdela.

[33] 'Protest na Manezhnoj – eto krik boli I otchayaniya', zayavil protodiakon Andrej Kuraev ('The Protest on Manezhnaya Square is a cry of pain and despair' said Archdeacon Andrei Kuraev) at: http://www.pravoslavie.ru/news/43453.htm (accessed 29/06/2012).

[34] Galina Kozhevnikova, *Iazyk vrazhdy i vybory: federal'nyi i regional'nyi urovni. Po materialam monitoringa oseni-zimy 2007–2008 godov* (Hate Speech and Elections: Federal and Regional Levels. Based on the Monitoring Period of Autumn-Winter 2007-2008) (Moskva: SOVA Centre, 2008), pp. 56 – 70.

[35] Since the mid-1990s Russian political scientists tend to view the LDPR rather as trading their voices in parliament then standing for any specific ideas. See for example Vladimir Pribylovskii, 'Natsional-patrioty na vyborakh v regionakh v 2000 – pervoj polovine 2006' (National-Patriots in the Elections in Regions in 2000 – the First Half of 2006), in *Russkii Natsionalizm: ideologiia i nastroenie* (Russian Nationalism: the Ideology and the Mood) (Moskva: SOVA Centre, 2006), p. 104.

[36] Michail Rubin, '"Pravoe delo" nachinaet eksperimenty s natsionalizmom' (Just Cause is Beginning to Experiment with Nationalism), *Izvestia*, 2 August 2011.

[37] This and foregoing quotes from Boris Nadezhdin are taken almost verbatim from the live radio broadcast with participation by Boris Nadezhdin and the author. See Ideologicheskie diskussii v riadakh partii "Pravoe delo" (The Ideological Debate Within the Just Cause Party) at: http://www.svobodanews.ru/articleprintview/24287042.html (accessed 29/06/2012).

[38] Osnovnye ideii 'Demokraticheskogo vybora' v sfere migratsionnoi politiki i politiki v oblasti mezhetnicheskikh otnoshenii (Key Ideas of Democratic Choice in the Area of Migration Policy and Interethnic Relations Policy) at: http://demvybor.ru/documents/DV-migration.pdf (accessed 29/06/2012).

[39] A group of local environmentalists managed to turn their struggle against the laying of a highway through the forest on the outskirts of Moscow, into a symbol of confrontation between 'ordinary people' and government officials, in close alliance with industry. The ultra-right groups seeking public legitimacy and thus paying attention to all popular topics could not miss their chance at the Khimki Forest. See one-such group's report on the trip to Khimki Forest: 'Pravaia Liga na zashite Khimkinskogo lesa' (The Right League Protecting Khimki Forest) at: http://pravliga.com/2010-09-06-16-25-32/689-2011-05-15-21-11-06 (accessed 29/06/2012).

[40] There is a separate study about Kalashnikov: Yevgenii Moroz, 'Podniavshii svastiku. Imperskii proekt Vladimira Kucherenko' (The One Who Raised the Swastika. The Imperial Project of Vladimir Kucherenko) at: http://www.sova-center.ru/racism-xenophobia/publications/2003/11/d1267/; http://www.sova-center.ru/racism-xenopho bia/publications/2003/11/d1266/; http://www.sova-center.ru/racism-xenophobia/publi cations/2003/11/d1265/ (accessed 29/06/2012). Kalashnikov's modern self-presentation: Maksim Kalashnikov, 'Yekonomichesko-organizatsionnaia baza 'Kievskoi Rusi-2', vazhneishie voprosy – bez otvetov!' (An Economic and Institutional Basis of 'Kievan Rus-2', The most Important Questions without Answers!), *Bol'shoi Forum* (Big Forum) 10 November 2008 at: http://bolshoyforum.org/forum/ind ex.php?page=29 (accessed 29/06/2012); 'Totalitarianism – mon Amour', at: http://m-kalashnikov.livejournal.com/239415.html (accessed 29/06/2012); 'Tesisy k bu-

duschemu-6' at: http://m-kalashnikov.livejournal.com/225820.html (accessed 29/06/2012).

[41] The same statement contained a remarkable version of the events at Manezhnaya Square. First, the protestors were not just objectively provoked, but consciously organized by 'the ruling bureaucracy'. Second, the protesters on Manezhnaya Square allegedly never chanted hostile slogans – although the video records show that the most popular slogans were 'Ebat Kavkaz, Ebat!' ('Fuck the Caucasus! Fuck!') and 'Za eto ubijstvo otvetyat vashi deti!' ('Your children will pay for this murder!') – but only called for fairness in law enforcement, at the most they proclaimed 'No more killing Russians'. See 'V Rossii idet poka holodnaia etnicheskaia voina'. (In Russia there is a cold – for now – ethnic war). Full text of the Presentation by the Director of the Institute of Globalization Problems, M. G. Delyagin at the XI Summit of the Russian-German Petersburg Dialogue (Hanover, Germany) at: http://delyagin.ru/articles/18595.html (accessed 29/06/2012).

[42] Transcript of the Joint Meeting of the State Council and Commission for the Implementation of Priority National Projects and Demographic Policy at: http://kremlin.ru/transcripts/9913 (accessed 29/06/2012).

[43] See, for example, Aleksandr Osipov, *Etnichnost' i ravenstvo v Rossii: osobennosti vospriiatiia* (Ethnicity and Equality in Russia: Patterns of Perception) (Moskva: SOVA Centre, 2012), pp. 130 – 132.

[44] Putin fully shares in a well-known trend of confusion in the Russian political jargon associated with the use of the word 'national' as synonymous with 'ethnic'; he is, of course, far from the only such case among top politicians and bureaucrats. He still occasionally uses the word 'ethnic', but only as a full synonym of the word 'national'. He clearly makes no distinction between the two, one day the Prime Minister even used the phrase 'national ethnic' as another full synonym. Putin never uses the word 'civic' in the context of 'civic nation'. His texts pertaining to our topic could use the above term maybe only in a phrase 'civic peace', or, more commonly, 'civic and interethnic peace' (sometimes 'interfaith' is also added). Incidentally, a Google.ru search for the Russian word *Mezhnatsional'nyi* (i.e. interethnic, literally 'between nationalities') brings up every single relevant speech by Putin between December 2010 and the present moment. No other major politicians, including President Medvedev demonstrate such an ideal Google search result.

[45] 'Predsedatel Pravitelstva Rossijskoj Federatsii V.V. Putin prinyal uchastie v mezhregionalnoj konferentsii partii "Edinaya Rossiya" na temu "Strategiya sotsialno-ekonomicheskogo razvitiya Severnogo Kavkaza do 2020 goda. Programma na 2010 – 2020 gody"' (Russian Prime Minister Vladimir Putin took part in the inter-regional conference of the United Russia Party on the subject of 'Strategy of Socio-Economic Development of the North Caucasus until 2020. Programme for 2010 – 2012') at: http://premier.gov.ru/visits/ru/11295/events/11301/ (accessed 29/06/2012).

[46] 'Predsedatel Pravitelstva Rossijskoj Federatsii V.V. Putin vystupil na VII siezde Federatsii Nezavisimykh Profsoyuzov Rossii' (Russian Prime Minister Vladimir Putin speaks at the VII Congress of the Federation of Independent Trade Unions of Russia) at: http://premier.gov.ru/events/news/13844/ (accessed 29/06/2012).

[47] 'Predsedatel Pravitelstva Rossijskoj Federatsii V.V. Putin prinyal uchastie v VI siezde Vserossijskogo pedagogicheskogo sobraniya' (Russian Prime Minister Vladimir Putin took part in the VI Congress of All-Russian Teachers Assembly) at: http://premier.gov.ru/events/news/15422/ (accessed 29/06/2012).

[48] 'Predsedatel Pravitelstva Rossijskoj Federatsii V.V. Putin vstretilsya s predstavitelyami konfessij I natsionalno-kulturnykh obshestvennyh oprganizatsij' (Russian Prime Minister Vladimir Putin met with representatives of religious denominations and ethno-cultural community organizations) at: http://premier.gov.ru/events/news/15972/ (accessed 29/06/2012).

[49] 'Putin na Kavkaze snova zagovoril o tom, chto priezzhie dolzhny uvazhat' traditsii mestnykh zhitelej' (Visiting the Caucasus, Putin says once again that visitors must respect local traditions) at: http://www.gazeta.ru/news/lenta/2011/08/03/n_ 1951405.shtml (accessed 29/06/2012).

[50] Channel 'Russia', 'Russia 24', Radio 'Mayak', 'Vesti FM' and 'Radio Russia' broadcasted a special live programme 'Razgovor s Vladimirom Putinym. Prodolzhenie' (A Conversation with Vladimir Putin. Continued) at: http://premier.gov.ru/events/news/13427/ (accessed 29/06/2012).

[51] Transcript of the Joint Meeting of the State Council and Commission for Implementation of Priority National Projects and Demographic Policy at: http://kremlin.ru/transcripts/9913 (accessed 29/06/2012).

[52] My article, containing additional evidence is being published as: Alexander Verkhovsky, 'Natsionalizm rukovodstva Russkoi pravoslavnoi tserkvi v pervom desiatiletii XXI v'. (Nationalism of the Russian Orthodox Church Leadership in the First Decade of the XXI Century), in *Pravoslavnaia tserkov' pri novom patriarkhe* (The Orthodox Church under the New Patriarch) (Moskva: Carnegie Centre, ROSSPEN, 2012), pp. 141 – 169.

[53] Vstrecha s rukovodstvom Federalnogo Sobraniya (Meeting with the Leadership of the Federal Assembly) at: http://kremlin.ru/news/10087 (accessed 29/06/2012).

[54] Zasedanie prezidiuma Gossoveta.

[55] Or, at least under its leadership. It is believed that Alexander Zhuravsky, the Director of the Department of International Relations, played a special role in preparing this report. The text of the report is available on the website of the Ministry: Report of the State Council of the Russian Federation. 'O merakh po ukrepleniiu mezhnatsion-al'nogo soglasiia' (On Measures to Strengthen Interethnic Harmony) at: http://www.minregion.ru/activities/interethnic_relations/national_policy/505/902.html (accessed 29/06/2012).

[56] Ibid., p. 2.

[57] Ibid., p. 3.

[58] Ibid.

[59] Emil Panin, 'Rossiia mezhdu imperiei i natsiei' (Russia Between Empire and Nation), *Pro et Contra,* 2007. No. 3; Victor Shnirelman, 'Vremia tsivilizatsii: tsivilizacionnyi podhod kak national'naia ideia' (Time for Civilization: Civilizational Approach as a National Idea), in *Rossiiskaia modernizatsiia: razmyshleniia o samobytnosti* (Russian Modernization: Reflections on Identity) (Moskva: Tri Kvadrata, 2008), pp. 198 – 232; Alexander Verkhovsky, Emil Panin, 'Tsivilizatsionnyi Natsionalizm: Rossiiskaia Versi-ia Osobogo Puti' (Civilizational Nationalism: The Russian Version of the 'Special Path'), in *Ideologiia 'osobogo puti' v Rossii i Germanii: Istoki, soderzhanie, posledstviia* ('Special Path' Ideology in Russia and Germany: Origins, Content, Consequences) (Moskva: Tri kvadrata, 2010), pp. 171 – 210.

[60] Report of the State Council of the Russian Federation 'O merakh po ukrepleniiu mezh-natsional'nogo soglasiia' (On Measures to Strengthen Interethnic Harmony), p. 4.

[61] According to diagrams shown on page 18 of the report, in 2005, 38 per cent of respondents considered ethnic differences to be very significant, while in 2007 this number

dropped to 28 per cent, and in 2010 to 24 per cent; the number of respondents, who considered ethnic differences to be insignificant was respectively 25 per cent, 31 per cent and 32 per cent (the remaining respondents consider them to be moderately important or, less frequently, find this question difficult to answer). For religious differences the same data series are: 26, 22, 18 per cent and 36, 38, 40 per cent.

[62] Ibid., p. 29.

[63] Here and below, cited from the State Council Presidium meeting on measures to strengthen interethnic harmony at: http://news.kremlin.ru/news/10312/print (accessed 29/06/2012).

[64] Problemy obespecheniya mezhetnicheskogo soglasiya v Rossii. Materialy Kruglogo stola Nauchnogo soveta po problemam natsionalnoj politiki Otdeleniya obschestvennykh nauk RAN v Institute sotsiologii RAN (Problems of Interethnic Harmony in Russia. Proceedings of the Round Table of the Scientific Council on National Policy, Division of Social Sciences of the Russian Academy of Sciences at the Institute of Sociology of the Russian Academy of Sciences) (14 March 2011) at: www.presidentsovet.ru/structure/consolidation_group/materials/actual_problems.doc (accessed 29/06/2012) The first two presentations, by Leokadia Drobizheva and Victor Shnirel'man, deserve particular attention.

[65] Legislation of this kind was prepared by the Russian nationalists in the parliament on a number of occasions, but never had any chance of passing.

[66] Ibid.

[67] Pavel Svyatenkov, 'Dvoinoi Burbon' (Double Bourbon), in *Russkiy Obozrevatel* at: http://www.rus-obr.ru/day-comment/9660 (accessed 29/06/2012).

[68] Mikhail Remizov, 'Grazhdanskaia natsiia: russkii zapros na segodnia' (Civic Nation: Russian Request for Today), APN.ru. 2 February 2011 at: http://www.apn.ru/publications/article23602.htm (accessed 29/06/2012).

[69] Boris Vinogradov, Andrei Saveliev, 'Mul'tikul'turalizm ne proidet' (Multiculturalism Shall Not Pass) at: http://www.apn.ru/publications/article23654.htm (accessed 29/06/2012).

[70] Victor Shnirelman, 'Rasologiia v deistvii: mechty deputata Savel'eva' (Rasology in Action: The Dreams of Deputy Saveliev), in *Verkhi i Nizy Russkogo Natsionalizma* (The Top and Bottom of Russian Nationalism) (Moskva: SOVA Centre, 2007), pp. 162–187.

[71] See, for example, his overview of the ethno-nationalist views (he calls them national-democratic) in comparison with the 'imperial' and the 'liberal' ones: 'Mezhdu Scilloi i Haribdoi. Natsional-demokratiia v eio otnosheniiakh k imperstvu i liberalizmu' (Between Scylla and Charybdis. National-Democratic Party in its Relationship to Empire-Building and Liberalism) at: http://krylov.livejournal.com/2278881.html (accessed 29/06/2012).

PART 4

AFTERWORD

HEROES KNOW WHICH VILLAINS TO KILL:
HOW CODED RHETORIC INCITES SCRIPTED VIOLENCE

Chip Berlet

'Get the nigger'! The voice came from within the racist mob after it had just forced a Jewish counter demonstrator to swim across the park's pond to escape being attacked. 'Kill that nigger! Stomp him!' Yelled a white teenager, as the terrified black youth realized he has pressed his luck too far by attending a neo-Nazi rally. He dodged fists as he ran to escape, but a leg snaked out and he fell. Face down in the grass he only had a moment to consider his plight before the first boot smashed into his ribs.

'Kill the nigger, kill the nigger', chanted the crowd. More boots, then fists, and as the black youth struggled, his shirt was reduced to shreds. Blood trickled down from his nose, and the corner of his mouth was split as yet another fist found its mark. A handful of white people rushed forward to the rescue, being pummeled in the process.

The racist mob then surrounded a small group of counter-protesters from a neighborhood synagogue. 'Go back to Skokie, Jew bitch', yelled one white teenager at a young woman, (Skokie is a northern suburb of Chicago, Illinois in the United States with a high percentage of survivors of the Nazi genocide). Do you sleep with the niggers? Why don't you go back to Africa with them?' 'Jews go home', the crowd chanted, 'Jews go home'.[1]

No one, not even the leader of the neo-Nazis in his fiery speech, directly told the members of the mob to go and attack blacks and Jews that day. However, each individual in the gang just knew what was expected of them. Why? How does this work?

As intellectuals we often remove ourselves from the bloody reality of words that provoke violence. I have therefore used the troubling and offensive language above to describe an incident I witnessed in 1978, in the Chicago neighborhood where my wife and I lived and participated in anti-racist work. While scholarly research exists on its own intellectual merits, we need to recognize that helping unravel the complexity of bigotry and xenophobia assists those working to extend human rights. The leaders of organized political or social movements sometimes tell their followers that a specific group of 'Others' is plotting to destroy civilized society. History tells us that if this message is repeated vividly enough, loudly enough, often enough, and long enough – it is only a matter of time before the bodies from the named scapegoated groups start to turn up.[2]

Levin persuasively argues that both culture and self-interest shape prejudiced ideas and acts of discrimination or violence, which are 'in many cases, quite rational'. According to Levin, respect for 'differences can be so costly in a psychological and material sense that it may actually require rebellious or deviant behavior', in contrast to the existing norms of a society.[3] Social science since World War II and the Nazi genocide has shown that under specific conditions, virulent demonization and scapegoating can – and does – create milieus in which the potential for violence is increased. What social science cannot do is predict which individual upon hearing the rhetoric of clear or coded incitement will turn to violence.

In approaching some of these questions, this concluding study will unpack the concepts of 'constitutive rhetoric'; the vilification, demonization, and scapegoating of a named 'Other'; coded rhetorical incitement by demagogues; the relationship between conspiracism and apocalyptic aggression; and the process of scripted violence by which a leader need not directly exhort violence to create a constituency that hears a call to take action against the named enemy. It will argue that these processes can and do motivate some individuals to adopt a 'superhero complex' which justifies their preemptive acts of violence or terrorism to 'save society' from imminent threats by named enemies 'before it is too late'.

In the United States, following the 1995 Oklahoma City terrorist bombing by a small cell of right-wing militants, there were calls by Democrats and Liberals to show restraint in the rhetoric used in electoral campaigns. A handful of principled conservatives also joined in this call. Overwhelmingly, however, the response by Republicans and conservatives (and a few liberals) was to denounce such concerns as falsely linking media rhetoric to violent action and thus endangering First Amendment free speech guarantees. A few of the more macho voices declared such concerns to be a sign of political weakness. Actually, such claims rebutting the link between rhetoric and violence are based on a misunderstanding or misrepresentations of existing social science.

A vivid example of this can be found in the statistics chronicling ethno-violence compiled by the US Justice Department. Following the 11 September 2001 terrorist attacks on the US World Trade Center in New York City and the Pentagon (the military headquarters outside the US capital city of Washington, DC.), assaults, the defacement of buildings, the murders of people perceived by attackers to be Muslims in the United States, have shown a ghastly upwards curve. This is not just a convoluted turn of phrase. From the first days after the 9/11 terror attacks by militant Islamic supremacists, adherents to the Sikh religion were attacked because the truly ignorant xenophobic attackers assumed that anyone with swarthy skin and a 'rag-head' had to be a Muslim enemy of America.

In their study of how media manipulation for political ends can help incite genocide, Frohardt and Temin looked at 'content intended to instill fear in a population', or 'intended to create a sense among the population that conflict is inevitable'.[4] They point out that 'media content helps shape an individual's view of the world and helps form the lens through which all issues are viewed'. They found two patterns: content creating fear and content creating a sense of inevitability and resignation that violence was about to occur. According to the authors:

- In Rwanda prior to the genocide a private radio station tried to instill fear of an imminent attack on Hutus by a Tutsi militia.
- In the months before [conflicts] in Serbia, state television attempted to create the impression that a World War II–style ethnic cleansing initiative against Serbs was in the works.
- Throughout the 1990s Georgian media outlets sought to portray ethnic minorities as threats to Georgia's hard fought independence.

Frohardt and Temin found the result was a sense within the target population that 'imminent' and serious threats were to be expected, even though 'there was only flimsy evidence provided to support them':

When such reporting creates widespread fear, people are more amenable to the notion of taking preemptive action, which is how the actions

305

later taken were characterized. Media were used to make people believe that 'we must strike first in order to save ourselves'. By creating fear the foundation for taking violent action through 'self-defense' is laid.

Frohardt and Temin explain that, by 'convincing people that conflict is in-evitable, those manipulating the media create a self-fulfilling prophecy'. They also add: 'Consequently, people convinced of the inevitability of conflict are much easier to move to violence. Two strategies have been used to create this sense of inevitability: portraying conflict as part of an 'eternal' process, and discrediting alternatives to conflict'.[5]

According to Arendt, this process is clearly observable in totalitarian movements of the right and left. Arendt, comparing Hitlerism and Stalinism, linked it to the elevated status of the totalitarian leader and the elite cadre of followers:

> Their superiority consists in their ability to dissolve every statement of fact into a declaration of purpose. In distinction to the mass membership which, for instance, needs some demonstration of the inferiority of the Jewish race before it can safely be asked to kill Jews, the elite for-mations understand that the statement, all Jews are inferior, means, all Jews should be killed.[6]

This example illustrates the most extreme case. Few would dispute that the rhetoric of Hitler and his propagandists had a connection to the murder of Jews and other 'enemies' of the Thousand Year Reich. What *is* disputed is whether or not this process can be extended to less obvious forms of provoc-ative rhetoric.

From Words to Actions

'They' always lie to 'Us'. It doesn't matter who 'They' are, because one of the hallmarks of bigotry is that 'Their' religion, ideology, or culture is said to promote lying. They cannot be trusted. In fact, they are probably conspiring against us right now. They threaten our entire way of life. They are not like us. They do not value human life like we do. In order to defend our nation, which reflects eternal truths, we must act now before it is too late. Attack first. Our war is justified. God is on our side. That's the universal narrative of justified aggression against a demonized 'Other'.[7]

Conspiracy theories attached to apocalyptic timetables are especially effective in building a constituency for aggression against the evil plotters. The history of the United States is replete with episodic widespread panic about subversion, which has created a mass counter-subversive movement whose bigoted charges become part of the public conversation about politics: Freemasons (1798 – 1844); Catholic immigrants (1834 – 1860); Jews (1919 – 1935); Italian and Russian immigrants, with some deported as anarchists and Bolsheviks (1919 – 1935); Communists and their 'fellow travellers' (1932 – 1960); Communist and Jewish control of the Civil Rights Movement (1958 – 1968); secular humanists, feminists and the 'homosexual agenda' (1975 – present); the 'New World Order' (1990 – present); Islamic menace and Sharia law (post 9/11). That is the short list.[8]

The potential for violence in a society increases when the mass media carries rhetorical vilification by high profile and respected figures who scapegoat a named 'Other'. This dangerous 'constitutive rhetoric' can build an actual constituency of persons feeling threatened or displaced. Or to put it another way, when rhetorical fecal matter hits the spinning verbal blades of a bigoted demagogue's exhortations, awful atrocities happen.

The resulting violence can incite a mob, a mass movement, a war, or an individual actor. Individual actors who engage in violence can emerge in three ways. They can be assigned the task of violence by an existing organizational leadership; they can be members or participants in an existing organization, yet decide to act on their own; or they can be unconnected to an existing organization and act on their own. According to the US government definition, a 'Lone Wolf' is a person who engages in political violence and is not known by law enforcement agencies to have any current or previous ties to an organization under surveillance as potential lawbreakers.[9] The person committing the violence may expect or even welcome martyrdom, or may plan for a successful escape to carry on being a political soldier in a hoped-for insurgency. Either way, the hope is that 'a little spark can cause a prairie fire'.[10] Revolution is seldom the result, but violence and death remains as a legacy.

Following the Research Trail: Social Science Responds to WWII

After World War II social scientists analyzed the Nazi genocide and tried to develop theories of how citizens in a society allow such atrocities to occur. While in some cases this research has been challenged and newer theoretical models proposed, there is a substantial amount of theoretical claims that stand up to the test of time, at least as far as social science is concerned.

The most influential early studies were sponsored by the American Jewish Committee as part of a series that began publishing before the US entry into WWII but after the trajectory of Nazi Party anti-Semitism became clear.[11] Titles included: *Frustration and Aggression* (1939), *The Dynamics of Prejudice* (1950), *Anti-Semitism and Emotional Disorder, a Psychoanalytic Interpretation* (1950), *The Authoritarian Personality* (1950), *The Nature of Prejudice* (1954).

Of these, *The Dynamics of Prejudice, Frustration and Aggression*, and *The Nature of Prejudice* have stood up relatively well to the test of time.[12] *The Authoritarian Personality* has received substantial criticism, but social scientists have made adjustments that keep it salient as a theory. The most obvious revisions include the harsh reality that authoritarians can appear anywhere on the political spectrum; and that authoritarian followers are in a symbiotic relationship with those who enjoy the psychic tingle of being an authoritarian leader. The submissive can enjoy the whip of the dominant. There will be more discussion of this later.

A benchmark 1951 study is Arendt's *The Origins of Totalitarianism*, which had three major sections: 'Antisemitism', 'Imperialism', and 'Totalitarianism'.[13] Other works that also played a role in establishing the post-war liberal consensus include Hoffer, *The True Believer*, and Rokeach, *The Open and Closed Mind*.[14]

Pluralist or Classical School Emerges

What emerged in social science was what is called classical theory, the pluralist school, or centrist-extremist theory; and a flurry of books were published around similar themes that stressed individual psychological disturbance, mob violence, or the reaction to stress or competition in societies as viewed through the lens of the social psychology of the time.[15] In a related vein, there were a series of books by Hofstadter, especially *The Paranoid Style in American Politics*.[16] The basic idea was that right-wing movements of the 20th century – whether populist or elitist – reflected dysfunctional outbursts of irrational 'extremism'. Many of these books have descriptive sections that remain valuable. Hofstadter's work has remained the most valuable of these, that is, if one ignores the social psychological theories that have been revised by more recent research.[17]

During the Cold War, it became politically expedient to tie communism to the theories of what social mechanisms where involved in totalitarianism and the rise of fascism in Europe. In some cases this led to theoretical breakthroughs, such as Arendt's tripartite study of totalitarianism, which today (along with *Eichmann in Jerusalem*) remains neglected as a philosophical formulation.[18] Hitler and Stalin were both totalitarians; this was never meant to support the claim that rightists or leftists were all totalitarians.[19] Arendt herself protested this interpretation of her work in the preface to one of her subsequent editions.

In 1967 sociologist Rogin challenged the claims of the Pluralist School.[20] Other scholars joined this critique as sociology turned to newer theories about social movements.[21]

New Paradigm: Social Movement Theories

Nothing in the previous discussions should be read to imply that social movements are all dangerous, or that only right-wing movements are dangerous. Social and political movement activists have different ideologies and methodologies in a myriad of combinations from left to right, from non-violent to violent, from socially constructive to destructive. People who join all sorts of social movements turn out to be pretty much like their neighbors along a full range of demographics.[22]

People who join social movements tend to be average people with grievances. They join with others to resolve their grievances. To accomplish this they mobilize resources, exploit opportunities that open up the political system, develop their own internal culture, and create perceptual frames, clever slogans, and parable-like stories to achieve their aims.[23] Sociologists talk about 'framing' as an ongoing process in which social movement leaders illustrate a power struggle by narrowing the subject to a specific point of view or perspective easily understood by their followers.[24] A narrative is simply a story told inside a movement that is sometimes shared with the public. These stories serve as parables, with the plot and storyline revealing heroes and villains. Movement participants learn lessons on expected ideas and actions valued by the movement as a whole. These become internalized and exist as if they are 'common sense'.[25] Narrative stories can be told in ways that defend the status quo or challenge the status quo.[26]

The main reason people join a social movement is that they have a grievance with society and get motivated enough to join others to do something about it. They plug into silo-like information channels where leaders frame an issue in a way that suggests a solution can be achieved through collective action. They agree to use techniques for social change that step outside the normal boundaries of political activism of using elections or lobbying, yet they often interact with political movements for elections and legislative campaigns. The most successful movements have skilled leaders who articulate clear goals, create positive communal interactions, and support their ideologically-driven strategies with resonant framing of issues and narrative stories that act like parables.

Authoritarianism Revisited

The original theories about the 'authoritarian personality' had some serious flaws, especially what appeared to be a bias limiting the syndrome to right-wing ideology. Later research showed that there were several inter-related factors involved; there were dominant authoritarian leadership personalities and submissive follower personalities; and the syndrome could be found across the political spectrum. Altemeyer discusses how the most 'socially-destructive' individuals combine authoritarianism and social dominance with ethnocentric prejudice.[27] In 2010 he revisited his research to detail its relevance to understanding the right-wing populist Tea Party movement in the United States.[28]

Betz has studied similar right-wing populist movements in Europe that attract support by using radically xenophobic and authoritarian rhetoric.[29] According to Taras, the 'rise of xenophobia is nearly synonymous with the anti–immigrant backlash' in Western Europe, 'especially against non–Europeans

310

and 'people who are not racially Caucasian or religiously Judeo–Christian'.[30] A number of recent books have used combinations of cognitive science and sociology to argue that certain types of 'authoritarian personalities' actually do tend to be more prevalent on the political right.[31]

The Tools of Fear: A Catalogue of Ingredients and Processes

In terms of radical right rhetoric, it is best to start with the concept and reality of prejudice: the preconceived formation of negative or hostile views towards a person or group of persons based on ignorance, stereotyping, or other filter of bigotry. Prejudice can be unconscious or conscious, and any set of prejudiced ideas may be transformed into an ideological viewpoint. Prejudice is a set of views. Discrimination is an act. What follows in this section traces the path to violence.[32]

Dualism: Dualism is a concept that divides the world into 'Us' versus 'Them'; and in the religious sense, between the forces of 'good' and 'evil'. In fact, a particular form of religious dualism, Manichaeism, was broadly practiced between the third and seventh centuries, and incorporated into many features of early Christianity. Today the terms Manichaeism and dualism are sometimes used interchangeably; dualism plays a central role in 'a totalist movement with an idealized charismatic leader and an absolutist apocalyptic outlook', write Anthony and Robbins. Participants engage in the 'projection of negativity and rejected elements of self onto ideologically designated scapegoats', and this helps create 'a basis for affirming a pure, heroic self'.[33] Anthony and Robbins call this 'exemplary dualism'.[34]

Hofstadter, in turn, noted that the 'fundamentalist mind [...] is essentially Manichaean'.[35] The United States has a significant presence of politically active fundamentalist Christian conservatives, many of who are caught up in social and political movements that employ exemplary dualism.[36] In Europe this worldview is found among anti-immigrant and xenophobic movements in addition to organized white supremacist and neo-Nazi groups.

Demagoguery and Constitutive Rhetoric : Demagoguery has been used historically by both populists to denounce corrupt elites, and by government officials to justify political repression – in both instances; its use is based on fears of conspiracies by real and imaginary subversive elements.[37] Dema-

311

gogues need to be charismatic movement leaders; otherwise, their performance is interpreted as buffoonery.

A clearer view of the demagogic process that can lead to 'scripted violence' is made visible when combining the contemporary sociological understanding of frames and narratives in mass movements with the concept of
constitutive rhetoric from the fields of speech, communication theory, and
media criticism. The early theorizing in this arena built a firm foundation for
studying the societal role of rhetorical content in mass media, from Lippmann's agenda-setting theory (1922);[38] through Bernays' public opinion and
propaganda theories (1923 and 1928);[39] to cultivation theory and other theories by Gerbner and his fellow thinkers in more recent decades.[40]

Much of the newer theorizing is prompted in one way or another by the
work of Althusser, which influences a wide range of authors far beyond the
original small audience of theoretical Marxists.[41] Charland writes that central
to his analysis of constitutive rhetoric is 'Althusser's category of the subject' in
which the collectivized identity of the constituency is actually created through
a 'series of narrative ideological effects'.[42] Charland's study concerns the
movement for the sovereignty of a Quebec nation. According to Charland, he
draws from Althusser's work to explain how the 'subject is not "persuaded" to
support sovereignty' but the support 'for sovereignty is inherent in the subject
position addressed by [the pro-sovereignty movement's] rhetoric'. This
demonstrates Althusser's contention that in these situations it is the members
(subjects) of the collectivized constituency who are 'interpellated' as political
subjects 'through a process of identification in rhetorical narratives that "always already" presume the constitution of the subject.[43]

Therefore the assumptions in the text and subtext of a movement leader's
constitutive rhetoric call into being an actual living constituency made up of the
individual 'subjects' being addressed. Thus when Hitler's favorite journalist Julius Streicher, in his newspaper *Der Stürmer*, railed against the Jews using a
particular narrative rhetoric, a constituency was created which moved from being individual passive anti-Semites into being active Jew haters in a collectivity
with a shared identity. Of course, this process of interpellation is not limited to
Nazi rhetoric. Gray notes that 'Althusser's theories of ideology and interpellation may be readily applied to the study of mass communication, in the context
of the perpetuation of hegemonic ideology via the mass media'.[44]

Movement leaders speak to their followers, but they also speak to different groups of people. Moving from the center of a movement outwards, leaders speak to their inner circle; staff, loyal members or cadre, general membership and followers, potential recruits, the general population via mass communications media; and their opponents. Johnston calls this a 'micro-frame analysis'.[45] The rhetoric aimed at each group needs to be analyzed separately altogether. Journalists frequently report only on the message aimed at them as media carriers, and not the more vivid rhetoric reserved for loyal followers that may more accurately reflect the ideological content of the speaker.

Some skillful rhetoricians can speak to several audiences at the same time using coded language, known in rude jargon as 'dog whistles'. For example, in some of his speeches, Pat Buchanan has woven in coded jargon aimed at Christian evangelicals, anti-immigrant xenophobes, anti-Semites, militia supporters and intellectual neo-fascists. Meanwhile, many listeners who are not mobilized into a specific constituency just hear a conservative patriotic speech. Speakers on the ideological Left sometimes do the same thing.

An example of constitutive rhetoric is explored in a study of e-mails forwarded by online right-wing groups. Duffy, Page, and Young analyzed messages that 'ranged from anti-liberal or anti-Obama polemics to blatantly racist communications'. The content of these e-mails ranged from claims that Obama was 'incompetent' to those that claimed 'he's plotting the downfall of America':[46]

> Many e-mails recounted events that evidently sought to reveal Obama as un-American, un-Christian, power-obsessed, weak, or Nazi-like. The dichotomous portrayals of Obama as both diabolical and incompetent expressed many of the fears of conservative voters: that the United States would become a socialist nation with government control of all businesses and institutions, overrun with minorities and immigrants and run by politicians who glad-handed despotic foreign leaders, particularly those from Muslim nations. In other words, Obama was illustrative of everything 'anti-American'.[47]

The authors argued that this is a 'form of digital folklore that is politically motivated', and found that 'their political dynamics may contribute to constructing not only group identity but also the individuals' social identity within their e-mail group'. They also argued that these 'images may amplify the impact and believability of the messages, especially when they are linked to familiar and sometimes demonized or beloved cultural references and experiences, through a process known as visual appropriation'.[48]

Right-wing movements in the United States have long used the rhetoric of fear mongering linked to scapegoating and conspiracy theories in ways that demonize a subversive 'Other' hiding inside progressive political movements.[49]

Scapegoating: In Western culture the term 'scapegoat' can be traced to an early Jewish ritual described in the book of Leviticus in the Bible.[50] As Allport explains:

> On the Day of Atonement a live goat was chosen by lot. The high priest, robed in linen garments, laid both his hands on the goat's head, and confessed over it the iniquities of the children of Israel. The sins of the people thus symbolically transferred to the beast, it was taken out into the wilderness and let go. The people felt purged, and for the time being, guiltless. [51]

The word scapegoat has evolved to mean a person or group wrongfully blamed for some problem, especially for other people's misdeeds. 'Psychologically', Landes explains, 'the tendency to find scapegoats is a result of the common defense mechanism of denial through projection'.[52] This can involve guilt over their own misconduct, or a rejection of their own inner thoughts, or a redirection of their own anxiety or frustration onto the scapegoat.[53]

A certain level of scapegoating is endemic in most societies, but it more readily becomes an important political force in times of social competition or upheaval. At such times, especially, scapegoating can be an effective way to mobilize mass support and activism during a struggle for power.[54]

Fisher explains that 'the scapegoated group serves more as a metaphor'. Nor does scapegoating by large groups and social movements indicate mass mental dysfunction.[55] As a social process, the hostility and grievances of an anxious, angry, or frustrated group are directed away from the most significant causes of a social problem onto a target group demonized as malevolent wrongdoers. In a book on right-wing populism several years ago, Lyons and I put it this way:

314

The scapegoat bears the blame, while the scapegoaters feel a sense of righteousness and increased unity. The social problem may be real or imaginary, the grievances legitimate or illegitimate, and members of the targeted group may be wholly innocent or partly culpable. What matters is that the scapegoats are wrongfully stereotyped as all sharing the same negative trait, or are singled out for blame while the other major culprits and causes are let off the hook.[56]

Benedict writes that desperate people 'easily seize upon some scapegoat to sacrifice to their unhappiness; it is a kind of magic by which they feel for the moment that they have laid [down] the misery that has been tormenting them'.[57] According to Benedict, we all 'know what the galling frictions are in the world today: nationalistic rivalries, desperate defense of the status quo by the haves, desperate attacks by the have-nots, poverty, unemployment, and war'. Benedict also observes that 'Whenever one group [...] is discriminated against before the law or in equal claims to life, liberty, and jobs, there will always be powerful interests to capitalize on this fact and to divert violence from those responsible for these conditions into channels where it is relatively safe to allow'.[58] In this way, scapegoating feeds on people's anger about their own disempowerment, but diverts this anger away from the real systems of power and oppression.

While scapegoats are often less powerful and more marginalized than the actual sources of conflict, this is not always the case.[59] Scapegoating of persons with high status can serve the status quo and protect those in power from criticism.[60] This can happen when a faction of elites holding political power targets another elite faction seeking electoral victories. Sometimes scapegoating targets at the same time *both* socially disempowered or marginalized groups as well as the powerful or privileged, in a form of populism called 'producerism'.[61]

Producerism is the idea that a hard-working and 'productive' middle class is being robbed by parasites above and below them on the socio-economic ladder.[62] For example, conservative activists Gary Allen and Larry Abraham used a producerist framework built around a conspiracy theory in *None Dare Call It Conspiracy* to explain the success of the communist conspiracy in penetrating America. They claimed this involved the use of the 'Communist tactic of pressure from above and pressure from below':

The pressure from above comes from secret, ostensible respectable Comrades in the government and Establishment, forming with the radicalized [leftist] mobs in the streets below, a giant pincer around middle-class society. The street rioters are pawns, shills, puppets, and dupes for an oligarchy of elitist conspirators working above to turn America's limited government into an unlimited government with total control over our lives and property.[63]

In their book, Allen and Abraham provide a diagram of the producerist vice. It illustrates how a conspiracy of the Rothschilds, the Rockefellers, and the Council on Foreign Relations applies pressure from above. Meanwhile a subversive leftist network (including the Students for a Democratic Society, Black Panther Party, Youth International Party (YIPPIES), Young Socialist Alliance and Common Cause) applies pressure from below. This creates the vice crushing the middle class.[64] Right-wing authors in the United States have used producerism coupled with a racialized subtext for decades.[65]

Vilification and Demonization of an 'Enemy': Vilification in the societal sense is the use of vicious rhetoric to denounce and portray a target group as disgusting and to be avoided. Demonization is the process through which a group of people target other groups of people as the embodiment of evil.[66]

The hated target is first denigrated, then vilified, then demonized, and finally dehumanized. Typically, proponents claim that the target is plotting against the public good.[67] Demonization generally involves demagogic appeals. The demonization of an adversary involves well-established psychological processes.[68] There are a number of social science experiments with troubling outcomes that demonstrate that across many cultures it is relatively easy to turn one group against another.[69] Among the most famous are the 'Milgram Experiments',[70] and the 'Brown Eye Blue Eye Experiments'.[71]

The demonized scapegoat serves a dual purpose by representing the evil 'them' and simultaneously illuminating, solidifying, and sanctifying the good 'us'. [72] According to Aho, even when it is unconscious, the objectification of evil through scapegoating has this wondrous outcome: 'The casting out of evil onto you not only renders you my enemy; it also accomplishes my own innocence. To paraphrase [Nietzsche]: In manufacturing an evil one against whom to battle heroically, I fabricate a good one, myself'.[73]

In addition, Girard argues, 'the effect of the scapegoat is to reverse the relationship between persecutors and their victims'.[74] When persons in scapegoated groups are attacked, they are often described as having brought on the attack themselves because of the wretched behavior ascribed to them as part of the enemy group.[75] They deserved what they got. Scapegoating evokes hatred rather than anger. The 'hater is sure the fault lies in the object of hate', notes Allport.[76]

Fuller, similarly, links scapegoating to Christian apocalyptic millennialism by noting how frequently throughout U. S. history scapegoated groups have been named as harboring agents of the Antichrist. Fuller also sees a psychological dimension:

> Many efforts to name the Antichrist appear to be rooted in the psychological need to project one's 'unacceptable' tendencies onto a demonic enemy. It is the Antichrist, not oneself, who must be held responsible for wayward desires. And with so many aspects of modern American life potentially luring individuals into nonbiblical thoughts or desires, it is no wonder that many people believe that the Antichrist has camouflaged himself to better work his conspiracies against the faithful.[77]

Apocalyptic Aggression: Apocalypticism involves the sense of expectation by individuals or groups that dramatic events are about to unfold during which 'good' will confront 'evil'. This confrontation will change the world forever and reveal hidden truths.[78] Members of apocalyptic movements believe that time is running out. The term millenarianism describes generic apocalyptic movements while millennialism refers to movements foreseeing a significant on thousand year time span. Robert J. Lifton observes that 'historically the apocalyptic imagination has usually been nonviolent in nature', but such beliefs also can generate indiscriminate violence.[79] An apocalyptic leader may take on the mantle of the messiah, and in some cases urge forms of apocalyptic aggression against the scapegoated enemy. In such cases, the apocalyptic activists often cast a 'projection of negativity and rejected elements of self onto ideologically designated scapegoats'.[80]

Conspiracism: Conspiracist thinking exists around the world and, in some circumstances, can move easily from the margins to the mainstream, as has happened repeatedly in the United States – as mentioned above.[81] Goldberg traces the concept of conspiracy thinking back to the 'Latin word conspirare – to breathe together', which implies some type of dramatic scenario.[82] Conspiracism evolves as a worldview from roots in dualistic forms of apocalypticism. Fenster argues that persons who embrace conspiracy theories are simply trying to understand how power is exercised in a society that they feel they have no control over. Often they have real grievances with the society – sometimes legitimate – sometimes seeking to defend unfair power and privilege.[83] Nonetheless, Conspiracism can appear as a particular narrative form of scapegoating that frames demonized enemies as part of a vast insidious plot against the common good, while it valorizes the scapegoater as a hero for sounding the alarm.[84]

Conspiracist thinking has appeared in mainstream popular discourse as well as in various subcultures in the United States and Europe.[85] In contemporary examples we can see conspiracy theories built around fears of liberal subversion by President Obama;[86] fears of government attempts to merge the United States, Canada, and Mexico into a North American Union;[87] and fears that Muslims living in the United States are plotting treachery and terrorism.[88]

From Paranoid Style to Apocalyptic Frame

Since the 1960s, numerous scholars have explored the role of conspiracy theories in American life. Some of the best-known early studies of conspiracy theories were penned by noted historian Hofstadter whose essay on 'The Paranoid Style in American Politics' established the leading analytical framework in the 1960s for studying conspiracism in public settings.[89]

Hofstadter identified 'the central preconception' of the paranoid style as a belief in the 'existence of a vast, insidious, preternaturally effective international conspiratorial network designed to perpetrate acts of the most fiendish character'. According to Hofstadter, this style was common in certain figures in the US political right, and was accompanied with a 'sense that his political passions are unselfish and patriotic' which 'goes far to intensify his feeling of righteousness and his moral indignation'.[90] According to Hofstadter:

[...] the feeling of persecution is central, and it is indeed systematized in grandiose theories of conspiracy. But there is a vital difference between the paranoid spokesman in politics and the clinical paranoiac: although they both tend to be overheated, oversuspicious, overaggressive, grandiose, and apocalyptic in expression, the clinical paranoid sees the hostile and conspiratorial world in which he feels himself to be living as directed specifically *against him*; whereas the spokesman of the paranoid style finds it directed against a nation, a culture, a way of life whose fate affects not himself alone but millions of others.[91]

Thompson, a journalist and scholar of religion, suggests Hofstadter was right to articulate the 'startling affinities between the paranoid style and apocalyptic belief', especially the demonization of opponents and 'the sense of time running out'. Thompson, however, argues Hofstadter should have made a more direct connection by considering 'the possibility that the paranoia he identified actually derived from apocalyptic belief; that the people who spread scare stories about Catholics, Masons, Illuminati, and Communists' were, in fact, extrapolating from widespread Protestant End Times beliefs. Furthermore, the persistence of End Times belief 'in the United States rather than Europe surely explains why the paranoid style seems so quintessentially American', concludes Thompson, who has also written extensively on apocalyptic millennialism.[92]

Scripted Violence and the Superhero Complex

Individuals in an elite totalitarian cadre organization can robe themselves in the garb of the elite warrior defending hearth and home from attack. In contemporary society, people who are fearful and alienated can adopt the same ideas and actions. They are self-mobilized into the role, and embrace this superhero persona in which the duties and actions are clearly laid out in popular media from television, comic books, motion pictures, and the Internet. Popular fictional superheroes are essentially vigilantes stepping outside the law to 'do what needs to be done'. Why are we surprised when amateur emulators attack or execute black people, Mexican immigrants, Muslims, Sikhs, abortion providers, or gay people?

In the United States especially, this Superhero Complex is generated in

319

part by the routine exposure to images of violence, primarily on television. That television viewing could be associated with violence was asserted with authority as early as 1972 in an advisory report issued by the US Government.[93]

Critics of the connection between viewing of large volume of violent media images and negative outcomes in children often argue that no direct causal link has been demonstrated. This is true if misleading. Many studies have shown that in the large population of young people who routinely watch many hours of televised violence, the percentage of those viewers with negative outcomes of socialization is higher than the group of young people not exposed to long hours of violent images.[94] Gerbner argues that some people exposed to many hours of violent images in the mass media develop what he calls 'Mean-World Syndrome' in which they become unrealistically afraid of threats from people outside their home and direct friendship circle.[95]

As also discussed elsewhere in this volume, many of these theoretical elements of the Superhero persona appear in vivid detail in the fifteen hundred page manifesto, written by convicted Norwegian terrorist Anders Behring Breivik.[96] A number of authors have written about 'Breivik's Ideology' of the 'Romantic Male Warrior Ideal'. Gardell writes that Breivik saw himself as a 'self-appointed knight' who 'gave himself the stage name [of the Norwegian King] Sigurd – the Crusader'.[97] Gardell observes of Breivik:

> Animated by heroic tales of the crusaders, movie epics such as 300, Lord of the Rings, Passion Of The Christ, Serbian ultranationalist narratives of Radovan Karadzic's bloody actions during the Bosnian civil war, and the exploits he performed in the World of Warcraft, Breivik felt equipped for battle.[98]

Breivik's manifesto correspondingly warns of a 'deconstruction of European cultures, identities and the traditional structures', which he identifies as the 'nuclear family, traditional morality and patriarchal structures'. He rejects what he sees as the current 'pacified/feminized' culture of Europe. He sees himself as a heroic warrior standing erect against the onslaught of 'Cultural Marxism',[99] which is revealed in Breivik's manifesto to be a fantastic conspiracy construction that justifies aggression against liberals and Muslims in defense of Christianity and western culture.[100]

The role of gender panic in shaping an identity of the Superhero warrior, is analyzed by Gibson in his book, *Warrior Dreams*.[101] In a similar line of analysis, found in Breivik's Manifesto 'evidence of his profoundly sexist view of the world, where women are naive and lacking in rationality, but are useful for sex and reproduction'. She called it 'emasculation paranoia'. Ingersoll also highlighted Breivik's claim that 'feminism is to blame for what he asserts is the success of a supposed Muslim plan for world domination'. Breivik 'wants to set the culture clock back to the '50's – because we know it works'. This mythic nostalgia, according to Ingersoll, 'is a central feature [...] of how Breivik's analysis could well have been lifted from the talking points of the religious right'.[102] Behind this is a long history in the United States of seeing the country being emasculated by liberal treachery.[103]

Conclusions

If we assemble the ingredients and processes in this study, we arrive at the following list which traces the linkages from words to violence:

- Pre-existing prejudice or tensions in the society that can be tapped into.
- Intensity of the vilifying language, its distribution to a wide audience, and repetition of message.
- Dualistic division: The world is divided into a good 'Us' and a bad 'Them'.
- Demagoguery. Respected status of speaker or writer, at least within the target audience. A constituency is molded.
- Vilification and Demonizing rhetoric: Our opponents are dangerous, subversive, probably evil, maybe even subhuman.
- Targeting scapegoats: 'They' are causing all our troubles – we are blameless.
- The employment of conspiracy theories about the 'Other'.
- Apocalyptic aggression: Time is running out, and we must act immediately to stave off a cataclysmic event.
- Violence against the named scapegoats by self-invented Superheroes.

Arendt, in *Eichmann in Jerusalem*, concluded that evil was banal, and that if

there was one clear universal truth, it is that ordinary people have a moral obligation to not look away from individual or institutional acts of cruelty or oppression. We recognize the processes that lead from words to violence, they
are well-studied, and the theories and proofs are readily available. Silence is
consent. Denial is simply evil.

ENDNOTES

[1] This story is drawn from Chip Berlet, 'Hate Groups, Racial Tension and Ethnoviolence in
an Integrating Chicago Neighbourhood 1976 – 1988', in *Research in Political Sociology*, 9 (*The Politics of Social Inequality*, eds. Betty A. Dobratz, Lisa K. Walder, and
Timothy Buzzell, 2001), pp. 117 – 163.

[2] The majority of this study is a literature review and sketch of concepts with an expanded
set of cites devised to support the underlying premise of the conference and the resulting articles. Portions of this study have been adapted from previously published
work as noted in the endnotes as appropriate.

[3] Jack Levin, *The Violence of Hate: Confronting Racism, Anti-Semitism, and Other Forms
of Bigotry* (Boston: Allyn and Bacon, 2002).

[4] Mark Frohardt and Jonathan Temin, *Use and Abuse of Media in Vulnerable Societies*,
Special Report 110, United States Institute of Peace (October 2003). Available at:
http://permanent.access.gpo.gov/websites/usip/www.usip.org/pubs/specialreports/sr1
10.pdf (accessed 26/09/2012). Although an excellent study, the report is flawed by
the failure to include a single footnote. See also Kofi A. Annan, Allan Thompson, and
International Development Research Centre of Canada, *The Media and the Rwanda
Genocide* (Ottawa: International Development Research Centre, 2007).

[5] Hannah Arendt, *The Origins of Totalitarianism* (New York: Harcourt Brace Jovanovich, 1973).

[6] Ibid., p. 385.

[7] Chip Berlet, 'Islamophobia, Antisemitism and the Demonized "Other": Parallels among
bigotries reflect the conspiratorial mindset', *EXTRA!* Magazine of Fairness and Accu-
racy in Reporting, August 2012. Available at: http://www.fair.org/index.php?page=45
89 (accessed 26/09/2012).

[8] Chip Berlet 'Protocols to the Left, Protocols to the Right: Conspiracism in American Political Discourse at the Turn of the Second Millennium', in Richard Landes and Steven
Katz eds., *The Paranoid Apocalypse: A Hundred-Year Retrospective on the Protocols
of the Elders of Zion* (New York: New York University Press, 2011).

[9] CBS News, 'Napolitano: Lone Wolf Terror Threat Growing', 2 December 2011. Available
at: http://www.cbsnews.com/8301-201_162-57336080/napolitano-lone-wolf-terror-thr
eat-growing/ (accessed 26/09/2012).

[10] The 'spark' phrase is from an essay by Mao. 'Spark' (*Iskra* in Russian), was the name of
a newspaper established by Lenin. The phrase was popularized by the 1960s
Weather Underground in its revolutionary journal *Prairie Fire*. The concept originates
in the revolutionary theory known as 'propaganda of the deed' that can include acts
of violence and terrorism. The theory was developed in the 1800s by left revolutionaries and anarchists, notably Carlo Pisacane, Mikhail Bakunin, and Paul Brousse.

[11] Theodor W. Adorno, Else Frenkel-Brunswick, Daniel J. Levinson, R. Nevitt Sanford, *The Authoritarian Personality* (New York: Harper and Row, 1950); Bruno Bettelheim and Morris
Janowitz, *The Dynamics of Prejudice* (New York: Harper and Row, 1950); Norman W.

Ackerman and Marie Jahoda, *Anti-Semitism and Emotional Disorder* (New York: Harper and Row, 1950); John Dollard, L. Doob, N. E. Miller, O. H. Mowrer, and R. R. Sears, *Frustration and Aggression* (New Haven: Yale University Press, 1939); Theodor W. Adorno *et al.*, *The Authoritarian Personality* (New York: Harper and Row, 1950); Gordon W. Allport, *Nature of Prejudice* (Cambridge, MA: Addison-Wesley, 1954).

[12] Naturally there are critics of this argument, but many of the contentions remain valid. Other contentions have been challenged or remain unproven in social science research studies. An exemplary review of this is found in Elisabeth Young-Bruehl, *The Anatomy of Prejudices* (Cambridge, MA: Harvard University Press, 1996).

[13] Arendt, *The Origins of Totalitarianism*, republished in three volumes: Hannah Arendt, *Antisemitism*: Part One of *The Origins of Totalitarianism* (New York: Harcourt, Brace and World, 1968); Hannah Arendt, *Imperialism*: Part Two of *The Origins of Totalitarianism* (New York: Harcourt, Brace and World, 1968); Hannah Arendt, *Totalitarianism*: Part Three of *The Origins of Totalitarianism* (New York: Harcourt, Brace and World, 1968).

[14] Eric Hoffer, *The True Believer: Thoughts on the Nature of Mass Movements* (New York: Harper and Row, 1951); Milton Rokeach, *The Open and Closed Mind* (New York: Basic Books, 1960).

[15] See for example, William Kornhauser, *The Politics of Mass Society* (Glencoe: The Free Press, 1959); Hans Toch, *The Social Psychology of Social Movements* (London: Methuen, 1966); Gustave Le Bon, *The Crowd: A Study of Popular Mind* (New York: Viking Press, 1960); Herbert Blumer, 'Social Movements', in Barry McLaughlin ed., *Studies in Social Movements: A Social Psychological Perspective* (New York: Free Press, 1969); Talcott Parsons, *The Structure of Social Action* Second Edition (New York: Free Press, 1967); Ted Robert Gurr, *Why Men Rebel* (Princeton, NJ: Princeton University Press, 1970); Daniel Bell, ed., *The Radical Right: The New American Right*, Expanded And Updated (Garden City, NY: Anchor Books, Doubleday and Company, 1964); Seymour Martin Lipset and Earl Raab, *The Politics of Unreason: Right-Wing Extremism in America, 1790 – 1970* (New York: Harper and Row, 1970); and Arnold Forster and Benjamin R. Epstein, *Danger on the Right* (New York: Random House, 1964).

[16] Richard Hofstadter, 'The Paranoid Style in American Politics', in *The Paranoid Style in American Politics and Other Essays* (New York: Alfred A. Knopf, 1965); Richard Hofstadter, *Anti-Intellectualism in American Life* (New York: Alfred A. Knopf, 1963); Richard Hofstadter, *The Age of Reform: From Bryan to FDR* (New York: Alfred A. Knopf, 1955).

[17] An excellent overview of these newer theories is Evan R. Harrington, 'The Social Psychology of Hatred', *Journal of Hate Studies*, 3/1 (2004), pp. 49 – 82.

[18] Hannah Arendt, *The Origins of Totalitarianism* (New York: Harcourt, Brace and World, 1951); Hannah Arendt, *Eichmann in Jerusalem; A Report on the Banality of Evil* (New York: Viking Press, 1963).

[19] Jeane J. Kirkpatrick made the claim that Arendt had indicted all Marxists in *Dictatorships and Double Standards: Rationalism and Reason in Politics* (New York: Simon and Schuster, 1982). For a critique of Kirkpatrick's claims, see Sara Diamond, *Roads to Dominion: Right-Wing Movements and Political Power in the United States* (New York: Guilford Press, 1995), pp. 198, and 216 – 217. For Arendt's actual thesis, see Hannah Arendt, *The Origins of Totalitarianism* (New York: Harcourt Brace Jovanovich, [1951] 1973). See especially pp. 468 – 474.

[20] Michael Rogin, *The Intellectuals and McCarthy: The Radical Specter* (Cambridge, MA: MIT Press, 1967). See especially pp. 261 – 282.

[21] Richard O. Curry and Thomas M. Brown, 'Introduction', in Richard O. Curry and Thomas M. Brown, eds., *Conspiracy: The Fear Of Subversion In American History* (New York: Holt, Rinehart And Winston, 1972), pp. xii – xi; Leo Ribuffo, *The Old Christian Right: The Protestant Far Right from the Great Depression to the Cold War* (Philadelphia: Temple Univ. Press, 1983), pp. 237 – 257; Margaret Canovan, *Populism* (New York: Harcourt Brace Jovanovich, 1981), pp. 46 – 51, and 179 – 190; Jerome L. Himmelstein, *To The Right: The Transformation Of American Conservatism* (Berkeley: Univ. Of California Press, 1990), pp. 1 – 5, 72 – 76, 152 – 164; Sara Diamond, *Roads To Dominion: Right-Wing Movements And Political Power In The United States* (New York: Guilford Press, 1995), pp. 5 – 6, 40 – 41; Sara Diamond, 'How "Radical" Is the Christian Right?' *The Humanist* (March/April 1994); Michael Kazin, *The Populist Persuasion: An American History* (New York: Basic Books, 1995), pp. 190 – 193; Betty A. Dobratz and Stephanie Shanks-Meile, *The White Separatist Movement in the United States: 'White Power, White Pride!'* (New York: Twayne Publishers, 1997); Berlet and Matthew N. Lyons, 'One Key to Litigating Against Government Prosecution of Dissidents: Understanding the Underlying Assumptions', *Police Misconduct and Civil Rights Law Report*, West Group, in Two Parts, 5/13 (January – February 1998), and 5/14 (March – April 1998); William B. Hixson, Jr., *Search for the American Right Wing: An Analysis of the Social Science Record: 1955 – 1987* (Princeton: Princeton Univ. Press, 1992). For statistical data that refutes claims made by the centrist/extremist theory concerning the social base of the 'radical right', see Rogin, *Intellectuals and McCarthy*; Fred W. Grupp, Jr., 'The Political Perspectives of Birch Society Members', in *The American Right Wing: Readings in Political Behaviour*, ed., Robert A. Schoenberger (New York: Holt, Rinehart and Winston, 1969); James McEvoy III, 'Conservatism or Extremism: Goldwater Supporters in the 1964 Presidential Election' in Schoenberger ed., *American Right Wing*; Charles Jeffrey Kraft, *A Preliminary Socio-Economic and State Demographic Profile of the John Birch Society* (Cambridge, MA: Political Research Associates, 1992).

[22] This section is borrowed from Chip Berlet, 'Reframing Populist Resentments in the Tea Party Movement', in Lawrence Rosenthal and Christine Trost, eds., *Steep: The Precipitous Rise of the Tea Party* (Berkeley: Univ. of California Press, 2012).

[23] John D. McCarthy and Mayer N. Zald, 'Resource Mobilization and Social Movements: A Partial Theory', *American Journal of Sociology*, 82/6 (May 1977), pp. 1212 – 1241; Doug McAdam, John D. McCarthy, and Mayer N. Zald, *Comparative Perspectives on Social Movements: Political Opportunities, Mobilizing Structures, and Cultural Framings* (London and New York: Cambridge University Press, 1996).

[24] Erving Goffman, *The Presentation of Self in Everyday Life* (Garden City, N.Y.: Doubleday, 1959); Erving Goffman, *Frame Analysis: An Essay on the Organization of Experience* (Cambridge, MA: Harvard Univ. Press, 1974); McCarthy and Zald, 'Resource Mobilization'; David A. Snow, E. Burke Rochford, Jr., Steven K. Worden, and Robert D. Benford, 'Frame Alignment Process, Micromobilization, and Movement Participation', *American Sociological Review* 51 (1986), pp. 464 – 481; David A. Snow and Robert D. Benford, 'Master Frames and Cycles of Protest', in Aldon D. Morris and Carol McClurg Mueller eds., *Frontiers in Social Movement Theory* (New Haven: Yale University Press, 1992).

[25] Joseph E. Davis, ed., *Stories of Change Narrative and Social Movements* (Albany: State University of New York Press, 2002); Francesca Polletta, 'Contending Stories: Narrative in Social Movements', *Qualitative Sociology,* 21/4 (1998), pp. 419 – 446.

[26] Patricia Ewick and Susan S. Silbey, 'Subversive Stories and Hegemonic Tales: Towards

a Sociology of Narrative', *Law and Society Review* 29/2 (1995), pp. 197 – 226.

[27] Robert (Bob) Altemeyer, 'Highly Dominating, Highly Authoritarian Personalities', in *Journal of Social Psychology* 14 (2004), pp. 421 – 447. See also Robert (Bob) Altemeyer, *Right-Wing Authoritarianism* (Winnipeg: University of Manitoba Press, 1981); Robert (Bob) Altemeyer, *Enemies of Freedom: Understanding Right-Wing Authoritarianism* (San Francisco: Jossey-Bass, 1988); Robert (Bob) Altemeyer, *The Authoritarian Specter* (Cambridge, MA: Harvard University Press, 1996).

[28] Robert (Bob) Altemeyer, 'Comment on the Tea Party Movement', Personal Website, 20 April 2010. See: http://home.cc.umanitoba.ca/~altemey/drbob/Comment%20on%20th e%20Tea%20Party.pdf (accessed 05/10/2012).

[29] Hans-Georg Betz, 'The Two Faces of Radical Right-Wing Populism in Western Europe', *The Review of Politics,* 55/4 (Autumn 1993), pp. 663 – 685, 663.

[30] Ray Taras, *Europe Old and New: Transnationalism, Belonging, Xenophobia* (Lanham, MD: Rowman and Littlefield, 2008), pp. 83 – 172, 93.

[31] Drew Westen, *The Political Brain: The Role of Emotion in Deciding the Fate of the Nation* (New York: Public Affairs, 2007); George Lakoff, *The Political Mind: A Cognitive Scientist's Guide to your Brain and its Politics* (New York: Viking Penguin, 2008); Chris Mooney, *The Republican Brain: The Science of Why They Deny Science and Reality* (Hoboken, NJ/ Chichester: Wiley, 2012).

[32] This section is adapted from Chip Berlet, 'The United States: Messianism, Apocalypticism, and Political Religion', in *The Sacred in Twentieth Century Politics: Essays in Honour of Professor Stanley G. Payne,* eds., Roger Griffin, Matthew Feldman, and John Tortice (Basingstoke: Palgrave Macmillan, 2008), pp. 221 – 257; Chip Berlet, 'Christian Identity: The Apocalyptic Style, Political Religion, Palingenesis and Neo-Fascism', in *Fascism, Totalitarianism, and Political Religion,* ed., Roger Griffin (London: Routledge, 2005), pp. 175 – 212; Chip Berlet, 'When Alienation Turns Right: Populist Conspiracism, the Apocalyptic Style, and Neofascist Movements', in Lauren Langman and Devorah Kalekin Fishman eds., *Trauma, Promise, and the Millennium: The Evolution of Alienation* (Lanham, MD: Rowman and Littlefield, 2005), pp. 115 – 144; Chip Berlet, 'Protocols to the Left, Protocols to the Right'; Chip Berlet, *Toxic to Democracy: Conspiracy Theories, Demonization, and Scapegoating* (Somerville, MA: Political Research Associates, 2009). See: http://www. publiceye. org/conspire/toxic2democracy/index. html (accessed 26/09/2012). Chip Berlet, 'Fears of Fédéralisme in the United States: The Case of the "North American Union" Conspiracy Theory', *Fédéralisme Régionalisme,* 9/1 (2009). Special Issue on 'Le Fédéralisme Américain', see: http://popups. ulg. ac. be/federalisme/document. php?id=786 (accessed 26/09/2012).

[33] Dick Anthony and Thomas Robbins, 'Religious Totalism, Exemplary Dualism, and The Waco Tragedy', in *Millennium, Messiahs, and Mayhem,* eds., Robbins and Palmer (New York: Routledge: 1997), pp. 261 – 84, quotes from 264, 269.

[34] Dick Anthony and Thomas Robbins, 'Religious Totalism, Violence and Exemplary Dualism: Beyond the Extrinsic Model', in Michael Barkun ed., *Millennialism and Violence* (London: Frank Cass, 1996), pp. 10 – 50.

[35] Hofstadter, *Anti-Intellectualism,* p. 135.

[36] Michelle Goldberg, *Kingdom Coming: The Rise of Christian Nationalism* (New York: W. W. Norton, 2006); William Martin, *With God on Our Side: The Rise of the Religious Right in America* (New York: Broadway Books, 1996).

[37] Gordon W. Allport, 'Demagogy', in Richard O. Curry and Thomas M. Brown eds., *Con-*

spiracy: The Fear of Subversion in American History (New York, N.Y.: Holt, Rinehart and Winston, 1972), pp. 263 – 276.

[38] Walter Lippmann, *Public Opinion* (New York: Harcourt Brace Jovanovich, 1922).

[39] Edward L. Bernays, *Crystallizing Public Opinion* (New York: Liveright, 1923); Edward L. Bernays, *Propaganda* (New York: Liveright, 1928). In an interview I conducted with the late Bernays, he asserted that the rhetoric of persuasion that used 'propaganda techniques not in accordance with good sense, good faith, or good morals' should be called 'impropaganda'. Logic and Credible Journalism, see: http://www. research-forprogress. us/media/training/logic. html (accessed 26/09/2012).

[40] George Gerbner, Larry Gross, Michael Morgan, and Nancy Signorielli, 'Growing up with Television: The Cultivation Perspective', in Michael Morgan ed., *Against the Mainstream: The Selected Works of George Gerbner* (New York: Peter Lang, 2002), pp. 193 – 213; James Shanahan and Michael Morgan, *Television and Its Viewers: Cultivation Theory and Research* (Cambridge: Cambridge University Press, 1999).

[41] Louis Althusser, *For Marx* (New York: Pantheon, 1965); Louis Althusser, *Reading Capital* (London: NLB, 1970). Louis Althusser, 'Ideology and Ideological State Apparatuses', in *Lenin and Philosophy* (New York: Monthly Review, 1971).

[42] Maurice Charland, 'Constitutive Rhetoric: The Case of the *Peuple Québécois*', in *Quarterly Journal of Speech*, 73/2 (1987), pp. 133 – 150.

[43] Ibid.

[44] Jennifer B. Gray, 'Althusser, Ideology, and Theoretical Foundations: Theory and Communication', in *NMEDIAC: Journal of New Media and Culture*, 3/1 (Winter 2006). Online at: http://www. ibiblio. org/nmediac/winter2004/gray. html (accessed 26/09/2012).

[45] Hank Johnston, 'A Methodology for Frame Analysis: From Discourse to Cognitive Schemata', in Hank Johnston and Bert Klandermans eds., *Social Movements and Culture*, Social Movements, Protest, and Contention vol. 4 (Minneapolis, MN: University of Minnesota Press, 1995), pp. 217 – 246.

[46] Margaret Duffy, Janice Teruggi Page, and Rachel Young, 'Obama as Anti-American: Visual Folklore in Right-Wing Forwarded E-mails and Construction of Conservative Social Identity', *Journal of American Folklore*, 125/496 (2012), pp. 177 – 203.

[47] Ibid.

[48] Ibid.

[49] David Neiwert, *The Eliminationists: How Hate Talk Radicalized the American Right* (Sausalito, CA: PoliPointPress, 2009); John Amato and David Neiwert, *Over the Cliff: How Obama's Election Drove the American Right Insane* (Sausalito, CA: PoliPointPress, 2010); Alexander Zaitchik, *Common Nonsense: Glenn Beck and the Triumph of Ignorance* (Hoboken, NJ: Wiley, 2010); Will Bunch, *The Backlash: Right-Wing Radicals, High-Def Hucksters, and Paranoid Politics in the Age of Obama* (New York: Harper, 2010).

[50] This text is borrowed from Chip Berlet and Matthew N. Lyons, *Right-Wing Populism in America: Too Close for Comfort* (New York: Guilford Press, 2000), pp. 7 – 9.

[51] Allport, *Nature of Prejudice*, p. 244. On the ritualized transference and expulsion of evil in a variety of cultures, see Frazier, *Golden Bough*, pp. 624 – 686. On the process and social function of scapegoating in historic persecution texts of myth and religion, see Girard, *Scapegoat*.

[52] Richard Allen Landes, 'Scapegoating' in the *Encyclopedia of Social History* ed., Peter N. Stearn (New York: Garland, 1994), p. 659.

[53] Allport, *Nature of Prejudice*, p. 350.

[54] Berlet and Lyons, *Right-Wing Populism*, pp. 7 – 9.

[55] Conversation with Susan M. Fisher, MD (Clinical Professor of Psychiatry at the University of Chicago Medical School and Faculty, Chicago Institute for Psychoanalysis), 1997.

[56] See Allport, *Nature of Prejudice*, pp. 243 – 260; Girard, *Scapegoat*.

[57] Ruth Benedict, *Race: Science and Politics* (New York: Viking Press, 1961), p. 151.

[58] Ibid., pp. 150 – 151, 153.

[59] Allport, *Nature of Prejudice*, p. 351.

[60] Jack Levin and Jack McDevitt, *Hate Crimes: The Rising Tide of Bigotry and Bloodshed* (New York: Plenum Press, 1996), pp. 234 – 235.

[61] Kazin, *The Populist Persuasion*; Berlet and Lyons, *Right-Wing Populism*, especially p. 6.

[62] Ibid.

[63] Gary Allen with Larry Abraham, *None Dare Call It Conspiracy* (Rossmoor/Seal Beach, CA: Concord Press, [1971] 1972), p. 24.

[64] Ibid. An image of the graphic is at: http://www.researchforprogress.us/producerism/ (accessed 05/10/2012).

[65] Kazin, *The Populist Persuasion*; and Berlet and Lyons, *Right-Wing Populism in America*.

[66] James A. Aho, *This Thing of Darkness: A Sociology of the Enemy* (Seattle: University of Washington Press, 1994), pp. 107 – 121; Elaine H. Pagels, *The Origin of Satan* (New York: Random House, 1995); David Norman Smith, 'The Social Construction of Enemies: Jews and the Representation of Evil', *Sociological Theory* 14/3 (1996); Lise Noël, *Intolerance, A General Survey*, translated by Arnold Bennett (Montreal: McGill-Queen's University Press, 1994).

[67] Robert Solomon Wistrich, *Demonizing the Other* (Amsterdam: Published for the Vidal Sassoon International Centre for the Study of Antisemitism, the Hebrew University of Jerusalem by Harwood Academic Publishers, 1999).

[68] Robert J. Lifton, *Thought Reform and the Psychology of Totalism* (Chapel Hill: University of North Carolina Press, [1961] 1989); Robert (Bob) Altemeyer, *The Authoritarian Specter* (Cambridge, MA: Harvard University Press, 1996).

[69] Evan R. Harrington, 'The Social Psychology of Hatred'.

[70] Stanley Milgram, *Obedience to Authority: An Experimental View* (New York: Harper and Row, 1974).

[71] Public Broadcasting System, 'Brown Eye Blue Eye Experiment' devised by the schoolteacher Jane Elliott, 'A Class Divided', Public Broadcasting System, original airdate March 26, 1985, at: http://www.pbs. org/wgbh/pages/frontline/shows/divided/ (accessed 26/09/2012).

[72] René Girard, *The Scapegoat* (Baltimore: Johns Hopkins University Press, 1986), pp. 43 – 44, 49 – 56, 66 – 73, 84 – 87, 100 – 101, 177 – 178.

[73] Aho, *This Thing of Darkness,* pp. 115 – 116.

[74] Girard, *Scapegoat*, p. 44.

[75] Noël, *Intolerance*, pp. 129 – 144.

[76] Allport, *Nature of Prejudice*, pp. 363 – 364.

[77] Robert C. Fuller, *Naming the Antichrist: The History of an American Obsession* (New York: Oxford University Press, 1995), p. 168.

[78] Fuller, *Naming the Antichrist*; Norman Cohn, *Cosmos, Chaos and the World to Come: The Ancient Roots of Apocalyptic Faith* (New Haven: Yale University Press, 1993); Norman Cohn *The Pursuit of the Millennium: Revolutionary Millenarians and Mystical Anarchists of the Middle Ages* Third Edition (New York: Oxford University Press,

[1957] 1970). See especially the Introduction; Stephen D. O'Leary, *Arguing the Apocalypse: A Theory of Millennial Rhetoric* (New York: Oxford University Press, 1994); Paul S. Boyer, *When Time Shall Be No More: Prophecy Belief in Modern American Culture* (Belknap/Cambridge, MA: Harvard University Press, 1992); Charles B. Strozier, *Apocalypse: On the Psychology of Fundamentalism in America* (Boston: Beacon Press, 1994); Damian Thompson, *The End of Time: Faith and Fear in the Shadow of the Millennium* (Hanover, NH: University Press of New England, 1998); Richard K. Fenn, *The End of Time: Religion, Ritual, and the Forging of the Soul* (Cleveland: Pilgrim Press, 1997); David G. Bromley, 'Constructing Apocalypticism', in *Millennium, Messiahs, and Mayhem: Contemporary Apocalyptic Movements*, eds., Thomas Robbins and Susan J. Palmer (New York: Routledge, 1997), pp. 31 – 45; Catherine Wessinger, 'Millennialism With and Without the Mayhem', in Robbins and Palmer, *Millennium, Messiahs, and Mayhem*, pp. 47 – 59; Joel Kovel, *Red Hunting in the Promised Land: Anticommunism and the Making of America* (New York: Basic Books, 1994); Pagels, Origin of Satan.

79 Robert Jay Lifton, *Superpower Syndrome: America's Apocalyptic Confrontation with the World* (New York: Thunder's Mouth Press/Nation Books, 2003), p. 21; Catherine Wessinger, ed., *Millennialism, Persecution, and Violence: Historical Cases* (Syracuse: Syracuse University Press, 2000).

80 Anthony and Robbins, 'Religious Totalism', p. 269.

81 David Brion Davis, ed., *The Fear of Conspiracy: Images of Un-American Subversion from the Revolution to the Present* (Ithaca, NY: Cornell University Press, 1972); Frank P. Mintz, *The Liberty Lobby and The American Right: Race, Conspiracy, and Culture* (Westport, CT: Greenwood Press, 1985); Robert Alan Goldberg, *Enemies Within: The Culture of Conspiracy in Modern America* (New Haven: Yale University, 2001); Michael Barkun, 'Conspiracy Theories as Stigmatized Knowledge: The Basis for a New Age Racism?', in J. Kaplan and T. Bjørgo eds., *Nation and Race: The Developing Euro-American Racist Subculture* (Boston: Northeastern University Press, 1998), pp. 58 – 72; Michael Barkun, *A Culture of Conspiracy: Apocalyptic Visions in Contemporary America* (Berkley: University of California Press, 2003); Michael Barkun, 'Anti-Semitism from Outer Space: The Protocols in the UFO Subculture', in Richard Landes and Steven Katz eds., *The Paranoid Apocalypse: A Hundred-year Retrospective on the Protocols of the Elders of Zion* (New York: Published for the Elie Wiesel Centre for Judaic Studies Series [Boston]: New York University Press, 2012), pp. 163 – 171.

82 Goldberg, *Enemies Within*, p. 1.

83 Mark Fenster, *Conspiracy Theories: Secrecy and Power in American Culture* (Minneapolis: University of Minnesota Press, 1999).

84 Berlet and Lyons, *Right-Wing Populism*, p. 9.

85 Chip Berlet 'Protocols to the Left'.

86 Chip Berlet, 'Collectivists, Communists, Labour Bosses, and Treason: The Tea Parties as Right–Wing Populist Countersubversion Panic', in *Critical Sociology* 38/4 (July 2012), pp. 565 – 587; Berlet, 'Reframing Populist Resentments in the Tea Party Movement'.

87 Berlet, 'Fears of Fédéralisme in the United States'.

88 Brigitte Nacos and Oscar Torres-Reyna, *Fueling Our Fears: Stereotyping, Media Coverage, and Public Opinion of Muslim Americans* (Lanham, MD: Rowman and Littlefield, 2007); Centre for Race, Gender and Council on American-Islamic Relations, *Same Hate, New Target: Islamophobia and its Impact in the United States; January 2009 –*

December 2010 (Berkeley: University of California, Centre for Race and Gender, and Washington DC: Council on American-Islamic Relations, 2011).

[89] Hofstadter, 'The Paranoid Style in American Politics'.

[90] Ibid., p. 4.

[91] Ibid., emphasis in the original.

[92] Thompson, *The End of Time*, pp. 307 – 308.

[93] United States Surgeon General's Scientific Advisory Committee on Television and Social Behaviour and The United States Public Health Service, Office of the Surgeon General, *Television and Growing Up: The Impact of Television Violence; Report to the Surgeon General*. (Washington: US Govt. Printing Office, 1972).

[94] W. James Potter, *Ten Myths of Media Violence* (Thousand Oaks: Sage Publications, 2003).

[95] George Gerbner, Larry Gross, Michael Morgan, and Nancy Signorielli, 'The "mainstreaming" of America: Violence', profile no. 11. *Journal of Communication* 30/3 (1980), pp. 10 – 29; George Gerbner, 'Reclaiming our Cultural Mythology: Television's Global Marketing Strategy Creates a Damaging and Alienated Window on the World', *The Ecology of Justice* 38 (Spring 1994), pp. 40 – 44; George Gerbner, Larry Gross, Michael Morgan, Nancy Signorielli, and James Shanahan, 'Growing up with Television: Cultivation Processes', in Jennings Bryant and Dolf Zillmann eds., *Media Effects: Advances in Theory and Research* (Hillsdale: Lawrence Erlbaum Associates, 1994). An extensive and excellent overview of Gerbner's theories is Scott Stossel, 'The Man Who Counts the Killing', *The Atlantic Monthly* 279/5 (May 1997), pp. 86 – 104. See: http://www.theatlantic.com/past/docs/issues/97may/gerbner.htm (accessed 05/10/2012).

[96] Anders Behring Breivik (writing as Andrew Berwick), '2083: A European Declaration of Independence', self-published, July 2011. A copy of the Breivik manifesto in PDF format is archived at: http://www.researchforprogress.us/dox/europe/norway/breivik/manifesto.pdf (accessed 05/10/2012).

[97] Mattia Gardell, 'Roots of Breivik's Ideology: Where Does the Romantic Male Warrior Ideal Come From Today?' OpenDemocracy.net, 8 January 2012. See: http://www.opendemocracy.net/mattias-gardell/roots-of-breiviks-ideology-where-does-romantic-male-warrior-ideal-come-from-today (accessed 27/01/2012).

[98] Ibid.

[99] David Neiwert, 'Norway Terrorist Breivik was an Ardent Subscriber to Theories of "Cultural Marxism"', Crooks and Liars, 23 July 2011. See: http://crooksandliars.com/david-neiwert/norway-terrorist-breivik-was-ardent- (accessed 05/10/2012); based in part on the programme 'Political Correctness Is Cultural Marxism', 25 March 2009. Fox News. Andrew Breitbart appearance on the 25 March edition of the Sean Hannity programme, 'The Obama Lexicon' segment. See also Media Matters, 'Breitbart: "Cultural Marxism is Political Correctness, Multiculturalism, and a War on Judeo-Christianty"', at Mediamatters.org 18/12/2009. See: http://mediamatters.org/video/2009/12/18/breitbart-cultural-marxism-is-political-correct/158346 (accessed 05/10/2012). The Andrew Breitbart appearance on the Sean Hannity programme is also preserved as an online video.

[100] Bill Berkowitz: 'Nightmare in Norway and the Threat of Fundamentalist Christian, Blonde, Blue-Eyed Terrorists in Our Midst', Buzzflash. See: http://blog.buzzflash.com/node/12881 (accessed 27/01/2012); Sarah Posner, 'How Breivik's "Cultural Analysis" is Drawn from the "Christian Worldview"', Religion Dispatches. See: http://www.religiondispatches.org/dispatches/sarahposner/4934/ (ac-

cessed 27/01/2012); Henry A. Giroux, 'Breivik's Fundamentalist War on Politics, and Ours', 3 August 2011. See: http://www.truth-out.org/breiviks-fundamentalist-war-politics-and-ours/1312390288 (accessed 27/01/2012).

[101] James William Gibson, *Warrior Dreams: Paramilitary Culture in Post-Vietnam America* (New York: Hill and Wang, 1994).

[102] Julie Ingersoll, 'Breivik's Emasculation Paranoia Fueled Vision for Patriarchal "Reforms"', Religion Dispatches, 29 July 2011. See: http://www.religiondispatches.org/dispatches/julieingersoll/4944/ (accessed 27/01/2012). See also Julie Ingersoll, 'Breivik's Christianity About Culture Not Piety', Religion Dispatches, 25 July 2011. Available online at: http://www.religiondispatches.org/dispatches/julieingersoll/4913/ (accessed 27/01/2012); Julie Ingersoll, 'What's Actually in Breivik's "Declaration of Independence"', Religion Dispatches, 26 July 2011. Available online at: www.religiondispatches.org/dispatches/julieingersoll/4931/ (accessed 27/01/2012).

[103] Jerry Lembke, *The Spitting Image: Myth, Memory, and the Legacy of Vietnam* (New York: New York Univ. Press, 2000); Jerry Lembke, *CNN's Tailwind Tale: Inside Vietnam's Last Great Myth* (Lanham, MD: Rowman and Littlefield, 2003); Jerry Lembke, *Hanoi Jane: War, Sex, and Fantasies of Betrayal* (Amherst: University of Massachusetts Press, 2010).

INDEX

Sie haben die Wahl:

Bestellen Sie die Schriftenreihe
Explorations of the Far Right
einzeln oder im **Abonnement**

per E-Mail: vertrieb@ibidem-verlag.de | per Fax (0511/262 2201)
als Brief (*ibidem*-Verlag | Leuschnerstr. 40 | 30457 Hannover)

Bestellformular

☐ Ich abonniere die Schriftenreihe *Explorations of the Far Right*
   ab Band # _____

☐ Ich bestelle die folgenden Bände der Schriftenreihe
   Explorations of the Far Right
   # _____; _____; _____; _____; _____; _____; _____; _____; _____; _____

Lieferanschrift:

Vorname, Name ....

Anschrift ....

E-Mail.. | Tel.: ....

Datum .... | Unterschrift ....

Ihre Abonnement-Vorteile im Überblick:

- Sie erhalten jedes Buch der Schriftenreihe pünktlich zum Erscheinungstermin – immer aktuell, ohne weitere Bestellung durch Sie.
- Das Abonnement ist jederzeit kündbar.
- Die Lieferung ist innerhalb Deutschlands versandkostenfrei.
- Bei Nichtgefallen können Sie jedes Buch innerhalb von 14 Tagen an uns zurücksenden.

ibidem-Verlag

Melchiorstr. 15

D-70439 Stuttgart

info@ibidem-verlag.de

www.ibidem-verlag.de
www.ibidem.eu
www.edition-noema.de
www.autorenbetreuung.de